First World War
and Army of Occupation
War Diary
France, Belgium and Germany

4 DIVISION
11 Infantry Brigade
Rifle Brigade (The Prince Consort's Own)
1st Battalion
1 January 1918 - 23 April 1919

WO95/1497/1

The Naval & Military Press Ltd
www.nmarchive.com
Published in association with The National Archives

Published by

The Naval & Military Press Ltd

Unit 10 Ridgewood Industrial Park,

Uckfield, East Sussex,

TN22 5QE England

Tel: +44 (0) 1825 749494

www.naval-military-press.com

www.nmarchive.com

This diary has been reprinted in facsimile from the original. Any imperfections are inevitably reproduced and the quality may fall short of modern type and cartographic standards.

© Crown Copyright
Images reproduced by permission of The National Archives, London, England, 2015.

Contents

Document type	Place/Title	Date From	Date To
Heading	WO95/1497 4 Div 11 Inf Bde 1 Bn Rifle Bde. Jan 1918-Apr 1919 (Feb 1919 Missing)		
Heading	4th Division 11th Infantry Bde 1st Rifle Bde January, To March 1918		
War Diary	Cambrai Road Sector [Right Sub-Sector	01/01/1918	03/01/1918
War Diary	Arras	04/01/1918	07/01/1918
War Diary	Bois Des Boeufs Camp.	08/01/1918	11/01/1918
War Diary	Monchy Defences.	12/01/1918	15/01/1918
War Diary	Front Line	15/01/1918	19/01/1918
War Diary	Brown Line	20/01/1918	23/01/1918
War Diary	Front Line	24/01/1918	27/01/1918
War Diary	Arras	28/01/1918	31/01/1918
Operation(al) Order(s)	Operation Order No. 1. By Lieut. Colonel R.T. Fellowes, D.S.O., M.C Commanding 1st Battalion, The Rifle Brigade	02/01/1918	02/01/1918
Operation(al) Order(s)	Operation Order No. 2. By Lieut. Colonel R.T. Fellowes, D.S.O., M.C Commanding 1st Battalion, The Rifle Brigade	06/01/1918	06/01/1918
Operation(al) Order(s)	Operation Order No. 3. By Lieut. Colonel R.T. Fellowes, D.S.O., M.C Commanding 1st Battalion The Rifle Brigade	10/01/1918	10/01/1918
Miscellaneous	1st Battalion The Rifle Brigade Amended Defence Scheme-Monchy Sector (Ref. Preliminary Defence Scheme: Issued 24-10-17)	13/01/1918	13/01/1918
Operation(al) Order(s) Miscellaneous	Amendments To Operation Orders No 3	10/01/1918	10/01/1918
Operation(al) Order(s)	Operation Orders No. 4. By Major H.C. Peyton. M.C. Commdg. 1st Battalion, The Rifle Brigade.	14/01/1918	14/01/1918
Miscellaneous	Preliminary Defence Scheme. Reserved Battalion.	14/01/1918	14/01/1918
Miscellaneous Map	Key to Attached Disposition Map		
Operation(al) Order(s)	Operation Orders No. 5. By Lieut. Col. R.T. Fellowes. DSO., MC. Commanding, 1st Battalion, The Rifle Brigade.	18/01/1918	18/01/1918
Operation(al) Order(s)	Operation Order No. 6 By Lieut. Col. R.T. Fellowes. DSO., MC Commanding, 1st Battalion, The Rifle Brigade.	22/01/1918	22/01/1918
Operation(al) Order(s)	Operation Order No. 7 By Lieut. Colonel R.T. Fellowes. DSO. MC., Commanding, 1st Battalion, The Rifle Brigade.	26/01/1918	26/01/1918
Operation(al) Order(s)	Operation Order No. 8 By Lieut. Col. R.T. Fellowes. DSO. MC., Commanding, 1st Battalion, The Rifle Brigade. 30th January, 1918		
Miscellaneous	Warning Order By Lieut. Colonel R.T. Fellowes, D.S.O., M.C Commanding 1st Battalion The Rifle Brigade	21/02/1918	21/02/1918
Operation(al) Order(s)	Amendments To Operation Order No. 9		
War Diary	Bois Des Boeufs Camp.	01/02/1918	05/02/1918
War Diary	Simencourt	06/02/1918	28/02/1918

Operation(al) Order(s)	Operation Order No. 9. By Lieut. Col R.T. Fellowes, D.S.O., M.C. Commanding, 1st Battalion, The Rifle Brigade.	03/02/1918	03/02/1918
Miscellaneous	Warning Order By Lieut. Colonel R.T. Fellowes, D.S.O., M.C. Commanding 1st Battalion The Rifle Brigade	21/02/1918	21/02/1918
Miscellaneous	Amendment To Warning Order	23/02/1918	23/02/1918
Map			
Miscellaneous			
Miscellaneous	Amendment To Warning Order	23/02/1918	23/02/1918
Miscellaneous	War Diary		
Heading	11th Inf. Bde. 4th Div. 1st Battn. The Rifle Brigade. March 1918		
War Diary	Simencourt	01/03/1918	11/03/1918
War Diary	Berneville	12/03/1918	19/03/1918
War Diary	Stirling Camp.	20/03/1918	24/03/1918
War Diary	Support Battalion	25/03/1918	28/03/1918
War Diary	Front Line Bn.	29/03/1918	31/03/1918
Miscellaneous	Battalion Operation Orders.		
Operation(al) Order(s)	Operation Order 10 By Lieut. Col. R.T. Fellowes, DSO, MC. Commdg. 1st Battn., The Rifle Brigade.	06/03/1918	06/03/1918
Operation(al) Order(s)	Addenda to Operation Order No 10		
Operation(al) Order(s)	To Accompany Operation Order No. 10		
Operation(al) Order(s)	Operation Order No. 11 By Lieut. Col. R.T. Fellowes, DSO, MC. Commdg. 1st Battalion. The Rifle Brigade.	10/03/1918	10/03/1918
Operation(al) Order(s)	Operation Order No. 13 By Major I. C. Montford Commanding 1st Battalion The Rifle Brigade	19/03/1918	19/03/1918
Operation(al) Order(s)	Operation Order No. 19 By Lieut. Col. R.T. Fellowes. DSO., MC. Commdg. 1st. Battalion, The Rifle Brigade.	18/03/1918	18/03/1918
Operation(al) Order(s)	Operation Orders No 16 By Lieut. Colonel R.T. Fellowes, D.S.O., M.C. Commanding 1st Battalion, The Rifle Brigade	28/03/1918	28/03/1918
Operation(al) Order(s)	Operation Orders No 17 By Lieut. Colonel R.T. Fellowes, D.S.O., M.C. Commanding 1st Battalion, The Rifle Brigade	29/03/1918	29/03/1918
Miscellaneous	The following is an amended list of bombs, ammunition etc. to be taken into action.		
Map			
Miscellaneous	Cover for Discharge Documents.		
Operation(al) Order(s)	Amendments To Operation Order No. 9		
Operation(al) Order(s)	Operation Order 10 By Lieut. Col. R.T. Fellowes, DSO, MC. Commdg. 1st Battn., The Rifle Brigade.	06/03/1918	06/03/1918
Map	Sketch Map Showing Dispositions Of Centre Bn		
Miscellaneous	The Following Is An Amended List of Bombs, Ammunition Etc. To Be Taken Into Action.		
Operation(al) Order(s)	Operation Order No. 11. by Lieut. Col. R.T. Fellowes. DSO. MC. Commdg. 1st Battalion, The Rifle Brigade.	10/03/1918	10/03/1918
Operation(al) Order(s)	To Accompany Operation Order No. 10		
Operation(al) Order(s)	Operation Order No. 12. By Lieut. Col. R.T. Fellowes, DSO. MC. Commdg. 1st Battalion, The Rifle Brigade.	18/03/1918	18/03/1918
Operation(al) Order(s)	Operation Order No. 13. By Major I. C. Montford Commanding 1st Battalion The Rifle Brigade	19/03/1918	19/03/1918
Operation(al) Order(s)	Operation Order No. 16 By Lieut. Colonel R.T. Fellowes, D.S.O., M.C. Commanding 1st Battalion, The Rifle Brigade 28th March, 1918	28/03/1918	28/03/1918

Operation(al) Order(s)	Operation Order No. 17 By Lieut. Colonel R.T. Fellowes, D.S.O., M.C. Commanding 1st Battalion, The Rifle Brigade 29th March, 1918	29/03/1918	29/03/1918
Map	Airy Corner Trench Map		
Heading	1st Battalion Rifle Brigade April 1918		
War Diary	Chemical Works. Sector	01/04/1918	10/04/1918
War Diary	Haute Avesnes	11/04/1918	12/04/1918
War Diary	S.E. Of Robecq	13/04/1918	14/04/1918
War Diary	S.E. Of Robecq La. Bassee Canal. Sector	15/04/1918	16/04/1918
War Diary	Busnettes	17/04/1918	18/04/1918
War Diary	Lannoy	19/04/1918	20/04/1918
War Diary	Front Line	21/04/1918	26/04/1918
War Diary	Gonnehem	27/04/1918	28/04/1918
War Diary	Busnettes	29/04/1918	30/04/1918
Miscellaneous			
Operation(al) Order(s)	Operation Orders No 18 By Lieut. Colonel R.T. Fellowes, D.S.O., M.C. Commanding 1st Battalion, The Rifle Brigade	01/04/1918	01/04/1918
Operation(al) Order(s)	Operation Orders No 19 By Lieut. Colonel R.T. Fellowes, D.S.O., M.C. Commanding 1st Battalion, The Rifle Brigade Provision Defence Scheme-Reserve Battalion Fampoux Sector	02/04/1918	02/04/1918
Operation(al) Order(s)	Amendment No. 1 to Operation Order No. 19	03/04/1918	03/04/1918
Operation(al) Order(s)	Amendment No. 2 to Operation Order No. 19	04/04/1918	04/04/1918
Miscellaneous	Warning Order App III	04/04/1918	04/04/1918
Operation(al) Order(s)	Operation Order No 20 By Lieut. Colonel R.T. Fellowes, DSO., MC. Commanding 1st Battalion, The Rifle Brigade	04/04/1918	04/04/1918
Operation(al) Order(s)	Operation Order No. 21 By Lieut. Colonel R.T. Fellowes, D.S.O., M.C. Commanding 1st Battalion The Rifle Brigade Provisional Defence Scheme For Support Battalion-Fampoux Sector	04/04/1918	04/04/1918
Operation(al) Order(s)	Amendment No 1 to Operation Order No 21	06/04/1918	06/04/1918
Operation(al) Order(s)	Operation Order No 22 By Lieut. Colonel R.T. Fellowes, DSO, MC. Commanding 1st Battalion, The Rifle Brigade	07/04/1918	07/04/1918
Operation(al) Order(s)	Operation Order No 23 By Lieut. Colonel R.T. Fellowes, DSO, MC. Commanding 1st Battalion, The Rifle Brigade	08/04/1918	08/04/1918
Operation(al) Order(s)	Operation Order No 24 By Lieut. Colonel R.T. Fellowes, DSO, MC. Commanding 1st Battalion, The Rifle Brigade	10/04/1918	10/04/1918
Miscellaneous	Warning Order 11th April, 1918		
Miscellaneous	Amendments No. 1 To Warning Order-11th April, 1918	11/04/1918	11/04/1918
Miscellaneous	O.C. Ida, Base	13/04/1918	13/04/1918
Operation(al) Order(s)	Operation Order No 25 By Lieut. Colonel R.T. Fellowes, D.S.O., M.C. Commanding 1st Battalion, The Rifle Brigade	16/04/1918	16/04/1918
Operation(al) Order(s)	Operation Order No 26 By Lieut. Colonel R.T. Fellowes, D.S.O., M.C. Commanding 1st Battalion, The Rifle Brigade	19/04/1918	19/04/1918
Operation(al) Order(s)	Operation Order No 27 By Lieut. Colonel R.T. Fellowes, D.S.O., M.C. Commanding 1st Battalion, The Rifle Brigade	21/04/1918	21/04/1918
Operation(al) Order(s)	Amendment No. 1 to Operation Orders No. 27		
Operation(al) Order(s)	Amendment No 3 to Operation Orders No 27	21/04/1918	21/04/1918

Map			
Miscellaneous	R.B. F. 93. App XIV	29/04/1918	29/04/1918
Map	Disposition 23-4-18 to accompany R.B.F 93		
Operation(al) Order(s)	Operation Orders No. 28 By Lieut. Colonel R.T. Fellowes, D.S.O., M.C. Commanding 1st Battalion The Rifle Brigade	23/04/1918	23/04/1918
Operation(al) Order(s)	Amendment No 1 to Operation Orders No 28	23/04/1918	23/04/1918
Operation(al) Order(s)	Operation Order No 29 By Lieut. Colonel R.T. Fellowes, D.S.O., M.C. Commanding 1st Battalion The Rifle Brigade	26/04/1918	26/04/1918
Operation(al) Order(s)	Operation Order No. 30 By Lieut. Colonel R.T. Fellowes, D.S.O., M.C. Commanding 1st Battalion The Rifle Brigade	28/04/1918	28/04/1918
Map	Situation Map No 142		
Miscellaneous	Situation Map No 142		
Map			
Miscellaneous	Fampoux Plex Map		
Map			
Heading	11th Brigade. 4th Division 1st Battalion The Rifle Brigade May 1918		
War Diary	Busnettes	01/05/1918	01/05/1918
War Diary	Front Line	02/05/1918	06/05/1918
War Diary	Support Bn.	06/05/1918	08/05/1918
War Diary	Front Line	06/05/1918	31/05/1918
Miscellaneous			
Miscellaneous	1st Bn Rifle Bde Vol 36		
Operation(al) Order(s)	Operation Order No 31 By Lieut. Colonel R.T. Fellowes, D.S.O., M.C. Commanding 1st Battalion The Rifle Brigade Appendix I	02/05/1918	02/05/1918
Operation(al) Order(s)	Operation Order No 32 by Major I. C. Montford 1st Battalion The Rifle Brigade Appendix II	06/05/1918	06/05/1918
Map	Appendix III		
Operation(al) Order(s)	Operation Order No. 35 By Major I. C. Montford 1st Battalion The Rifle Brigade Appendix IV	11/05/1918	11/05/1918
Operation(al) Order(s)	Operation Order No. 36 App V	13/05/1918	13/05/1918
Operation(al) Order(s)	Amendments To Operation Order No. 36 Preliminary Defence Scheme (For Brigade In Divisional Reserve)	25/05/1918	25/05/1918
Operation(al) Order(s)	Amendment No. 2 to Operation Order No. 36 (Preliminary Defence Scheme)	25/05/1918	25/05/1918
Operation(al) Order(s)	Operation Order No. 43 By Lieut. Col. R.T. Fellowes DSO, MC Commanding 1st Battalion The Rifle Brigade	27/05/1918	27/05/1918
Map	App III		
Operation(al) Order(s)	Amendment No. 1 to Operation Order No 40	22/05/1918	22/05/1918
Operation(al) Order(s)	Operation Order No. 44 By Lieut. Col. R.T. Fellowes, D.S.O., M.C. Commanding 1st Battalion The Rifle Brigade Appendix I	01/06/1918	01/06/1918
Operation(al) Order(s)	Amendment No 2 to Operation Order No. 46 Preliminary Defence Scheme Appendix III		
Operation(al) Order(s)	Operation Order No. 37 By Lieut. Col. R.T. Fellowes, D.S.O., M.C. Commanding 1st Battalion The Rifle Brigade App VI	13/05/1917	13/05/1917
Operation(al) Order(s)	Operation Order No. 38 By Lieut. Col. R.T. Fellowes, D.S.O., M.C. Commanding 1st Battalion The Rifle Brigade App VII	14/05/1918	14/05/1918
Map	App VIII		

Operation(al) Order(s)	Operation Order No. 39. By Lieut. Col. R.T. Fellowes, D.S.O., M.C. Commanding 1st Battalion The Rifle Brigade App IX	24/05/1918	24/05/1918
Miscellaneous	Work To Be Done		
Operation(al) Order(s)	Operation Order No. 40 By Lieut. Col. R.T. Fellowes, D.S.O., M.C. Commanding 1st Battalion The Rifle Brigade App XI	22/05/1918	22/05/1918
Operation(al) Order(s)	Operation Order No. 42 By Lieut. Col. R.T. Fellowes, D.S.O., M.C. Commanding 1st Battalion The Rifle Brigade App XII	27/05/1918	27/05/1918
Miscellaneous	France. Sheet 51c. Edition 2		
Map	France		
Miscellaneous	Glossary.		
Heading	11th Brigade. 4th Division. 1st Battalion The Rifle Brigade June 1918		
Heading	4th Division 11th Infantry Bde 1st Rifle Bde April To June 1918		
War Diary	Vinage Sector	01/06/1918	08/06/1918
War Diary	Busnettes	09/06/1918	13/06/1918
War Diary	Pacaut Wood Sector	14/06/1918	25/06/1918
War Diary	Busnettes.	26/06/1918	30/06/1918
Operation(al) Order(s)	Amendment No. 1 to Operation Order No. 46 Preliminary Defence Scheme	10/06/1918	10/06/1918
Operation(al) Order(s)	Amendment No. 2 to Operation Order No 46 Preliminary Defence Scheme	11/06/1918	11/06/1918
Operation(al) Order(s)	Operation Order No 45 By Major I. C. Montford Commanding 1st Battalion The Rifle Brigade	07/06/1918	07/06/1918
Operation(al) Order(s)	Operation Order No 46 By Major I. C. Montford Commanding 1st Battalion The Rifle Brigade Preliminary Defence Scheme For Brigade In Divisional Reserve	08/06/1918	08/06/1918
Operation(al) Order(s)	Amendment No. 1 to Operation Order No 46 Preliminary Defence Scheme	10/06/1918	10/06/1918
Operation(al) Order(s)	Amendment No 2 to Operation Order No. 46 Preliminary Defence Scheme Appendix III	11/06/1918	11/06/1918
Operation(al) Order(s)	Amendment No. 2 to Operation Order No 46 Preliminary Defence Scheme		
Operation(al) Order(s)	Operation Order No 47 By Major I. C. Montford Commanding 1st Battalion The Rifle Brigade Appendix IV	10/06/1918	10/06/1918
Map			
Operation(al) Order(s)	Operation Order No 48 By Major I. C. Montford Commanding 1st Battalion, The Rifle Brigade Appendix IV	12/06/1918	12/06/1918
Map	Dispositions of Battalion 13.6.18-25.6.18		
Operation(al) Order(s)	Operation Order No. 49 By Major I. C. Montford Commanding 1st Battn. The Rifle Brigade	13/06/1918	13/06/1918
Operation(al) Order(s)	Operation Order No. 48 By Major I. C. Montford Commanding 1st Battalion, The Rifle Brigade Appendix V	12/06/1918	12/06/1918
Operation(al) Order(s)	Operation Order No. 49 By Major I. C. Montford Commanding 1st Battalion, The Rifle Brigade	13/06/1918	13/06/1918
Operation(al) Order(s)	Amendment No. 1 to Operation Order No. 49 Appendix VI	13/06/1918	13/06/1918

Type	Description	Date From	Date To
Operation(al) Order(s)	Operation Order No 50 By Major I. C. Montford Commanding 1st Battn. The Rifle Brigade Preliminary Defence Scheme For Right Battalion-Pacaut Sector	15/06/1918	15/06/1918
Operation(al) Order(s)	Operation Order No 51 By Major I C Montford Commanding 1st Bn The Rifle Brigade.	25/06/1918	25/06/1918
Miscellaneous	War Diary 1		
Operation(al) Order(s)	Operation Order No. 52 Major I. C. Montford Commanding 1st Battn The Rifle Brigade	25/06/1918	25/06/1918
Miscellaneous	W. Diary 2		
Map	Dispositions of Right Battalion.		
Operation(al) Order(s)	Amendment No. 1 to Operation Order No 58 By Major I. C. Montford Commanding 1st Battalion The Rifle Brigade	28/06/1918	28/06/1918
Operation(al) Order(s)	Amendment No 1 to Operation Order No 52 by Major I. C. Montford Commanding 1st Battalion The Rifle Brigade	28/06/1918	28/06/1918
Miscellaneous	Appendix IX	29/06/1918	29/06/1918
Miscellaneous	Appendix IX		
Heading	4th Division 11th Infantry Bde 1st Rifle Bde July, To September 1918		
Heading	11th Brigade. 4th Division. 1st Battalion The Rifle Brigade. July 1918		
War Diary	Front Line Vinage Sector.	01/07/1918	13/07/1918
War Diary	Busnettes	14/07/1918	20/07/1918
War Diary	Front Line Pacaut Sector.	20/07/1918	31/07/1918
Operation(al) Order(s)	Operation Order No 53 By Major I. C. Montford Commanding 1st Batt. The Rifle Brigade	30/06/1918	30/06/1918
Operation(al) Order(s)	Operation Order No 54 By Major I. C. Montford Commanding 1st Battalion The Rifle Brigade Appendix II	01/07/1918	01/07/1918
Map			
Operation(al) Order(s)	Operation Order No 55 By Captain CFC Letts Commanding 1st Bn The Rifle Brigade	03/07/1918	03/07/1918
Miscellaneous	W. Diary		
Operation(al) Order(s)	Operation Order No 56 By Captain CFC Letts Comdg 1st Bn The Rifle Brigade.	06/07/1918	06/07/1918
Operation(al) Order(s)	Amendment No. 1 Operation Order No 55 By Captain C.E.C. Letts Comdg 1st Batt. The Rifle Brigade	03/07/1918	03/07/1918
Operation(al) Order(s)	Operation Order 57 By Lieut Col R.T. Fellowes D.S.O. Inf Comdg 1st Bn The Rifle Brigade	12/07/1918	12/07/1918
Operation(al) Order(s)	Operation Order No. 58 By Lieut Col R.T. Fellowes D.S.O. In. C. Commanding 1st Bn The Rifle Brigade	13/07/1918	13/07/1918
Operation(al) Order(s)	Operation Order No 59 By Lieut. Colonel R.T. Fellowes, DSO, MC Commanding 1st Battalion The Rifle Brigade	19/07/1918	19/07/1918
Operation(al) Order(s)	Operation Order No 59 A By Lieut. Colonel R.T. Fellowes, DSO, MC Commanding 1st Battalion The Rifle Brigade Appendix VII	16/07/1918	16/07/1918
Operation(al) Order(s)	Operation Order No 50 By Major I. C. Montford Commanding 1st Battalion. The Rifle Brigade Preliminary Defence Scheme For Right Battalion-Pacaut Sector Appendix IX	15/06/1918	15/06/1918
Operation(al) Order(s)	Amendment No 1 to Operation Order No 50 By Lieut Col. R.T. Fellowes DSO, MC. Commdg 1st Battalion, The Rifle Brigade	21/07/1918	21/07/1918

Type	Description	Date From	Date To
Operation(al) Order(s)	Amendment No 1 to Operation Order No 60 By Lieut Col. R.T. Fellowes DSO, MC. Commdg 1st Battalion, The Rifle Brigade Appendix IX	27/07/1918	27/07/1918
Heading	11th Brigade. 4th Division. 1st Battalion The Rifle Brigade. August 1918		
War Diary	Pacaut Sector	01/08/1918	03/08/1918
War Diary	Busnettes	04/08/1918	08/08/1918
War Diary	Vinage Sector	09/08/1918	12/08/1918
War Diary	Left Support Vinage Sector	12/08/1918	18/08/1918
War Diary	Vinage Sector	18/08/1918	20/08/1918
War Diary	Right Support Vinage Sector.	20/08/1918	29/08/1918
War Diary	Sensee River.	30/08/1918	30/08/1918
War Diary	Eterpigny.	31/08/1918	31/08/1918
Miscellaneous			
War Diary	Reinforcements.	20/08/1918	30/08/1918
War Diary	Casualties	10/08/1918	31/08/1918
War Diary	Casualties	24/08/1918	24/08/1918
War Diary	Honours & Awards	20/08/1918	31/08/1918
War Diary			
Operation(al) Order(s)	Operation Order No 51 By Lieut Col. R.T. Fellowes DSO, MC Commanding 1st Battalion The Rifle Brigade	03/08/1918	03/08/1918
Miscellaneous	Amendment No 1 to Operation Order No 61 By Lt. Col. R.T. Fellowes, DSO, MC Commdg 1st Battn. The Rifle Brigade	03/08/1918	03/08/1918
Operation(al) Order(s)	Operation Order No. 62 By Lieut. Colonel R.T. Fellowes, D.S.O., M.C. Commanding 1st Battalion The Rifle Brigade	06/08/1918	06/08/1918
Operation(al) Order(s)	Operation Order No. 63 By Lieut. Colonel R.T. Fellowes, D.S.O., M.C. Commanding 1st Battalion The Rifle Brigade	09/08/1918	09/08/1918
Map	Battle Positions		
Operation(al) Order(s)	Operation Order No 64 By Lieut. Colonel R.T. Fellowes, DSO, MC. Commanding 1st Battalion The Rifle Brigade.	09/08/1918	09/08/1918
Miscellaneous	Amendment No. 1 to Operation Order No 64 By Lt. Col. R.T. Fellowes, DSO, MC Commdg 1st Battn. The Rifle Brigade	09/08/1918	09/08/1918
Operation(al) Order(s)	Operation Order No. 65 By Lieut. Col. R.T. Fellowes, DSO, MC Commanding 1st Battn. The Rifle Brigade 9th August 1918	09/08/1918	09/08/1918
Operation(al) Order(s)	Operation Order No. 66 By Lt. Colonel R.T. Fellowes, DSO, MC Commanding 1st Battalion, The Rifle Brigade 11th August, 1918	11/08/1918	11/08/1918
Map	Right Battalion Pacaut Sector		
Map	Northern Div. Boundary		
Miscellaneous	OOs 63, 64, 65		
Operation(al) Order(s)	Operation Order No 67 By Lt. Colonel R.T. Fellowes, DSO, MC Commanding 1st Battn. The Rifle Brigade Preliminary Defence Scheme-Left Support Battalion	17/08/1918	17/08/1918
Map			
Operation(al) Order(s)	Operation Order No 68 By Lieut. Colonel R.T. Fellowes, DSO., MC. Commanding 1st Battalion The Rifle Brigade Defence Scheme For Outpost Battalion-Left Brigade	17/08/1918	17/08/1918
Operation(al) Order(s)	Operation Order No 69 By Lt. Colonel R.T. Fellowes, DSO, MC Commanding 1st Battn. The Rifle Brigade	17/08/1918	17/08/1918

Type	Description	Date From	Date To
Miscellaneous Map	4th Division Intelligence Map No 10		
Operation(al) Order(s)	Operation Order No. 70 By Lieut. Colonel R.T. Fellowes, DSO, MC Commanding 1st Battn. The Rifle Brigade	20/08/1918	20/08/1918
Operation(al) Order(s)	Operation Order No. 71 By Lieut. Colonel R.T. Fellowes, DSO, MC Commanding 1st Battn. The Rifle Brigade	22/08/1918	22/08/1918
Operation(al) Order(s)	Operation Order No. 72 By Lieut. Colonel R.T. Fellowes, DSO, MC Commanding 1st Battn. The Rifle Brigade	22/08/1918	22/08/1918
Miscellaneous Map	Amendment No 1 to Operation Order No 72	22/08/1918	22/08/1918
Miscellaneous	Warning Order	24/08/1918	24/08/1918
Operation(al) Order(s)	Operation Order No. 73 By Lieut. Colonel R.T. Fellowes, DSO, MC Commanding 1st Battalion The Rifle Brigade	25/08/1918	25/08/1918
Operation(al) Order(s)	Operation Order No 74 By Lieut. Colonel R.T. Fellowes, DSO MC Commanding 1st Battalion, The Rifle Brigade Appendix 9	28/08/1918	28/08/1918
Operation(al) Order(s)	Operation Order No. 75 By Lieut. Colonel R.T. Fellowes, DSO, MC Commanding 1st Battalion The Rifle Brigade	29/08/1918	29/08/1918
Map	Eterpigny		
Miscellaneous	Reference Sketch On Back.		
Operation(al) Order(s)	Operation Order No. 76 By Lieut. Colonel R.T. Fellowes, DSO, MC Commanding 1st Battn. The Rifle Brigade	30/08/1918	30/08/1918
Miscellaneous	Amendment No 1 to Operation Order No 76	30/08/1918	30/08/1918
Miscellaneous Map	Hamblain-Les-Pres. Ed. 5 Special Sheet. Parts of 51B N. W. N.E., S.W. & S.E.		
War Diary	Eterpigny Area	01/09/1918	04/09/1918
War Diary	Frevillers	05/09/1918	19/09/1918
War Diary	Hamblain-Les-Pres	20/09/1918	24/09/1918
War Diary	Orange. Hill Area.	25/09/1918	30/09/1918
War Diary	Reinforcements		
War Diary	Casualties		
War Diary	Distribution of Battalion 30/9/18		
Operation(al) Order(s)	Operation Order No. 77 By Lieut. Colonel R.T. Fellowes, DSO, MC Commdg 1st Battn. The Rifle Brigade Appendix I	01/09/1918	01/09/1918
Map	Eterpigny		
Miscellaneous	Reference Sketch On Back.		
Operation(al) Order(s)	Operation Order No 78 By Lieut. R.T. Fellowes, DSO MC Commdg 1st Batt The Rifle Brigade Appendix I	01/09/1918	01/09/1918
Operation(al) Order(s)	Operation Order No 79 By Capt. J.A. Davison, MC Commdg 1st Battalion, The Rifle Brigade Appendix IV	03/09/1918	03/09/1918
Operation(al) Order(s)	Operation Order No 79 By Capt. J.A. Davison, MC Commdg 1st Battalion, The Rifle Brigade Appendix II	03/09/1918	03/09/1918
Miscellaneous	Account Of Operations At Arras August 28th-September 2nd, 1918		
Operation(al) Order(s)	Operation Order No 80 By Capt. J.A. Davison, MC Comdg 1st Battalion, The Rifle Brigade Appendix III	04/09/1918	04/09/1918
Operation(al) Order(s)	Operation Order No 80 By Capt. J.A. Davison, MC Comdg 1st Battalion, The Rifle Brigade	04/09/1918	04/09/1918

Operation(al) Order(s)	Operation Order No 81 By Major G. W. Liddell, D.S.O. Commanding 1st Battalion The Rifle Brigade	18/09/1918	18/09/1918
Miscellaneous	Amendment No 1 to Operation Order No 81 18th September, 1918	18/09/1918	18/09/1918
Miscellaneous	Amendment No 1 to Operation Order No 81 18 September, 1918	18/09/1918	18/09/1918
Operation(al) Order(s)	Operation Order No 62 By Major G. W. Liddell, D.S.O. Comdg 1st Battalion The Rifle Brigade Appendix V	18/09/1918	18/09/1918
Operation(al) Order(s)	Operation Order No 62 By Major G.W. Liddell, D.S.O. Comdg 1st Battalion The Rifle Brigade	18/09/1918	18/09/1918
Map	Valley Wood.		
Miscellaneous	Appendix V		
Diagram etc	Reserve Coy In Kite Trench.		
Miscellaneous	Amendment No 1 to Operation Order No 83 18th September, 1918	18/09/1918	18/09/1918
Operation(al) Order(s)	Operation Order No 83 By Lieut. Col. G. W. Liddell, DSO. Comdg 1st Battalion, The Rifle Brigade	23/09/1918	23/09/1918
Miscellaneous	Warning Order In The Event Of An Enemy Withdrawal 27 September. 1918	27/09/1918	27/09/1918
Miscellaneous	Amendment No 1 to Operation Order No 83 24th September, 1918	24/09/1918	24/09/1918
Operation(al) Order(s)	Operation Order No 84 By Lieut. Col. G. W. Liddell, D.S.O. Commdg 1st Battalion The Rifle Brigade Centre Battalion Of Reserve Brigade	28/09/1918	28/09/1918
Operation(al) Order(s)	Operation Order No 84 By Lieut. Col. G. W. Liddell, D.S.O. Comdg 1st Battalion The Rifle Brigade Centre Battalion Of Reserve Brigade	28/09/1918	28/09/1918
Miscellaneous	Warning Order	29/09/1918	29/09/1918
Miscellaneous	Warning Order In The Event Of An Enemy Withdrawal	27/09/1918	27/09/1918
Operation(al) Order(s)	Operation Order No 85 By Lt. Colonel G. W. Liddell, D.S.O. Commdg 1st Battalion, The Rifle Brigade	30/09/1918	30/09/1918
Miscellaneous	Amendment No 1 to Operation Order No 85	30/09/1918	30/09/1918
Map	Sketch Map Showing Dispositions Of Centre Bn		
Miscellaneous	Reference		
Map			
Heading	4th Division 11th Infantry Bde 1st Rifle Bde October, To December 1918		
War Diary	Front Line. (L'Ecluse Sector)	01/10/1918	06/10/1918
War Diary	Berneville	07/10/1918	10/10/1918
War Diary	Escaudoeuvres	11/10/1918	16/10/1918
War Diary	Haspres Area	17/10/1918	25/10/1918
War Diary	Haspres	25/10/1918	28/10/1918
War Diary	Front Line (Artres Sector)	28/10/1918	31/10/1918
Miscellaneous	Warning Order	02/10/1918	02/10/1918
Operation(al) Order(s)	Operation Order No 86 By Lt. Col. G. W. Liddell, D.S.O. Commdg 1st Battn. The Rifle Brigade	02/10/1918	02/10/1918
Map			
Map	Sketch Map Showing Dispositions		
Operation(al) Order(s)	Operation Order No 87 By Lt. Col. G. W. Liddell, DSO. Commdg 1st Battn. The Rifle Brigade 3rd October, 1918	03/10/1918	03/10/1918
Operation(al) Order(s)	Operation Order No 88 By Lt. Col. G. W. Liddell, DSO. Commdg 1st Battn. The Rifle Brigade	04/10/1918	04/10/1918

Operation(al) Order(s)	Operation Order No 89 By Lieut. Col. G. W. Liddell, DSO. Commdg 1st Battalion The Rifle Brigade 5th October, 1918	05/10/1918	05/10/1918
Operation(al) Order(s)	Operation Order No 90 By Lt. Col. G. W. Liddell. D.S.O. Commdg 1st Battalion The Rifle Brigade 6th October, 1918	06/10/1918	06/10/1918
Operation(al) Order(s)	Operation Order No 91 By Lt. Col. G. W. Liddell, DSO. Commanding 1st Battalion, The Rifle Brigade	10/10/1918	10/10/1918
Operation(al) Order(s)	Operation Order No 92 By Lt. Col. G. W. Liddell, DSO Commdg 1st Battn. The Rifle Brigade	13/10/1918	13/10/1918
Operation(al) Order(s)	Operation Order No 93 By Lt. Col. G. W. Liddell, D.S.O. Commdg 1st Battalion The Rifle Brigade In The Event Of A Hostile Attack	16/10/1918	16/10/1918
Operation(al) Order(s)	Operation Order No 94 By Lt. Col. G. W. Liddell, D.S.O. Commdg 1st Battn. The Rifle Brigade	17/10/1918	17/10/1918
Miscellaneous	Amendment To Operation Order No 94	17/10/1917	17/10/1917
Map	Sketch Map		
Operation(al) Order(s)	Operation Order No 95 By Lt. Col. G. W. Liddell, D.S.O. Commdg 1st Battalion The Rifle Brigade	19/10/1918	19/10/1918
Miscellaneous	Amendment No 1 to Operation Order No 95	19/10/1918	19/10/1918
Map	Sketch Map		
Operation(al) Order(s)	Operation Order No 96 By Lt. Col. G. W. Liddell, D.S.O. Commdg 1st Battalion The Rifle Brigade	23/10/1918	23/10/1918
Map	Sketch Map		
Miscellaneous	O.C. "A", "B", "I" Coy	24/10/1918	24/10/1918
Operation(al) Order(s)	Operation Order No 97 By Lt. Col. G. W. Liddell, DSO. Commdg 1st Battalion The Rifle Brigade	28/10/1918	28/10/1918
Miscellaneous	Amendment No 1 to Operation Order 97, dated 28/10/18	28/10/1918	28/10/1918
Map	Dispositions.		
Miscellaneous	Casualties		
Miscellaneous	Honours & Awards		
Miscellaneous	Distribution of Battalion 31/10/18	31/10/1918	31/10/1918
War Diary	Preseau	01/11/1918	02/11/1918
War Diary	Haspres	03/11/1918	10/11/1918
War Diary	Curgies	11/11/1918	30/11/1918
Operation(al) Order(s)	Operation Order No 98 By Lt. Col. G. W. Liddell. D.S.O. Commdg 1st Battalion The Rifle Brigade	30/10/1918	30/10/1918
Miscellaneous	Amendment No 1 to Operation Order No 98	31/10/1918	31/10/1918
Map	Sketch Map		
Operation(al) Order(s)	Operation Order No 99 By Lt. Col. G. W. Liddell, D.S.O. Commdg 1st Battalion The Rifle Brigade	01/11/1918	01/11/1918
Operation(al) Order(s)	Operation Order No 100 By Lt. Col. G. W. Liddell, D.S.O. Commdg 1st Battn. The Rifle Brigade	02/11/1918	02/11/1918
Operation(al) Order(s)	Operation Order No 101 By Major C. F. C. Letts Commdg 1st Battn. The Rifle Brigade	10/11/1918	10/11/1918
Miscellaneous	Casualties, Etc.		
Miscellaneous	Honours And Awards		
Miscellaneous	Distribution of Battalion 30 Nov. 1918	30/11/1918	30/11/1918
Miscellaneous	1st Battalion The Rifle Brigade Narrative Of Operation 1st And 2nd November, 1918	01/11/1918	01/11/1918
War Diary	Curgies	01/12/1918	31/12/1918
Heading	4th Division 11th Infy Bde 1st Bn Rifle Bde Jan-Mar 1919 Served In Mesopotamia 18 Ind Division 53 Bde		
Heading	4th Division War Diaries All Month 1919		
War Diary	Curgies	01/01/1919	04/01/1919

War Diary	Haine St. Paul	05/01/1919	31/01/1919
Operation(al) Order(s)	Operation Order No 102 By Lt. Col. G. W. Liddell, DSO. Commanding 1st Battalion The Rifle Brigade.	02/01/1919	02/01/1919
War Diary	Haine St. Paul	01/02/1919	28/02/1919
Miscellaneous	Amendment No. 1. to Operation Order No. 102 by Lt. Col. G. W. Liddell, DSO Commanding 1st Battn the Rifle Brigade.	03/01/1919	03/01/1919
War Diary	Haine St. Paul	01/02/1918	28/02/1918
Miscellaneous	Casualties Etc.		
Miscellaneous	Distribution of Battalion 28/2/19	28/02/1919	28/02/1919
War Diary	Binche	01/04/1919	20/04/1919
War Diary	Binche To Dunkirk	20/04/1919	23/04/1919
Operation(al) Order(s)	Operation Order No 104 By Captain F.V. Kibbey MC, Commanding 1st Battalion The Rifle Brigade	19/04/1919	19/04/1919
Miscellaneous	Distribution of Battalion on 24.4.19	24/04/1919	24/04/1919

WO95/1497

4 DN II Inf Bde

1 Bn Rhodesian Rifle Bde.
Jan 1918 – Apr 1919
(Feb 1919 missing)

4th Division

11th Infantry Bde

1st Rifle Bde.

January to March
1918

WAR DIARY
or
INTELLIGENCE SUMMARY

Army Form C. 2118.

1st Bn. 9th Rifle Bgd. 7
Vol 32

Place	Date	Hour	Summary of Events and Information	Remarks and references to Appendices
CAMBRAI ROAD SECTOR (FRONT SUB-SECTOR)	1917 Jan 1st to 2nd		The Bn. were in the Front Line having taken over from the 18th Bn. Somerset Light Infantry on the night of December 30–31.1.17. The two days were quite quiet, except for the heavy Trench Mortars which were intermittently active throughout the period. The disposition of the Battalion was as follows:- I Coy in the front line on Left and A Coy on the right: boundary, right. I.14.d.75.60., left- I.8.b.20.15., incl. Company boundary. POMMEL ALLEY. I.8.c.75.45. inclusive to right Company. B Company was the left supp't Company and C the right supp't Company. Bn. H.Q. in CRATER SUBWAY. I.3.b.35.95. Bn. the right 3/4 2nd In the 13th. H.Q. in CRATER SUBWAY. I.3.b.35.95. Bn. the right 7th Bn. The Bn. was relieved by the HOUSEHOLD BATTALION (10th BRIGADE), and marched back to billets in SCHRAMM BARRACKS, ARRAS.	See Trench Orders attached 31/12/17 Appendix I
ARRAS	4th to 7th		The first two days were spent in cleaning up & taking over the chief items: Certain working parties were provided for clearing the ARRAS street. On the 15th 6th the B.n. held the a Christmas Day. There was a Short service in the morning in the 4th Divisional Cinema Hut; from 2p.m. till 4.30. P.M. the Follies gave a Special performance for the Bn. the Dinner was at 5.30 P.M. and was a great success in every way. The Officers Dinner was held at 8.0 P.M. Births 7th the 75th, lasted	

WAR DIARY or INTELLIGENCE SUMMARY.

1st Rifle Bde

Army Form C. 2118.

Place	Date	Hour	Summary of Events and Information	Remarks and references to Appendices
ARRAS	Jan 6 to 7th		Bois des Boeufs Camp and relieved 1st/4th Bn the East Lancashire Regiment, the relief being complete before 10.30 A.M.	APPENDIX II
Bois des Boeufs Camp	8th to 11th		The weather was exceptionally cold throughout. Apart from a number of working parties were found to work on the INTERMEDIATE LINE under R.E. Supervision, on two nights the whole Battalion went, on the third night one of the Companies was shelled whilst getting into position too early, two marched in to Costadine. 9 other ranks killed, 3 died of wounds and 6 wounded. On the evening of the 11th the Bn relieved the 2nd/3rd the Kings Regt in the MONCHY DEFENCES, the disposition being as follows: A Company in MUSKET RESERVE (I.31.c.) B Company in ORCHARD RESERVE (O.1.A+B), C Company in CURB SWITCH SOUTH. (I.31.c.) D Company in the STRONG POINTS F.G. + H. (A.36.Cd.) and Bn H.Q. at the junction of CURB SWITCH and ORANGE AVENUE (I.31.c.30.00)	APPENDIX III Trench State Reliefs
MONCHY DEFENCES	Jan 12th to 15th		The term thaw set in. It rained hard and the trenches were not very good. However on the 15th it froze again and conditions were certainly better. The Bn was hard at work all the time and much work was done on the parapets and bringing up and laying all kinds of which had to be protected also in clearing up and laying all kinds of which had to be collected. The trenches paths were found much in the condition to both the superior.	DEFENCE SCHEME APPENDIX IV

Army Form C. 2118.

1st Rifle Bde

WAR DIARY
or
INTELLIGENCE SUMMARY.
(Erase heading not required)

Instructions regarding War Diaries and Intelligence Summaries are contained in F.S. Regs., Part II. and the Staff Manual respectively. Title pages will be prepared in manuscript.

Place	Date	Hour	Summary of Events and Information	Remarks and references to Appendices
Monchy Defences	14th to 15th		On the evening of the 15th the Bn was relieved by the 12th Somerset Light Infantry and relieved that Battalion in the front line, the disposition being as follows. B Company was on the right, boundaries Cross Alley O.26.4.6 to Southern Edge of Northern Twin Copse O.26.65.53. Clumps in rear the left, boundaries Southern Edge of Northern Twin Copse O.26.65.33 to Bit Lane I.31.a.90.10. I Company in support in Highland Support and Dake Tr. O.1.b.O.2.a.v.c. A Company in Reserve in Creese Tr. O.1.c.7.a and Bn H.Q. at O.1.c.80.10. In C/Regt Tr. The period was very quiet. But the trenches owing to the heavy rain became exceedingly bad. In some parts the duck was head high in the Communication trenches and the front line; The whole becoming so on the right Company's front that it had to be evacuated, being kept only by posts during the night. Two duckboard tracks were laid from Monchy to the Support Line, A running No Copse - Sharpnel and Dake Trenches to Hill Support and B track via Orangeard - Orchard Reserve to Highland Support. The condition were exceedingly	Appendix V
Front Line	Jan 15th to 19th			

Army Form C. 2118.

WAR DIARY
or
INTELLIGENCE SUMMARY.
(Erase heading not required.)

1st Rifle Bde

Place	Date	Hour	Summary of Events and Information	Remarks and references to Appendices
FRONT LINE	JAN 13th to 19th		Quiet day very cold almost trying to the troops. No fast food could be got up to the troops and tank tracks were out and impossible to walk had to be carried up to patrol time by the Reserve Company from the MONCHY DUMP N.6 & 7.E. On the night of the 19th/20th the 13th Bn were relieved and by the 1st SOMERSET LIGHT INFANTRY and moved back to the BROWN LINE NORTH of K. ARRAS. CAMBRAI ROAD N 4 a, Bn HQ being in the QUARRY N 3 b 80. 30.	APPENDIX VI
BROWN LINE	JAN 20th to 23rd		The had days left the relief were spent in cleaning up and in trying demolish Defence Scheme which was very badly needed. Working parties were found daily by of under the R.E's. Also giving the troops very scanty rest. On the evening of the 23rd the Bn relieved the 1st Bn, The SOMERSET LIGHT INFANTRY IN front line; A + Southern Edge of MNTWIN COPSE O.2 a. 85.53. Company was in the right location CATS ALLEY O2b 40.60 1 Company in the left location SOUTHERN EDGE of M.N TWIN COPSE O 2 a. 85 53. to Bn LANE. I 31. a. 90. 10. (C Company to SUFFOLK HIGHLAND SUPPORT + DALE TR (OIB O2 a+c) and B Company in Reserve CIRCLE TR O.I.C. + Bn HQ. being in CIRCLE TR. O.I.C. 80. 10.	APPENDIX VII APPENDIX VIII

Army Form C. 2118.

WAR DIARY
or
INTELLIGENCE SUMMARY.
(Erase heading not required.)

Place	Date	Hour	Summary of Events and Information	Remarks and references to Appendices
FRONT LINE	24th to 27th		The front line as a whole fairly quiet, though enemy machine guns and trench mortars were continuously active. The latter especially on the night of 26th - 27th when Bow Tr., HIGHLAND SUPPORT and TWIN COPSE were very heavily shelled by harassing and heavy T.M. fire, but the trenches were certainly in a better condition than during E. from 45mm. The night still very bad. On the night of the 27th, the Bn were relieved by the Honble. Battalion and moved back to ARRAS ending at FEUCHY.	APPENDIX IX
ARRAS	28th to 31st		CHAPEL CROSS ROADS and Schramm Barracks ARRAS. The first was spent in cleaning up and taking into the hut the Company training was carried out and as the MOAT RANGE and BUTT DE TIR were also available. On the 31st the Bn. relieved the 1/5th SOMERSET L.I. in 103 & 105 BOEUFE CAMP on the ARRAS - CAMBRAI Th. Railway. In the evening Rushworth Bn. was hosting a Rifle Avenue, the task being "Cleaning up 300 X"	APPENDIX X

Casualties during Month — 2Lt. A.C. TURNER - Killed 16.1.18 O.Rks. 10 Killed
" " " — Lt. G.H.G. CROSFIELD - Killed 26.1.18 O.Rks. 17 Wounded
Evacuated Sick " " — Capt. F.T. HILL Wounded 31.1.18 O.Rks. 37
 — 2Lt. J.Y.I. KINGHAM 19.1.18
 — Lt. A.J. SALTER 31.12.17
 — Lieut. R.W. HOLMES & COURT. 19.1.18
Reinforcements During Month — 2Lt. C.D. CRAVEN , 2Lt. C.G. COOPER and 98 O.Rks.

LIEUT. COL.
COMMAND.
1st Bn. THE RIFLE BRIG.

Appendix I

SECRET   OPERATION ORDER No 1.   COPY No 11
                                by
                   Lieut. Colonel R. T. FELLOWES, D.S.O., M.C
                              Commanding
                      1st Battalion, THE RIFLE BRIGADE

Ref. 51 B N.W.   2nd JANUARY, 1918
           S.W.

1. RELIEF   The Battalion will be relieved in the front line to-morrow
                  night, 3rd/4th instant, by the HOUSEHOLD BATTALION.
                  "A" Coy, RIFLE BRIGADE will be relieved by No 1 Coy. HOUSEHOLD BN.
                  "B"   "   "   "   "   "   " No 2   "   "   "
                  "C"   "   "   "   "   "   " No 4   "   "   "
                  "I"   "   "   "   "   "   " No 3   "   "   "
                        The order of relief will be as follows:-
                        "I", "A", "B", "C" Companies, Battalion Headquarters

2. ADVANCED   The HOUSEHOLD BATTALION will send forward an advanced party
   PARTY   consisting of Lewis Gun teams, 1 N.C.O. per company and
                  Headquarters, to take over trench stores; Sgt. Master cook and
                  1 R.A.M.C. private to take over the water point.

3. GUIDES   from the Battalion will be found as follows:-
                      (1) For the advanced party, 5 Guides from Battalion
                  Headquarters at the western end of GORDON AVENUE at 11.0 a.m.
                  These guides will conduct the parties to the Company Headquarters.
                      (2) For remainder of the Battalion, 1 Guide per platoon
                  (3 per Company), and 1 for Headquarters, to report to the
                  Assistant Adjutant at Battalion Headquarters at 4.55 p.m.

4. ROUTE OF   "B" and "I" will be relieved via GORDON AVENUE and
   RELIEF   COOKHOUSE CRESCENT. These Companies will move out via
                  PICK AVENUE. Remaining two Companies will carry out the relief
                  via GORDON AVENUE.

5. TRENCH   All trench stores etc. will be carefully handed over.
   STORES   Receipts should reach Battalion Headquarters as soon as possible
                  after completion of relief. The reserve supply of water
                  (50 tins) will be handed over. Remainder of petrol tins will
                  not be brought out of the line.

6. MOVE   On completion of the relief the Battalion will move to
                  Billets in ARRAS. Companies will move independently with an
                  interval of 30 yards between platoons.

7. TRANSPORT   The Transport Officer will arrange to have 2 limbers for
                  each "A" and "I" Companies and 1 limber for each "B" and "C"
                  Companies and 1 for Headquarters at a point 150 yards West of
                  LA BERGERE FARM at 6.30 p.m. These limbers will take the
                  packs and greatcoats of "A" and "I" Companies. Valises, blankets
                  etc will be in billets by the time the Battalion arrives.

8. HOT TEA   The Quartermaster will arrange for 2 cookers containing
                  hot tea to be at ESTAMINET CORNER from 7.0 p.m. onwards.

9. BILLETING   The Quartermaster, 2/Lieut. E. A. Mallett, 2/Lieut. J. A.
   PARTIES   Lawton, 4 C.Q.M.Ss and buglers will report to the Town
                  Major "A" Area ARRAS at 9.0 a.m. The Quartermaster will
                  arrange for guides to meet the Battalion on the wooden bridge
                  where the CAMBRAI ROAD crosses the Railway
                        Attention is called to 11th Infantry Brigade No 891/
                  circulated to Companies on the 5th December, 1917.

10. REPORT   Completion of the relief will be reported by wire by any sentence containing the code word "Bubbly".

ACKNOWLEDGE.

(sd) J. A. Davison
Capt & Adjt
1st Battalion THE RIFLE BRIGADE

8/1/18.

DISTRIBUTION

```
Copy No  1    O.C. "A" Company
     "   2         "B"    "
     "   3         "C"    "
     "   4         "I"    "
     "   5    Commanding Officer
     "   6    Adjutant
     "   7    Assistant Adjutant
     "   8    Quartermaster
     "   9    Transport Officer
     "  10    Household Battalion
     "  11    War Diary No 1
     "  12       "       " 2
     "  13    File
```

OPERATION ORDERS No 2
by
Lieut. Colonel R.T.FELLOWES, D.S.O., M.C.
Commanding
1st Battalion THE RIFLE BRIGADE

6th JANUARY, 1918   Copy No 12

1. RELIEF   The Battalion will relieve the 1st Battalion THE EAST LAN-
             CASHIRE REGIMENT in the BOIS DES BOEUFS CAMP to-morrow, 9th inst.
             "A" Coy 1st Bn RIFLE BRIGADE will relieve "A" Coy EAST LANCASHIRE RGT
             "B" "   "   "   "   "   "   "   "B" "   "   "
             "C" "   "   "   "   "   "   "   "C" "   "   "
             "I" "   "   "   "   "   "   "   "D" "   "   "

                Order of relief
                   Headquarters, "B", "A", "C", "I" Companies
                Headquarters will be ready to move off at 8.15 a.m.
                An interval of 300 yards will be kept between platoons.
                Cookers and necessary transport will follow 300 yards in
             rear of the last platoon of "I" Company

2. ADVANCED   An advanced party of one N.C.O. per Company and one from
   PARTY   Headquarters will report at Orderly Room, Battalion Head-
                quarters at 7.15 a.m. They will be marched to the BOIS DES
                BOEUFS CAMP by the senior N.C.O. and will take over accommodation
                stores, etc. and will be ready on the ARRAS-CAMBRAI ROAD to
                guide their companies to their quarters. Lists of stores
                taken over will be rendered to Orderly Room by 12.0 noon.

3. BAGGAGE   Officers' kits, mess equipment etc will be packed and
                dumped outside Headquarters and Company messes by 8.0 a.m.
                Transport will collect.
                   Blankets will be rolled in bundles of ten, labelled and
                dumped in the BARRACK SQUARE by 8.0 a.m.
                   O.C. "A" Company will detail a party of 1 N.C.O. and 8
                men to load these blankets, and unload them on arrival.

4. BILLETS   2/Lieut E. A. MALLETT will remain behind to check all
                furniture in Billets and obtain certificate for cleanliness etc.
                These certificates will be handed in to Orderly Room as soon
                as possible.

5. RATIONS will be delivered by 1st Line TRANSPORT.

6. WATER   can be obtained from the water point in the CAMP.

7. FATIGUE   Each Company will detail 1 group to report to 2/Lieut
               G.J.COLE at Orderly Room at 8.30 a.m. They will move all tables,
               etc. which have been borrowed.

               ACKNOWLEDGE

                                                sd/ J. A. DAVISON, Capt
                                                                 & Adjt.
                                          1st Battn THE RIFLE BRIGADE

                        DISTRIBUTION

                  Copy No 1 O.C."A" Company
                    "   2   " "B"   "
                    "   3   " "C"   "
                    "   4   " "I"   "
                    "   5   Commanding Officer
                    "   6   2nd in Command
                    "   7   Adjutant
                    "   8   Assistant Adjutant
                    "   9   Quartermaster
                    "   10   Transport Officer
                    "   11   1st. Bn. East Lancashire Regt.
                    "   12   War Diary No 1
                    "   13   "   "   " 2
                    "   14   File

APPENDIX II

OPERATION ORDERS No 3
by
Lieut. Colonel R.T. FELLOWES, D.S.O., M.C.
Commanding
1st Battalion THE RIFLE BRIGADE

Reference
J Corps Trench Map 84 C   18th JANUARY, 1918.   Copy No /2

1. **RELIEF** The Battalion will relieve the 2nd Battalion THE ESSEX REGIMENT in MONCHY DEFENCES to-morrow night 18th/19th instant.
"A" Coy. R.B. will relieve "D" Coy. ESSEX REGT. in MUSKET RESERVE.
"B"   "   "   "   "   "A"   "   "   "   ORCHARD RESERVE
"C"   "   "   "   "   "B"   "   "   "   CURB SWITCH
                                                    RESERVE
"I"   "   "   "   "   "C"   "   "   "   "F", "G" and "H"
                                                    Strong Points
                    Company Headquarters in "F" Strong Point
Battalion Headquarters will be at the junction of CURB SWITCH RESERVE and ORANGE AVENUE.

2. **ROUTE & ORDER** The Battalion will relieve via ORANGE AVENUE in the
   of RELIEF.   following order:-
"A", "B", "C" Companies, Battalion Headquarters and "I" Company.

3. **ADVANCED** Nos 1 and 2 of the Lewis Gun teams (with guns), 1 N.C.O. per
   PARTY   company and 1 for Headquarters, Sgt. Master Cook and 2
signallers will parade at Orderly Room at 10.30 a.m. under the Assistant Adjutant. They will proceed to the Battalion Headquarters of the 2nd Battalion ESSEX REGIMENT, where guides will be provided to take them to their respective Company Headquarters.

4. **MOVE** The Battalion will move off from here in the above mentioned order, the first platoon of "A" Company leaving camp at 4.0 p.m. Guides at the rate of 1 per platoon will be met at a point where SWORD LANE is cut by CROMARTY TRENCH (Corps Line).

5. **TRENCH KITS** 1 limber per Company and 1 for Battalion Headquarters will accompany the Battalion as far as the Corps Line. All kits will be packed by 3.15 p.m.

6. **KITS FOR**   All valises, blankets, packs and greatcoats will be dumped,
   TRANSPORT   by Companies, near the Orderly Room by 12.0 noon.

7. **TRENCH**   Receipted lists of trench stores will be forwarded to Battalion
   STORES   Headquarters as soon as possible after the completion of relief
The necessary number of camp kettles, hot food containers, etc., will be taken over on relief.
Separate lists will be compiled for each Strong Point.

8. **RATIONS** Rations for 19th instant will be carried on the man.
Rations will come up by train as far as B 40? Siding. Each Company will detail 1 N.C.O. and 10 men, Headquarters 1 N.C.O. and 6 men, to be at HAPPY VALLEY at 4.30 p.m. daily.
At HAPPY VALLEY there are five trucks (1 per Company and 1 for Battalion Headquarters). Six men of each of the above mentioned parties will push the trucks to B 40? Siding where they will transfer the rations from the train to the trolley line and push them back to HAPPY VALLEY. From here they and the remainder of the party will carry them to their respective Company or Battalion Headquarters.

9. **WATER** There are two water points, one in HAPPY VALLEY and one in MUSKET RESERVE. Each Company and Headquarters will be responsible for its own supply. Petrol tins will be handed over by the ESSEX REGIMENT.

SECRET   1st BATTALION   THE RIFLE BRIGADE   APPENDIX IV

                     Amended DEFENCE SCHEME - MONCHY SECTOR
                 (Ref. Preliminary Defence Scheme: Issued 24-10-17)

Ref. Latest Edition of Plex Trench Map.   Copy No 9

1. DISPOSITIONS.

        Battalion Headquarters   CIRCLE TRENCH   O.1.c.8.1.

        Right Company   Three platoons (less 2 sections) in front line
                         and posts.
                         Headquarters and 2 sections in HILL SUPPORT
                         (Bombing section at junction of HILL and CANISTER)

        Left Company   Three platoons in front line and posts.
                         Headquarters - SHAFT ALLEY.

        Support Company CHAIN SUPPORT (3 sections) HIGHLAND SUPPORT and
                         DALE SUPPORT.
                         (Bombing sections to be at junction of CHAIN
                         and BRIDOON ALLEY, BOW ALLEY and DALE SUPPORT,
                         and SHAFT ALLEY and HIGHLAND SUPPORT).
                         Headquarters - HIGHLAND SUPPORT.

        Reserve Company CIRCLE TRENCH

5.   The Battalion front is covered by 13 Machine Guns.
Their positions and arcs of fire can be seen on Map at Battalion
Headquarters.

9.(2) AN ATTACK ON   Should the enemy pierce the front or support lines on
OUR RIGHT.   our right, a defensive flank will be formed along
                        CANISTER. - Right front Company from junction of front
line and CANISTER to junction of DALE SUPPORT and CANISTER.
Troops of support company from junction of DALE and CANISTER -
Westward.   Till CANISTER is sufficiently fire-stepped troops
will take up positions OUTSIDE the trench.
          Heavy fire will be brought to bear on the enemy's
flank, and troops will be prepared to counter attack if necessary.
          Bombing blocks will be established as far South along
HILL SUPPORT and front line as possible, to prevent the enemy
extending his gains Northwards.

10. AN ATTACK ON   The same system of defence as outlined in preceding
OUR LEFT   paragraph will be adopted.   Every opportunity of
                        counter attacking will be taken.   If necessary a
defensive flank will be formed OUTSIDE BRIDOON ALLEY. - Left
front Company from junction of front line and BRIDOON to junction
of CHAIN and BRIDOON.   Support Company from latter junction
Westwards.
          Bombing blocks will be established as far North as
possible along CHAIN and front line.

                                                M Davison
                                                Capt + Adjt
                                                for.

                                                      Lieut. Colonel
                                                     Comdg 1st Battalion
13th January, 1918.   THE RIFLE BRIGADE

                          Distribution

                Copy No 1   O.C. "A" Company
                "   " 2   "B"   "
                "   " 3   "C"   "
                "   " 4   "D"   "
                "   " 5   Commanding Officer
                "   " 6   Adjutant
                "   " 7   Intelligence Officer
                "   " 8   11th Infantry Bde
                "   " 9   War Diary No 1
                "   "10   "   " 2
                "   "11   File

AMENDMENTS
to
OPERATION ORDERS No 3

RATIONS   Para. 8 is now cancelled
          Rations will come up by train to MONCHY RAILHEAD, arriving
at 8.0 p.m. each night. The party of 1 officer and 30 Other Ranks
of "A" Company billeted in the Brown Line will unload all rations.
They will also carry the rations of "B" and "C" Companies to the
respective Company Headquarters.   Battalion Headquarters, "A",
and "D" Companies will be responsible for carrying their own
rations.
          Rations for consumption on the 1"th instant will be carried
to the trenches on the man
          The Quartermaster will arrange for rations to come up
cooked for the above mentioned party of "A" Company to the Brown
Line, by day.

WATER   Para. 9 is now cancelled
          There is only one water point, in HAPPY VALLEY. All water
will be drawn from there

COOKING ARRANGEMENTS   Para. 10
          ADD:-   1 N.C.O. and 6 men of party of "A" Company in
Brown Line will report to Sgt Shadbolt daily at 1.0 a.m. in HAPPY
VALLEY to clean up the cookhouses, etc.

ADD   Para. 13
          There is a dug-out near Battalion Headquarters in ORCHARD
RESERVE which is available for use as a drying room, where men can
change their socks and rub their feet, if required.
          O.C. "B" Company will provide 2 men to take charge of this
dug-out. The Quartermaster will also arrange for special fuel to
come up for use of this dug-out alone, with "B" Company's rations.

                                  (sd) J. A. DAVISON. Capt & Adjt
                                    1st Battn. THE RIFLE BRIGADE

                 To all recipients of
          1st Battn. RIFLE BRIGADE Operation Orders No 3

Page 2; Op 0 No 3

10. COOKING   The cookhouse in ORCHARD RESERVE will cook for "B" Company
    ARRANGEMENTS   and Battalion Headquarters. The remainder of the cooking
                        will be done in the cookhouse in HAPPY VALLEY.
                        Companies will be responsible for drawing their own meals
    from there.

11. REPORT   Completion of relief will be reported by wire, by any sentence
                        containing the word "(S)PARROT".

                        ACKNOWLEDGE.

                                              (sd) J. A. DAVISON,   Capt & Adjt
                                                   1st Battalion THE RIFLE BRIGADE

10/1/16

                              DISTRIBUTION

                        Copy No 1   O.C. "A" Company
                         "   2   "   "B"   "
                         "   3   "   "C"   "
                         "   4   "   "D"   "
                         "   5   Commanding Officer
                         "   6   2nd in Command
                         "   7   Adjutant
                         "   8   Assistant Adjutant
                         "   9   Quartermaster
                         "   10   Transport Officer
                         "   11   2nd Battn The Essex Regt.
                         "   12   War Diary No 1
                         "   13   "   "   No 2
                         "   14   File

GUMBOOTS. 8. There is a Gumboot store at Dead Horse Corner. O.C. "A" Company will detail one N.C.O. and one storeman to take charge of it.

Each Front Line Company will be responsible for changing their own gumboots. Should any extra men be required requisitions for parties will be forwarded to Battalion Headquarters.

Gumboots will be available for each company as shown below. Gumboots issued to each Front Line Company will be kept in the gumboot store, when not actually in use. "A" and "I" Companies will keep their gumboots in their Company Headquarters for use of Working Parties, etc.

  "A" Coy... 30 pairs.
  "B" : ... 200 :
  "C" : ... 200 :
  "I" : ... 30 :

DRYING ROOM. 9. Sock-changing and Drying Rooms are available as shown below:-
 (a) For Right Company- in SHRAPNEL TRENCH, O.s.d.1.4.
 (b) : Left : :: CHAIN SUPPORT, O.1.b.25.25.
 (c) : Support : :: CANISTER, O.1.d.7.5.

"I" Company will be responsible for (c).

Companies concerned will be responsible for keeping a supply of clean socks and towels in their respective Drying rooms. Full use should be made of these drying rooms for the prevention of trench feet.

WORKING PARTIES. 10. Further instructions regarding Working Parties for tomorrow will be issued later.

REPORT. 11. Completion of the relief (less the isolated Posts, in the case of "B" and "C" Companies) will be reported by wire with any sentence containing the Code Word "MALCOLM". "B" and "C" Companies will report completion of relief of Posts by wire, using any sentence containing the Code Word XXXXXX "TANK".

ACKNOWLEDGMENT. 12. The receipt of these orders will be acknowledged.

   (sd) J.A. DAVIDSON. Capt & Adjt.
  1st Battalion, THE RIFLE BRIGADE.

DISTRIBUTION:-

  Copy No.1..Commanding Officer.
  " " 2..Second in Command.
  " " 3..Adjutant.
  " " 4..O.C. 1st SOMERSET LIGHT INFANTRY.
  " " 5..: : "A" Company.
  " " 6..: : "B" :
  " " 7..: : "C" :
  " " 8..: : "I" :
  " " 9..: : D.S. Troops.
  " " 10.Trans.Offr. and Qr.Mr.
  " " 11.War Diary.
  " " 12. : : :
  " " 13. File.
  " " 14. ::

SECRET.   OPERATION ORDERS No. X.4.   APPENDIX V
                                      by
                           Major N.A.O. PRYDE, M.C.
                        Commdg. 1st Battalion, THE RIFLE BRIGADE.

Ref "J" Corps Trench Map
     No. 27(c).   13TH JANUARY, 1918.   Copy No. 11.
==

RELIEF.   1. The Battalion will relieve the 1st Battalion, SOMERSET
               LIGHT INFANTRY in the Front Line, in the Right Sub-Sector,
               tomorrow night, 13th/14th inst.
                   "A" Coy R.B. will relieve Light Coy S.L.I. in Reserve.
                   "B" " "   "   "   "   "   "   "   " on the Right.
                   "C" " "   "   "   "   "   "   "   " :: :Left.
                   "I" " "   "   "   "   "   "   "   " in Support.
               Battalion Headquarters will be in CIRCLE TRENCH, O.1.s.7.4.
                   Relief will be complete by 4.5.pm, with the exception
               of the Isolated Posts which will be relieved as soon as
               darkness permits.   R.B.
                   In turn, "I" Company will be relieved by "H" Company
               S.L.I. in 'F', 'G' and 'H' Strong Points. The garrisons
               will not leave these Strong Points until the completion of
               relief.

ADVANCED   2. Each Company and Bn.H.Q. will send forward one N.C.O.
PARTY.   to take over Trench Stores, etc., to arrive at their re-
               spective Coy H.Q. by 12.0.pm.
                   N.C.Os. of the Somerset Light Infantry will arrive at
               the various H.Q. at 12...pm, with the exception of those
               for old Company.
                  Companies   who will await relief
GUIDES.   3. Guides, with the exception of "I" Company/s, will move
               off from their present position in time to meet guides at
               the times and places shown below. The relief will be carried
               out in the undermentioned order:-
                   "B"- At junction of CANISTER and EAST, at 1...pm.
                   "C"- At junction of BRIDOON and ORCHARD, at 1.10.pm.
                   "A"- At junction of CANISTER and EAST, at 1.20.pm.
                       Battn.H.Q.- No guides will be provided.
                   "I"- At junction of BRIDOON and EAST, at 1.30.pm.
               In all cases one guide per Platoon will be provided.

HANDING   4. All trench stores, etc., will be handed over. Receipts
OVER.   for those handed over and those taken over will be forwarded
               to Battalion Headquarters as soon as possible after the
               completion of relief.

RATIONS.   5. Rations will come up each night to MONCHY Dump.
               O.C. "A" Company will carry rations for "B", "C" and "I"
               Companies; Battn.Hd.Qrs. will carry their own.

WATER.   6. There is a Water Point in FORK RESERVE. Water will be
               supplied in the same manner as rations. With the exception
               of "A" Company, each Company and Hd.Qrs. will take their
               ten water tins to the new sector.

COOKING.   7. Cooking for "B" and "I" Companies will be done in FORK
               RESERVE; for "A", "C" Coys, and Battn.Hd.Qrs in CIRCLE
               TRENCH.   "A"
                   Battn.Hd.Qrs, and "I" Company will draw their own meals.
               "A" Company will carry those of "B" and "C" Companies.

                                                   /A. GORDONS.

SECRET.   Copy No........
                    PRELIMINARY DEFENCE SCHEME:
                    RESERVE BATTALION.   (MONCHY SECTOR.)

Ref: Trench Maps. 51B. S.W.   14th January 1918.

1. The Battalion will be located in the SUNKEN LINE, N. of ARRAS –
    CAMBRAI Road.

2. In the event of a serious hostile attack along the Divisional
    front, the Battalion will "stand to" and be prepared to move in
    artillery formation to the following positions in the intermediate
    line.:-
        Bn. Hd.'rs. - Dugout at H.36.a.05.15. HAPPY VALLEY.
        "B" Coy.   - roughly from H.6.b.20.03 - H.6.a.62.51 thence
                       to H.6.a.19.94. 98.92
        "C" "   - in support in old trenches H.6.a.17.56- H.6.a.19.94.
        "I" "   - between G. & H. strong points H.36.d.81.50 - H.36.c.90.85.
        "A" "   - in support. H.36.c.12.65. - H.36.c.40.91.

    Until the intermediate line is Dug, troops and supporting companies
    will man shell holes.

3. The enemy by a serious attack on a big front may capture
    (i) The spur running S. from TWIN COPSE and his line might
         run as follows :-
         Junction of BIT DARE with front line - DALE TRENCH -
         SADDLE SUPPORT - CAVALRY LANE.
    (ii) The spur N. & S. of, and including MONCHY when his line
         might run :-
         – LA BERGERE FARM - Intermediate Line as far as H Post
         and thence along the spur to the SCARPE.

4. In the event of 3 (i) occurring, the Battalion will form up for
    counter-attack along SADDLE LANE from its junction with VINE AVENUE
    to its junction with SADDLE SUPPORT on a 3 company front.
            "B" Coy. on the Right.
            "C" Coy. in the Centre
            "I" Coy. on the Left.
    "A" Coy. will form up in Support in POME RESERVE, and will follow in
    rear of "I" Coy.
    Battalion Hd.Qrs. will move to CIRCLE TRENCH O.1.c.8.1.
    Objectives of Companies :-
        "B" Coy. from SAP 5 inclusive to INFANTRY LANE exclusive.
        "C" Coy. from INFANTRY LANE inclusive to S. edge of southern
                  TWIN COPSE inclusive.
        "I" Coy. from S. edge of Southern TWIN COPSE exclusive to Junction
                  of old front line and SHAFT ALLEY exclusive.
        "A" Coy. DALE TRENCH and S. part of HIGHLAND SUPPORT.
    "B" & "C" Coys. will each be responsible for clearing and holding
    the old original support line behind their their objective.
    As soon as objectives have been gained, consolidation in the form
    of section lunettes will be   put in hand immediately.
    Outpost posts will be sent out. Great care will be taken to keep
    touch with troops on both flanks
    This counter-attack will be covered by artillery and machine gun barrages
    and will only be delivered after a successful counter-attack has
    been made by the Reserve Battalion of the Right Brigade, which will
    have established a line from about O.14.a.45.97. – Sap 1 – along
       old front line to SAP 5 with a defensive flank facing N.N.E. on
    the line. SAP 5 – O.8.b.0.9. – O.8.a.7.9.

                                                    para.5/

-2-

5. In the event of 3 (ii) occurring the battalion will form up for counter-attack on the line N.17.a.45.00 - N.17.a.20.75.(eastern end of bank).

This counter-attack will be delivered in conjunction with the Reserve battalion of the Right Brigade who will form up on our right.

Dividing line between battalions :- N.17.a.45.00.-N.18.a.6.8. - X road 0.7.c.06.50.

The battalion will be on a 3 Company front.
"C" Coy. on the right.
"A" Coy. in the Centre.
"B" Coy. on the left.
"I" Coy. will form up behind in support and will follow in rear of the centre of the attack.

Objectives of Companies:-
"C" Coy. from X ROADS 0.7.c.06.50 inclusive to C Strong Point inclusive
"A" Coy. from C Strong Point exclusive to D Strong Point inclusive.
"B" Coy. from D Strong Point exclusive to E Strong Point inclusive.
"I" Coy. on a line roughly facing N.N.E. supporting the above objectives to run through and include LE ROMBLE M.M.

Battalion Hd. rs. will move to LES POUSES M.M.

The same system and precautions for consolidation etc. will be adopted as outlined in para.4.

6. All officers will reconnoitre as soon as possible the routes they would take overland to get into the positions named in paras. 2, 4 & 5.

ACKNOWLEDGE.

Lieut.Colonel.
Commanding 1st.Bn.The Rifle Brigade.

Copy No. 1.   "A" Coy.
         2.   "B" "
         3.   "C" "
         4.   "I" "
         5.   C.O.
         6.   Adjutant.
         7.   Intelligence Officer.
         8.   11th.Inf.Brigade.
         9.   Reserve Bn. Right Bde. 4th.Div.
        10.   Left Bn. Left Bde. 4th.Div.
        11.   War Diary.
        12.   "   "
        13.   File.

Key to Attached Disposition Map

— → Left Div. Boundary
— Right Front Line Coy. C. Coy.
— Left " " " B "
— Support Coy. A "
— Reserve " I "

- - - New Reserve Line.
- - - New Support Line.

⚑ Bn. H.Q.
⚑ Coy. H.Q.

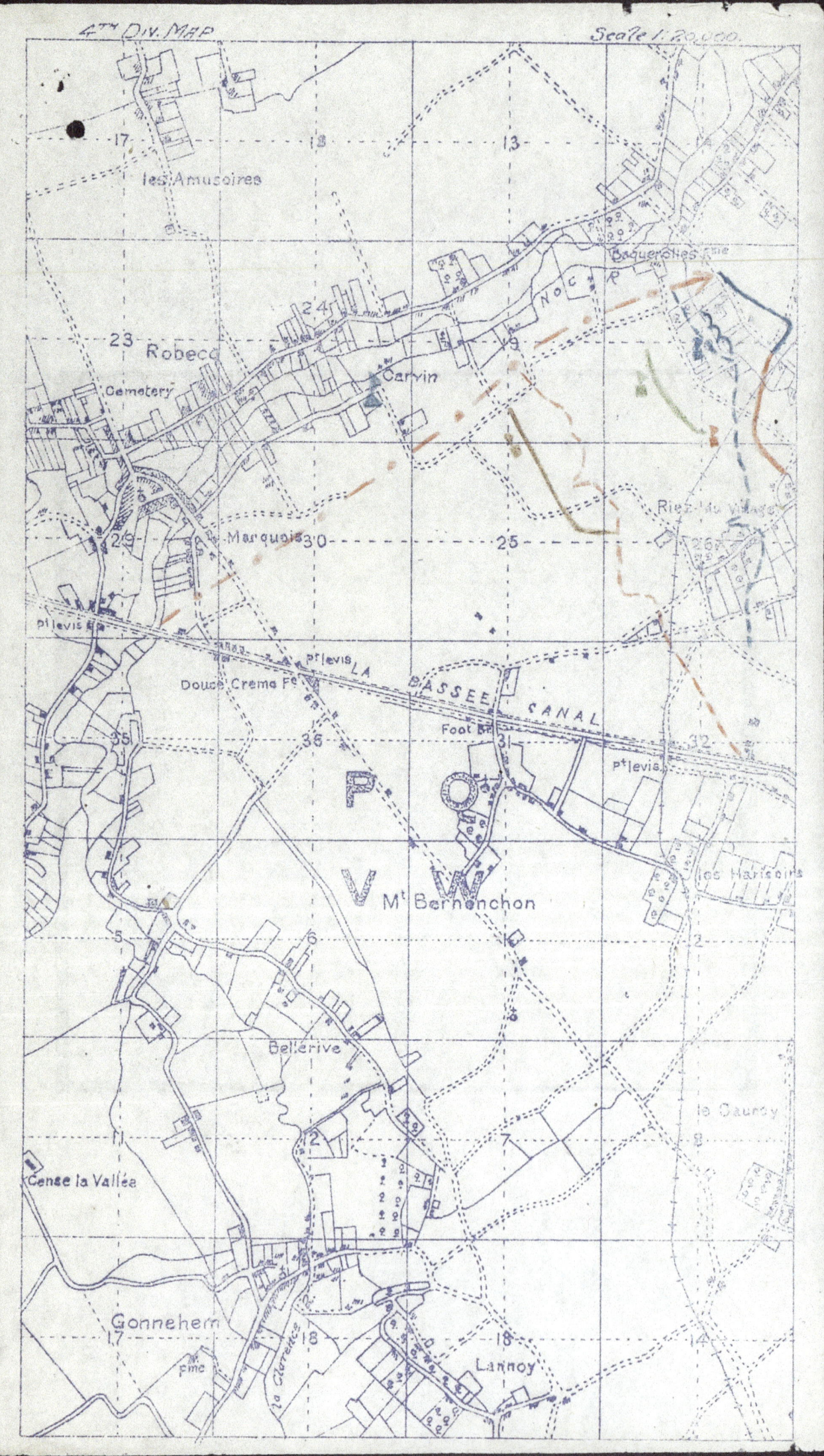

SECRET.

OPERATION ORDERS NO.6.
by
Lieut.Col. R.Y.FELLOWES, DSO., MC.
Commanding,
1st Battalion, THE RIFLE BRIGADE.

Ref. "J" Corps Trench
Map 27 (c).   18th JANUARY, 1918.   Copy No...12.

RELIEF. 1. The Battalion will be relieved in the Front Line tomorrow night, 19th/20th inst, by the 1st Battalion, SOMERSET LIGHT INFANTRY.

"A" Coy RB, will be relieved by "B" Coy SLI, from CURB SWITCH.
"B" "   "   "   "   "   " "C" "   "   from ORCHARD.
"C" "   "   "   "   "   " Light "   from MUSKET.
"I" "   "   "   "   "   " "H" "   "   from 'F', 'G' and 'H' Posts.

"H" Company Som. L.I. will not vacate these Posts until 7.0 pm when relieved by 1st Battn. HAMPSHIRE Regt.
Battn. H.Q. will be relieved at 7.0.pm.
Companies will be relieved in the following order:-
"B"; "C"; "A"; "I".

GUIDES & ROUTE. 2. (a) From "A" Company- one guide per Platoon and one guide per Post to be at DEAD HORSE CORNER at 6.0.pm.

(b) From "B" Company- one guide per Platoon, 'A', 'B' and No. 7. Posts at the junction of SHRAPNEL and CANISTER at 5.30.pm.

One N.C.O. will be detailed to remain at this trench junction and direct any men who may have strayed.

(c). From "C" Company- one guide per Platoon, 'C', and 'D' Posts, at the junction of Track 'B' and ORCHARD RESERVE (O.1.a.75.65)., at 6.0.pm.
Route: via Track 'B'.

(d). From "I" Company- one guide per Platoon at the junction of Track 'B' and ORCHARD RESERVE (O.1.a.75.65) at 7.30.pm.
Route: Track 'B'.

ADVANCED PARTY. 3. O.C. "H" Company SOM.L.I. will send forward an Advanced Party consisting of the four Lewis Gun teams; one N.C.O., etc. and O.C. "I" Company R.B. will arrange to meet this party at the junction of 'S' Track and ORCHARD RESERVE (O.1.a.75.65) at 5.0.pm. to guide it to the Suppers Company Headquarters.

HANDING OVER. 4. All Trench Stores, etc. will be carefully handed over. In the case of "B" Company the main Bomb and S.A.A. Dump should be pointed out on the map.

Receipts will be forwarded to Battalion Headquarters as soon as possible after the completion of the relief.

GUMBOOTS, WATER TINS (EXCEPT THOSE ACTUALLY TAKEN OVER AS TRENCH STORES) TEA PACKS, etc. WILL ALL BE BROUGHT OUT.

GUMBOOTS. 5. Each Company and Headquarters will be responsible for taking out with it the boots it now has in possession. O.C. "A" Company will be responsible for carrying the gumboots in the stores. The Transport Officer will arrange to have eight Pack Ponies at HONCHY DUMP at 7.30.pm. to take gumboots, etc, back to the BROWN LINE.

/6. MOVE.

MOVE. 6. On completion of relief the Battalion will move into Brigade Reserve in the BROWN LINE. Battalion Headquarters will be in the QUARRY at the junction of SWORD LANE and FEUCHY ROAD.

BILLETING PARTY. 7. The Quartermaster, 2/Lieut C.G. MAYNARD and the four C.Q.M.Ss. will meet at the BROWN LINE at 5.0.pm. to allot accommodation. Companies will be provided with a hot meal on arrival.

WORKING PARTIES. 8. Further instructions will be issued later.

REPORT. 9. Completion of the relief will be reported by any sentence containing the Code Word 'GUMBOOTS'.
Care must be taken to see that the message reporting relief complete is not unduly delayed. During the last relief messages were in two cases delayed for over four hours. Should the lines become disconnected messages must be sent at once by visual or runner.

ACKNOWLEDGMENT. 10. The receipt of these orders will be acknowledged by wire.

                                  (sd) J.A. DAVISON. Capt.
              Adjt. 1st Battalion, THE RIFLE BRIGADE.

DISTRIBUTION:-
Copy No. 1. Commdg. Offr.
" " 2. 2nd in Commd.
" " 3. Adjutant.
" " 4. Asst. Adjt.
" " 5. O.C. H.Q. Troops.
" " 6. : "A" Company.
" " 7. : "B"   "
" " 8. : "C"   "
" " 9. : "D"   "
" " 10. : 1st SOMERSET LIGHT INFANTRY
" " 11. Trans Offr & Qr.Mr.
" " 12. War Diary 1.
" " 13. :   :
" " 14. File.

RETURNED STORES.	9. Special care will be taken by all concerned that petrol tins, tea packs, dirty socks and salvage are collected by companies, at some central spot, each evening, and sent back by the ration carrying parties, to be put on the returning ration train from MONCHY Dump. Should the train have left before the carrying parties arrive, the abovementioned articles will be dumped at "B" Coy.H.Q., in CIRCLE TRENCH. O.C. "B" Company will be responsible that these articles are then put on the train the following evening. /Issue All Company Commanders will issue special orders to give effect to these instructions.
GUMBOOTS.	10. The Quartermaster will arrange to have all gumboots sent to Battalion Headquarters, tomorrow morning. Coys will draw these on the following scale:- "A" Coy- 110 pairs; "B" Coy- 30 pairs; "C" : 40 : "I" : 110 : Battalion Headquarters- 30 pairs. They will be carried to the trenches, on the man. O.C. "B" Company will detail one N.C.O. and one man to proceed in advance of "I" Company, to DEAD HORSE CORNER, to take over the gumboot store. Companies will dump any pairs they do not require, there, as they pass. The Quartermaster will arrange for the remainder of the gumboots to come up with the reserve water supply. They will be carried by "B" Company, to the gumboot store.
TAKING OVER.	11. All trench stores will be carefully taken over and receipts forwarded to Battalion Headquarters as soon as possible after completion of relief.
SICK PARADE.	12. Sick parade will be carried out as during the last tour, at each Company Headquarters.
REPORT.	13. The completion of relief will be reported by wire, by any sentence containing the Code Word "WATTLE".
ACKNOWLEDGMENT.	14. The receipt of these orders will be acknowledged.

        (sd) J.A. DAVISON. Captain.
   Adjutant, 1st Battalion, THE RIFLE BRIGADE

DISTRIBUTION:-

Copy No. 1..Commanding Officer.
" " 2..Adjutant.
" " 3..Assistant Adjutant & Intelligence Off.
" " 4..O.C. 1st Battn SOMERSET LIGHT INFANTRY
" " 5..: : "A" Company.
" " 6..: : "B" :
" " 7..: : "C" :
" " 8..: : "I" :
" " 9..Transport Offr & Quartermaster.
" " 10..O.C. Battn.H.Q. Troops.
" " 11..War Diary No.1.
" " 12..: : : : " 2.
" " 13..File.
" " 14.. "

SECRET.   OPERATION ORDER No.6.
                              by
                  Lieut.Col.R.T.FELLOWES.DSO.,MC
                          Commanding,
                  1st Battalion, THE RIFLE BRIGADE.

Ref. "J" Corps Trench
Map No.87(c).   22nd JANUARY,1918.   Copy No...11

RELIEF.   1. The Battalion will relieve 1st Battalion, SOMERSET
           LIGHT INFANTRY, in the Front Line, tomorrow night 23/24 inst.
           "A" Coy R.B. will relieve "C" Coy S.L.I. on the Right Front.
           "B" : : :   : :   :   "E" : : :   in Reserve.
           "C" : : :   : :   :   "H" : : :   :: Support.
           "I" : : :   : :   :   Light : : :   : on Left Front.
              "A" Coy H.Q. will be in SHRAPNEL TRENCH.
              Battn.H.Q. will be at junction of CHERRY LANE and
           CIRCLE TRENCH.
              Order of Relief- "I"; "A"; "C";"B"; Battn.H.Q.

GUIDES.   2. No guides will be provided. Companies will proceed to
           their respective Coy H.Qs. direct, via Tracks "A" or "B".

MOVE.   3. The Battalion will move from present position, by
           platoons at 200 yards interval- the leading platoon of "I"
           Company leaving the BROWN LINE, at 4.30.pm.

TRANSPORT. 4. One Pack Pony will be at the disposal of each Company
           and two for Battn.H.Q. to take trench kit, etc.
              All valises, blankets, packs, etc., will be dumped out-
           side the Guard Room by 12.0. noon. The Transport Officer
           will arrange to collect them. Cookers will move off in-
           dependently, after dinner.
                Rations
RATIONS.   5. /For the 24th inst will be carried on the man. Each
           succeeding night rations will come up by train, arriving
           at MONCHY Railhead at 6.0.pm.

WATER.   6. The water point in FORK RESERVE is at present in work-
           ing order. The Medical Officer will detail two R.A.M.C.
           MEN to be in charge of water supply.
              The following will come up by the ration train tomorrow
           night, 23rd inst, and will be disposed of as shown, as
           soon after 6.0.pm, as possible:-
           7. Hot Food Containers, to be carried by "B" Company to
                                  FORK RESERVE.
              50 Full tins of water, namely 10 tins to be carried by
              "B" Company to each of "A" and "I".
                  "B", "C" and Battn.H.Q. carry 10 tins for
                                  themselves.
              Remainder of gumboots, to be carried by "B" Company to
                                  DEAD HORSE CORNER.
              26 tea packs: 6 packs to be carried for each Company and
                 2 for Battn.H.Q.- to be carried as for Water Tins.

CARRYING, 7. ~~The carrying will be done as usual, by "B" Company,~~
SUPPLY,etc.~~except rations of which "C" Company and Battn.H.Q. will~~
           ~~carry their own.~~ R.E. material & Rations will be carried by 'B' Coy:
              except for 'C' Coy. & Battn. H.Q. who will carry their own.

HOT FOOD. 8. In order to give the men an extra hot drink during the
           day and in addition to the tea packs, that will come up
           each night, the following arrangements will be made. Each
           Company and Battn.H.Q. will detail one cook for the cook-
           houses. Hot soups, or cocoa or Oxo will be prepared during
           the night and put into Hot Food Containers as late as
           possible. In the early morning each Company and Battn.H.Q.
           will send a party down in time to fetch their containers
           and return to their companies before it is too light to
           travel overland. Containers will be kept in dugouts and
           will not be opened until it is desired to issue the hot
           drink. Companies and Battn.H.Q. will be responsible for re-
           turning the containers to the cookhouses in the evening.

                                                 /9. RETURNED STORES.

SECRET

APPENDIX IX

OPERATION ORDERS No 7
by
Lieut.Colonel R. T. FELLOWES, DSO, MC.,
Commanding
1st Battalion THE RIFLE BRIGADE

26th JANUARY, 1918   Copy No 12

RELIEF 1.   The Battalion will be relieved in the front line by the
HOUSEHOLD BATTALION to-morrow night, 27th/28th instant.

"I" Coy. RIFLE BRIGADE will be relieved by No 1 Coy HOUSEHOLD BATT.
"A" "   "   "   "   "   " No 2 "   "   "
"C" "   "   "   "   "   " No 4 "   "   "
"B" "   "   "   "   "   " No 3 "   "   "

Companies will be relieved in the above order.

GUIDES 2.   Guides at the rate of 1 per platoon and 1 per Battalion
Headquarters will be provided for each Company. These guides
will report to ~~the~~ Lieut. G.J. Cole ~~Adjutant~~ at Battalion Headquarters
at 4.30 p.m.   These guides will meet the relieving Battalion
at a point where the CORPS LINE crosses SWORD LANE at 5.40 p.m.
         "C" and "I" Companies will conduct their relief via track
"B", and "A" and "B" Companies via track "A".
         Guides for the isolated posts will be provided from Com-
pany Headquarters.

ADVANCE 3.   No advance parties will be sent by the HOUSEHOLD BATTALION.
PARTY

HANDING 4.   Special care will be taken in handing over trench stores, etc.
OVER   Receipts will be obtained and will be forwarded to Battalion Headquarters, as soon as possible after the completion of relief.
All petrol tins, except those taken over as trench stores, tea packs,
gum boots, salvage, etc., will be carried out.
         Special care will be taken to hand over all trenches, posts,
dug-outs, etc., in as clean and sanitary condition as possible.
All latrines will be emptied before relief, and the latrine pits
will be filled in.

MOVE   5.   On completion of the relief the Battalion will move to
billets in ARRAS.   Platoons will move off independently at an
interval of 200 yards.   14 lorries have been allotted to the
Battalion.   These will be drawn up near FEUCHY CHAPEL CROSS
ROADS.   Platoons on arrival will report to Lieut. G. J. Cole,
who is assisting 2/Lieut. G. Bland, who is acting as embussing
officer.

TRANSPORT 6.   The Transport Officer will arrange to have 2 limbers per
Company and 2 for Battalion Headquarters at MONCHY DUMP.
These limbers will take the trench kits, Lewis Guns, ammunition,
water tins, tea packs, gum boots not being worn, etc.   Two men
only will accompany each limber.

GUM BOOTS 7.   Gumboots at present on charge of Companies will be taken
out by them, ankle boots being worn as far as possible.   The gum
boots in the store will be put on a special train, by "B" Company.
This train will also take any surplus water tins, etc., which did
not go back by the train to-night.   Further particulars of this
train will be notified to O.C. "B" Company later.

STRENGTHS 8.   Companies will render by wire their exact trench strength
to reach Battalion Headquarters by not later than 9.30 a.m.
to-morrow.   The daily metal report will be rendered as usual.

Advance party 9/

O.O. 7: Page 2

ADVANCE PARTY 9. Lieut. G. W. Glover, D.S.O., the four C.Q.M.Ss and 1 N.C.O. for Battalion Headquarters will report to the Town Major "A" Area at 10.30 a.m. to take over accomodation for Officers' messes. The Quartermaster, 4 C.Q.M.Ss, 1 N.C.O. per Battalion Headquarters and 16 Buglers will report to Captain Hall, 4th Division, at "J" Pavillion, SCHRAMM BARRACKS, to take over men's accomodation.

REPORT 10. Completion of the relief will be reported by wire by any sentence containing the code word "MONKMAN".

ACKNOWLEDGE.

                              (sd) J. A. DAVISON, Capt &
                                                   Adjt
                  1st Battn. THE RIFLE BRIGADE

DISTRIBUTION

Copy No		
1	O.C. "A" Company
2	" "B" "
3	" "C" "
4	" "I" "
5	Commanding Officer
6	2nd in Command
7	Adjutant
8	Assistant Adjutant
9	Intelligence Officer
10	Transport Officer & Quartermaster
11	Household Battalion
12	War Diary No 1
13	" " 2
14	File.

SECRET

OPERATION ORDER NO. 3.
by
Lieut.Col.R.T.FELLOWES, DSO., MC,
1st Battalion, THE RIFLE BRIGADE,
30th JANUARY, 1918.   Copy No. 11

RELIEF. 1. The Battalion will relieve the 1st Battalion SOMERSET LIGHT INFANTRY in BOIS DES BOEUFS Camp, tomorrow morning, 31st inst.

"A" Coy. R.Bde. will relieve Light Coy, SOM.L.I.
"B" :   : ::   "   :   "B" : : ::
"C" :   : ::   "   :   "C" : : ::
"I" :   : ::   "   :   "H" : : ::

Order of relief: Headquarters; "B"; "A"; "C"; "I".
Headquarters will move off at 8.0.am.
An interval of 300 yards will be maintained between platoons on the move.
Cookers and necessary transport will follow in rear of the Battalion.
"I" Company will detail one platoon as Baggage Guard.

ADVANCED PARTY. 2. An advanced party of one N.C.O. per company and one from Battalion Headquarters will report at Orderly Room at 6.30.am. They will be marched to Bois Des Boeufs Camp under the senior and will take over stores, accommodation, etc. They will meet their companies on the CAMBRAI Road.
Lists of stores taken over will be rendered to Orderly Room by not later than 2.0.pm.

BAGGAGE. 3. Officers' kits, mess equipment, etc., will be packed and dumped outside officers' messes at 8.30.am.
Blankets will be rolled in bundles of ten and dumped on the Square, by Companies, by 8.30.am.
One N.C.O. and eight men of the Baggage Guard will load these.

FATIGUE. 4. Each Company will detail two men to report to the Provost Corporal, at 9.0.am. This party will remain behind and clean up the Barracks.

RATIONS. 5. Rations will be delivered as usual.

WATER. 6. Water may be obtained from the Water Point in Camp.

WORKING PARTIES. 7. Particulars of the Work to be done on ni[ght] 1st Feb. are issued herewith.

ACKNOWLEDGE.

(sd) J.A. DAVIS
Adjutant, 1st Battalion, THE RIF[LE BRIGADE]

DISTRIBUTION:-

Copy No. 1..Commanding Officer.
 "   " 2..Second in Command.
 "   " 3..Adjutant.
 "   " 4..Assistant Adjutant.
 "   " 5..Intelligence Officer.
 "   " 6..O.C. "A" Company.
 "   " 7.. " : "B"   :
 "   " 8.. " : "C"   :
 "   " 9.. " : "I"   :
 "   " 10..Trans. Offr & Quartermast[er]
 "   " 11..War Diary No. 1.
 "   " 12.. "   :   " :
 "   " 13..File.
 "   " 14.. "

SECRET

WARNING ORDER
by
Lieut.Colonel R.T.FELLOWES, D.S.O., M.C.
Commanding
1st Battalion THE RIFLE BRIGADE

REF. MAP 51 B. N.W. 21st FEBRUARY, 1918. COPY No 10

Infantry

MOVE 1. The 11th Brigade will be prepared to move at short notice to billets in ARRAS (Either SCHRAMM BARRACKS or ECOLE COMMUNALE).
   The Battalion will march to BERNEVILLE and will move from there in buses. Buses will be loaded 5 at a time along the road from R.1.d.95.60 to R.1.d.2.5. Further instructions regarding embussing will be notified later.
   The Transport will move to G.20.a.3.1.

PERSONNEL 2. The personnel of the Battalion detailed in S.S.135, Section 30, para 2, will be left behind when the Brigade moves up into action. Companies and Headquarters will submit the necessary nominal Rolls (retaining one copy) stating those ~~going into and those~~ being left out of action.
   The above personnel will be used
   (a) to clear up billets vacated by troops going into action,
   (b) to collect stores, blankets and men's packs under orders to be issued by the senior officer remaining behind.
   After completion of the above mentioned duties the party will move to the 4th Divisional Depot Battalion at AGNEZ LES DUISANS.
   The transport of the 26th Battalion NORTHUMBERLAND FUSILIERS will be used to take rations for this party to the Depot Battalion on the following day.
   The party will use one cooker from this transport.

AMMUNITION 3. Companies and Headquarters will complete their S.A.A. up to 200 rounds per man, from that stored for practice purposes or from the Mobile Reserve.

TRANSPORT 4. Detailed orders for the move of the Transport to G.20.a.3.1. will be issued later.
   The pack animals of the 26th Battn. NORTHUMBERLAND FUSILIERS will move with Brigade Headquarters transport.

BAGGAGE & STORES 5. In the first instance baggage wagons will not be required, as Packs, Blankets, etc can be stored in WARLUS. The location of this store will be notified later. The transport of the 26th Batt. NORTHUMBERLAND FUSILIERS will be available for collecting. The transport of the 3/10 MIDDLESEX will be available for collecting stores after completing those of the 13th Brigade.
   Should opportunity arise later for officers to use their Baggage arrangements will be made with the Divisional train to send baggage wagons.

SUPPLIES 6. These will probably be delivered at the present Quarter Master's Stores for the day following troops going into action. Should however the warning order come out before 10.0 a.m. rations will then be sent to transport camps at G.20.a.3.1.
   Subsequently it may be possible to find good Quarter Master's Stores near the PORTE DU BAUDIMENT in which case arrangements for supplies to be taken to the stores will be made by the Quarter Master direct with O.C. No 3 Company Train.

7. ACKNOWLEDGE.

[signature]

Captain
Adjutant 1st Battalion THE RIFLE BRIGADE

DISTRIBUTION on Reverse.

DISTRIBUTION

Copy No	1	Commanding Officer
:	2	Adjutant
:	3	Assistant Adjutant
:	4	Transport Officer
:	5	Quarter Master
:	6	O.C. "A" Company
:	7	: "B" :
:	8	: "C" :
:	9	: "D" :
:	10	War Diary No 1
:	11	: 2
:	12	File
:	13	:
:	14	:

loaded by 10.0.am.

5. TRANSPORT: Cookers will move off as soon after breakfast as possible. The transport required for the removal of kits, etc. will rejoin the remainder of the 1st Line Transport as soon as possible after the times mentioned in para 4.
The 1st Line Transport will fall in in rear of the Battalion at the Place de la ~~Gauss~~ Gare, ARRAS.

6. DINNERS: The Battalion will halt from 1.55.pm to 2.35.pm for dinners which will be prepared on route.

7. MATERIAL: Companies and Headquarters will indent on the Orderly Room for any tables or forms that they require in the new area. Indents should reach Orderly Room by not later than 12.0.noon, 6th instant.

8. REPORT: Companies will render to Orderly Room within an hour of arrival in new area a state showing:-
    (a) Number of men fallen out, not rejoined.
    (b) Number of men fallen out and since rejoined.
    (c) Number of men fallen out and brought in by baggage guard.

9. ACKNOWLEDGE.

(sd) J.A. DAVISON.   Captain.
Adjutant, 1st Battalion, THE RIFLE BRIGADE.

DISTRIBUTION:-

Copy No.1..Commanding Officer.
" " 2..Second in Command.
" " 3..Adjutant.
" " 4..Assistant Adjutant.
" " 5..Intelligence Officer.
" " 6..O.C. "A" Company.
" " 7.. "   "B"   "
" " 8.. "   "C"   "
" " 9.. "   "D"   "
" " 10. Transport Officer.
" " 11. Quartermaster.
" " 12..War Diary No.1.
" " 13.. "   "   " 2.
" " 14..File.

SECRET. Copy No 12

AMENDMENTS to OPERATION ORDERS No 9

I. Ref. Para.1: Battalion Headquarters will move off from the open space west of the Camp at 10.45 a.m.

II Ref. Para.1: ROUTE is cancelled and the following substituted:
Road Junction, H.31.d.2.0. (ESTAMINET CORNER) - TILLOY - BEAURAINS - ACHICOURT - Road Junction, L.35.b.6.7. - Le BAC du NORD - thence by BEAUMETZ to SIMENCOURT.
Headquarters will pass ESTAMINET CORNER at 11.0 a.m.

III Ref. Para.1: Delete from "An interval .... will be maintained" and substitute "An interval of 200 yards between Platoons, Companies and Transport will be maintained until the halt for dinners. After this halt an interval of 200 yards between Companies and Transport only will be maintained".

IV Ref. Para 1: The Buglers will join the Battalion at the Cross Roads, M.4.c. They will march first with "B" Company, then with "A", "C" and "I" Companies respectively after each halt.

V Ref. Para. 5: After "As soon as possible" add "to rejoin Transport".
The head of the 1st Line Transport will be at the Cross Roads, M.4.c,, facing south, in rear of the Buglers. They will fall in and follow 200 yards in rear of "I" Company.

VI Ref. Para. 6: Para. 6 is cancelled and the following is substituted:
"When the head of the Battalion reaches the point G.31.b.0.3. the Battalion will halt, closing up to companies at 90 yards interval.
Haversack rations will be carried and will be eaten during this halt.
The Battalion will resume the march at 1.30 p.m. opening out to companies at 200 yards interval.
Dinners will be provided on arrival in new area.

VII Ref. Para. 7: Companies will also indent for any material for the improvement of billets.

VIII Ref. Para. 8: Insert after paragraph 8, new paragraph 9:-
"HINTS FOR MARCH:
(a) All men should wash their feet in cold water and cut their toe nails that morning.
(b) Wherever possible put on clean socks.
(c) Soap freely the soles of the socks and put them on carefully avoiding wrinkles.
(d) Lace the boots firmly and evenly - any knots in bootlaces should not be used next to the foot.
(e) Any small sores or skin abrasions should be dressed at the Aid Post before starting".

(sd) J. A. DAVISON, Captain
Adjutant 1st Battalion THE RIFLE BRIGADE

DISTRIBUTION - as for O.O. No 9

WAR DIARY or INTELLIGENCE SUMMARY

Army Form C. 2118.

Place	Date	Hour	Summary of Events and Information	Remarks and references to Appendices
BUS LES ARTOIS / BOEURS CAMP	FEB 1st		Working parties found by the Bn. Escort Party of 300 men to take on Corporation Star Flakes in the morning & prepare for 4th Army F.M. the Afternoon. Carpet tape and improved plan of demonstration. Bn. was inspected by the G.O.C. 51st Battn. Highlanders and handed to billet in — SIMENCOURT	See Appendix A
SIMENCOURT	5th to 9th	8am	Company and Battalion Training. Dress Rehearsal Pack for Physical Training, Regtl. & Platoon and learn from the Range knowing musketry, fighting and may tanks.	SHEET 51C SCALE 1/10,000
	8th		Weather fine up to 8th. May Rifle Association Competition. Firing Platoon of the Bn. won 2nd in 10/30m short shoot, taking place in 5th Major F.F.B. Page R.C. left for Beachin to command 20/73rd	
	14th		THE RIFLE BRIGADE	
	21st		Brigade Scheme in the Training Area K.19,20,25,26. Scheme - Enemy retreating to the Hindenburg Reserve Line, taken by British, from whom 89 O.E. the 3rd and 4th Infantry Brigades take the Rifle Brigade on the left were ordered to combined attack to regain the original front line	See Appendix
	26th		Brigade Scheme: the Starfordshire Regt and the Rifle Brigade ordered to make an attack by the Yeomanry Regt Cav & 5th	

Casualties Nil
Attached Sect 18 O.Rks. 2 Q.M.A.A.C. Type.2.18
Reinforcements 2 Lt. Martin 27.2.18 and 89 O.Ranks
W.O. for Env. 14.2.18 – 2 Lt Donald – 2 Lt Corporal 4. 2 Bn Rifle Brigade 14.2.18 – 2 Lt Holland to England (sick (inf)) 9.2.18
Lieut. Eytle Strength 12 – 2 Lt Holland – Buck 1 – Off. Strength 13.2.18 – 2 Lt McLaughlin – 20 TMB – Off. Strength 14.2.18
2 Lt Holland to England (Sick ins) 9.2.18
O.B.N. Strength 132.18 O.R.'s Strength 684

LIEUT. COMMANDING
1st Bn. THE RIFLE BRIGADE

SECRET.
OPERATION ORDER No.9.
by
Lieut.Col. R.T. FELLOWES. D.S.O., M.C.
Commanding,
1st Battalion, THE RIFLE BRIGADE.

Ref Sheets 51.B.
and 51.C.   3rd FEBRUARY, 1918.   Copy NO. 12

1. **RELIEF**: The Battalion will be relieved in the BOIS DES BOEUFS Camp by the 6th Battalion ROYAL HIGHLANDERS, on 6th inst. Companies will be relieved in the order shown below, by corresponding companies of the relieving Battalion:-
   Headquarters; "B"; "A"; "C"; "I".
   On completion of the relief the Battalion will march to billets in SIMENCOURT.
   As each company, or headquarters is relieved it will move to the open space on the west side of the Camp.
   Battalion Headquarters will move off from there at 11.30.am.
   Route: Faubourg St. SAUVEUR - Iron Bridge over Railway (G.99.b.9.7) - North East gateway of SCHRAMM BARRACKS - road junction (G.91.d.?.?) - factory, L.30.b.- Le BAC du NORD (R.6.c) - cross roads, R.1.c.9.6. - SIMENCOURT.
   Headquarters will not pass the north east gateway of SCHRAMM BARRACKS until 12.30.pm.
   Dress: Marching Order less packs; the haversack will be worn on the back.
   An interval of 200 yards between platoons will be maintained until the first halt after ARRAS, when an interval of 200 yards between companies only will be maintained. At all times the Transport will follow 200 yards in rear of the last Platoon of "I" Company.
   O.C. "I" Company will detail one platoon as Baggage Guard. This platoon will also bring along all stragglers.
   BUGLERS will join the Battalion in ARRAS and will march with Headquarters until the first halt after ARRAS, when they will march with each company in turn, starting with "B" Company.

2. **HANDING OVER**: Each company will detail two men to report to Cpl LEACH at 9.0.am, on 5th instant. 2/Lieut E.J. GRAY will remain behind with this party to clean up the Camp. The Camp and surroundings will be left scrupulously clean. A certificate to this effect, including a statement that all stores, etc., have been handed over correctly, will be obtained from the Area Commandant. The Quartermaster and the Transport Officer will obtain similar receipts from the Area Commandant "A" Area, ARRAS.
   All the abovementioned receipts will be forwarded to reach Orderly Room, by not later than 2.0.pm, 5th instant.

3. **ADVANCED PARTY**: Billeting Party consisting of the four C.Q.M.Ss. and one N.C.O. for Battalion Headquarters will meet the Assistant Adjutant at the Town Major's office, SIMENCOURT, at 2.0.pm, tomorrow, 4th instant.
   Rations for consumption on 5th instant will be carried.
   This party will meet the Supply wagons, containing rations for 6th instant at 10.0.am, 5th instant, outside the Town Major's office. They will guide the wagons to the Quartermaster's store.

4. **BAGGAGE**: Four lorries are at the disposal of the Battalion. These lorries will arrive at 9.0.am. The Assistant Adjutant will arrange to have a man on the lookout for these lorries to stop them outside the Camp.
   Two lorries will take packs and two lorries, blankets.
   They will be loaded and ready to move off at 9.30.am.
   The Baggage wagons to take officers' valises will be *loaded by 10.0 Am. Each Company will have at its disposal half a limber, which will take the Lewis guns, Ammunition, Mess Equipment etc. These limbers will also be loaded by 10.0 Am.*

SECRET

WARNING ORDER
by
Lieut.Colonel R.T.FELLOWES, D.S.O., M.C.
Commanding
1st Battalion THE RIFLE BRIGADE

REF. MAP 51 B. N.W.   21st FEBRUARY, 1918.   COPY No 11

              Infantry
MOVE   1.   The 11th Brigade will be prepared to move at short notice to billets in ARRAS (Either SCHRAMM BARRACKS or ECOLE COMMUNALE).
                  The Battalion will march to BERNEVILLE and will move from there in buses. Buses will be loaded 20 at a time along the road from R.1.d.95.60 to R.1.d.9.5. Further instructions regarding embussing will be notified later.
                  The Transport will move to G.20.a.3.1.

                      the
PERSONNEL 2.   The personnel of each Battalion detailed in S.S.135,
                Section 30, para 2, will be left behind when the Brigade moves up into action. Companies and Headquarters will submit the necessary nominal Rolls (retaining one copy) stating those ~~going into and those~~ being left out of action.
                The above personnel will be used
        (a) to clear up billets vacated by troops going into action,
        (b) to collect stores, blankets and men's packs under orders to be issued by the senior officer remaining behind.
                After completion of the above mentioned duties the party will move to the 4th Divisional Depot Battalion at AGNEZ LES DUISANS.
                The transport of the 26th Battalion NORTHUMBERLAND FUSILIERS will be used to take rations for this party to the Depot Battalion on the following day.
                The party will use one cooker from this transport.

AMMUNITION 3.   Companies and Headquarters will complete their S.A.A. up to 200 rounds per man, from that stored for practice purposes or from the Mobile Reserve.

TRANSPORT 4.   Detailed orders for the move of the Transport to G.20.a.3.1. will be issued later.
                The pack animals of the 26th Battn. NORTHUMBERLAND FUSILIERS will move with Brigade Headquarters transport.

BAGGAGE 5.   In the first instance baggage wagons will not be required,
& STORES   as Packs, Blankets, etc can be stored in WARLUS. The location of this store will be notified later. The transport of the 26th Batt. NORTHUMBERLAND FUSILIERS will be available for collecting. The transport of the 3/10 MIDDLESEX will be available for collecting stores after completing those of the 12th Brigade.
                Should opportunity arise later for officers to use their Baggage arrangements will be made with the Divisional train to send baggage wagons.

SUPPLIES 6.   These will probably be delivered at the present Quarter Master's Stores for the day following troops going into action. Should however the warning order come out before 10.0 a.m. rations will then be sent to transport camps at G.20.a.3.1.
                Subsequently it may be possible to find good Quarter Master's Stores near the PORTE DU BAUDIMENT in which case arrangements for supplies to be taken to the stores will be made by the Quarter Master direct with O.C. No 3 Company Train.

        7. ACKNOWLEDGE.

                                              Captain
                      Adjutant 1st Battalion THE RIFLE BRIGADE

DISTRIBUTION on Reverse.

DISTRIBUTION

Copy No	1	Commanding Officer
:	2	Adjutant
:	3	Assistant Adjutant
:	4	Transport Officer
:	5	Quarter Master
:	6	O.C. "A" Company
:	7	: "B" :
:	8	: "C" :
:	9	: "D" :
:	10	War Diary No 1
:	11	: 2
:	12	File
:	13	:
:	14	:

SECRET   COPY NO
                    AMENDMENT TO WARNING ORDER
                    ----=-=-=-=-=-=-=-=-=-----   T 3,/30

    Reference Paragraph 2 of Battalion Warning Order dated 21-2-16,
the following personnel will be left out of action.

    (1)   Officers ....   To be detailed later.
    (2)   C.S.M.s   ....   To be detailed later.
    (3)   From all Companies   1 Sergeant (a)   3 Rifle Grenadiers
                                 1 Corporal (a)   3 Scouts or Snipers
                                 1 A/Corporal (a)   8 Lewis Gunners
                                 2 Signallers   1 Runner
    (4)   From Headquarters   1 Lewis Gun Instructor   - Sgt. RYE
                                 1 Musketry Instructor   - Sgt. GRAY
                                 1 Bombing Instructor   - Sgt. ROUNDS
                                 2 Signallers
    (5)   From "A" Coy.   1 Gas Instructor   - Sgt. HAYTER
           "   "D" "   1 P.T. & B.F. Instructor - Sgt. WELCH
           "   "C" "   1 Lewis Gun Instructor   - Cpl. SCALES
           "   "B" "   1 Sniping Instructor   - Cpl. WOODALL
          In addition to those
          mentioned in (3)

    Note (a) At least one of these N.C.Os will be an instructor in some
branch or other.

    N.B.   N.C.O.s and men on leave and on courses of instruction will
be reckoned as being left out of action - i.e. if a Company has one
signaller and two Lewis gunners on leave or on a course, they will
only detail one more signaller and 4 more Lewis gunners to remain
out of action.

        Nominal rolls of the above will be prepared at once, and
corrected and kept up to date as necessity arises, so that, should
the necessity arise, nominal rolls of those to be left out of action
can be submitted at short notice.

                            approximate
    STATE SHOWING NUMBER OF OFFICERS AND OTHER RANKS GOING INTO
ACTION WITH COMPANY WILL BE RENDERED BY 8.0 p.m. TODAY.

                                            J.A.Dawson
                                                   Captain
                                    Adjt. 1st Battalion THE RIFLE BRIGADE

23rd FEBRUARY, 1916

                          DISTRIBUTION

              Copy No 1 Commanding Officer
                "   2 Adjutant
                "   3 Asst. Adjutant
                "   4 Transport Officer
                "   5 Quartermaster
                "   6 O.C. "A" Coy.
                "   7 "   "B" "
                "   8 "   "C" "
                "   9 "   "D" "
                "   10 War Diary No 1
                "   11   "   "   No 2
                "   12 File
                "   13   "
                "   14   "

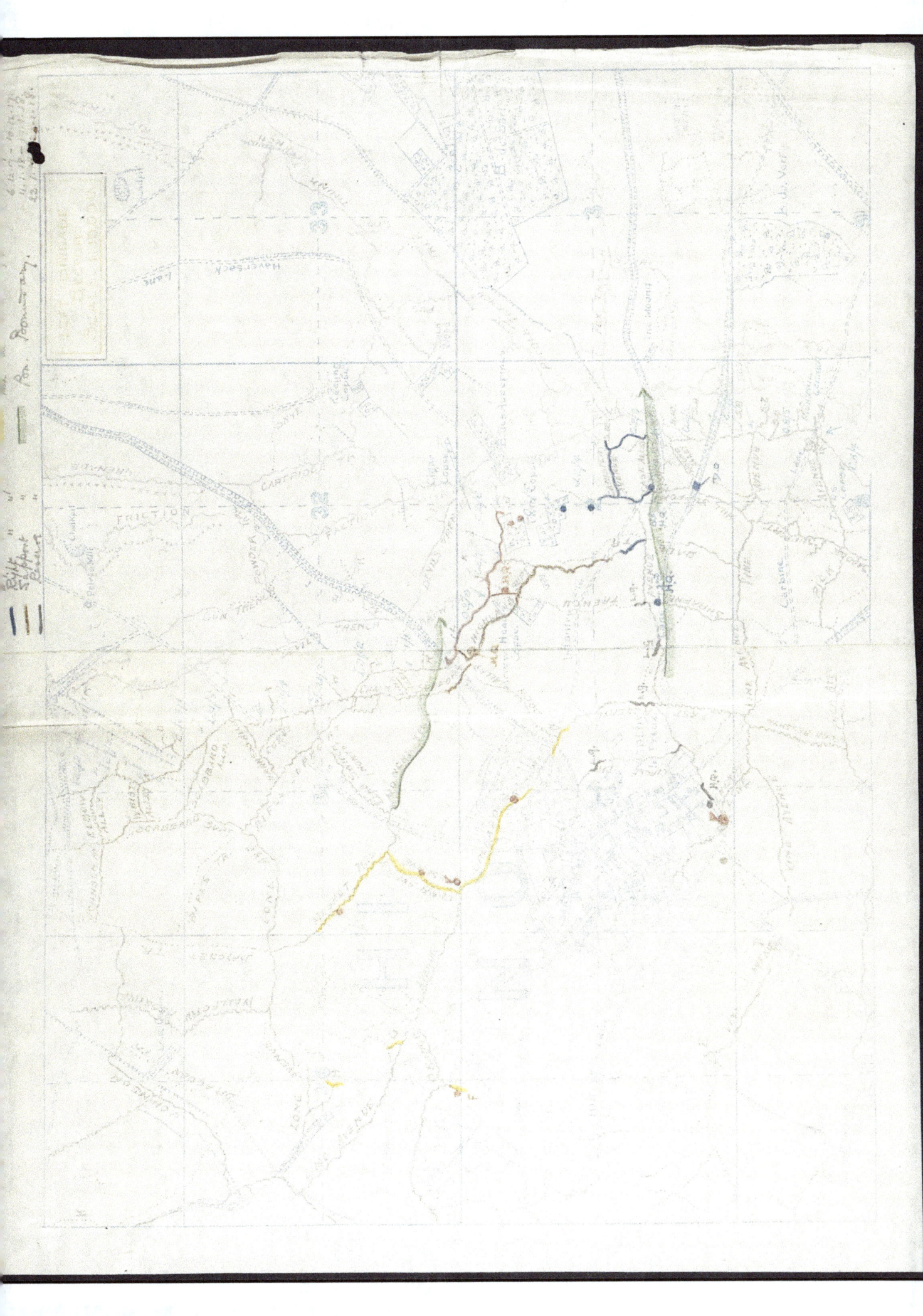

SECRET
AMENDMENT TO WARNING ORDER

~~COPY NO~~ J31/30

Reference Paragraph 2 of Battalion Warning Order dated 21-2-18, the following personnel will be left out of action.

(1)	Officers	<u>To be detailed later.</u>	
(2)	C.S.M.s	<u>To be detailed later.</u>	
(3)	From all Companies	1 Sergeant (a)	3 Rifle Grenadiers
		1 Corporal (a)	3 Scouts or Snipers
		1 A/Corporal (a)	6 Lewis Gunners
		2 Signallers	1 Runner
(4)	From Headquarters	1 Lewis Gun Instructor	- Sgt. RYE
		1 Musketry Instructor	- Sgt. GRAY
		1 Bombing Instructor	- Sgt. ROUNDS
		2 Signallers	
(5)	From "A" Coy.	1 Gas Instructor	- Sgt. HAYTER
	" "B" "	1 P.T. & B.F. Instructor	- Sgt. WELCH
	" "C" "	1 Lewis Gun Instructor	- Cpl. SCALES
	" "D" "	1 Sniping Instructor	- Cpl. WOODALL

In addition to those
mentioned in (3)

Note (a) At least one of these N.C.Os will be an instructor in some branch or other.

N.B.   N.C.O.s and men on leave and on courses of instruction will be reckoned as being left out of action - i.e. if a Company has one signaller and two Lewis gunners on leave or on a course, they will only detail one more signaller and 4 more Lewis gunners to remain out of action.

Nominal rolls of the above will be prepared at once, and corrected and kept up to date as necessity arises, so that, should the necessity arise, nominal rolls of those to be left out of action can be submitted at short notice.

Approximate
STATE SHOWING NUMBER OF OFFICERS AND OTHER RANKS GOING INTO ACTION WITH COMPANY WILL BE RENDERED BY C.O p.m. TODAY.

J A Dawson
Captain
Adjt. 1st Battalion THE RIFLE BRIGADE

23rd FEBRUARY, 1918

DISTRIBUTION

Copy No	1	Commanding Officer
"	2	Adjutant
"	3	Asst. Adjutant
"	4	Transport Officer
"	5	Quartermaster
"	6	O.C. "A" Coy.
"	7	" "B" "
"	8	" "C" "
"	9	" "D" "
"	10	War Diary No 1
"	11	" " No 2
"	12	File
"	13	"
"	14	"

11th Inf.Bde.
4th Div.

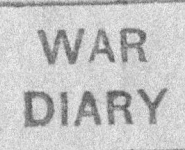

1st BATTN. THE RIFLE BRIGADE.

M A R C H

1 9 1 8

Attached:-

Battn. Operation Orders.

WAR DIARY
or
INTELLIGENCE SUMMARY.
(Erase heading not required.)

Vol 34

1st Bn the Rifle Brigade

Army Form C. 2118.

Place	Date	Hour	Summary of Events and Information	Remarks and references to Appendices
SAULCOURT	March 1st to 11th		Battalion and Company Training was carried out. This included Toch Amrikating, Bombing, Attacks with Tanks co-operating and out formation. Construction, Pistol and Lewis Bayonet Fighting. On the 5th the Bn carried out an attack and Rest firing exercise on the WALNUT RANGE. On the 11th W.R.G.C. inspected the Bn in preparation for the G.O.C. 2nd Division's inspection on the following day. On the 12th the Bn moves to BERNEVILLE into a new NISSEN HUT CAMP.	Sheet 57c DEFENCE SCHEME MARCH 6TH APPENDIX I
BERNEVILLE	13th to		The G.O.C. 2nd Division inspected the Bn. He expressed his satisfaction at the turn out and appearance of the men and complete the wonderful steadiness of the Rank and File. The Company training was carried out to include Chiefly Musketry. On the 19th the Bn. was relieved by the WELSH GUARDS and back and marched to billets in SCHRAMM BARRACKS, ARRAS.	
STIRLING CAMP	20th to 24th		The Bn. relieved the 2nd Bn. GRENADIER GUARDS in Student Camps and Railway Embankment TRENCH. Disposition Bn. HQ. A + B Coys Winter Slope of Railway Embankment, STIRLING CAMP. D Coy in PUDDING TRENCH. HILL 60 Heron. HUMANS and C+D Coy + 510 P.M to 30 1PM on the 21st but no infantry section. Askew Bridge back from 510 P.M. to 1PM. Troops employed in infection of rifles, dropping of trenches and intern flatting trodge. Bn Scout M. set S.O. P.M. getting to ABRAS by HY. Guns Barrage.	to HUMBERT. L55 1 PART SCALE 1/10,000

WAR DIARY or INTELLIGENCE SUMMARY

Army Form C. 2118.

(Erase heading not required.)

4th The Rifle Brigade

Place	Date	Hour	Summary of Events and Information	Remarks and references to Appendices
STIRLING CAMP	March 22 to 24		On the 22 & 23rd the Bn again stood to S.A.M. ready to move up at 15 minutes notice. On the morn of the 24th C & D Coys withdrew back to STIRLING CAMP whilst on the 23rd I Coy again received orders to proceed to PUDDING TRENCH. On the 24th the Bn relieved the 2nd Bn THE HAMPSHIRE REGIMENT in support, A&B being in COST TRENCH, "A" Coy in TOTLAND & HAVANA TRS, "D" Coy in COST & COST TRS, "C" Coy in STONE TR. as B Coy. In JUTLAND, HAVANA and CAMEL TRS. Trenches found dug out disconfort and inadequate shelters for the men.	
SUPPORT PLATOON	25th to 26th		On the 24th owing to information obtained from a prisoner had an attack was to be made on the 2nd the the Bn dispositions were altered. Bn HQ moved to PUDDING TRENCH A.1.6.4.7. B. B Coy took over C&D Coy and part of CAMEL, I Coy remained in STONE. A Coy from B.H.M. D.1. Coy 6 H.17.6.9.5.34. E Coy from H.17.5.95.34. on the 25th "A & C" Coys when to start digging a trench to advance to the firm SCARPE. "A & C" Coys were repulsed by the HAMPSHIRES. GONE TRENCH. On 30 AM on the 27th a raid was taken to be REGIMENT CAMEL TRENCH from 113 a 30 35 to A.17 b.52 #71 two officers and the 2nd Lieut 13 Bn and the platoon of B Coy then relieved took over CORAL TR. In the 295 a heavy hostile barrage was put down at 3.0 AM and at 3.20 AM the attack developed, the enemy gained the front and support lines and started pushing down the communication trenches. On 11.30 AM they knock up and D Coys stood to relieve and took over the part A STOKE trenches by I Coy.	

WAR DIARY or INTELLIGENCE SUMMARY.

Army Form C. 2118.

Place	Date	Hour	Summary of Events and Information	Remarks and references to Appendices
SUPPORT Bn	25/9/15 1 AM		1st Bn the Rifle Brigade. During the night the three Coys of the Hampshire Regiment in the front line withdrew to their support line, A Coy Reserve which became the front line, and did Camel Avenue (from its junction with Cadiz Reserve to the junction with Coot Trench and Camel Av.) B Coy of the Regt holding from the junction of Cadiz Reserve and Camel Av. to the Brigade boundary, C Coy Coral Tr. Southern half of Coral Tr remained in its original position. This line hung on magnificently for the rest of the day. During the afternoon 1 Coy was again ordered to move up steadily (Havana Tr) to fill up the gap between the 2nd Hampshire Regiment and the 1 Lancashire Fusiliers. 1 Coy found the head of the Lancashire Fusiliers Channel under orders from the O.C. 1st Hampshire Regiment (North). The enemy (South) The 2nd Lancashire Fusiliers (North) occupied Tuthatib Tr. The 2 Hants (South) bombed its way up to Hampshire Tr. at the rear. Point 2 platoons of I Coy Cumbs. attacked as the Hampshire Regiment & Cent Lately later in the afternoon the Hants Tr. Having arrived the enemy and camp South of the Railway over the top driving the enemy withdrew from the front line Mount Tekasunt & Seaforth Highlanders had evacuated the 11 Bojar exposing embankment accompanied to him and the right flank of the Wood temporarily. This left the right flank to form a defensive flank Coys 2 platoons of I Coy were orders to form a junction with Coot Tr. towards along but Bn from Embankment from its junction with a Coy of the Seaforths and Seaforth the S. Wigan then were relieved by Scott TR.

WAR DIARY
or
INTELLIGENCE SUMMARY.
(Erase heading not required.)

Army Form C. 2118.

Place	Date	Hour	Summary of Events and Information	Remarks and references to Appendices
SUPPORT TRENCHES Bn.	March 23rd to 24th		4th Bn. the Rifle Brigade. At night the Bn. was with draws the 2nd HAMPSHIRE REGT. Bn going into front line & was to hand over and the 1st RIFLE BRIGADE took over the front line with CAMEL AV. B Coy a stope Tr from 15Dx N to the junction with TAMPOUX LOOP. C Coy & H.Q. & H.H. A Coy from this point to tch flank from tch back along the SCARPE forming a defensive flank IN G.WHIT TR. I Coy was in SUPPORT to the junction with D TR. One Platoon were in PUDDING TR. One brigade was in the area of TAMPOUX. Patrols were sent out reconnoitring the area of TAMPOUX	REF. O.O. No 1 para 3.
FRONT LINE Bn.	24th to 31st		The last three days were indifferently quiet kept on the 29th the enemy made two unsuccessful bombing attacks, both being repulsed. On the second by 2 Platoons of the 1 SOMERSET L.I, & A & D Coys & C Coy on the evening of that day. I Coy relieved B Coy.	

JC Humphrey Major for OC
1 Bn. The Rifle Brigade

BATTALION OPERATION ORDERS.

SECRET. OPERATION ORDER 10
by
Lieut.Col. R.T. FELLOWES, DSO, MC.
Commdg. 1st Battn., THE RIFLE BRIGADE.

Ref Maps 51B.N.W.
     51B.S.W.   6th MARCH, 1918.   Copy No. 11.
----

1. In the event of a serious attack by the enemy whilst the Division is in Corps Reserve the Battalion may take part in any of the following moves:-

  (a) The Division takes over the centre portion of the Corps front. 11th Brigade will be in Divisional Reserve in ARRAS. Boundaries of Divisional front will be issued later.

     12th Brigade will take over Right Brigade front and 10th Brigade the Left Brigade front.

  (b) The Division moves to a position of assembly on the line TILLOY LES MOFFLAINES - RAILWAY TRIANGLE, ARRAS-LENS Railway

     11th Brigade moves to ARRAS, the Battalion to SCHRAMM BARRACKS.

     The 11th Brigade may however have to move to any of the following places:- BEAURAINS, BLANGY LOCK, ST. LAURENT BLANGY.

  (c) The Division occupies the 3rd system south of the SCARPE. 11th Brigade will hold from N.5.a.8.0. to H.35.a.7.8.

     The Battalion will hold front and support lines from H.35.c.8.4. to H.35.a.7.8. 1st Somerset Light Infantry will be on the right and 10th Brigade on the left. In this case the Brigade will probably debus at BEAURAINS and march via TILLOY.

  (d) The Division occupies the 3rd system north of the SCARPE. 11th Brigade would be in Divisional Reserve in ARRAS.

  (e) The Division occupies 3rd system 6th Corps front. 11th Brigade would debus at BEAURAINS and march to area N.29.a & b. From there it may have to occupy 3rd system between N.32.d.0.8. and N.27.b.0.4.

     The Battalion will hold front and support lines from N.27.c.0.1 to N.27.b.0.4. 1st Somerset Light Infantry will be on the right and 12th Brigade on the left.

     From the above system the Division may have to counter-attack so as to regain:- 1). WANCOURT TOWER RIDGE.
                                     2). GUEMAPPE.

     The greater portion of 3rd system 6th Corps is only partially dug and some of it is not dug at all. Digging in will therefore commence at once on arrival in our sector.

  (f) The Division as distributed in (d) counter attacks from the 3rd system north of the SCARPE.

  (g) Should the enemy attack penetrate the 3rd system north of the SCARPE the Corps Reserves will counter attack due east from the line of the LENS Railway with the objective of the FAMPOUX-POINT DU JOUR RIDGE.

     11th Brigade would debus at BLANGY LOCK or ST. LAURENT BLANGY.

2. In any of the above eventualities the Battalion will embus on the BERNEVILLE - BAC DU NORD Road in lorries, head of the Battalion at R.8.c.6.5. 27 lorries are allottted to the Battalion.

     The Battalion will be distributed on the <u>right</u> side of the road clear of the road itself. 6 groups (20 to 25 men each) per 80 yards of road space.

/3. Troops will move

3.   Troops will move from this Camp in fighting order except that aeroplane flares, sandbags and S.O.S. signals will be delivered to the Battalion at the embussing point. Jerkins will be worn.
    Tools will be carried on the man from this Camp.
    Water bottles will be filled before leaving this Camp.
    The extra 50 rounds S.A.A. per man and the bombs will be drawn from the Mobile Reserve or the Guard Room before leaving the Camp.
    The following table shows what each man will carry.

	Rifle-men	Rifle Grenad-iers.	Lewis Gunners	Bombers	Signal-lers.	Runners.
S.A.A.	200 &	100	50	100	50	50
Grenades No.5.	2	2	2	2	2	2
Stalks.	-	16	-	-	-	-
Blank Cartridges.	-	16	-	-	-	-
-X- Ground Flares.	2	2	2	2	2	2
Magazines L.G.	-	-	30	-	-	-
-X- Rockets S.O.S.	12 per Company Headquarters.					
-X- Sandbags.	3	3	3	3	3	3
Picks or Shovels.	1	1	1½	1	-	-
Bombs 'P'	-	-	-	1	-	-
Grenades No.23.	-	8	-	-	-	-

%. 1. Except Nos. 1. of Lewis Gun teams.
& 2. 120 rounds in pouches; 2 bandoliers of 50 each, in packs of Rifle Sections. Others carry their 100 rounds or their 50 rounds in their pouches.
   3. Water bottles will be carried FULL.
   4. Iron Rations will NOT be consumed without an order from Battalion Headquarters.
   5. Bombs, No.5, 23 and 'P', will be carried in the haversack by sections concerned.
   6. All officers taking part in the attack and all officers in charge of Carrying Parties will be dressed and equipped exactly as the men. Sticks will not be carried.

/7. The entrenching

7. The entrenching implement will <u>not</u> be carried.
8. The pack will contain:- Cap Comforter, ~~Cardigan jacket,~~ Fork, Iron Ration, "Z and Z plus 1" days rations, Mess Tin, and cover, Waterproof Sheet, and in Rifle Sections-100 rounds S.A.A. and 1 pair of socks.
9. Tools will be carried, 80% shovels and 20% picks. H.Q.Pioneers and Police will carry tools on this scale. The remainder of Battalion H.Q., Coy and Platoon H.Q. will NOT carry tools.

-X- These will be issued at the embussing point.

In future, the S.A.A., bombs, etc., as laid down, will be on the man's charge and will be carried on the man until further notice.

4. The 1st Line Transport will move by road to G.20.a.5.1. via WARLUS and DAINVILLE (except in the case of para 1(e) when the transport of the whole Brigade will ~~be~~ concentrate in WARLUS).

5. While the Battalion is in its present position breakfast will not be later than 7.0.am.

6. Paras. 1, 3 and 4. of Warning Order issued 21/3/18 are cancelled. Paras 2, 5 and 6 ~~xxxx xxxx xxxx~~ and amendments hold good.

C.C.Naaman 2Lt

Lieut.Col.
Commanding, 1st Battalion,
THE RIFLE BRIGADE.

DISTRIBUTION:

Copy No. 1..Commanding Officer,
  "   " 2..Adjutant.
  "   " 3..Assistant Adjutant.
  "   " 4..Transport Officer.
  "   " 5..Quartermaster.
  "   " 6..O.C. "A" Company.
  "   " 7.. "   " "B"   "
  "   " 8.. "   " "C"   "
  "   " 9.. "   " "D"   "
  "   " 10..War Diary.
  "   " 11.. "   "
  "   " 12..File.

Copy No. 11

Addenda to Operation Order No 10

(7) Steps will be taken to see that all Water Bottles are filled over night.

(8) When in future fighting Order is the dress for training Para 2 will be strictly adhered to.

Os C Companies will check ammunition, contents for pack etc, from time to time

2/Lt & A/Adjt
for O.C. 1st Bn The Rifle Brigade

Surplus bombs will be withdrawn from the men, de-detonated, packed in boxes, and returned to the Transport Officer by 6.0.pm, tonight, 14/3/18.

2/Lieut.
A/Adjt. 1st Battalion, THE RIFLE BRIGADE.

DISTRIBUTION- as for OPERATION ORDER No.10.

TO ACCOMPANY OPERATION ORDER No. 10.

Owing to the Mobile Reserve only being available for the present for the issue of S.A.A. and Bombs, the following is a revised list of S.A.A. and Bombs to be carried with Fighting Order.

Para.3. of OPERATION ORDER No. 10. will be amended accordingly and J.1/452 dated 9/3/18 will be destroyed.

Should the operations demand the use of Bombing and Rifle Grenade Sections, these Sections will be made up to FIVE Bombs to each N.C.O. and man from the 180 bombs carried by each company.

	Rfn.	Bombers	Rifle Gren'drs	Lewis Gnrs.	Sigs.	Runner
S.A.A.	170	170	170	50	50	50
MILLS' Hand.	2 per man up to 84 bombs per company. (remaining 4 boxes of MILLS' hand to Battn.H.Q.					
MILLS' Grenade.	2 per man up to 96 bombs per company.					
STALKS.	-	-	16	-	-	-
BLANK CART'DGES:	-	-	16	-	-	-
SANDBAGS.	3 per man to be carried under the waistbelt and *not* in the pack.					

S.A.A. to make up the above amounts will be drawn from the Transport Officer forthwith, and issued.

Surplus bombs will be withdrawn from the men, **de-detonated**, packed in boxes, and returned to the Transport Officer by 6.0.pm. tonight, 14/3/18.

2/Lieut.
A/Adjt. 1st Battalion, THE RIFLE BRIGADE.

DISTRIBUTION- as for OPERATION ORDER No.10.

OPERATION ORDER No.11.
by
Lieut.Col. R.T.FELLOWES, DSO. MC.
Commdg. 1st Battalion, THE RIFLE BRIGADE.
─o─o─o─o─o─o─o─o─o─o─o─o─

Ref. Sheet 51.C.   10th MARCH, 1918.   Copy No. 11.

MOVE   1. The Battalion will move to the new Camp at BERNEVILLE, tomorrow.
Order of March - H.Q; "B"; "A"; "C"; "I".
The Battalion will parade on the Battalion Parade Ground ready to move off at 2.0.pm.

BAGGAGE.   2. Officers' kits, Aid Post stores, etc., will be dumped at the Quartermaster's store by 9.45.am.
All blankets will be rolled up in bundles of ten and <u>labelled</u>. Those of "A", "C" and "I" Companies will be dumped in the open space East of the Guard Room; those of "B" Company and H.Q. will be dumped at Qr.Mr's. store, by 9.45.am.
All tables, forms (except those from the Officers' Mess) and beds from the Nissen huts will be dumped in the open space East of the Guard Room, by 9.0.am.
The Transport Officer will make all arrangements for the conveyance of all kits, etc. to the new Camp.
Mess equipment, forms and tables from the Officers' Mess, will be ready by 1.45.pm.
Extra transport consisting of three G.S. wagons and three limbers will report to the Transport Officer at 10.0.am.
Q.M. will arrange for the removal of all washing bowls & palliases.

FATIGUE.   3. The last draft of reinforcements will report to the Qr.Mr. at 9.15.am, for duty.

ADVANCED PARTY.   4. An advanced party of one N.C.O. per Company, one from H.Q. and one from Transport will report to Lieut.G.J. COLE at the Orderly Room, at 8.40.am.
They will take over stores, accommodation, etc., and will guide their units to their quarters.
List of stores taken over will be rendered to the Orderly Room.

BILLETS.   5. Certificate that billets are left clean, etc. will be rendered to Orderly Room by 1.30.pm., tomorrow.
2/Lieut. G.H. MERCER will remain behind and obtain necessary certificates from owners- list of billets occupied will be forwarded him by Adjutant, tomorrow. These certificates will be handed in to Orderly Room on completion of this duty.

(sd) C.C. NAUMANN. 2/Lieut
A/Adjt. 1st Battalion, THE RIFLE BRIGADE.

DISTRIBUTION:
Copy No. 1.. Commanding Officer.
"   "   2.. Adjutant.
"   "   3.. Quartermaster.
"   "   4.. Transport Officer.
"   "   5.. O.C. "A" Company.
"   "   6.. " : "B"   :
"   "   7.. " : "C"   :
"   "   8.. " : "I"   :
"   "   9.. Intelligence Officer.
"   "   10.. War Diary.
"   "   11.. :   :
"   "   12.. File.

SECRET

OPERATION ORDERS No 13
by
Major I. C. MONTFORD
Commanding 1st Battalion THE RIFLE BRIGADE

Reference Trench Map 51 B.NW. 19th MARCH, 1918. Copy No /4

MOVE 1. The Battalion will relieve the 2nd Battalion GRENADIER GUARDS in STIRLING CAMP and PUDDING TRENCH tomorrow 20th instant:-
Battalion Headquarters, "A" & "B" Coys will be in STIRLING CAMP
"C" & "D" : : : : PUDDING TRENCH
The Battalion will move off from here with an interval of 200 yards between platoons in the following order:-
Headquarters, "B", "A", "C" and "D".
Headquarters will move off at 1.30 p.m.
ROUTE:- PLACE DE LA GARE - BLANGY - G.34.c.8.8 -
G.18.a.8.3 - thence via HERVIN FARM.
DRESS:- Full marching order.
"C" and "D" Companies will move off, with an interval of 200 yards between platoons, from STIRLING CAMP in time to pass under the Railway Arch at H.14.a.2.5 at 7.10 p.m. These two companies will take one blanket per man and officers' valises; the necessary transport will accompany them as far as the 4th System. Lewis Gun limbers will also accompany them.
The Quartermaster will arrange for two cooks and six dixies to be provided for these two companies.

TEAS 2. The four cookers will accompany the Battalion to STIRLING CAMP where teas for the whole Battalion will be provided at 5.0 p.m. Two cookers will then return and will be at the disposal of the details.

ADVANCE 3. (A) For STIRLING CAMP.
PARTIES 2/Lieut. W. H. CURTIS and one N.C.O. per each "A" and "B" Companies and Headquarters will parade at Orderly Room at 9.30 a.m. They will proceed to report to the Adjutant of the 2nd Battalion, GRENADIER GUARDS, to take over the camp.
(B) For PUDDING TRENCH.
2/Lieut. E. J. GRAY, one N.C.O. and three Guides from each "C" and "D" Companies will parade at Orderly Room at 9.30 a.m. They will take over trench Stores, etc., in PUDDING TRENCH. Guides from this party will meet their respective companies at the point on the main FAMPOUX Road, H.15.c.8.9 at 7.20 p.m.
(C) 2/Lieut. G. C. HAYMANN and two C.Q.M.Ss will report to the Town Major "B" Area at 10.0 a.m. to allot accommodation for the details.

DETAILS 4. All details to be left out (shown on return B) and the Buglers will parade under 2/Lieut G.C. HAYMANN at 1.30 p.m. Before this hour they will be available for cleaning up Barracks. The following officers will accompany this party:-
2/Lieut. J. A. TAYLOR and 2/Lieut. H.C.V.SHARPE.

BILLETS 5. Lieut. G. J. COLE will remain behind and settle any claims for billets. If necessary he will use the details for cleaning up.

BAGGAGE 6. The two Companies and Headquarters going to STIRLING CAMP will take two blankets per man. These blankets and those of "C" and "D" (one per man) and the officers' valises (less those of the details) will be dumped and LABELLED by Companies on the square by 12.0 noon. Care should be taken to see that the blankets and valises to be left at STIRLING CAMP are loaded on top.
The necessary transport to take valises and blankets of details will accompany them; the valises and blankets being collected before 3.0 p.m.

B.O. No 12 cont. sheet 2   19-3-18

WATER   7.   There is a water point for the cookers in STIRLING CAMP.
                 The water carts will come up twice daily to replenish water bottles.
                 There is a water point in PUDDING TRENCH.

HANDING   8.   All station calls and conditions of alertness as those of the
OVER   2nd Battalion GRENADIER GUARDS, will be adopted.
                 All details of trenches, trench stores, DEFENCE SCHEMES,
                 will be carefully taken over and receipts given.   Duplicates of
                 receipts will be forwarded to Battalion Headquarters before
                 12.0 noon on the 21st inst.

BOUNDARY   9.   (a) Steel Helmets will be worn by all ranks EAST of a
of ALERT   North and South line through:-
AREA   GAVRELLE Road - Railway Bridge - H.13.b.9.9
                FAMPOUX   " -   "   "   - H.13.b.9.4
                FEUCHY   " -   "   "   - H.19.b.3.6
                 (b) Box Respirators will be worn by all ranks in the
                ALERT position EAST of a North and South line passing through
                     GAVRELLE Road - LE POINT DU JOUR
                     FAMPOUX ROAD at its junction with ATHIES ROAD in H.15.a.
                     FEUCHY ROAD - west end of FEUCHY VILLAGE at H.21.a.1.3.

ROPORT   10.   (1) Officers Commanding "C" and "I" Companies are reminded
                that they must report the names of the Platoon Commanders on their
                flanks.
                 (2) Completion of the relief of "C" and "I" Companies will
                be reported by wire by any sentence containing the code word
                "NAUGHTY".

                                     (sd) J. A. DAVISON   Captain
                                     (Adjutant 1st Battalion
                                        THE RIFLE BRIGADE

                            DISTRIBUTION

                  Copy No 1   Commanding Officer
                         2   Adjutant
                         3   Assistant Adjutant
                         4   Lewis Gun Officer
                         5   Quartermaster
                         6   Transport Officer
                         7   O.C. 2nd Batt Grenadier Guards
                         8   Area Commandant Stirling Camp
                         9   O.C. "A" Coy
                        10   "   "B" "
                        11   "   "C" "
                        12   "   "I" "
                        13   War Diary No 1
                        14   "   "   2
                        15   FILE

OPERATION ORDER No. 19.
by
Lieut. Col. R.T. FELLOWES, DSO., MC.
Commdg. 1st. Battalion, THE RIFLE BRIGADE.
========================
18th. MARCH, 1918.   Copy No. **13**

MOVE 1. The Battalion will move to billets in SCHRAMM BARRACKS tomorrow 19th. inst.
Order of march - H.Q. "B". "A". "C". "I".
The Battalion will be formed up in mass facing the road on the foot-ball ground opposite the Camp ready to move off at 5.30 pm.
DRESS. Full Marching Order.
The MALTESE CART will carry the packs of the Buglers.
The Battalion will march with Companies closed up.

BAGGAGE 2. Officers' kits, etc. will be dumped by the side of the road and collected at 4.30 pm.
Transport will move in rear of the Battalion.
Blankets will be rolled up in bundles of ten and dumped on the road by 1.30 pm.

FATIGUE 3. Two men per Company and one N.C.O. of "A" Coy. will report to 2ndLtF.C. LILLYWHITE at 4.30 pm.
This party will remain behind to clean up etc.
2nd. Lieut. F.C. LILLYWHITE will report to the Town Major before leaving to settle any claims there may be outstanding and to obtain certificates of cleanliness for the Camp and Billets.

CERTIFI- 4. Certificates that the Camp has been left clean and in a
CATES sanitary condition will be rendered by Companies to reach ORDERLY ROOM by 3.30 pm.

ADVANCE 5. One N.C.O. per Company and Battn. H.Q. will report to
PARTY Lieut. G.J. COLE at ORDERLY ROOM at 2.0 pm. with bicycles.
This party will report to Capt. HALL at the WESTERN GATE SCHRAMM BARRACKS at 3. 0 pm. to be allotted accomodation.

(sd) J. A. DAVISON. Captain.

Adjutant 1st. Battalion, THE RIFLE BRIGADE.

DISTRIBUTION

Copy No. 1. Commanding Officer.
"   " 2. Second in Command.
"   " 3. Adjutant.
"   " 4. A/Adjutant.
"   " 5. Intelligence.Officer.
"   " 6. O.C. "A" Company.
"   " 7. O.C. "B" Company.
"   " 8. O.C. "C" Company.
"   " 9. O.C. "I" Company.
"   " 10. Transport Officer.
"   " 11. Quarter-Master.
"   " 12. War Diary.
"   " 13. War Diary.
"   " 14. File.

SECRET

OPERATION ORDERS No 16
by
Lieut.Colonel R.T.FELLOWES, D.S.O., M.C.
Commanding 1st Battalion, THE RIFLE BRIGADE
28th March, 1918

Para. 1. Following moves will take place to-night.

Para. 2. "C" Company will, as soon after dark as possible, extend his right to Junction of FRONT LINE, THIRD SYSTEM and RIVER SCARPE H.22.b. (80.30.) 6.2.
This extra bit of line will be held by a series of posts.

Para. 3. "B" Company at a time to be notified by O.C. LAVA (probably 11.0 p.m.) will withdraw to STOKE TRENCH and occupy the line between "A" and "C" Companies.

Para. 4. "I" Company, at a time to be notified by O.C. LAVA (probably 11.0 p.m.) will withdraw to PUDDING and PORT Trenches, relieving LIGHT Coy. 1st SOMERSET L.I.
Three guides for "I" Company will be at Battalion H.Q. in PUDDING TRENCH from 11.0 p.m. onwards, and platoon Commanders of "I" Company will arrange to send on ahead someone to fetch a guide before their platoons reach the line of PORT.

Para. 5. "A" Company will, on the arrival of "B" Company in STOKE, close up to their left and gain touch with 12th Brigade. Till the arrival of "B" Company "A" and "C" Companies will be responsible for maintaining touch with one another.

Para. 6. RATIONS, WATER, etc. for "B" and "I" Companies will be taken to STOKE and PUDDING Trenches respectively by carrying party of 1st SOMERSET L.I.
Should rations for "B" Company arrive in STOKE before the arrival of "B" Company O.C. "A" will be responsible for meeting them and dumping them in the trench. "A" and "C" Coys. will draw their own rations in accordance with verbal instructions already issued.

Para. 7. The Battalion will thus become the FRONT LINE battalion of the Brigade.

Para. 8. All Companies will report their arrival in their new positions as soon as possible, and Company Commanders will report personally to the C.O. at Battalion H.Q. some time before dawn to-morrow.

Para. 9. "B" Company will take over "A" Company's present headquarters.

(sd) R. T. FELLOWES, Lieut. Colonel.
Comndg 1st Battn. THE RIFLE BRIGADE

Issued 8.0 p.m.
28/3/18

SECRET

OPERATION ORDERS No 17
by
Lieut. Colonel R. T. FELLOWES, D.S.O., MC.
Commanding 1st Battalion, THE RIFLE BRIGADE
29th March, 1918

Following moves will take place to-night.

Para. 1. "I" Company less 1 platoon will relieve "B" Coy., H.Q. details and troops of 1st SOMERSET L.I. in STOKE between a point 150 yards North of CAMEL (or wherever touch is gained with 12th Brigade) and Bank H.17.b.4.4. exclusive. Any men of "I" Coy. between these points will not be relieved but will join up with "I" Coy. on its arrival.

"I" Coy. will begin to leave PORT at 8.15 p.m. and Lieut. COLE will arrange to meet them at junction of STOKE and CAMEL.

"I" Coy. will be responsible for maintaining touch with 12th Brigade and for the Bombing blocks E. and W. along CAMEL and along STOKE N. of CAMEL.

On relief "B" Coy. under C.S.M. GOODE will move to PUDDING from the FAMPOUX-Road Northwards.

Lieut. COLE and H.Q. details will rejoin Battalion H.Q., and troops of 1st SOMERSET L.I. will move to

Para. 2. "C" Company will be relieved from H.22.a.6.2. to FAMPOUX LOCK exclusive by "B" Coy. 1st SOMERSET L.I. who will arrive at junction of River SCARPE and DINGWALL at 9.0 p.m., where O.C. "C" Coy. will arrange to meet O.C. "B" Coy 1st SOMERSET L.I. and conduct the relief with him.

"C" Company will hand over the responsibility for the defence of FAMPOUX LOCK to "A" Coy.

"C" Company on relief will take over that portion of STOKE from FAMPOUX Road exclusive to Bank H.17.b.4.4. inclusive. Troops of "A" Coy. relieved in this area will move S. of FAMPOUX Road; troops of "I" will join their Company in the N. part of STOKE (see para. 1); troops of "B" Coy. 1st R.B., 1st S.L.I. etc. will move to places indicated in para. 1.

Para. 3. "A" Company will be responsible for the line FAMPOUX LOCK inclusive to FAMPOUX-ATHIES Road inclusive and will remain in their present H.Q.

Para. 4. "I" and "C" Companies will occupy "B" Company's present H.Q.

Para. 5. Work on cutting through the FAMPOUX-ATHIES Road and the road in H.17.b. will be commenced as soon as possible after dark by "A" and "B" Companies respectively.

"C" Company will carry on with this work in H.17.b. as soon as they relieve the troops at work there.

It is most important that these roads be cut through to-night to allow movement along the trenches under cover.

Lewis Guns will be placed at these points to cover the approaches from the E. and S.E; and troops will not leave these places before being properly relieved.

Para. 6. Time and place for meeting rations etc. will be notified later but not more than 6 men from each Company are to be away at the same time fetching rations. Empty Water tins and tea packs will be sent back to the pack animals by the men sent to fetch rations.

Para. 7. Completion of relief and arrival in new positions will be notified by 'phone or runner to Battalion H.Q. - the CODE WORDS "GOOD" and "LUCK" being used respectively.

Para. 8. There will be no withdrawal of any sort and every inch of ground will be contested.

ACKNOWLEDGE.

(sd) R. T. FELLOWES, Lieut.Col.
Commdg 1st Batt THE RIFLE BRIGADE

Issued at 4. 0 p.m.
29/3/18

War Diary No 2

J.1/452

The following is an amended list of bombs, ammunition etc. to be taken into action.
Para.3. of OPERATION ORDER No.1. dated 6/3/18 will be amended accordingly.

	Rfn.	Rifle Gren'drs.	Lewis Gunners.	Bombers	Sigs.	Runners
S.A.A.	170 &	120	50	120	50	50
Magazines, L.G.	-	-	28	-	-	-
Grenades, No.23.	-	6	-	-	-	-
Stalks.	-	16	-	-	-	-
Blank Cartridges.	-	16	+	-	-	-

Every man except Rifle Grenadiers will carry 2 bombs, Mills' No.5.
Should the operation undertaken by the Battalion necessitate the use of Bombing Sections, each N.C.O. and man of Bombing Sections will be issued with 5 bombs, Mills' No.5. from those carried by everyone in the company.
& 120 rounds in pouches; 50 rounds in bandolier in pack.

2/Lieut.

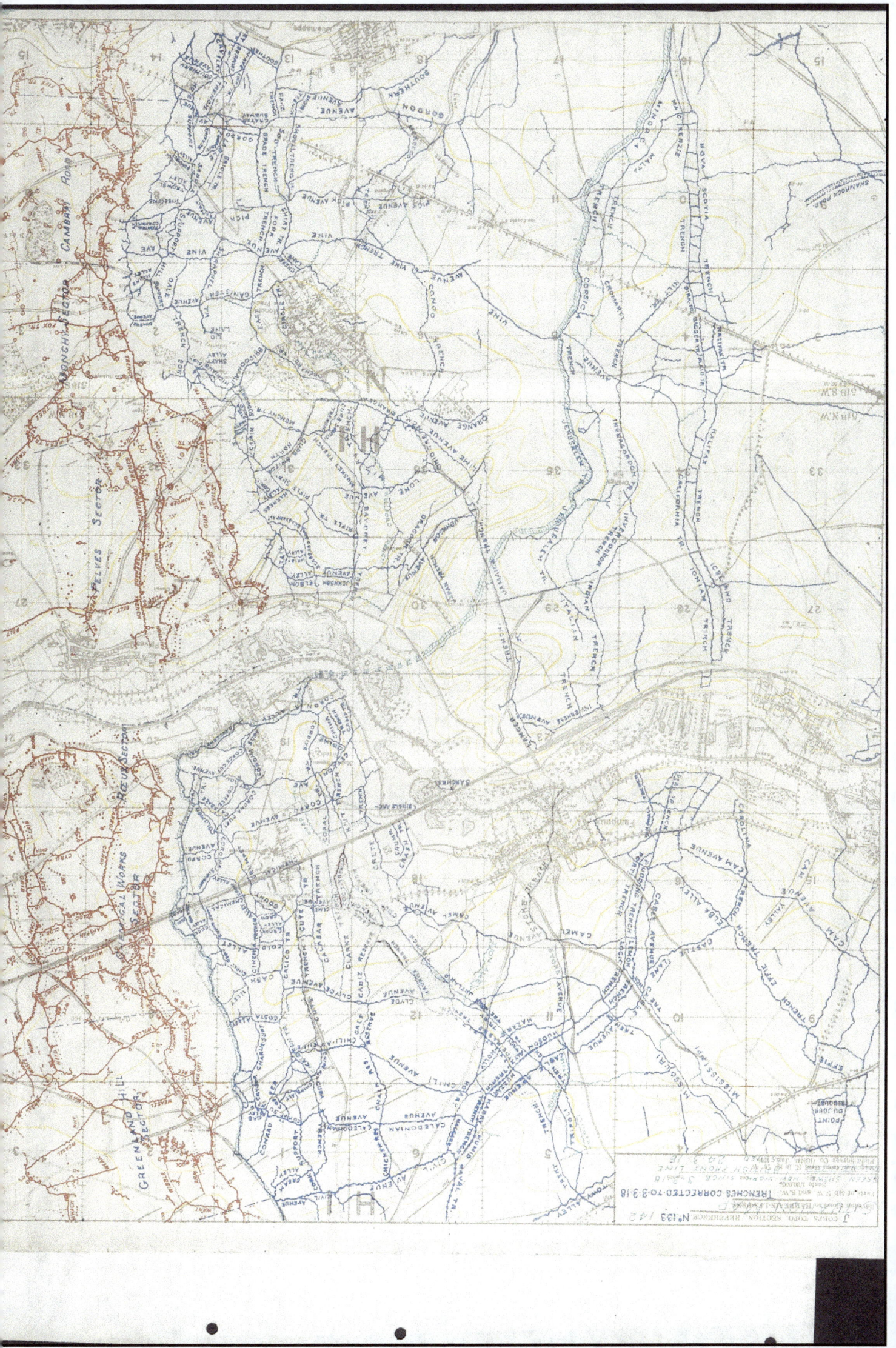

W 8466/P1968 1,000,000 1/19 Mc A & W Ltd (E 4374)

Army Form W3997.

Regtl. No.................... Rank..

Name ....
     (Christian Names in full)   (Surname)

Unit............................. Regt. ....
      or
     Corps

Date of { Discharge*
     Disembodiment* } ....191......
     Transfer to the Reserve* }
  * Strike out whichever inapplicable.

COVER

FOR

DISCHARGE DOCUMENTS.

NOTE.—In every case where A.F Z.22 is included among the documents the letter Z is to be stamped in the space provided below.

SECRET   Copy No. 13

AMENDMENTS to OPERATION ORDERS No 9

I.   Ref:
     <u>Paragraph 1.</u> Battalion Headquarters will move off from the open space
                   west of the Camp at 10.45.am.

II. <u>Ref Para.1.-</u> ROUTE is cancelled and the following substituted:
                   Road Junction, M.31.d.3.0. (ESTAMINET CORNER) - MILLOY -
                   BEAURAINS - ACHICOURT - Road Junction, L.5.b.8.7. - Le BAC
                   du NORD - thence by BEAUMETZ to SIMENCOURT.
                   Headquarters will pass ESTAMINET CORNER at 11.0.am.

III. <u>Ref. para.1:</u> Delete from "An interval.............will be maintained"
                   and substitute "An interval of 200 yards between Platoons,
                   Companies and Transport will be maintained until the halt for
                   dinners. After this halt an interval of 200 yards between
                   Companies and Transport only will be maintained"

IV. <u>Ref para 1:</u> The Buglers will join the Battalion at the Cross Roads,
                   M.4.c. They will march first with "B" Company, then with "A",
                   "C" and "I" Companies respectively after each halt.

V.   <u>Ref para 5:</u> After "As soon as possible" add "to rejoin Transport".
                   The head of the 1st Line Transport will be at the Cross
                   Roads, M.4.c., facing south, in rear of the Buglers. They will
                   fall in and follow 200 yards in rear of "I" Company.

VI. <u>Ref para 6:</u> Para 6. is cancelled and the following is substituted:
                   "When the head of the Battalion reaches the point G.31.b.0.3.
                   the Battalion will halt, closing up to companies at 20 yards
                   interval.
                   Haversack rations will be carried and will be eaten
                   during this halt.
                   The Battalion will resume the march at 1.30.pm, open-
                   ing out to companies at 200 yards interval.
                   Dinners will be provided on arrival in new area.

VII. <u>Ref.para.7:</u> Companies will also indent for any material for the
                   improvement of billets.

VIII.<u>Ref.para.8:</u> Insert after paragraph 8. insert new para.9:-
                   "HINTS FOR MARCH:
                   (a) All men should wash their feet in cold water and
                   cut their toenails that morning.
                   (b) Wherever possible put on clean socks.
                   (c) Soap freely the soles of the socks and put them on
                   carefully avoiding wrinkles.
                   (d) Lace the boots firmly and evenly- any knots in
                   bootlaces should <u>not</u> be used next to the foot.
                   (e) Any small sores or skin abrasions should be dressed
                   at the Aid Post before starting"

(sd) J.A. Davison
                                                    Captain.
Adjutant, 1st Battalion, THE RIFLE BRIGADE.

<u>DISTRIBUTION-</u> as for O.O. No.9.

loaded by 10.0.am.

5. **TRANSPORT:** Cookers will move off as soon after breakfast as possible. The transport required for the removal of kits, etc. will rejoin the remainder of the 1st Line Transport as soon as possible after the times mentioned in para 4.
   The 1st Line Transport will fall in in rear of the Battalion at the Place de la Gare, ARRAS.

6. **DINNERS:** The Battallion will halt from 1.30.pm to 2.30.pm for dinners which will be prepared en route.

7. **MATERIAL:** Companies and Headquarters will indent on the Orderly Room for any tables or forms that they require in the new area. Indents should reach Orderly Room by not later than 12.0.noon, 8th instant.

8. **REPORT:** Companies will render to Orderly Room within an hour of arrival in new area a state showing:-
   (a) Number of men fallen out, not rejoined.
   (b) Number of men fallen out and since rejoined.
   (c) Number of men fallen out and brought in by baggage guard.

9. **ACKNOWLEDGE.**

                    (sd) J.A. DAVISON.   Captain.
        Adjutant, 1st Battalion, THE RIFLE BRIGADE.

DISTRIBUTION:-

Copy No. 1 .. Commanding Officer.
 "   " 2 .. Second in Command.
 "   " 3 .. Adjutant.
 "   " 4 .. Assistant Adjutant.
 "   " 5 .. Intelligence Officer.
 "   " 6 .. O.C. "A" Company.
 "   " 7 .. " : "B"   "
 "   " 8 .. " : "C"   "
 "   " 9 .. " : "D"   "
 "   " 10. Transport Officer.
 "   " 11. Quartermaster.
 "   " 12 .. War Diary No.1.
 "   " 13 .. "   "   " 2.
 "   " 14 .. File.

SECRET.   OPERATION ORDER 10
                            by
              Lieut.Col. R.T. FELLOWES, DSO, MC.
              Commdg. 1st Battn., THE RIFLE BRIGADE.

Ref Maps 51B.N.W.
        51B.S.W.   6th MARCH, 1918.   Copy No. 10.
----

1.   In the event of a serious attack by the enemy whilst the
Division is in Corps Reserve the Battalion may take part in any of
the following moves:-
        (a) The Division takes over the centre portion of the Corps
front. 11th Brigade will be in Divisional Reserve in ARRAS.
Boundaries of Divisional front will be issued later.
            12th Brigade will take over Right Brigade front and 10th
Brigade the Left Brigade front.
        (b) The Division moves to a position of assembly on the line
TILLOY LES MOFFLAINES - RAILWAY TRIANGLE, ARRAS-LENS Railway
            11th Brigade moves to ARRAS, the Battalion to SCHRAMM BARRACKS.
            The 11th Brigade may however have to move to any of the
following places:- BEAURAINS, BLANGY LOCK, ST. LAURENT BLANGY.
        (c) The Division occupies the 3rd system south of the SCARPE.
11th Brigade will hold from N.5.a.8.0. to H.35,a.7.8.
            The Battalion will hold front and support lines from
H.35.c.8.4. to H.35.a.7.8. 1st Somerset Light Infantry will be on
the right and 10th Brigade on the left. In this case the Brigade
will probably debus at BEAURAINS and march via TILLOY.
        (d) The Division occupies the 3rd system north of the SCARPE.
11th Brigade would be in Divisional Reserve in ARRAS.
        (e) The Division occupies 3rd system 6th Corps front.
11th Brigade would debus at BEAURAINS and march to area N.29.a & b.
From there it may have to occupy 3rd system between N.32.d.0.8.
and N.27.b.0.4.
            The Battalion will hold front and support lines from N.27.c.0.1
to N.27.b.0.4. 1st Somerset Light Infantry will be on the right
and 10th Brigade on the left.
            From the above system the Division may have to counter-attack
so as to regain:- 1). WANCOURT TOWER RIDGE.
                  2). GUEMAPPE.
            The greater portion of 3rd system 6th Corps is only partial-
ly dug and some of it is not dug at all. Digging in will therefore
commence at once on arrival in our sector.
        (f) The Division as distributed in (d) counter attacks from the
3rd system north of the SCARPE.
        (g) Should the enemy attack penetrate the 3rd system north of the
SCARPE the Corps Reserves will counter attack due east from the line
of the LENS Railway with the objective of the FAMPOUX-POINT DU JOUR
RIDGE.
            11th Brigade would debus at BLANGY LOCK or ST. LAURENT BLANGY.

2.   In any of the above eventualities the Battalion will embus on
the BERNEVILLE - BAC DU NORD Road in lorries, head of the Battalion
at R.8.c.8.5. 27 lorries are allottted to the Battalion.
            The Battalion will be distributed on the right side of the
road clear of the road itself. 6 groups (20 to 25 men each) per
80 yards of road space.

                                        /3. Troops will move

3.   Troops will move from this Camp in fighting order except that aeroplane flares, sandbags and S.O.S. signals will be delivered to the Battalion at the embussing point. *Jerkins will be worn*

Tools will be carried on the man from this Camp.

Water bottles will be filled before leaving this Camp.

The extra 50 rounds S.A.A. per man and the bombs will be drawn from the Mobile Reserve or the Guard Room before leaving the Camp.

The following table shows what each man will carry.

	Riflemen	Rifle Grenadiers.	Lewis Gunners	Bombers	Signallers.	Runners.
S.A.A.	300 &	100	50	100	50	50
Grenades No.5.	2	2	2	2	2	2
Stalks.	-	16	-	-	-	-
Blank Cartridges.	-	16	-	-	-	-
Ground Flares.	2	2	2	2	2	2
Magazines L.G.	-	-	30	-	-	-
Rockets S.O.S.	12 per Company Headquarters.					
Sandbags.	3	3	3	3	3	3
Picks or Shovels.	1	1	1 %	1	-	-
Bombs 'P'	-	-	-	1	-	-
Grenades No.23.	-	8	-	-	-	-

%. 1. Except Nos. 1. of Lewis Gun teams.

& 2. 100 rounds in pouches; 2 bandoliers of 50 each, in packs of Rifle Sections. Others carry their 100 rounds or their 50 rounds in their pouches.

3. Water bottles will be carried FULL.
4. Iron Rations will NOT be consumed without an order from Battalion Headquarters.
5. Bombs, No.5, 23 and 'P', will be carried in the haversack by sections concerned.
6. All officers taking part in the attack and all officers in charge of Carrying Parties will be dressed and equipped exactly as the men. Sticks will not be carried.

/7. The entrenching

7. The entrenching implement will _not_ be carried.
8. The pack will contain:- Cap Comforter, ~~Cardigan jacket~~, Fork, Iron Ration, "Z and Z plus 1" days rations, Mess Tin, and cover, Waterproof Sheet, and in Rifle Sections-100 rounds S.A.A. _and 1 Pair of Socks_
9. Tools will be carried, 80% shovels and 20% picks. H.Q. Pioneers and Police will carry tools on this scale. The remainder of Battalion H.Q., Coy and Platoon H.Q. will NOT carry tools.
-X- These will be issued at the embussing point.

In future, the S.A.A., bombs, etc., as laid down, will be on the man's charge and will be carried on the man until further notice.

4. The 1st Line Transport will move by road to G.30.a.5.1. via WARLUS and DAINVILLE (except in the case of para 1(e) when the transport of the whole Brigade will be concentrated in WARLUS).

5. While the Battalion is in its present position breakfast will not be later than 7.0.am.

6. Paras. 1, 3 and 4. of Warning Order issued 21/2/16 are cancelled. Paras 2, 5 and 6 ~~xxxx xxxx xxxx~~ and amendments hold good.

                          [signature] Lt.Col.
                         Lieut.Col.
                   Commanding, 1st Battalion,
                     THE RIFLE BRIGADE.

DISTRIBUTION:

    Copy No. 1 .. Commanding Officer.
     "   " 2 .. Adjutant.
     "   " 3 .. Assistant Adjutant.
     "   " 4 .. Transport Officer.
     "   " 5 .. Quartermaster.
     "   " 6 .. O.C. "A" Company.
     "   " 7 .. " " "B"   "
     "   " 8 .. " " "C"   "
     "   " 9 .. " " "D"   "
     "   " 10 .. War Diary.
     "   " 11 .. "   "
     "   " 12 .. File.

SKETCH MAP
SHOWING
DISPOSITIONS OF
CENTRE BN. 1.X.18.

1:10,000

Reference.
Right Front Coy ——
Left " " ——
Support " " ——
Reserve " " ——
Lewis Gun Posts ——
Coy & Pl. H.Q. ——
Bn. H.Q. ——

(By platoons)

War Diary No 1.

J.1/452

The following is an amended list of bombs, ammunition etc. to be taken into action.
Para.3. of OPERATION ORDER No.1. dated 6/3/18 will be amended accordingly.

	Rfn.	Rifle Gren'drs.	Lewis Gunners.	Bombers	Sigs.	Runners
S.A.A.	170 &	120	50	120	50	50
Magazines, L.G.	-	-	23	-	-	-
Grenades, No.23.	-	6	-	-	-	-
Stalks.	-	16	-	-	-	-
Blank Cartridges.	-	16	+	-	-	-

Every man except Rifle Grenadiers will carry 2 bombs, Mills' No.5.
Should the operation undertaken by the Battalion necessitate the use of Bombing Sections, each N.C.O. and man of Bombing Sections will be issued with 5 bombs, Mills' No.5. from those carried by everyone in the company.
&. 120 rounds in pouches; 50 rounds in bandolier in pack.

2/Lieut.

OPERATION ORDER No.11.
by
Lieut.Col. R.T.FELLOWES, DSO. MC.
Commdg. 1st Battalion, THE RIFLE BRIGADE.
—o—o—o—o—o—o—o—o—o—o—o—o—

Ref. Sheet 51.G.   10th MARCH,1918.   Copy No. 10.

MOVE 1. The Battalion will move to the new Camp at BERNEVILLE, tomorrow.
Order of March- H.Q; "B"; "A"; "C"; "I".
The Battalion will parade on the Battalion Parade Ground ready to move off at 2.0.pm.

BAGGAGE. 2. Officers' kits, Aid Post stores, etc., will be dumped at the Quartermaster's store by 9.45.am.
All blankets will be rolled up in bundles of ten and <u>labelled</u>. Those of "A", "C" and "I" Companies will be dumped in the open space East of the Guard Room; those of "B" Company and H.Q. will be dumped at Qr.Mr's. store, by 9.45.am.
All tables, forms (except those from the Officers' Mess) and beds from the Nissen huts will be dumped in the open space East of the Guard Room, by 9.0.am.
The Transport Officer will make all arrangements for the conveyance of all kits, etc. to the new Camp.
Mess equipment, forms and tables from the Officers' Mess, will be ready by 1.45.pm.
Extra transport consisting of three G.S. wagons and three limbers will report to the Transport Officer at 10.0.am.
Q.M. will arrange for removal of all washing bowls & palliases.

FATIGUE. 3. The last draft of reinforcements will report to the Qr.Mr. at 9.15.am, for duty.

ADVANCED PARTY. 4. An advanced party of one N.C.O. per Company, one from H.Q. and one from Transport will report to Lieut.C.F. COLE at the Orderly Room, at 8.40.am.
They will take over stores, accommodation, etc., and will guide their units to their quarters.
List of stores taken over will be rendered to the Orderly Room.

BILLETS. 5. Certificate that billets are left clean, etc. will be rendered to Orderly Room by 1.30.pm., tomorrow.
2/Lieut. G.H. MERCER will remain behind and obtain necessary certificates from owners- list of billets occupied will be forwarded him by Adjutant, tomorrow. These certificates will be handed in to Orderly Room on completion of this duty.

                    (sd) C.C. NAUMANN. 2/Lieut
        A/Adjt. 1st Battalion, THE RIFLE BRIGADE.

                    DISTRIBUTION:
        Copy No.1..Commanding Officer.
         "   " 2..Adjutant.
         "   " 3..Quartermaster.
         "   " 4..Transport Officer.
         "   " 5..O.C. "A" Company.
         "   " 6.." : "B"   :
         "   " 7.." : "C"   :
         "   " 8.." : "I"   :
         "   " 9..Intelligence Officer.
         "   " 10..War Diary.
         "   " 11.. :   :
         "   " 12..File.

J. 1/649

TO ACCOMPANY OPERATION ORDER No. 10.

Owing to the Mobile Reserve only being available for the present for the issue of S.A.A. and Bombs, the following is a revised list of S.A.A. and Bombs to be carried with Fighting Order.

Para.5. of OPERATION ORDER No. 10. will be amended accordingly and J.1/459 dated 9/3/18 will be destroyed.

Should the operations demand the use of Bombing and Rifle Grenade Sections, these Sections will be made up to FIVE Bombs to each N.C.O. and man from the 180 bombs carried by each company.

	Rfn.	Bombers	Rifle Gren'drs	Lewis Gnrs.	Sigs.	Runner
S.A.A.	170	170	170	50	50	50
MILLS' Hand.	3 per man up to 84 bombs per company. (remaining 4 boxes of MILLS' hand to Battn. H.Q.)					
MILLS' Grenade.	3 per man up to 96 bombs per company.					
STALKS.	-	-	16	-	-	-
BLANK CART'DGES	-	-	16	-	-	-
SANDBAGS.	3 per man to be carried under the waistbelt and not in the pack.					

S.A.A. to make up the above amounts will be drawn from the Transport Officer forthwith, and issued.

Surplus bombs will be withdrawn from the men, de-detonated, packed in boxes, and returned to the Transport Officer by 6.0.pm, tonight, 14/3/18.

2/Lieut.
A/Adjt. 1st Battalion, THE RIFLE BRIGADE.

DISTRIBUTION- as for OPERATION ORDER No. 10.

OPERATION ORDER No.12.
by
Lieut. Col. R.T. FELLOWES, DSO., MC.
Commdg. 1st. Battalion, THE RIFLE BRIGADE.
==
18th. MARCH, 1918.   Copy No... 12

MOVE
1. The Battalion will move to billets in SCHRAMM BARRACKS tomorrow 19th. inst.
   Order of march - H.Q. "B". "A". "C". "I".
   The Battalion will be formed up in mass facing the road on the foot-ball ground opposite the Camp ready to move off at 5.30 pm.
   DRESS. Full Marching Order.
   The MALTESE CART will carry the packs of the Buglers.
   The Battalion will march with Companies closed up.

BAGGAGE
2. Officers' Kits, ~~Blankets~~, etc. will be dumped by the side of the road and collected at 1.30 pm.
   Transport will move in rear of the Battalion.
   Blankets will be rolled in bundles of 10 and dumped on the road by 1-30 P.M.

FATIGUE
3. Two men per Company and one N.C.O. of "A" Coy. will report to 2nd. Lieut. F.C. LILLYWHITE at 4.30 pm.
   This party will remain behind to clean up etc.
   2nd. Lieut. F.C. LILLYWHITE will report to the Town Major before leaving to settle any claims there he may be outstanding and to obtain certificates of cleanliness for the Camp and Billets.

CERTIFI-
CATES
4. Certificates that the Camp has been left clean and in a sanitary condition will be rendered by Companies to reach ORDERLY ROOM by 5.30 pm.

ADVANCE
PARTY
5. One N.C.O. per Company and Battn. H.Q. will report to Lieut. G.J. COLE at ORDERLY ROOM at 2.0 pm. with bicycles. This party will report to Capt. HALL at the WESTERN GATE SCHRAMM BARRACKS at 3.0 pm. to be allotted accomodation.

(sd) J. A. DAVISON. Captain.

Adjutant 1st. Battalion, THE RIFLE BRIGADE.

DISTRIBUTION.

Copy No. 1. Commanding Officer.
 "   " 2. Second in Command.
 "   " 3. Adjutant.
 "   " 4. A/Adjt.
 "   " 5. Intelligence Officer.
 "   " 6. O.C. "A" Company.
 "   " 7. O.C. "B" Company.
 "   " 8. O.C. "C" Company.
 "   " 9. O.C. "I" Company.
 "   " 10. Transport Officer.
 "   " 11. Quarter-Master.
 "   " 12. War Diary.
 "   " 13. War Diary.
 "   " 14. File.

SECRET

OPERATION ORDERS No 13
by
Major I. G. MONTFORD
Commanding 1st Battalion THE RIFLE BRIGADE

Reference Trench Map 51 B.NW 19th MARCH, 1918.   Copy No 13

MOVE 1. The Battalion will relieve the 2nd Battalion GRENADIER GUARDS
in STIRLING CAMP and PUDDING TRENCH tomorrow 20th instant:-
   Battalion Headquarters, "A" & "B" Coys will be in STIRLING CAMP
                          "C" & "D" :   :   :   :   PUDDING TRENCH
   The Battalion will move off from here with an interval of
200 yards between platoons in the following order:-
   Headquarters, "B", "A", "C" and "D".
   Headquarters will move off at 1.30 p.m.
   ROUTE:- PLACE DE LA GARE - BLANGY - G.24.a.6.5 -
G.18.a.5.5 - thence via HERVIN FARM.
   DRESS:- Full marching order.
   "C" and "D" Companies will move off, with an interval of 200
yards between platoons, from STIRLING CAMP in time to pass under
the Railway Arch at H.14.a.0.3 at 7.10 p.m. These two companies
will take one blanket per man and officers' valises; the neces-
sary transport will accompany them as far as the 4th System.
Lewis Gun limbers will also accompany them.
   The Quartermaster will arrange for two cooks and six dixies
to be provided for these two companies.

TEAS 2. The four cookers will accompany the Battalion to STIRLING CAMP
where teas for the whole Battalion will be provided at 3.0 p.m.
Two cookers will then return and will be at the disposal of the
details.

ADVANCE 3. (A) For STIRLING CAMP.
PARTIES   2/Lieut. W. H. GORRIS and one N.C.O. per each "A" and "B"
Companies and Headquarters will parade at Orderly Room at 9.30
a.m. They will proceed to report to the Adjutant of the 2nd
Battalion, GRENADIER GUARDS, to take over the Camp.
       (B) For PUDDING TRENCH.
       2/Lieut. E. J. GRAY, one N.C.O. and three Guides from each
"C" and "D" Companies will parade at Orderly Room at 9.0 a.m.
They will take over trench Stores, etc., in PUDDING TRENCH.
Guides from this party will meet their respective companies at
the point on the main PAMPOUX Road, H.10.a.8.0 at 7.30 p.m.
       (C) 2/Lieut G. G. NAUMANN and two C.Q.M.Ss will report to
the Town Major "B" Area at 10.0 a.m. to allot accomodation for
the details.

DETAILS 4. All details to be left out (shown on return B) and the
Buglers will parade under 2/Lieut G.G.NAUMANN at 3.30 p.m. Before
this hour they will be available for cleaning up Barracks.
The following officers will accompany this party:-
2/Lieut. J. A. TAYLOR and 2/Lieut. H.C.V.SHARPE.

BILLETS 5. Lieut. G. J. COLE will remain behind and settle any claims
for billets. If necessary he will use the details for cleaning
up.

BAGGAGE 6. The two Companies and Headquarters going to STIRLING CAMP
will take two blankets per man. These blankets and those of "C"
and "D" (one per man) and the officers' valises (less those of
the details) will be dumped and LABELLED by Companies on the
square by 12.0 noon. Care should be taken to see that the
blankets and valises to be left at STIRLING CAMP are loaded
on top.
   The necessary transport to take valises and blankets of
details will accompany them; the valises and blankets being
collected before 3.0 p.m.

O.O. No 13 cont. sheet 2   19-3-18

WATER   7.   There is a water point for the cookers in STIRLING CAMP.
            The water carts will come up twice daily to replenish water bottles.
            There is a water point in PUDDING TRENCH.

HANDING   8.   All station calls and conditions of alertness as those of the
OVER   2nd Battalion GRENADIER GUARDS, will be adopted.
                   All details of trenches, trench stores, DEFENCE SCHEMES,
            will be carefully taken over and receipts given.   Duplicates of
            receipts will be forwarded to Battalion Headquarters before
            12.0 noon on the 21st inst.

BOUNDARY   9.   (a) Steel Helmets will be worn by all ranks EAST of a
of ALERT   North and South line through:-
AREA   GAVRELLE Road - Railway Bridge - H.13.b.9.9
                FAMPOUX   " -   "   " - H.13.b.9.4
                FEUCHY   " -   "   " - H.19.b.2.6
                   (b) Box Respirators will be worn by all ranks in the
            ALERT position EAST of a North and South line passing through
                GAVRELLE Road - LE POINT DU JOUR
                FAMPOUX ROAD at its junction with ATHIES ROAD in H.13.a.
                FEUCHY ROAD - west end of FEUCHY VILLAGE at H.21.a.1.2;

REPORT   10.   (1) Officers Commanding "C" and "I" Companies are reminded
            that they must report the names of the Platoon Commanders on their
            flanks.
                   (2) Completion of the relief of "C" and "I" Companies will
            be reported by wire by any sentence containing the code word
            "HAUGHTY".

                                           (sd) J. A. DAVISON   Captain
                                              (Adjutant 1st Battalion
                                                 THE RIFLE BRIGADE

                              DISTRIBUTION

                    Copy No 1   Commanding Officer
                            2   Adjutant
                            3   Assistant Adjutant
                            4   Lewis Gunn Officer
                            5   Quartermaster
                            6   Transport Officer
                            7   O.C. 2nd Batt Grenadier Guards
                            8   Area Commandant Stirling Camp
                            9   O.C. "A" Coy
                           10   "   "B" "
                           11   "   "C" "
                           12   "   "I" "
                           13   War Diary No 1
                           14   "   "   " 2
                           15   FILE

SECRET

OPERATION ORDERS No 16
by
Lieut.Colonel R.T.FELLOWES, D.S.O.,M.C.
Commanding 1st Battalion, THE RIFLE BRIGADE
28th March, 1918

Para. 1. Following moves will take place to-night.

Para. 2. "C" Company will, as soon after dark as possible, extend his right to Junction of FRONT LINE, THIRD SYSTEM and RIVER SCARPE H.22.b. (80.30.) 6.9.
This extra bit of line will be held by a series of posts.

Para. 3. "B" Company at a time to be notified by O.C. LAVA (probably 11.0 p.m.) will withdraw to STOKE TRENCH and occupy the line between "A" and "C" Companies.

Para. 4. "I" Company, at a time to be notified by O.C. LAVA (probably 11.0 p.m.) will withdraw to PUDDING and PORT Trenches, relieving LIGHT Coy. 1st SOMERSET L. I.
Three guides for "I" Company will be at Battalion H.Q. in PUDDING TRENCH from 11.0 p.m. onwards, and platoon Commanders of "I" Company will arrange to send on ahead someone to fetch a guide before their platoons reach the line of PORT.

Para. 5. "A" Company will, on the arrival of "B" Company in STOKE, close up to their left and gain touch with 12th Brigade. Till the arrival of "B" Company "A" and "C" Companies will be responsible for maintaining touch with one another.

Para. 6. RATIONS, WATER, etc. for "B" and "I" Companies will be taken to STOKE and PUDDING Trenches respectively by carrying party of 1st SOMERSET L.I.
Should rations for "B" Company arrive in STOKE before the arrival of "B" Company O.C. "A" will be responsible for meeting them and dumping them in the trench. "A" and "C" Coys. will draw their own rations in accordance with verbal instructions already issued.

Para. 7. The Battalion will thus become the FRONT LINE battalion of the Brigade.

Para. 8. All Companies will report their arrival in their new positions as soon as possible, and Company Commanders will report personally to the C.O. at Battalion H.Q. some time before dawn to-morrow.

Para. 9. "B" Company will take over "A" Company's present headquarters.

(sd) R. T. FELLOWES, Lieut. Colonel.
Commdg 1st Battn. THE RIFLE BRIGADE

Issued 8.0 p.m.
28/3/18

SECRET

OPERATION ORDERS No 17
by
Lieut. Colonel R. T. FELLOWES, D.S.O., MC.
Commanding 1st Battalion, THE RIFLE BRIGADE
29th March, 1918

Following moves will take place to-night.

Para. 1 "I" Company less 1 platoon will relieve "B" Coy., H.Q. details and troops of 1st SOMERSET L.I. in STOKE between a point 150 yards North of CAMEL (or wherever touch is gained with 12th Brigade) and Bank H.17.b.4.4. exclusive. Any men of "I" Coy. between these points will not be relieved but will join up with "I" Coy. on its arrival.

"I" Coy. will begin to leave PORT at 8.15 p.m. and Lieut. COLE will arrange to meet them at junction of STOKE and CAMEL.

"I" Coy. will be responsible for maintaining touch with 12th Brigade and for the Bombing blocks E. and W. along CAMEL and along STOKE N. of CAMEL.

On relief "B" Coy. under C.S.M. GOODE will move to PUDDING from the FAMPOUX Road Northwards.

Lieut. COLE and H.Q. details will rejoin Battalion H.Q., and troops of 1st SOMERSET L.I. will move to

Para. 2. "C" Company will be relieved from H.22.a.6.2. to FAMPOUX LOCK exclusive by "B" Coy. 1st SOMERSET L.I. who will arrive at junction of River SCARPE and DINGWALL at 9.0 p.m., where O.C. "C" Coy. will arrange to meet O.B."B" Coy 1st SOMERSET L.I. and conduct the relief with him.

"C" Company will hand over the responsibility for the defence of FAMPOUX LOCK to "A" Coy.

"C" Company on relief will take over that portion of STOKE from FAMPOUX Road exclusive to Bank H.17.b.4.4! inclusive. Troops of "A" Coy. relieved in this area will move S. of FAMPOUX Road; troops of "I" will join their Company in the N. part of STOKE (see para. 1); troops of "B" Coy. 1st R.B., 1st S.L.I. etc. will move to places indicated in para. 1.

Para. 3. "A" Company will be responsible for the line FAMPOUX LOCK inclusive to FAMPOUX-ATHIES Road inclusive and will remain in their present H.Q.

Para. 4. "I" and "C" Companies will occupy "B" Company's present H.Q.

Para. 5. Work on cutting through the FAMPOUX-ATHIES Road and the road in H.17.b. will be commenced as soon as possible after dark by "A" and "B" Companies respectively.

"C" Company will carry on with this work in H.17.b. as soon as they relieve the troops at work there.

It is _most_ important that these roads be cut through to-night to allow movement along the trenches under cover.

Lewis Guns will be placed at these points to cover the approaches from the E. and S.E; and troops will not leave these places before being properly relieved.

Para. 6. Time and place for meeting rations etc. will be notified later but not more than 6 men from each Company are to be away at the same time fetching rations. Empty Water tins and tea packs will be sent back to the pack animals by the men sent to fetch rations.

Para. 7. Completion of relief and arrival in new positions will be notified by 'phone or runner to Battalion H.Q. - the CODE WORDS "GOOD" and "LUCK" being used respectively.

Para. 8. There will be no withdrawal of any sort and every inch of ground will be contested.

ACKNOWLEDGE.

(sd) R. T. FELLOWES, Lieut.Col.
Commdg 1st Batt THE RIFLE BRIGADE

Issued at 4. 0 p.m.
29/3/18

11th
1~~1~~th Brigade.

4th Division

1st BATTALION

RIFLE BRIGADE

APRIL 1918.

WAR DIARY or INTELLIGENCE SUMMARY

Army Form C. 2118.

1st R.B. "The Rape Empire"

Place	Date	Hour	Summary of Events and Information	Remarks and references to Appendices
PAMPOUX	1st April		PAMPOUX - ATHIES RD. W. of village shelled by a .21 calibre gun from 8.9.a.m. & 9.30 a.m. Enemy shelled in N. end of STIRLING AVENUE & by FAUCHILL PEPPER TR. Hostile M.G's active from S. of SCARPE. Aeroplane at one named. Capt. G.F. Snyder's claimed many hits. E.A. very active. The Bn. was relieved by the 11th Bn. THE SOMERSET LIGHT INFANTRY.	REGISTRATION MAP. No. 42 OPERATION ORDER No. 2. OPERATION ORDER No. 19. APPENDIX II REF. FRIENDLY PLAN. MAP.
	2nd		Moved with Reserve. Infantry scheme held. Day spent in cleaning up. No work. Rifles to be done away. Hostile aeroplane.	
	3rd		Recreational training carrying on cultivate improved. 2 Coys on working party CAROLINA TR. at night. "B" Coy on relieved by Coy of 1st HAMPSHIRE REGT. Went into cellars in ATHIES.	AMENDMENT O.O. No 19.
	4th & 5th		Stay quiet. 2 Coys working in CAROLINA TR. at night. Heavy shelling on front line & rear areas. The Bn. relieved the 1st HAMPSHIRE REGT in support the 2nd HAMPSHIRE FUSILIERS being on the left and 2nd SEAFORTH HIGHLANDERS on the right. Reference scheme issued.	WORK ORDER No. III O.O. No 20. APPENDIX IV
	6th		Hostile activity quiet through out the day. Low flying E.A. active. The Bn. on working party digging a new support line W. of STONE AV. "B" Coy moved platoons to Bank in H.22.a. CAROLINA TR. S. of FAMPOUX. TR.	O.O. No 21 APPENDIX V
	7th		From 9.30 a.m. & 6.0 p.m. intermittent shelling of PUDDING TR. 8th CANADIAN BN. Bn. was relieved by the 1st HAMPSHIRE REGT and S.E. of ELBA TR. Hostile activity normal. The Bn. was relieved by 1 Coy & 2 platoons of the 15th CANADIAN BN. & 1 Coy of the 14th CANADIAN BN. Returned to lorries at "Y" HUTMENTS.	O.O. No 22 APPENDIX VI
	8th		Rouse at 12.0 noon. Remainder of day spent in cleaning up.	O.O. No 23 APPENDIX VII REF. SHEET 57B. N.W.
	9th 10th		The Bn. moved into billets in HAUTE AVESNES.	O.O. No 24 APPENDIX VIII REF. SHEET 57B. N.W.

Army Form C. 2118.

WAR DIARY or INTELLIGENCE SUMMARY.

(Erase heading not required.)

1st Bn. the Rifle Brigade

Place	Date	Hour	Summary of Events and Information	Remarks and references to Appendices
HAUTE AVESNES	11th		Day spent in arranging inspections etc. At 6.30 p.m. a warning order was received for the Bn. to be ready to move at 4 hours notice. Nothing further received during the night.	WARNING ORDER APPENDIX IX
	12th		At 9.30 a.m. orders were received for the Bn. to move. Platoons at 10.30 a.m. concentrated at junction of HERMAVILLE Rd & main ARRAS – ST POL ROAD. The Bn. E. entries at 11.0 a.m. The Bn moved through BUSNES at 6.15 p.m. At 7.0 p.m. the Bn marched to GONNEHEM, the 1st Bn. HAMPSHIRE REGT. marching as advanced flank guards, & took over the line from the 2nd SUFFOLK REGT. on the LA BASSÉE CANAL bank, the 1st GORDON HIGHLANDERS being on the right – 1st SOMERSET LIGHT INFANTRY on the left. The night was quiet. Patrols were sent out but nothing was seen or heard of the enemy. Dispositions of the Bn. as follows:– Bn. H.Q. in farmhouse at W.7.a.1.0. "A" Coy in right, "B" Coy in left in front line from Q.31.a.8.0.6 W.3.a.7.8. "C" Coy in support to "A" Coy & "D" Coy in support to "B" Coy.	REF. SHEET 36 A.
S.E. of POLECQ	13th		Hostile activity quiet during the morning. During the afternoon the support line was lightly shelled. Our Heavy gun being employed per R.B. 38/20/A wired. Hostile M. Gs from RIEZ and 2nd Lt. WOOD very active against our low flying aircraft. From 3.0 p.m. both were responsibly for the defence of the canal bridges from the 1st Bn. SOMERSET LIGHT INFANTRY. Guards were provided as follows:– 1 platoon at Q.31.a.8.2. 1 platoon at P.36.a.8.7, 5 platoon at P.29.c.8.2. At 6.0 p.m. our artillery concentrated on RIEZ-du-VINAGE. At 6.30 p.m. field artillery put down a barrage for 10 minutes in preparation for an attack by the 1st SOMERSET LIGHT INFANTRY. The remainder of the night was quiet.	APPENDIX X
	14th			

Army Form C. 2118.

WAR DIARY
or
INTELLIGENCE SUMMARY.
(Erase heading not required.)

Instructions regarding War Diaries and Intelligence Summaries are contained in F.S. Regs., Part II. and the Staff Manual respectively. Title pages will be prepared in manuscript.

1st Bn. The Rifle Brigade

Place	Date	Hour	Summary of Events and Information	Remarks and references to Appendices
S.E. OF ROBECQ LA BASSÉE CANAL SECTOR	15th	S.E. OF ROBECQ LA BASSÉE CANAL SECTOR	Hostile shelling of the bridges over the canal throughout the day, being specially heavy against them between 9.0 a.m. – 11.0 a.m. and 3.30 p.m. – 6.0 p.m. Post 5:15 p.m. the 10th Brigade attempted to capture BOIS DE PACAUT, "F" Coy of this Bn assisting with L.G. fire. The night was quiet on the Bn front.	
	16th		Heavy artillery fire directed against bridges held by the Bn between 9.0 a.m. and 11.0 a.m. In the evening the Bn was relieved by the 2nd ESSEX REGT. turned back to HILLTOP BUSNETTES.	OPERATION ORDER NO 25 APPENDIX XI REF. SHEET. 36A
BUSNETTES	17th & 18th	BUSNETTES	Day spent in reorganising unit. The Bn was prepared to move in case of emergency. A hostile barrage was put down on the 10th Brigade and at 2.30 a.m. the Bn was ordered to move up to W.&CENTRAL in support. The 10th & 13th Brigade had been forced to withdraw all posts to the S. of the canal, the 13th Brigade to evacuate RIEZ-DU-VINAGE. Withdraw to the Southern bank of the CANAL. All bridges in the Divisional front and from the foot bridge Q.31.a.5.5 exclusive were blown up. The Bn was ordered back to LANNOY where it billeted for the night.	REF. SHEET. 36A
LANNOY	19th LANNOY		The Bn failed during the day in the evening relieved the 1st ROYAL WARWICKSHIRE REGT & part of the 2nd DUKE OF WELLINGTON'S REGT. in the front line from W.10.6.2.9 GAVELETTE BRIDGE W.7.4.3.0.	O.O's No 26 APPENDIX XII REF. PLEX NPP (attached to O.O. 27)
	20th		Day quiet. On the evening "A" Coy attempted to establish a post in the farm at W.11.a.5.5. but found the enemy in strength and hung there, about 60 attached on patrol which had to withdraw.	

Army Form C. 2118.

WAR DIARY
or
INTELLIGENCE SUMMARY.
(Erase heading not required.)

Instructions regarding War Diaries and Intelligence Summaries are contained in F. S. Regs., Part II. and the Staff Manual respectively. Title pages will be prepared in manuscript.

Place	Date	Hour	Summary of Events and Information	Remarks and references to Appendices
FRONT LINE	21st		1st Bn. The Rifle Brigade. Intermittent shelling & bursts throughout the day. In the evening "A" Coy established three posts just S. of the farm in W.11.a.+b. and "I" Coy in W.10.b.90.65. "C" Coy was relieved by "B" Coy. 1/4th SOMERSET LIGHT INFANTRY made their way across the CANAL at PONT L'HINGES W.4.C.45.70 & took up a position in hand just N. of the CANAL in preparation for an attack next morning. The 2 platoons of "B" Coy at W.10.b.25.20. moved & came under command of O.C. 1/4th HAMPSHIRE REGT.	
FRONT LINE	22nd	5.15 a.m	at 5.15 a.m. our artillery put down a heavy barrage, after 3 minutes the infantry advanced. The objectives being as follows:— On the left the 1/4th HAMPSHIRE REGT. the line of RIEZ-du-VINAGE – LA PANNETRIE roads in the BOIS du PACAUT. The 2 platoons of "B" Coy attached, to form a line of posts from PACAUT WOOD along this road to LA PANNETRIE. "C" Coy LA PANNERIE from a line of posts E. of the LA PANNERIE – PONT L'HINGES road to the CANAL. By 5.50 a.m. "C" Coy had gained its objective, the 2 platoons of "B" Coy formed a line of posts as ordered connecting up with "C" Coy on their right. 1/4th HAMPSHIRE REGT. on their left at road junction Q.33.d.95.40. The BN captured over 60 prisoners. The enemy barrage during the attack was not very intense & soon stopped. c & t 7.40 a.m. hostile artillery commenced shelling the whole BN front heaviest on "A" Coy. it ceased about 12.0 p.m. c & t 1.50 p.m. it commenced again & developed into a heavy barrage fire which lasted until 5.15 p.m. after which everything was quiet. E.A. MGs very active during the evening firing on troops on the CANAL BANK, & N of it.	OPERATION ORDERS No. XII APPENDIX XIII REF. FLEX.MAPS. ATTACHED

WAR DIARY or INTELLIGENCE SUMMARY

Army Form C. 2118.

Unit: 11th Bn. The Rifle Brigade

Place	Date	Hour	Summary of Events and Information	Remarks and references to Appendices
	22nd contd.		At 8.30 p.m. the S.O.S. was sent up W. of PRECAUT. WOOD. The hostile barrage fell at Coffs, being very intense around PONT L'HINGES. It soon ceased afterwards & the night was quiet. Several moves were ordered to take place during the night.	REF. R.B. F93 APPENDIX XIV REFLEX MAP ATTACHED
	23rd		Intermittent shelling throughout the day being especially heavy on the CANAL BANK from 5.30 a.m. to 8.30 a.m. Gas shells were also used in the evening. "B" & "C" Coys were relieved by 2 Coys of the 1/5 SOMERSET LIGHT INFANTRY, Bn. Coy H.Qs & 2 platoons went to HINGETTE + 2 platoons L'PLOUY FARM. "C" Coy came back to VERTANNOY. Before being relieved wiring was commenced between the post. 1 Coy sent out 2 patrols one to the house at Q.34.a. outside the other to the practice trenches W.5. n.s.c. The house was unoccupied on post was established there. The trenches were strongly held by the enemy.	OPERATION ORDERS No 28 APPENDIX XV REF SHEET 36.A
	24th		Heavy shelling of the CANAL BANK from 5.30 a.m. to 8.30 a.m. & at 9.0 a.m. & 7 p.m. Gas shelled the area W.15.a. for 15 minutes. Shelling on the right of the Bn. front was exceptionally heavy during the early part of the evening. Enemy seemed a direct hit on an advanced post at W.10.b.9.6, this post was later re-established 150x N. of its original position.	
	25th		Intermittent shelling of the CANAL BANK, and HINGETTE during the day & of HINGES & the HINGES-VERTANNOY ROAD during the night. A.E.A. flew very low over our lines for an hour in the afternoon.	
	26th		Quiet all day in front. Heavy shelling of HINGES during the afternoon. The Bn. was relieved by the 8th KINGS. OWN. REGT. & the 2 SUFFOLK. REGT. turned back to billets in GONNEHEM.	O.Os No 29 APPENDIX XVI REF SHEET 36.A

Army Form C. 2118.

WAR DIARY
or
INTELLIGENCE SUMMARY.
(Erase heading not required.)

Instructions regarding War Diaries and Intelligence Summaries are contained in F. S. Regs., Part II. and the Staff Manual respectively. Title pages will be prepared in manuscript.

Place	Date	Hour	Summary of Events and Information 1st Bn The Rifle Brigade	Remarks and references to Appendices
GONNEHEM	27th 28th		Day spent in cleaning up Village shelled during the night. Village shelled at 10th Bn area during the morning necessitating the removal of all troops from billets. The TBN moved to billets in BUSNETTES in Divisional Reserve.	OPERATION ORDERS No 30 APPENDIX XVII REF SHEET 36A
BUSNETTES	29th & 30th BUSNETTES		Spent cleaning up reorganizing. The BN under orders to move at 1 hour notice.	

G.V.C. Letter
O.C. 1st Bn The Rifle Brigade

Army Form C. 2118.

WAR DIARY
or
INTELLIGENCE SUMMARY.
(Erase heading not required.)

Instructions regarding War Diaries and Intelligence Summaries are contained in F. S. Regs., Part II. and the Staff Manual respectively. Title pages will be prepared in manuscript.

Place	Date	Hour	Summary of Events and Information	Remarks and references to Appendices
			CASUALTIES IN ACTION:	
			Capt. J. E. TREVOR-JONES Killed	
			Lieut. L. H. ADAMS M.C. Killed	
			2/Lieut. H. C. V. SHARPS Killed	
			Capt. R. J. F. CHANCE, M.C. Wounded	
			2/Lieut. J. T. MARTIN Wounded	
			: C. G. COOPER Wounded	
			: A. E. SALTER Wounded	
			Major I. O. MONTFORD Wounded and rejoined.	
			Other ranks	
			Killed 40	
			Wounded 100	
			Missing 4	
			Wounded at duty ... 8	
			Self Inflicted Wounds 3	
			Total 155	
			EVACUATIONS SICK	
			Lieut. R. D. SHIRLEY	Other Ranks 67
			REINFORCEMENTS 2/Lieut.	
			Capt. A. W. L. KISSIN : T. R. M. LEE	Other ranks 333
			Lieut. M. R. HARVEY : R. C. LOVELL	
			: W. H. ELDRIDGE : F. H. BROWN	
			2/Lieut A. O. HUNTING : T. R. LECKIE	
			: C. J. C. SCHUSTER : F. W. RAY	
			: J. HARVEY : J. H. S. PIERCE	
			: H. V. MORLOCK : J. H. AIMLEY	
			: W. BREWARD : A. R. BURRIDGE	
			: J. G. SHOOBRIDGE: R. JOHNSTONE	

APP "I"

OPERATION ORDERS No 18
by
Lieut.Colonel R. T. FELLOWES, D.S.O., M.C.
Commanding 1st Battalion, THE RIFLE BRIGADE

Ref. 51B. N.W.   1.4.18

1.   The Battalion will be relieved in the Front Line to-night by
      the 1st Batt. SOMERSET L.I.
      "A" Coy. RIFLE BRIGADE on the right will be relieved by "B" Coy.
                                                               SOMERSET L.I.
      "B"   :   :   :   in support   :   :   :   by "C" Coy.
                                                               SOMERSET L.I.
      "C"   :   :   :   in centre   :   :   :   by "H" Coy.
                                                               SOMERSET L.I.
      "I"   :   :   :   on the left :   :   :   by LIGHT Coy.
                                                               SOMERSET L.I.

2.   Guides from the Battalion will be required as follows:-
         1. From "A" Coy. RIFLE BRIGADE 1 per platoon and 1 for Com-
      pany H.Q. at H.17.c.8.4. at 9.15 p.m.
         2. From "B" Coy. NO guides will be required.
         3. From "C" Coy. 1 per platoon and 1 for Company H.Q. at
      junction of PUDDING TRENCH and FAMPOUX ROAD at 9.15 p.m.
         4. From "I" Coy. 1 per platoon and 1 for Company H.Q. at the
      junction of PUDDING TRENCH and the PONT DU JOUR Road at 8.30 p.m.

3.   On completion of relief the Battalion will move into Brigade
      Reserve and Companies will take up the following positions. All
      moves will be at an interval of 200 yards between platoons.
      "A" Company)   will move to CAM AVENUE from H.15.b.2.4. to
      "B"   :   )   H.15.a.8.9 junction with Track "B".
      "C" Company will move to CAM VALLEY from H.15.d.05.73 to
         H.15.b.40.25.
      "I" Company will move to trench from H.9.c.15.30 to H.15.a.14.81.
      Battalion H.Q. will move to Dug-out at H.15.a.3.7.
      Companies will make their own arrangements about getting to
      the above mentioned places, "C" and "I" Companies moving via
      "B" Track, "A" and "B" via main ATHIES ROAD.

4.   "B" Company will take over and man S.O.S. relay station in
      CAM AVENUE at H.15.b.1.5. All S.O.S. signals which are sent up
      in the Brigade sector will be repeated by this station.

5.   The men of "A" Company at present attached to "B" Company
      will rejoin "A" Company as soon as possible after reaching the
      new position.

6.   All available salvage, tea packs, empty water tins, will be
      carried out and dumped by "A" and "B" Companies on the limber
      near the junction of PUDDING TRENCH and the FAMPOUX ROAD. "C"
      and "I" Companies will send their material to the new Battalion
      H.Q. in the course of tomorrow.

7.   All red very lights, picks and shovels, will be carried out
      and taken to new position. White very lights, S.A.A., Bombs,
      etc. will be handed over and receipts obtained which will be
      forwarded to Battalion H.Q. as soon as possible after completion
      of relief.

8.   Rations and water will come up each night by limber,
      arriving at H.15.a.3.5. at 9.0 p.m. To-night they will be
      dumped here and should be fetched by Companies as soon as
      possible after arrival in their new positions.

                                                    cont. on sheet 2

O.O. No 18: sheet 2   1/4/18

9.   Completion of relief in the present sector will be reported either by wire or by runner by any sentence containing the Code Word "PUG".

       Arrival in new position will be similarly reported by the Code Word "PEKE".

10.   Defence scheme will be issued later.

11.   ACKNOWLEDGE.

                                                     (sd) J. A. DAVISON, Captain
                                    Adjutant 1st Batt. THE RIFLE BRIGADE.

SECRET

OPERATION ORDER No 19
by
Lieut.Colonel R.T.FELLOWES, D.S.O., M.C.
Commanding 1st Battalion, THE RIFLE BRIGADE
PROVISION DEFENCE SCHEME - RESERVE BATTALION
FAMPOUX SECTOR

9/4/18

APP II

Ref J SITUATION MAP No 135:9-4-18:   Copy No

1. **DISPOSITIONS**
    Battalion H.Q.   H.15.a.3.5.
    "A" and "B" Companies   CAM AVENUE
    "C" Company   ...   ...   CAM VALLEY
    "I"   ...Trench H.14.b.8.3. - H.9.c.3.0.

2. **ACTION IN CASE OF ATTACK**
    A.   There will be no withdrawal from any line.
    B.   If the S.O.S. signal is sent up or if hostile shelling is so heavy as to make it appear probable that a hostile attack is imminent, the following moves will be carried out. In both cases notification will at once be sent to Battalion H.Q. and Companies will move on their own initiative without waiting for orders from Battalion H.Q. (except "I" Coy.)

    (1)   "B" Company will move to CAROLINA TRENCH (Reserve-line 3rd SYSTEM) and will be responsible for the front from the River SCARPE to 150 yards South of CAM AVENUE.

    (2)   "A" Company will move to CAROLINA TRENCH (Reserve Line 3rd SYSTEM) from a point 150 yards South of CAM AVENUE to CASTLE LANE inclusive. Touch will be obtained with the 12th Brigade on their left.

    (3)   "C" Company will be in readiness at the Southern end of CAM VALLEY to counter attack with the sword any of the enemy who may have penetrated the front and support lines of the THIRD SYSTEM and are seen to be advancing.

    O.C. "C" Company will arrange to have a look-out post well forward West of CAM VALLEY to give him this information, and O.C. "A" and "B" Companies will also arrange to send back all information to "C" Company.

    O.C. "A" Company 1st HAMPSHIRE REGT. which guards the River SCARPE has a direct call on "C" Company in case the enemy should attempt to force a crossing over the SCARPE and "C" Company will answer the call without reference to Battalion H.Q. Should "C" Company be called upon for the above O.C. "A" Company 1st HAMPSHIRE REGT. will notify the O.C. Support and Reserve Battalions of this action.

    (4)   "I" Company will be kept as a reserve and may be used in the following alternative ways according to the situation:-
    (a) Form a defensive flank facing N.E. along CAM AVENUE should the enemy force his way on the North of the Brigade Sector.
    (b) Reinforce the reserve line THIRD SYSTEM or carry out a local counter attack in that line.

3.   The necessary reconnaissances will be carried out as soon as possible.

4.   ACKNOWLEDGE by bearer.

                       (sd) J. A. DAVISON, Captain
                    Adjutant 1st Battalion THE RIFLE BRIGAD

Issued at 2.15 a.m.
    9 - 4 - 18

SECRET   AMENDMENT No 1
                               to
                OPERATION ORDER   No A9   3 - 4 - 18

1. **DISPOSITIONS.**   "B" Company will now be accomodated in Dugouts and cellars in ATHIES.

2. **ACTION IN CASE OF ATTACK.**   "A" Company will move to CAROLINA TRENCH and garrison it from the River to the FAMPOUX ROAD inclusive.

                "A" Company 1st HAMPSHIRE REGT. will garrison CAROLINA TRENCH from the FAMPOUX ROAD to H.10.c.9.0.

                "B" Company will take up positions on the Eastern outskirts of ATHIES.

                The roles of "C" and "I" Companies will remain the same.

3.   The S.O.S Station at H.15.b.1.5. will be taken over by the 1st HAMPSHIRE REGT.

4.   ACKNOWLEDGE.

                                         (sd) J. A. DAVISON   Captain
                              Adjutant 1st Battalion THE RIFLE BRIGADE

Issued to all recipients
   of O.O. No 19
   10.0. p.m.   3 - 4 - 18

SECRET

AMENDMENT No 3
to
OPERATION ORDER No 19

Fourth Company of 1st HAMPSHIRE REGT. is now in Dug-outs in H.15.d.

<u>ACTION IN CASE OF ATTACK</u>.
"A" Company will move from CAM AVENUE and man CAROLINA TRENCH from FAMPOUX ROAD exclusive to H.16.a.3.8. and the fourth Company 1st HAMPSHIRE REGT. will man CAROLINA TRENCH from FAMPOUX ROAD inclusive to the River.

ACKNOWLEDGE.

Captain
Adjutant 1st Batt THE RIFLE BRIGADE

Issued to all recipients
of Operation Order No 19
5.0 p.m. 4/4/18

WARNING ORDER

App III

1. The Battalion will probably relieve the 1st HAMPSHIRE REGT. in Support tomorrow night 5/6th inst.

2. The dispositions of the 1st HAMPSHIRE REGT. are as follows:-
 (a) 1 Company Front and Support Lines 3rd SYSTEM South of the FAMPOUX ROAD and Guarding the river between H.29.a.75.30. inclusive and FAMPOUX LOCK exclusive.
 (b) 2 Companies less one Platoon, Front and Support lines 3rd SYSTEM between CAMEL AVENUE inclusive and sunken road H.16.b.7.0. inclusive.
 (c) 1 Platoon reserve line 3rd SYSTEM H.10.c.2.0. to H.16.a.3.6.
 (d) 1 Company CAM AVENUE H.15.b.

3. (1) "C" Company will relieve Company in (a) above.
 (2) "I" Company will relieve Northernmost Company in (b), and the Platoon in (c) if it comes from that Company of the HAMPSHIRE REGT. which they relieve.
 (3) "A" Company will relieve Southernmost Company in (b) and the Platoon in (c) if it comes from that Company of the HAMPSHIRE REGT. they relieve.
 (4) "B" Company will relieve Company in (d) above.

4. Officers and N.C.Os will carry out the reconnaissances of their respective Company fronts before 12.0 noon tomorrow under Company arrangements.

5. Sandbags on the scale of 5 per man must be drawn from Battalion H.Q. tonight before 9.0 p.m. by "B" and "C" Companies. Also any deficiencies in picks and shovels.

                                (sd) J. A. DAVISON, Captain
                                Adjutant 1st Batt. THE RIFLE BRIGADE

4/4/18

SECRET   OPERATION ORDER No 20   APP IV
by
Lieut.Colonel R.T.FELLOWES, DSO., MC.
Commanding 1st Battalion, THE RIFLE BRIGADE

Ref. 51 B N.W.   4 - 4 - 18   Copy No

RELIEF   1.   The Battalion will relieve the 1st Batt. HAMPSHIRE REGT. in Support tomorrow night.
         The relief will be carried out as follows:-
"A" Company RIFLE BRIGADE will relieve "B" Coy. HAMPSHIRE REGT.
     2 Platoons in PUDDING TRENCH from sunken road H.16.b.7.0 Northwards.
     1 Platoon H.10.c.9.0. to H.16.a.3.6.
"B" Company RIFLE BRIGADE will relieve "A" Coy. HAMPSHIRE REGT.
     in Dug-outs South of road in H.15.d.
"C" Company RIFLE BRIGADE will relieve "D" Coy. HAMPSHIRE REGT.
     in DINGWALL, PEPPER TRENCH and River bank.
"I" Company RIFLE BRIGADE will relieve "C" Coy. HAMPSHIRE REGT.
     in PORT Trench and PUDDING Trench from CAMEL AVENUE (inclusive) Southwards.
Battalion H.Q. will move to H.16.d.05.50. (present H.Q. of 1st SOMERSET L.I.)
     The order of relief will be "I","C", "A", "B"
     All moves will be with an interval of 200 yards between platoons.
     ROUTE:-   "B" Track, EFFIE, ELBA

GUIDES.   2.   Guides for the Battalion will be found as follows:-
     (a)   For "A", "C" and "I" Companies one per Platoon and one for Company H.Q. at the junction of PUDDING TRENCH and ELBA TRENCH at 8.45 p.m.
     (b)   For "B" Company at the junction of the Eastern bank of CAM VALLEY and the FAMPOUX Road at 8.30 p.m.
     (c)   Guide for the reserve Platoon of "A" Company will be at the junction of "B" track and EFFIE at 8.45 p.m.

ADVANCE PARTIES   3.   Companies and Battalion H.Q. will send in advance one N.C.O. to take over Trench Stores. These N.C.Os will arrive at their respective H.Q. at 4.0 p.m.

TOOLS   4.   Picks and shovels will be handed over. RED Very Lights will be carried on the man.

TRENCH STORES   5.   All Trench Stores will be carefully taken over and duplicates of receipts forwarded to Battalion H.Q. Full particulars must be obtained regarding S.O.S. Stations, etc.

REPORTS   6.   Completion of relief will be reported by any sentence containing the Code Word "SPY". Name of Platoon Commanders on the flanks will be reported as soon as possible after completion of relief.

RATIONS   7.   Rations and water will come up by limber to the point where CAROLINA TRENCH crosses the FAMPOUX Road. Companies will be notified when the pipe line is working.

     8.   ACKNOWLEDGE.

                               (sd) J. A. DAVISON, Captain
                   Adjutant 1st Batt. THE RIFLE BRIGADE

SECRET

APP V

OPERATION ORDERS No 91
by
Lieut.Colonel R.T.FELLOWES, D.S.O.,M.C.
Commanding 1st Battalion THE RIFLE BRIGADE
PROVISIONAL DEFENCE SCHEME for SUPPORT BATTALION - FAMPOUX SECTOR

Reference PELVES Special Sheet 51B N.W.
Plex Situation Maps   Copy NO

DISPOSITIONS 1.
(a) Battalion H.Q. - H.16.d.05.50
(b) 1 Company in Front and Support Lines, 3rd SYSTEM South of FAMPOUX ROAD (DINGWALL and PEPPER TRENCHES), with posts guarding River bank from H.22.a.75.30 to FAMPOUX LOCK both inclusive.
(c) 2 Companies less 1 Platoon in Front and Support Lines.- 3rd SYSTEM between CAMEL AVENUE inclusive and sunken road H.16.b.7.0. inclusive (PORT and PUDDING)
(d) 1 Platoon in Reserve line - 3rd SYSTEM H.10.c.2.0. to H.16.a.3.6. (EFFIE and CAROLINA TRENCHES)
(e) 1 Company in Dugouts South of road in H.16.d.

ACTION IN CASE OF ATTACK. 2.
(1) There will be no withdrawal from any line.
(2) The Battalion is responsible for the defence of the 3rd SYSTEM from CAMEL AVENUE inclusive to the River inclusive and for the right flank of the Brigade along the SCARPE from H.22.a.75.30 to FAMPOUX LOCK both inclusive.
(3) The enemy will be met with steady and controlled Rifle and Lewis Gun fire.
(4) Should the enemy effect a footing in our trenches:-
   (a) He will at once be attacked with Sword and Rifle & Bombs and thrown out.
   (b) Troops will NOT try to withdraw out of range of the enemy's bombers but will rather run inside his range thus letting his bombs pass over their heads and charge him with the sword. If necessary blocks will be made to prevent him extending his gains to either flank.
   (c) Bombers and Rifle Grenadiers will be placed at the junction of Support Line and all Communication Trenches running towards the front.
   (d) In addition special arrangements will be made by the establishment of Police Posts to prevent any of our troops withdrawing from the Front Line along the Communication Trenches.
(5) The Company mentioned in Paragraph 1 (c) will garrison CAROLINA TRENCH between the FAMPOUX ROAD inclusive and the River Scarpe.
   This Company will move on its own initiative should the S.O.S. go up or should hostile shelling be so heavy as to make it appear probable that a hostile attack is imminent. It will NOT await orders from Battalion H.Q.
(6) The Company mentioned in Paragraph 1 (b) has a direct call on the Company of the Reserve Battalion situated in CAM VALLEY should the enemy attempt to force a crossing over the SCARPE. Should the O.C. call on this Company he will inform O.C. Support and Reserve Battalions of his action.
(7) The word RETIRE will on no account be used. Anyone heard using this word will be shot at sight.
(8) These orders will be made known and thoroughly explained to all ranks and every man should know what he has to do and how he has to do it should certain eventualities arise.

Issued at 8.0 p.m.   (sd) J. A. DAVISON Captain
4-4-18   Adjutant 1st Battn. THE RIFLE BRIGADE

Copy No 1   O.C. "A" Company
         2   "B"   :
         3   "C"   :
         4   "D"   :
         5   War Diary No 1
         6   :   :
         7   File

SECRET

AMENDMENT No 1
to
OPERATION ORDERS No 21

1. Reference Para. 1 (b) and Para. 2 (2) Delete from "H.22.a.75.30 ------ both inclusive" and substitute "H.22.a.1.3. inclusive to FAMPOUX LOCK exclusive."

2. Reference Para. 2 (5) This Company on arrival in CAROLINA TRENCH will come under the orders of O.C. Reserve Battalion.

3. Delete Para. 2 (b).

4. Should the enemy penetrate our front line O.C. front line Battalion will at once use his local supports to eject him. Should this counter attack take place the platoons situated from H.10.c.8.0. to H.16.a.3.6 will be moved at once by O.C. Company to join the remainder of the Company in PORT and PUDDING.TRENCHES without waiting for further orders.
   Should this counter attack fail two of the three Companies in PUDDING, PORT and DINGWALL TRENCHES will be prepared to counter attack and the Company in CAROLINA TRENCH will be moved up into PUDDING and PORT.

5. The following S.O.S. Stations will be manned:-
   1 CAMEL AVENUE about H.17.a.1.0. by Left Company.
   2 ELBA TRENCH about H.16.a.4.6. by Centre Company.

Issued to all recipients
of Operation Orders No 21   (sd) J.A. DAVISON, Captain
10.0 a.m. 6-4-18   Adjt 1st Battn. THE RIFLE BRIGADE

SECRET   OPERATION ORDER No 52   APP VI
by
Lieut.Colonel R.T.FELLOWES, DSO, MC.
Commanding 1st Battalion, THE RIFLE BRIGADE

Ref. Sheet 51B N.W.   7-4-18   Copy No

RELIEF 1.   The Battalion will be relieved by the 1st Battalion THE HAMPSHIRE REGT., and the 8th CANADIAN BATTALION tonight, as shown below:-
"A" Company) RIFLE BRIGADE will be relieved by "B" Coy. 8th
"I"   :   ) CANADIAN BATTALION.
"C" Company RIFLEBRIGADE will be relieved by "D" Coy HAMPSHIRE REGT
Battalion H.Q. and "B" Coy. will remain in their present positions.

GUIDES 2.   Guides from the Battalion will be found as follows:-
A.   From "C" Coy. 4 guides (1 per platoon and 1 for Company H.Q.) at the junction of DINGWALL TRENCH and the FAMPOUX ROAD at 8.30 p.m.
B.   (I) From "A" Coy. 1 guide to take 1 platoon 8th CANADIAN BATTN. to relieve their 2 platoons in PUDDING TRENCH.
       1 guide to take 1 platoon 8th CANADIAN BATTN. to relieve their third platoon in
    (II) From "I" Coy. 1 guide to take 1 platoon 8th CANADIAN BATTN. to relieve 2 platoons in PORT TRENCH
       1 guide to take Company H.Q. to "I" Company's present H.Q.
    (III) These guides will be at the Railway Arch H.14.a.0.3 at 8.30 p.m.
C.   From "B" Coy. 8 guides at ATHIES CROSS ROADS at 10.30 p.m. to guide 6 platoons and 2 Company H.Q. of "A" and "I" Companies to their cellars and dugouts in ATHIES.

MOVE 3.   On completion of relief the following moves will take place:-
(I)   "C" Company will move to CAM VALLEY.
(II)   "A" and "I" Companies will move to cellars and dugouts in ATHIES, being conducted there by "B" Coy. ("A" Coy. will occupy the H.Q. lately vacated by "B" Coy. when in reserve.)

RATIONS 4.   Rations and water will arrive at ATHIES CROSS ROADS at 12.0 midnight. Each Company will send a guide to this point to show the ration limbers where they require their rations dumped.

SALVAGE 5.   All salvage, empty water tins, etc. will be brought by Companies moving from the present positions and will be sent back on the returning ration limbers.

STORES 6.   All Trench Stores, Picks, Shovels and GREEN Very Lights will be carefully handed over. Receipts obtained will be forwarded to Battalion H.Q. as soon as possible after the completion of the relief.

REPORT 7.   Completion of the relief will be reported by wire or runner by any sentence containing the Code Word "JUST". Companies will similarly report their arrival in their new positions by Code Word "ICE".

8.   ACKNOWLEDGE.

                                (sd)   J. A. DAVISON,   Captain
                         Adjutant 1st Battn. THE RIFLE BRIGADE

Issued at 5.0 p.m.
7-4-18

SECRET

OPERATION ORDER No 23
by
Lieut.Colonel R.T.FELLOWES, DSO, MC.
Commanding 1st Battalion THE RIFLE BRIGADE

App VII

Ref. Sheet 51B N.W.   8.4.18   Copy No

RELIEF I.   The Battalion will be relieved tonight as follows:-
        (1) "B" Coy. RIFLE BRIGADE will be relieved by 3 Platoons 15th
                                                       CANADIAN INF. BATTN.
        (2) "C" :   :   :   :   :   by 1 Company 15th
                                                       CANADIAN INF. BATTN.
        (3) "A" and "I" Coys: :   :   :   by 1 Company 14th
                                                       CANADIAN INF. BATTN.
        (4) Battalion H.Q. : :   :   :   Battalion H.Q. 15th
                                                       CANADIAN INF. BATTN.

GUIDES II. (1) 3 from "B" Coy to report to Lieut G.J.COLE at G.18.c.4.4
                         at 7.0 p.m.
             (2) 5   : "C" :   - ditto -   - ditto -
             (3) 5   : "I" :   - ditto -   - ditto -
             (4) 2   : Batt. H.Q. - ditto -   - ditto -
             (5) 1   : "B" Coy to report to Lieut G.J.COLE at G.18.c.4.4,
                         at 7.0 p.m. to conduct the relief of the
             3 guards on Bridges.
                     These guides will be given the attached slips which
             they will show Lieut.G.J.COLE on arrival.

MOVE   III. On completion of relief the Battalion will embus at a place
             to be notified later and move to "Y" HUTS.

HANDING
OVER   IV. Defence Schemes, all Trench Stores, Very Lights, etc. will be
             handed over and receipts obtained. These receipts will be for-
             warded to Battalion H.Q. on arrival at "Y" HUTS. All water tins,
             salvage, etc. will be carried out and placed on the busses.

MEAL   V.   A hot meal will be provided on arrival in camp. Valises,
             packs, blankets, cookers, etc. will be in camp by the time the
             Battalion arrives.

DETAILS VI. The personnel at present with the Provisional Battalion will
             rejoin the Battalion on the 9th inst.

REPORT VII. Completion of relief will be reported if possible BY WIRE by
             any sentence containing the Code Word "MACHONACHIE". If reported
             by runner the Code Word need not be used.

        VIII. ACKNOWLEDGE.

                                  (sd) J. A. DAVISON, Captain
                             Adjutant 1st Battn. THE RIFLE BRIGADE

Issued at 3.15 p.m.
    8 - 4 - 18

APP. VIII

SECRET

OPERATION ORDERS No 34
by
Lieut.Colonel R.T.FELLOWES, D.S.O., M.C.
Commanding 1st Battalion THE RIFLE BRIGADE
10th APRIL, 1918   Copy No

1. The Battalion will move to HAUTE AVESNES to-day. Companies will move, at an interval of 300 yards, in the following order H.Q. leaving camp at 11.0 a.m.
   Headquarters, "B", "A", "C", "I".
   Transport will move in rear of Companies.
   O.C. "I" Company will detail the last platoon as baggage guard.
   The Buglers will march first with "B" Company.

2. All valises, mess tins, etc. will be packed and ready to move off at 10.30 a.m.   Blankets will be rolled and labelled in bundles of 10 and dumped near the road at the Eastern end of the camp where they will be loaded on two lorries. The Quartermaster will send a guide to Brigade H.Q. at 9.30 to show the buses where they are required.

3. Advance party consisting of the four C.Q.M.Ss and 1 N.C.O for Battalion H.Q. will report to Lieut. L. H. ADAMS at 8.0 a.m. They will proceed to HAUTE AVESNES, reporting to the Town Major at 9.0 a.m.

4. Companies will render to Orderly Room not later than 10.15 am certificates to the effect that their lines have been left clean and in a sanitary condition.
   The Assistant Adjutant will report to Camp Warden at this time to hand over the camp. He will obtain a certificate that the camp has been left in a clean and sanitary condition.

(sd) J. A. DAVISON,   Captain
Adjutant 1st Battn. THE RIFLE BRIGADE

DISTRIBUTION.
Copy No 1   Commanding Officer
        2   2nd in Command
        3   Adjutant
        4   Assistant Adjutant
        5   Intelligence Officer
        6   Transport Officer
        7   Quartermaster
        8   O.C, "A" Company
        9   "B"   "
       10   "C"   "
       11   "I"   "
       12   War Diary No 1
       13   "   "   " 2
       14   File

SECRET   MARCHING ORDER   APP IX

14th APRIL, 1918

No 13

1. Instructions already issued are cancelled.

2. The Battalion will be prepared to move at three-and-a-half hours notice.
   On the Battalion Call, followed by the "Fall in" being sounded the following procedure will take place:-
   (a) All blankets will be handed in to the Quartermaster's Stores in bundles of 10.
   Officers' Valises and Mess Kit will be dumped outside the billets, ready to be loaded one hour after the call has been sounded.
   (b) One baggage Wagon will collect the officers' Valises, Mess Stores, etc. The other will report at the Quartermaster's Stores.
   (c) Each Company will send 1 N.C.O. and 4 men (to be detailed at once) to the Quartermaster's Stores to report to Lieut. G. J. COLE. In the event of lorries being supplied they will load the blankets.

3. All ranks will sleep within easy reach of their equipment, which on no account will be undone. Officers' servants will sleep near their officers.

4. The Bugle Major will detail the following repeating Buglers.
   1 to be at the Orderly Room.
   1 : : in "C" Company's lines.
   1 : : : "I" : :
   1 : : at Headquarters
   1 : : at Company Officers' H.Q.
   These Buglers will be relieved every 4 hours.
   They will repeat the call mentioned in Para 2 as soon as they hear it.

5. The Companies will be formed up in column of route as shown below, ready to move off three-and-a-half hours after this call.
   DRESS: Fighting Order
   ORDER OF MARCH: H.Q., "B", "A", "C", "I".
   Head of the Column will be at a point 200 yards North of the Quartermaster's Stores.

6. Further instructions regarding the exact hour to move off will be issued later.

7. All surplus Mess Kit, Signalling equipment, Orderly Room boxes, Aid Post Stores, etc. should be packed up on receipt of these Orders.
   Orderly Room boxes will be carried on the Quartermaster's Wagon.
   Packs will probably be stored in this village.

8. All stores which cannot be carried will be taken to the Quartermaster's Stores and handed over to the Town Major. This will include blankets should lorries not be provided.

9. ACKNOWLEDGE:

(sd) J. A. DAVISON Captain
Adjt. 1st Batt THE RIFLE BRIGADE

DISTRIBUTION
Copy No 1 "O.C. "A" Coy   No 6 Commanding Officer
     2   -   "B" :   7 Adjutant
     3   -   "C" :   8 2nd in Command
     4   -   "I" :   9 Town Major

AMENDMENTS No 1
To WARNING ORDER - 11th April, 1918
----

1. Officers will arrange to store their surplus kit (i.e Winter Clothing) in a mail bag in the Quartermaster's Stores as soon as possible. The total officer's kit should not exceed 1bs40, bare necessities only being retained.

2. Packs will be stored, and handed over to the Town Major.

3. One lorry is being provided which will carry the blankets of the Battalion.

4. The under-mentioned billeting party will be warned and will hold itself in readiness to proceed at short notice on bicycles:-
   1 N.C.O per Company; 1 for Headquarters.
   To report to Lieut. G.J.COLE at Orderly Room one hour after the "Fall in" has sounded. Further particulars will be issued later

5. Reference Warning Order, Para 9 (c), for 'Lieut. G.J.COLE' read 'the Reg. Sergeant Major.'

(sd) J. A. DAVISON, Captain
Adjutant 1st Batt. THE RIFLE BRIGADE

Distribution
as for Warning Order 11th April, 1918

RB.38/20/a

13-4-18

APP X

O.C. Ida,
     Besa,

        "B" and "I" Coys will each send out patrols consisting of
2 sections and 1 officer each to cross the canal at 12.30 a.m.
tomorrow morning.   Object of Patrols is to gain the line of the
road LA PANNERIE to RIEZ.
        The 10th Brigade are sending out similar Patrols on the
right and 1st SOMERSET L.I. on the left.
Dividing line between "I" Coy and 10th Brigade:-
    Western edge of PACAUT WOOD.
Between "B" Coy and 1/SOMERSET L.I. bridge Q.39.c.6.9. to road
    junction Q.36.d.1.1. both inclusive to "B" Coy.
Between "B" and "I" Coys. North and South Grid line between
    squares 39 b. and 33 a. as far as the line of objective, thence
    to Q.39.d.65.30.
        If the line of the road mentioned above is gained troops will
dig in at once.   "I" Coy. will then move forward 2 remaining
sections of that platoon, who will dig in in support of the 2 leading sections and their support platoon will move up and line the
canal bank South of the canal.
        "B" Coy. will move the 2 remaining sections of their platoon
to dig in on the same line as their 2 leading sections and will
move one platoon over the canal, to dig in in support of these 4
sections East of the road junction Q.36.d.1.1. Their support
platoon will be moved up to line the canal bank South of the canal.
        The Division on left will not fire near RIEZ during the night
or day except on case of attack.   Reports as to progress of events
will be sent to Battalion H.Q. as soon as, and as frequently as
possible.   If time permits and it is necessary tools must be
drawn from "A" or "C" Coys.
        If operations are successful touch must be gained and main-
tained with troops on flanks.

        ACKNOWLEDGE by bearer.

                                (sd) J. A. DAVISON   Captain
                Adjt.   1st Battn. THE RIFLE BRIGADE.

SECRET   APP. XI

OPERATION ORDERS No 25
by
Lieut.Colonel R.T.FELLOWES, D.S.O., M.C.
Commanding 1st Battalion, THE RIFLE BRIGADE

REF SHEET 36a   16th APRIL, 1918   Copy No

RELIEF   I   The Battalion, less 2 platoons of "B" Company will be relieved in their present position tonight by the 2nd Battalion ESSEX REGIMENT.
"A" Coy. RIFLE BRIGADE will be relieved by "A" Coy. ESSEX REGT.
"B"   :   :   :   :   :   :   "B"   :   :   :
"C"   :   :   :   :   :   :   "C"   :   :   :
"I"   :   :   :   :   :   :   "D"   :   :   :
         Order of relief: "A", "B", "I", "C".

GUIDES   II   Guides from the Battalion will be found as follows:-
1 per Company and 2 for Battalion H.Q., found from Battalion H.Q., at road junction W.13.a.2.7 at 8.45 p.m. Guides on the scale of 1 per platoon will be held in readiness at Company H.Q. to take relieving platoons to their positions.

MOVE   III   On completion of relief Company will march to BUSNETTES.
ROUTE: GONNEHEM - road junction V.17.a.3.7 - Cross roads
         V.16.c.2.3.

ADVANCE   IV   The Quartermaster who is sending forward an advance party
PARTY   to take over billets, will arrange to have guides to meet the Battalion marching in at V.21.a.7.7.

TOOLS, etc   V.   All Water tins, picks and shovels, and L.G. Material will be carried on the man as far as road junction W.13.a.60.95, where one limber per Company will meet the Companies and take the above mentioned material. One N.C.O. per Company will be with these limbers.

TRENCH   VI   All S.A.A, S.O.S.Grenades, Flares and Very Lights will be
STORES   handed over to the relieving Companies - also all information possible will be carefully handed over. All receipts will be forwarded to this office.

PACKS   VII   Efforts are being made to get blankets and valises to the billets. Packs will not be brought up.

REPORT   VIII   Completion of relief will be reported by wire by any sentence containing Code Word "LOOT".

                 IX   ACKNOWLEDGE.

                                          (sd) J. A. DAVISON,   Capt.
                                    Adjutant 1st Batt. THE RIFLE BRIGADE

Issued at 4.0 p.m.
16-4-18

SECRET   OPERATION ORDERS No 26   APP XII
by
Lieut.Colonel R. T. FELLOWES, B.S.O., M.C.
Commanding 1st Battalion THE RIFLE BRIGADE

Ref. Plex man (App. attached O.O.27)

19th APRIL, 1918   Copy No

RELIEF   I.   The Battalion will relieve the 1st Battn. ROYAL WARWICKS and 2nd DUKE OF WELLINGTONS REGT. along Canal bank between W.17.b.1.0. exclusive to road W.4.d.1.0 inclusive.

              II.   "I" Company and 1 Platoon "A" Company will relieve 2nd DUKE OF WELLINGTONS REGT. from road in W.4.d.1.0. to W.11.a.5.0. Remainder of Battalion will relieve 1st Bn. ROYAL WARWICKS.

DISPOSITIONS III.   Battalion H.Q. W.17.b.1.3. :
                         "C" Company   on Right   :
                         "I"   :   in Centre   :   Regimental Aid Post
                         "A"   :   on Left   :   W.9.d.8.8
                         "B"   :   in Support   :

GUIDES   IV   Guides will be provided as follows:-
                   From DUKE OF WELLINGTONS REGT
                      4 for "I" Company   )
                      1 : 1 platoon of "A" Coy)   at W.3.c.1.6. at 9.0 p.m.
                   From 1st ROYAL WARWICKS
                      5 for "C" Company   )
                      4 :   "A"   :   )   at W.17.c.1.1, at 9.0 p.m.
                      1 :   Battalion H.Q.   )
                  No guides will be provided for "B" Coy. who will be responsible for finding their own way to positions.

RATIONS   V   Rations and Water will be delivered at the above places for the same parties at 12.0 p.m. tonight.
                Rations for "B" Company will be delivered at W.17.c.1.1. at the same time.

BOMBS, etc. VI   Eight boxes of Mills Rifle Grenades will come on ration limbers for each "A", "B", "C" and "I" Companies.

BAGGAGE   VII   Blankets will be rolled and dumped in Companies' billets by 3.0 p.m.
               The Mess Cart will collect surplus officers' mess kit at 7.30 p.m.
               The Assistant Adjutant will detail 3 Buglers per Company and H.Q. to look after these and guide the Transport to collect them.

TAKING OVER   VIII   All Trench Stores will be taken over including S.O.S. Grenades and Very Lights. Os C. Companies are reminded that each Company H.Q. in the front line is a relay S.O.S. Post.
               Picks and shovels will be carried on the man.

BILLETS   IX   All billets will be left scrupulously clean and in a sanitary condition.

REPORT   X   Completion of relief will be reported by runner.

           XI   ACKNOWLEDGE

                                                        (sd) J. A. DAVISON,   Capt.
                                          Adjutant 1st Batt. THE RIFLE BRIGADE

Issued at 2.0 p.m.
19-4-18

SECRET   OPERATION ORDERS No 27
                         by
         Lieut.Colonel R. T. FELLOWES, DSO, MC.
         Commanding 1st Battalion THE RIFLE BRIGADE

Ref. 36.A. S.E.   21st APRIL, 1918

I   The Battalion will tomorrow morning April 22nd establish a line
from Q.34.c.60.45 cross roads (exclusive) - road junction La PANNERIE
W.4.a.9.8. - PONT L'HINGES (inclusive).

II   Two platoons of "B" Coy. will attack on the left and "C" Coy.
will attack on the right.   The inter-company boundary will be LA
PANNERIE road junction inclusive to "C" Coy.
         The 1st HAMPSHIRE REGT. will carry out a similar operation on
the left, entering the BOIS de PACAUT in 3 columns, the right
column working up the South East side of the wood.

III   (a) The 2 Platoons of "B" Coy. under Lieut. ADAMS, will report
to Lieut. ABBOTT, 1st HAMPSHIRE REGT, at W.3.b.1.7. at 4.30 a.m.
tomorrow.
         They will follow in rear of the right column of the 1st
HAMPSHIRE REGT. and will establish a line of posts along their
objective gaining touch with "C" Coy. on their right at the road
junction LA PANNERIE.
         (b) "C" Coy. will be relieved in their present position by a
Company of the 1st SOMERSET LIGHT INFANTRY tonight.   "C" Coy will
send 4 guides to be at Battalion H.Q. at 10.0 p.m.   Completion of
relief will be wired to Battalion H.Q., Code Word "WOMAN" being
used.
         They will be formed up along the breastwork and dugouts on
the North bank of the Canal at PONT L'HINGES by 4.45 a.m.   Should
they be unable to cross the canal at the PONT L'HINGES they will
allow sufficient time to move round by the bridges at W.3.b.1.7. and
still be in position by the above time.   When the action commences
they will work up the left hand side of the road from the PONT
L'HINGES - LA PANNERIE, thus forming a defensive flank by occupying
the houses, etc.   As each house and locality is seized it will be
put into a state of defence and consolidated immediately.   "C" Coy's
H.Q. will in the first instance be established in the breastworks
at present occupied by 2 sections 1st HAMPSHIRE REGT.
         (c) "C" Coy. will as soon as possible after dark tonight relieve
the 2 sections of 1st HAMPSHIRE REGT. in the breastwork in front of
the PONT L'HINGES on the North side of the canal.
         (d) In the event of the flanks of "B" and "C" Coys not being
able to reach their objective (LA PANNERIE) each Coy. will place
posts in echelon to gain touch with each other.
         (e) "A" and "I" Coys will assist in these operations by opening
rifle and Lewis gun fire on to any suitable targets that may appear.
They will be prepared to check any counter-attack from the East or
South East.
         (f) Tanks will co-operate.   One will move down the line of the
objective starting from RIEZ de VINAGE at 5.0 a.m.
         (g) One Vickers machine gun will be at the disposal of O.C.
"C" Coy.   The officer in charge will report to an officer of "C"
Coy. at PONT L'HINGES some time tonight.   This gun will be moved
up after "C" Coy. has gained its objective, to the vicinity of LA
PANNERIE road junction to assist in the defence of the line gained.
         (h) In the event of the whole of the objectives not being
gained, posts already established will be maintained at all costs.
Other posts will be established and touch maintained to conform to
the general line of the operation.

IV   There will be no barrage covering the advance of the Battalion.
Heavies will fire at intervals during the night on the LA PANNERIE -
PONT L'HINGES road.

V   Zero hour will be 5.15 a.m.   Infantry will not commence to
cross the canal until Zero plus 3 minutes.

VI   A contact patrol will fly over at 7.0 a.m.   The most advanced
troops will light flares when the aeroplane calls for them.   These
flares will be lit in groups of 2 or 3 along the front.

Sheet 2   O.O No 27

VII   Each Coy. will send a representative to "C" Coy's present H.Q. (Report Centre) at 4.0 a.m. where Lieut. C. C. NAUMANN will synchronise watches.

VIII   Care must be taken to see that every man carries a pick or a shovel. Bombs and rifle grenades will be carried by "C" Coy.

IX   Battalion H.Q. will be at W.15.b.10.95. An advanced report centre will be established at "C" Coy's present H.Q. from 4.0 a.m. onwards.

X   ACKNOWLEDGE.

Issued at 6.45 p.m.

21.4.18   to Coys.

                                (sd) J. A. DAVISON, Capt. & Adjt
                                1st Battn. THE RIFLE BRIGADE

AMENDMENT No 1   to

OPERATION   ORDERS   No 27

After Para V add new para VI :-

On completion of relief of "C" Coy and relief of the right Coy. 1st HAMPSHIRE REGT. by another Coy 1st SOMERSET L. I., these 2 Coys. will come under command of O.C. 1st RIFLE BRIGADE.   O.C. 1st RIFLE BRIGADE will then be responsible for the defence of the canal from W.3.b.1.7. to W.11.c.6.8.

Re number all succeeding paragraphs.

         (sd) J. A. DAVISON, Capt & Adjt.
          1st Battn. THE RIFLE BRIGADE

AMENDMENT NO 2 to   R.B. 48/39
OPERATION ORDERS No 27

I   Para IX   Report Centre will now be at W.3.b.5.3. (late Coy. H.Q. right Coy. 1st HAMPSHIRE REGT. being relieved tonight by Coy. of 1st SOMERSET L.I. attached to the Battalion).

II   Para VII   Delete "(Report Centre)"   Representatives will still be sent to "C" Coy's old H.Q. to synchronise watches.

III   Each Coy will send one runner with their representative, who is synchronising, to report to Lieut. NAUMANN. He will take these runners on to report centre, and will use them for sending messages, etc. from there to Companies.

                                          (sd) J. A. DAVISON,   Capt. & Adjt
                                          1st Batt. THE RIFLE BRIGADE

11.35 p.m.

21-4-18

Situation after attack
22.4.18

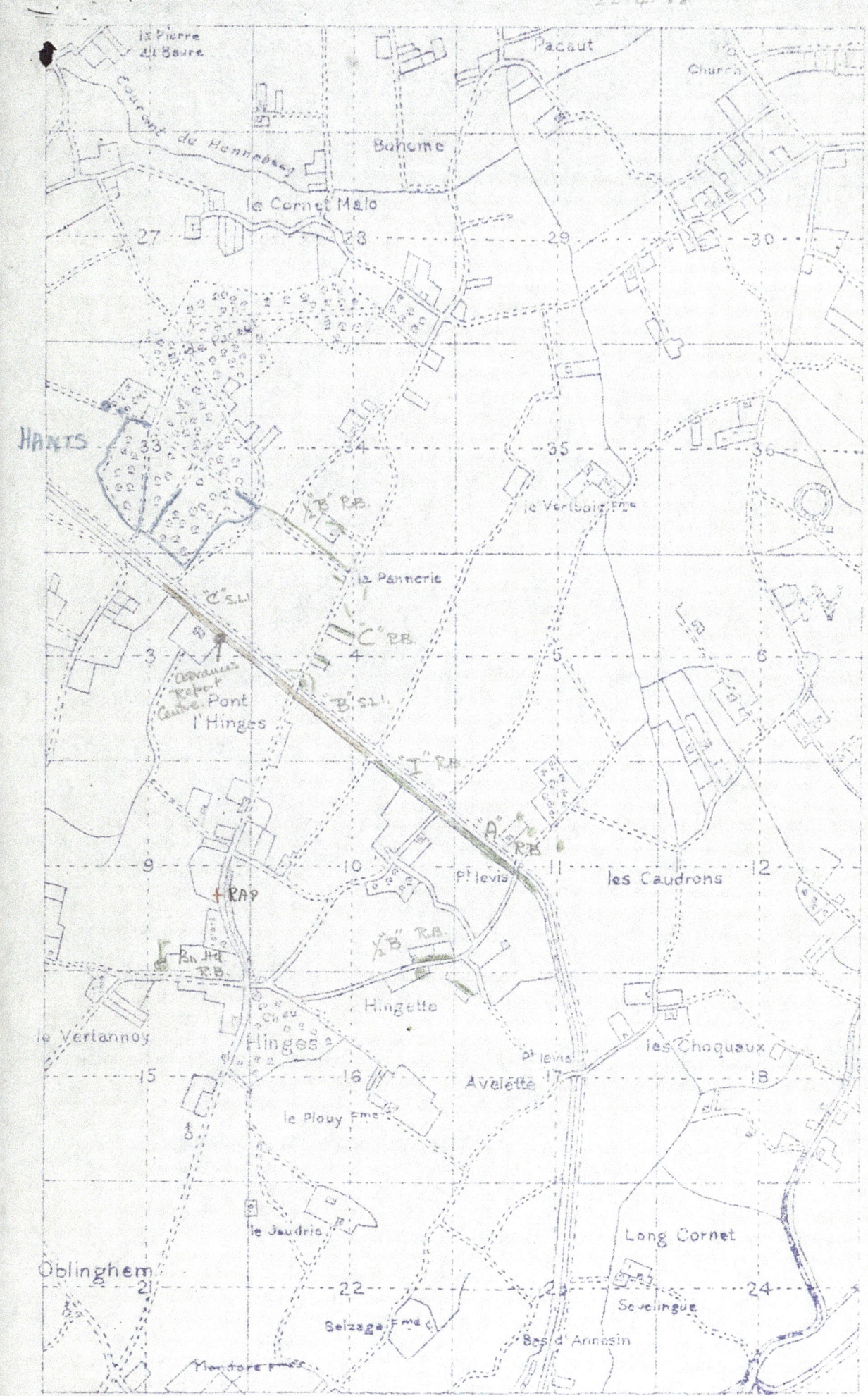

Scale 1:20,000

SECRET   R.B. F. 93

App XIV

The following moves will take place tonight.

I   H.Q. and remaining 2 platoons of "B" Coy. will take over that portion of the line from W.3.b.2.7. to PONT L'HINGES (inclusive) at present held by "C" Coy 1st SOMERSET L.I. and 1 platoon "B" Coy. 1st SOMERSET L.I.

II   "I" Coy will extend its left and take over from remainder of "B" Coy. 1st S.L.I. up to the PONT L'HINGES (exclusive).

III   "A" Coy. will withdraw 2 platoons to positions vacated by "B" Coy. in HINGETTE.

IV   "C" Coy. will thin out its front by placing supporting posts in shell holes, etc. West of LA PANNERIE - PONT L'HINGES road and in the breastwork and dugouts in the N.E. bank of the canal South of PONT L'HINGES.

V.   (1)   Boundaries of Coys will then become as follows:-
   a)   "B" Coy. Front line:- Road junction Q.34.c.0.5.(exclusive) LA PANNERIE road junction (exclusive)
       Canal bank:- W.3.b.2.7. (inclusive) - PONT L'HINGES (exclusive)
   b)   "C" Coy:- LA PANNERIE road junction (inclusive) - PONT L'HINGES (exclusive)
   c)   "I" Coy:- PONT L'HINGES (exclusive) - W.10.b.82.55 (inclusive)
   d)   "A" Coy:- W.10.b.82.55 (exclusive) - W.11.c.8.8 (exclusive)

   (2)   Completion of these moves and arrival in new positions will be wired to Battalion H.Q., the Code Word "CHEERY" being used.
   (3)   "B" Coy will draw rations first in normal place and will then proceed to take over the new line.

VI   "B" and "C" Coys S.L.I. will on relief move back to LANNOY.

VII   All Casualties will be searched for and evacuated. Dead bodies and effects will be sent to Battalion H.Q. Casualty reports will be submitted as early as possible.

VIII   Companies will arrange to draw their own rations and water which will arrive as follows:-
   "B" Coy. 1st R.B.   )
   "A" :   :   :   less 1 platoon   ) at W.17.c.1.1. at 9.30 p.m.

   "I" Coy. 1st R.B.   )
   "C" :   :   :   ) at W.3.c.1.6 at 9.30 p.m.
   1 platoon "A" Coy 1st R.B.   )

   Care will be taken to send back all water tins, tea packs and salvage, by ration parties to the limbers.

IX   "B" and "C" Coys. 1st R.B. will arrange for a careful patrolling of their front and will if necessary establish advanced L.G. posts in front of their line.
   O.C. "B" Coy. will report location of his new H.Q. as soon as possible.

X   Care will be taken to maintain Signal communication.

XI   Disposition maps showing location and strength of posts will be sent to Battn. H.Q. by 8.0 a.m. tomorrow.

XII   R.E. have been asked to dump a spare footbridge behind houses at PONT L'HINGES tonight in case present footbridge is broken.

cont. on sheet 2

Sheet 2

XIII   1st German Guards Division should have relieved troops opposite to us last night and should have attacked to-day. The relief may take place to-night - also the attack. This may take place to-night or to-morrow morning.

XIV   Any posts now established will on <u>no</u> account be given up. There will be NO withdrawal.

XV   ACKNOWLEDGE.

                                        (sd) R. T. FELLOWES, Lieut Col.
                                      Commdg 1st Batt THE RIFLE BRIGADE

Issued at 5.0 p.m.
    29-4-18

Copies to "A","B","C","I" Coys
    "C" & "B" Coys 1st SOM.L.I.

Disposition 23-4-18. To accompany R.B.F. 93.

Scale 1:20,000.

APP. XV

OPERATION ORDERS No 28
by
Lieut.Colonel R.T.FELLOWES, D.S.O., M.C.
Commanding 1st Battalion THE RIFLE BRIGADE

Ref. Sheet 36A, S.E.   Copy No 2

RELIEF I   "B" and "C" Coys. will be relieved to-night by Light, "A"
and "C" Coys 1st SOMERSET L.I. respectively.
For dispositions see Amendment No 1

GUIDES II   Guides from these 2 Coys will be found as follows:-
From "B" Coy - 2 for "A" Coy (S.L.I.) at 9.30 p.m. for para 1(b)
         1 : "C" : : : 9.45 p.m. : : 1(c)
         1 : Light : : : 10.0 p.m. : : 1(d)
From "C" Coy - 3 (1 per platoon and 1 for H.Q.) 10 p.m: : 1(a)
All guides will be at point W.3.c.1.6.

MOVE III   The 2 platoons of "A" Coy at present in HINGETTE will move
up to the canal bank North of point W.11.c.3.8. This move will
be complete by 11.0 p.m.
On relief "B" Coy will move 2 platoons to LE PLOUY FARM
and 2 Platoons to HINGETTE. O.C. "B" Coy. will occupy his late
H.Q.   "C" Coy will move to VERTANNOY. Four guides from
Battalion H.Q. will be at road junction W.15.a.75.95 from 11.0
p.m. onwards.

RATIONS IV   Water and rations for these 2 Coys. will arrive as follows:-
For "B" Coy. at LE PLOUY FARM at 12.0 p.m.
  : "A" : : road junction W.15.a.75.95 at 12.0 p.m.

HANDING OVER V   All S.A.A., S.O.S. Grenades, Wire (brought up by "A" and
"I" Coys.) will be handed over. Picks, shovels, water tins
and salvage will be brought. All bodies will be sent to
Battalion H.Q. for burial. All bombs will be brought out on
the man.

REPORT VI   Completion of the relief will be reported to Battalion H.Q.
by wire and runner. In the case of the former the code word
used will be "THICK".

ACKNOWLEDGE.

                                (sd) J. A. DAVISON, Capt & Adjt.
                   1st Batt. THE RIFLE BRIGADE

Copy No 1   O.C. "A" Coy
       2   :   "B" :
       3   :   "C" :
       4   :   "I" :
       5   Adjutant.

23rd APRIL, 1918

AMENDMENT No 1 to
OPERATION ORDERS No 28

I   Ref. Para I (a) 2 Platoons Light Coy. (S.L.I.) will relieve "C" Coy (R.B.)
            (b) 2   :   "B"   :   :   :   :   "B" Coy (R.B.) along LA PANNERIE-RIEZ road
            (c) 1   :   "C" Coy (S.L.I.) will relieve "B" Coy (R.B.) on Canal bank from the present left as far as W.3.b.8.2
            (d) 1   :   Light Coy (S.L.I.) will relieve "B" Coy (R.B.) from W.3.b.8.2 to PONT L'HINGES

II   The frontages of "A" and "I" Coys will be slightly readjusted tonight, the boundary between the 2 Coys being the bridge at W.10.b.8.5., the defence of which "A" Coy will be responsible for

                                       (sd) J. A. DAVISON, Capt & Adjt
                                              1st Batt   THE RIFLE BRIGADE

23-4-18

SECRET   OPERATION ORDER No 29   APP XVI
by
Lieut.Colonel R. T. FELLOWES, D.S.O.,M.C.
Commanding 1st Battalion THE RIFLE BRIGADE

Ref. Sheet 36A S.E.   26th APRIL, 1918   Copy No

RELIEF   I   The Battalion will be relieved tonight by the 8th Batt KINGS OWN (R.L.) REGT. and the 2nd Batt. SUFFOLK REGT, as follows:-
(1) "A" Coy. RIFLE BRIGADE will be relieved by "C" Coy KINGS OWN
(2) H.Q. and 2 Platoons "B" Coy RIFLE BRIGADE will be relieved by "B" Coy KINGS OWN in HINGETTE
       :   :   : RIFLE BRIGADE will be relieved by "A" Coy KINGS OWN in LE PLOUY FME
(3) "C" Coy. RIFLE BRIGADE will be relieved by 2 Platoons "X" Coy SUFFOLKS
(4) "I"   :   :   :   :   ::   : "Z" Coy SUFFOLKS
(5) Battn H.Q.   :   :   :   ::   : Battn H.Q. -do-

GUIDES   II   Guides from the Battalion will be supplied as follows:-
(1) From "A" Coy 5 guides (1 per platoon and Coy H.Q.) at
                         W.17.c.1.1 at 8.45 p.m. (for I(1)
(2) From "B"   :   10   :   (1 per platoon and Coy H.Q.) at
                         W.17.c.1.1 at 8.45 p.m. (for I(2)
(3) From "C"   :   NO guides will be required.
(4) From "I"   :   5 guides (1 per platoon and Coy H.Q.) will report to the A/Adjt at Battn. H.Q. at 7.0 p.m.
    Guides will be given slips of paper showing who they are to meet and where they are to take them.

MOVE   III   On completion of relief the Battalion will move to billets in GONNEHEM. The Quartermaster will arrange the necessary billeting parties. Officers' kits, blankets and cookers, etc. will be there by the time the Battalion arrives. Guides will meet the Battalion at the bridge at V.18.a.95.70.

HANDING OVER   IV   All S.A.A., S.O.S. grenades, spare rifle grenades, will be carefully handed over. Picks and shovels will be carried out on the man. The 2 Mills hand grenades already issued to each man as part of his fighting kit will also be carried out.
    Special care will be taken to hand over all advanced posts correctly. All petroltins and salvage will be brought out.

TRANSPORT   V   Limbers to take L.G.material, petrol tins, salvage, etc. will be provided as follows:-
(1) For "A" and "B" Coys at Ration Dump (W.17.c.1.1.) at 10. p.m.
(2) For "C" Coy. at VERTANNOY road junction W.16.a.7.9 at 11 p.m.
(3) For "I" Coy at LE CAUROY road junction W.8.d.85.20 at 11.30 p.m.
(4) For Battalion H.Q. at Battalion H.Q. at 9.0 p.m.

REPORT   VI   Completion of relief will be reported to Battalion H.Q. by wire or runner, for the former the code word "DEAF" being used.

      VII   ACKNOWLEDGE.

                                             (sd) J. A. DAVISON, Captain
                                        Adjutant 1st Batt THE RIFLE BRIGADE

Issued at 3.0 p.m.
26-4-18

SECRET　　　　　　　OPERATION ORDERS No 30　　　　　　　APP XIII
　　　　　　　　　　　　　　by
　　　　　　　Lieut.Colonel R.T.FELLOWES, D.S.O., M.C.
　　　　　　　Commanding 1st Battalion THE RIFLE BRIGADE

Ref:Sheet 36 A　　　　　　28th APRIL, 1918　　　　　　Copy No 9

I　　　　　The Battalion will move to-day to billets in BUSNETTES.
　　　Order of March:- H.Q., "A", "B", "C", "I".
　　　Route:- via LEMGLET and LE HAMEL.
　　　　Companies will move off with an interval of 100 yards between
　　　platoons.
　　　　H.Q. will move off at 5.0 p.m.

II　　　　Blankets, officers' kits, etc. will be dumped on the side of
　　　the road outside billets by 4.45 p.m., when the Transport Officer
　　　will collect them.　Transport will move 100 yards in rear of
　　　the last platoon of "I" Company.
　　　　Officers' chargers will be required.

III　　　　The Quartermaster will send forward the necessary billeting
　　　party.
　　　　He will arrange for guides to meet the Battalion at
　　　V.21.a.7.4. at 5.30 p.m.

IV　　　　Companies will render to Orderly Room by not later than
　　　5.0 p.m. certificates that their billets have been left clean and
　　　in a sanitary condition.

V　　　　ACKNOWLEDGE.

　　　　　　　　　　　　　　　　　　(sd) J. A. DAVISON,　Capt & Adjt
　　　　　　　　　　　　　　　　1st Battalion THE RIFLE BRIGAD

　　　DISTRIBUTION
　　　Copy No 1 Commanding Officer
　　　　　　　2 Adjutant
　　　　　　　3 O.C. Headquarters
　　　　　　　4 Transport Officer & Quartermaster
　　　　　　　5 O.C. "A" Coy.
　　　　　　　6 　　 "B" :
　　　　　　　7 　　 "C" :
　　　　　　　8 　　 "I" :
　　　　　　　9 War Diary No 1
　　　　　　10 　　　　　　 2
　　　　　　11 File

Situation Map
No 142

Situation Map
No 14²

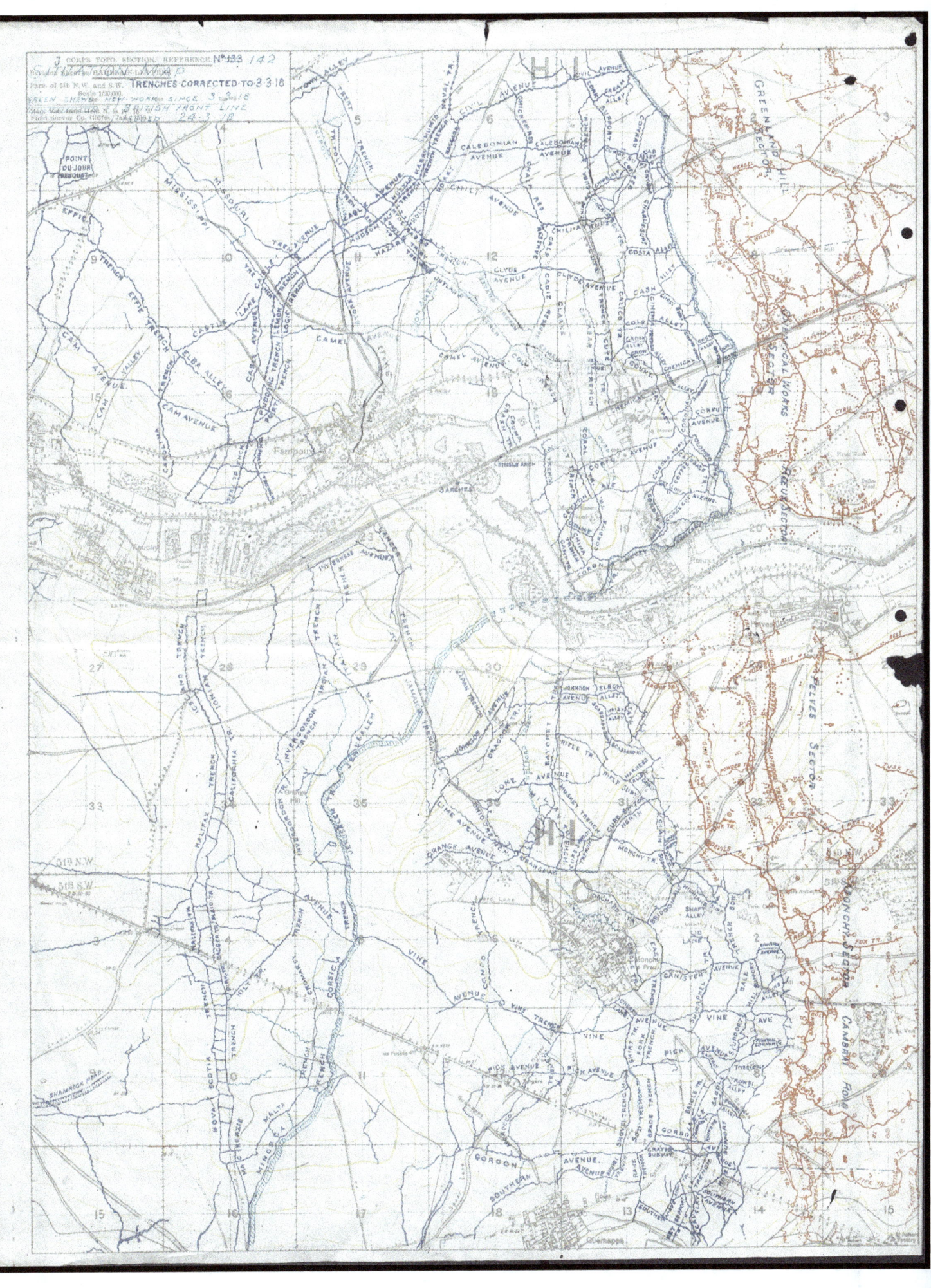

Fampoux
Plex map

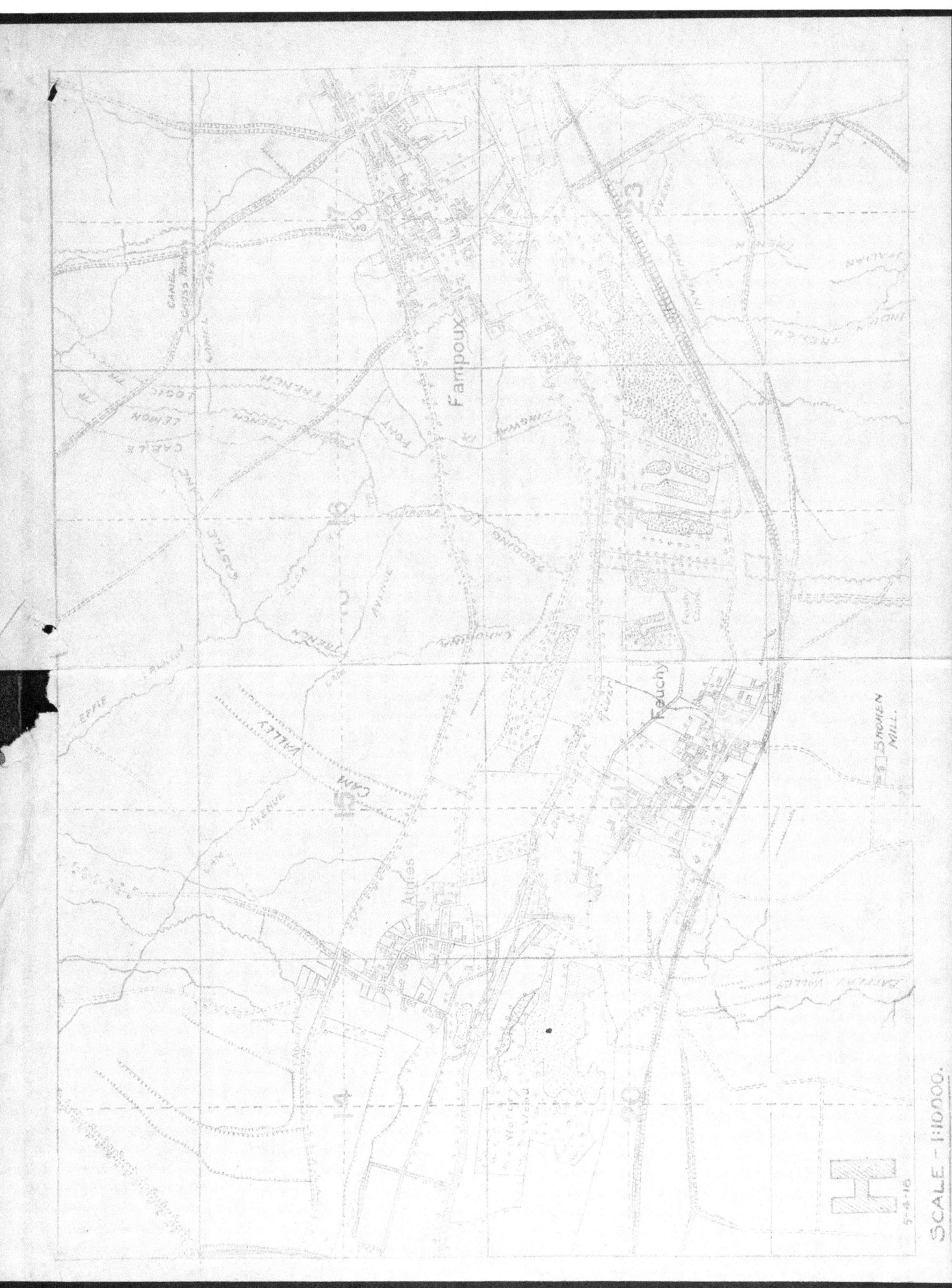

11th Brigade.
4th Division

1st BATTALION

THE RIFLE BRIGADE

M A Y 1 9 1 8

Appendices attached:-
Operation Orders.
Situation Maps

WAR DIARY
INTELLIGENCE SUMMARY.
(Erase heading not required.)

Army Form C. 2118.

1st Bn. R. Welsh Rifle Brigade
1916

Place	Date	Hour	Summary of Events and Information	Remarks and references to Appendices
BUSNETTES.	May 1st		The Battalion was in Divisional Reserve: Reorganising, cleaning up, drills and saluting.	SHEET 36 S.E. SCALE 1/20,000
TRENCHES	May 2nd to May 5th		The Battalion relieved the 2nd Bn SEAFORTH HIGHLANDERS in the left front line in the left sector of the Left Brigade in front of ROBECQ. The enemy was very quiet during the day throughout the time displaying more activity at night with Machine Guns and Artillery. On the morning of the 3rd the front line & the left Company View heavily shelled and howitzers in the Company sustaining 6 killed and 2 wounded. Much chief work was carried up the line the as putting out wire. & The hooks on left and right were respectively:- 2/5 Bn. THE GLOUCESTER REGT. AND 1/5 Bn HAMPSHIRE REGT. On the evening of the 6th Bn was relieved by 1st SOMERSET L.I. & how is back into Support. Companies employed in making connection wire and carrying it up at night to the front line. B.M.'s after which the Carrying Parties worked on the support line. On the morning of the 7th & Bn Hdq'rs were heavily shelled and in the evening moved to V.4.b.6.3. Owing to information received from prisoners who said the Germans were going to attack at 1.30 P.M. on the night of the 9/10 or 10/10 V it was decided to hand 3 Bn's of the Brigade in the front line; no relief orders were issued but the Bn took over the Centre portion of the Brigade front, as shown on the Rec. Map: 1 Coy taking over the front line from Q.20.a.6.6. to Q.27.c.10.40.A Coy on the right in Support from Q26.b.2.8 to Q26.6.5.0; C Coy on the left	APPENDIX I Disposition on TRENCH MAPS. APPENDIX II APPENDIX III

1st Bn the Rifle Brigade

May 1918.

Army Form C. 2118.

WAR DIARY
or
INTELLIGENCE SUMMARY.
(Erase heading not required.)

Place	Date	Hour	Summary of Events and Information	Remarks and references to Appendices
FRONT LINE	6th to 8th		In support from Q.20.c.9.75. to Q.26.6.2.8. B Coys on Q.25.h.5.to Q.26.c.2.8. Bn.H.Q. at Q.25.c.7.2. Troops on left not respective were 1st Somerset L.I. and 1/2 Hants Regt.	
FRONT LINE	9th to 11th		Each day quiet during the night an artillery carried out harassing fire. Our Coys were forced against Cornet Malo. On the evening of the 11th our Bn was relieved by the 15th Bn KING'S OWN R.L. REGT and returned back to huts in BUSNETTES.	APPENDIX IV
	12th		Resting, cleaning up & general re-organization of companies	
	13th		Drill & cleaning up. A & B Coys moved up to the CANAL BANK in the evening relieved the No 2 advanced coys of the 1st Som.L.I. APP V They came under the tactical command of the B.G.C. 12th Infantry Brigade. The coy boundries were as follows:- APP VI A Coy from. Q.36.a-1-9 to Q.31.a.00.45. B Coy from Q.31.a.00-45 to Q.31.L.85-05.	
	14		Officers went forward to reconnoitre the right Brigade front	

Army Form C. 2118.

1st B. The Rifle Brigade

May 1918

WAR DIARY
or
INTELLIGENCE SUMMARY.
(Erase heading not required.)

Instructions regarding War Diaries and Intelligence Summaries are contained in F. S. Regs., Part II. and the Staff Manual respectively. Title pages will be prepared in manuscript.

Place	Date	Hour	Summary of Events and Information	Remarks and references to Appendices
	14th		in preparation to taking over the front line on the evening of the 17th.	
	15th		The Battalion relieved the First Royal Warwickshire Regt: in the front line. The dispositions were as follows "A" Coy in the front line from Q.33.a.8.0.-5.5. to Q.34.a.0.1. - B Coy in support from Q.33.b.5.3.1. to W.4.a.4.4. "C" Coy in support on the CANAL BANK from W.3.6.1.7. to W.3.6.9.0. "D" Coy in front line 2nd system from W.3.a.6.0 to W.3.d.3.4. Bn HQ at W.8.a.16. The 1st Bn Royal Scots (Brooklyn - 3rd Bn) were on our right & 1st Hampshire Regt on our left. Hostile activity was quiet during the night.	APP VII APP VIII APP IX APP X
	16th		Intermittent hostile shelling of western & southern sides of PACAUT WOOD from 9.0 am to 1.30pm. Heavy shelling of PACAUT WOOD from 11.0am to 11.20am. Heavy shelling of CANAL BANK at W.3.a. & eastern end of LES-HARISOIRS from 3.0pm. Heavy shelling with HE + Gas Gas at W.3.a. & southern end of PACAUT WOOD from 10.15pm to 10.30pm. Harrassing fire during the night. One E.A. was brought down by Machine Gun fire about 400 + west of B.A. at 4-30 pm.	

WAR DIARY
INTELLIGENCE SUMMARY

(Erase heading not required.)

Army Form C. 2118.

1st Bn. The Rifle Brigade
May 1918

Instructions regarding War Diaries and Intelligence Summaries are contained in F. S. Regs., Part II. and the Staff Manual respectively. Title pages will be prepared in manuscript.

Place	Date	Hour	Summary of Events and Information	Remarks and references to Appendices
	17th		Hostile activity quiet during the day - At 9-30 p.m. 8.10-5" on our artillery had 3 minute concentrations on enemy forward areas in reply the latter on the CANAL BANK at A 36 & LES HARISOIRS were heavily shelled from 10-10 p.m. to 10-25 p.m. and all calibre chiefly 15 inch - Gas was also used. Hostile Machine Guns & Snipers were active during the night - Work was concentrated on improving posts during front & support lines - Patrols were out	
	18th		Hostile artillery was quiet during the day. Our 18 pdrs & 4-5 hows fired on S.O.S line at 12-45 p.m. - at 11-50 p.m. our artillery fired a 3 minute concentration on the enemy forward area, in reply the CANAL BANK at Q 33a & Q 33a & b was heavily shelled especially at the bridge at Q 3.b.17 - Work - improving posts of front & outpost lines	
	19th		Intermittent firing of CANAL BANK from midnight to 4-10 a.m. Hostile machine guns were very active at 3-10 a.m. on the eastern edge of PACAUT WOOD & swept the front & support lines - Hostile artillery shelled the CANAL BANK at intervals during the morning obtaining 5 direct hits on house W 3 b & also 80-25 & you house W 3 b 45-30 shelling was especially heavy from 9-15 a.m. to P.45 a.m.	

WAR DIARY or INTELLIGENCE SUMMARY

1st Bn The Rifle Brigade

May 1918

Army Form C.2118.

Place	Date	Hour	Summary of Events and Information
	19th		Occasional short bursts of MG fire during the night. Aerial activity normal. Working & improving & connecting up posts during front. 9 support lines. C+I party carrying RE material Etc. Our artillery fired 3 minute concentration at 9.0pm, 9.30pm, 13.15am. The enemy replying heavily to the 9.30pm shoot for 15 minutes.
	20	3.0am to 4.0am	Heavy shelling of actn on our right with HE + Gas. A few gas shells fell on our pctve line + around Bn HQ. One direct hit being obtained on tank. MGs active during the night. One E.A. was attacked though seen by 2 of our planes and landed behind the enemy lines. A/c were out. Working & improving boyaux by deepening trench & removing parapet. Harados wiring etc front Support lines C + I Coys carrying RE material etc.
	21st		Heavy artillery on both sides shelled rear areas intermittently. Quiet on forward areas. Our artillery fired 3 minute concentration at 10pm + 10.30pm to which the enemy replied weakly. Hostile Machine guns active in PACAUT WOOD. E.A. active during the night. Work improving trenches, wiring front support lines.

Army Form C. 2118.

1st Bn. the Rifle Brigade
May 1918

WAR DIARY
INTELLIGENCE SUMMARY.
(Erase heading not required.)

APP XI

Place	Date	Hour	Summary of Events and Information	Remarks and references to Appendices
	21st		C + D Coys carrying R.E. material etc	
	22nd		HINGES - LA PANNERIE - PACAUT WOOD + CANAL BANK were heavily shelled during the morning. 8 + 5pm, 9 - 5pm, + 10pm roads leading to forward areas were shelled with accuracy. For 10 minutes 11.38 Pm to 12.15 am PACAUT WOOD CANAL BANK + Riff-Raff of support line were heavily shelled in retaliation for our concentration shoot at 11.30 pm. Several direct hits were obtained on support line. 11 + 5 pm a few "BLUE CROSS" Gas shells were fired on W 3 d one direct hit being obtained on the trench. 1.30am HINGES + CANAL BANK shelled for 15 minutes with Blue X. Gas also area in 3 c was cleverly shelled with same. M.G. active during hostile shelling. PACAUT WOOD Light TMs were active during the night. Hostile snipers active during the night. E.A. also tried to cross our lines owing to A.A. fire - Wiring work on trenches in front support lines E.S. carrying R E. material etc	
	23		Quiet throughout the day - The Bn. was relieved by the 2nd Lancashire Fusiliers throughout. Such a billets in Pyramides Huts, Fosse huts and continuous Dugouts being about size Pakumus + opposite Pont Louis few Coy. hqrs. put out about 1000x of Rifle Bde, Our left front, down the right flank.	

Army Form C. 2118.

WAR DIARY
or
INTELLIGENCE SUMMARY.
(Erase heading not required.)

1st Bn. The Rifle Brigade

May 1918

Place	Date	Hour	Summary of Events and Information	Remarks and references to Appendices
	24		Work cleaning up + reorganizing - Ar B Coy Baths	
	25		Baths	
	26		Presentation of Medals by Bde Commander. Baths - COs conference of New Draft. + Billets	
	27		The Batn in the evening relieved the 2nd Duke of Wellington's Rgt in the front line centre Bn of the left sector - dispositions as follows. C Coy front line Q 20 d 6.9. to house Q 27 a Q 35 inclusive B + I in support from road at Q 20 d 2-3 to road Q 26 d 8.+.9. A in reserve from road Q 25 b 9.4. to Q 26 e 3.5. Bn. HQ Q 31 a 0.5. 1st Hants Regt on our right 10th Rom L on our left - Quiet during the night on front area. Active in rear near Canal Bank shelled intermittently during the day otherwise Hostile Artillery quiet on our front Hostile Snipers normal	APP XII APP XIII
	28		Work improving existing posts making new ones - wiring + carrying. Boundaries of support line extended on east to the ...	

WAR DIARY
or
INTELLIGENCE SUMMARY

1st Bn The Rifle Brigade

May 1918

Army Form C. 2118.

Place	Date	Hour	Summary of Events and Information	Remarks and references to Appendices
	28		Reserve Line extended one post each flank. EA active but seldom able to cross our lines owing to AA fire	
	29		CANAL BANK Q.31.a. Lightly shelled during the early morning. Hostile activity intermittently active during the day, in vicinity of Canal Bank & the Burnghon Rd. MGs active during the night on forward area. Rt 11th m 15 rounds Grenatenwerfen fell close to own barricade at Q.24.a. Enemy fairly active during the night - Work making new post connecting up existing ones using trenches R.E. material etc.	
	30		Day Patrols were sent out 1am to 2am area Q.31a over Hostile Artillery intermittently active throughout the day especially on RIEZ to VINAGE roads. Banks and battery R.J.10.30.b.m. A Lyris Bapres was put down Q.Q.08 and on our light field guns 4.23 and MGs. Hostile throughout the night. EA active for 15 minutes by Red balloons were dropped and landed behind our line. One hatch ballon brought down by Shell fire. Work - diff 12th Bridge between posts improving hasty posts wiring and carrying. Patrol sent out about discovering useful information. Posts improving the day. Special attention being paid to posts & tracks.	
	31st		Hostile Artillery intermittently active throughout the day especially in front of agt' fr front line. EA less active in Batabn area MGs active during the night and carrying. Work - fatigues 12th Bridge between posts improving hasty posts wiring & carrying R.E material etc.	

Army Form C. 2118.

WAR DIARY
or
INTELLIGENCE SUMMARY.

(Erase heading not required.)

May 1918

Place	Date	Hour	Summary of Events and Information	Remarks and references to Appendices
			Casualties during Month.	
			Officers O.R.	
			2/Lieut G.H.L. Prince W'd Killed W.-- N.-- my W.-- (Wounded)	
			2/" J.H. Brown W'd 19 - 69 N.-- 7	
			Evacuations - Sick.	
			2/Lieut H.P. Rankin 73	
			2/" H. Steward	
			2/" Lc Lillywhite	
			Reinforcements:-	
			Capt L J O Pete.	
			215	
			R. First	
			Lieut Col	
			Commanding 1st Bn. The Rifle Bde.	

11/6/1918

1st B. Rifle B[de]
Vol 36

SECRET

APPENDIX I.

OPERATION ORDER No 31
by
Lieut.Colonel R.T.FELLOWES, D.S.O., M.C.
Commanding 1st Battalion THE RIFLE BRIGADE

Ref. Sheet 36A S.E.   2nd MAY 1918   Copy No

RELIEF   I.   The Battalion will relieve the 2nd Battn. SEAFORTH HIGH-LANDERS in the front line to-night. On completion of relief the Battalion will be the left Battalion of the Left Brigade.
"B" Coy. R.B. will relieve "B" Coy. SEAFORTHS on the left.
"C" : : : : :   "A" :   :: : : right.
"A" : : : : :   "D" :   ::   in support.
"I" : : : : :   "C" :   ::   in reserve.
Battalion H.Q. will be at P.24.d.55.45.
The order of relief will be as shown above.

GUIDES   II   Guides at the rate of 4 per Company and 1 for Battalion Headquarters will be at a point P.36.c.4.4. at 9.30 p.m.

MOVE   III   Companies will move off from here with an interval of 100 yards between platoons, the leading platoon of "B" Company moving off at 8.20 p.m.
    ROUTE:- CENSE LA VALLEE - track through V.11.a. - cross roads V.5.b.5.2.

TRANSPORT   IV   One limber per Company and one for Battalion H.Q. will accompany each Company and H.Q. as far as the point where the guides are to be met. These limbers will move off at 8.20 p.m. A small percentage of Lewis gunners will accompany them to unload them. The limbers for "I" Company and Battalion H.Q. will proceed as far as Battalion H.Q. if so desired.

BAGGAGE   V   All blankets, officers' kits, etc. will be dumped outside billets ready for loading by 7.30 p.m.

RATIONS   VI   For consumption on the 3rd inst, rations will be carried on the man. Each succeeding night they will come by limber as far as P.24.b.8.1. Time of arrival about 10.0 p.m.

WATER   VII   For 3rd inst. water will arrive at the ration dump at 1.0 a.m. Each succeeding night water will come up with rations.

CARRYING   VIII   "I" Company will be responsible for carrying all rations and water for "B" and "C" Companies. "A" Company will be responsible for supplying themselves. O.C. "I" Company will take steps to find out the position of the two front line Company Headquarters.

TAKING OVER   IX   All S.O.S. grenades, S.A.A. etc. will be taken over. Duplicates of receipts given will be forwarded to reach Battalion H.Q. as soon as possible after completion of relief. All details of work in progress will be carefully taken over.

REPORT   X   Completion of relief will be reported by wire AND runner, in the case of the former the code word "BASIL" will be used. Names of flank Platoon Commanders will be reported as soon as possible.

    ACKNOWLEDGE.

                                          (sd) J. A. DAVISON Captain
Issued at 10.30 a.m.   Adjt 1st Batt THE RIFLE BRIGADE
2.5.18

SECRET   APPENDIX II
                    OPERATION ORDER No 32
                                by
                       Major I. C. MONTFORD
                    1st Battalion THE RIFLE BRIGADE

Ref. Sheet 36A S.E.   6th MAY 1918

RELIEF   1.   The Battalion will be relieved in the front line tonight as
              shown below by the 1st Battalion SOMERSET LT. I.
              "A" Coy. (RIFLE BRIGADE) will be relieved by "B" Coy SOMERSET L.I.
              "B"   :   :   :   :   :   :   : LIGHT :   :   :
              "C"   :   :   :   :   :   :   : "C" :   :   :
              "I"   :   :   :   :   :   :   : "A" :   :   :

GUIDES   II. Four guides per Company (1 per platoon and one for Company
              H.Q.) and one for Battalion H.Q. will be at a point where the
              Light Railway cuts the RIEZ DU VINAGE - CARVIN ROAD (approximately
              Q.26.a.8.1.) at 9.45 p.m.
              Route of relief will be the Light Railway Track.

TRANSPORT III. Except for Battalion H.Q. no limbers will be provided. All
              salvage possible and all empty water tins will be carried out.
              One limber is to be at Battalion H.Q. at 10.15 p.m.

HANDING IV. All S.O.S. grenades, spare Rifle Grenades, S.A.A., wire, etc.
OVER   will be carefully handed over and receipts obtained. These will
              be forwarded to reach Battalion H.Q. by not later than 12.0 noon
              tomorrow, 7th inst. Picks, shovels, gas rattles, etc., will
              be carried out on the man.

MOVE   V.   On completion of relief the Battalion will occupy the position
              of Support Battalion vacated by 1st SOMERSET L.I. as shown below:-
              "A" Coy. R.B. will move into position vacated by "A" Coy SOM.L.I.
                            from PONT LEVIS in Q.32.c.(exclusive)
                            to footbridge Q.31.a.(inclusive)
              "C" :   :   will move into position vacated by "B" :   :   :
                            footbridge in Q.31.a.(exclusive) to
                            PONT LEVIS in P.36.a.(exclusive)
              "I" :   :   will move into position vacated by LIGHT :   :
                            PONT LEVIS in P.36.a (inclusive) to
                            PONT LEVIS in P.29.c (exclusive)
              "B" :   :   will move into position vacated by "C" :   :   :
                            V.5.b.1.2. to V.5.d.7.7. (2 platoons)
                            and V.5.d.1.8. to V.5.d.5.6. (1 platoon)
              ROUTE via PONT LEVIS in P.36.a.

ADVANCE VI. Each Company will send 1 N.C.O. forward to take over (H.Q.
PARTY AND   will provide the N.C.O. for "C" Company). He will ascertain all
GUIDES   particulars of dispositions, etc. 3 Buglers will report to each
              of these N.C.Os at 5. p.m. The N.C.Os will show the disposi-
              tions of the 1st SOMERSET L.I. to these Buglers who will guide
              in the Companies. They will be at the PONT LEVIS in P.36.a.
              from 11.0 p.m. onwards.
                 All wire, details of work, conditions or alertness observed,
              and defence schemes will be carefully taken over. All details
              of Anti Aircraft Lewis gun positions will also be taken over.

RATIONS VII. Rations and water will come up each night as follows, arriv-
              ing at 9.30 p.m. To night rations will arrive at 1.0 a.m.
              Each Company will be responsible for supplying itself.
              "A", "C" and "I" Companies to point P.36.b.0.4.
              "B" Coy. and Battalion H.Q. to their respective H.Q.

MOVEMENT VIII. All movement on the Canal Bank will be kept down to an
              absolute minimum. Companies will arrange to have an aeroplane
              sentry at the Company H.Q. to give warning of the approach of
              hostile aircraft.

REPORTS IX. Reference to this Battalion NoL31/389 issued 1.5.18
              Intelligence and Situation Reports will not be required until
              further orders. Work reports will be rendered when working

                                          cont on sheet 2

Sheet 2   O.O. No 32

parties are provided for the front line Battalions.
Officers Commanding Companies will render
disposition maps and the names of flank platoon
Commanders as soon as possible after the completion
of relief.   Special attention will be paid to the
disposition of troops detailed for the defence of the
different bridges over the Canal.

COMPLETION X. The completion of relief will be reported by a
OF   SENTENCE containing the code word "COCK". Arrival in
RELIEF   new position will be similarly reported by the code
             word "PHEASANT".

   XI. ACKNOWLEDGE.

Issued at   (sd) J.A.DAVISON   Captain
  2.30 p.m.   Adjt. 1st Battn THE RIFLE BRIGADE
  6-5-18

SECRET

APPENDIX IV

OPERATION ORDER No 35
by
Major I. C. MONTFORD
1st Battalion THE RIFLE BRIGADE

Copy No 10

RELIEF   1.   The Battalion will be relieved in the front line tonight by the 1st Battn. KINGS OWN (R.L.) Regt. as follows:-
"I" Coy RIFLE BRIGADE will be relieved by No 1 Coy KINGS OWN Regt
"C" :) : : : : : : : No 3 : : : :
"A" :) : : : : : : : : : : : :
"B" : : : : : : : : No 2 : : : :
The relief will be carried out in the above mentioned order.

GUIDES   II   Guides as follows will report at Battalion H.Q. at 9.30 pm tonight:-
From "I" Coy. 3 guides (1 per platoon and 1 for Coy. H.Q.)
: "C" : 1 guide for 1 platoon
: "A" : 2 guides for 1 platoon and Coy. H.Q.
: "B" : 3 : (1 per platoon and 1 for Coy. H.Q.)
Battalion H.Q. 2 guides.
These guides will proceed under the A/Adjt. to be at DOUCE CREME FARM at 10.0 p.m.
The route of relief will be as follows:-
"I" and "A" Coys will relieve via the Light Railway track
"B" and "C" Coys will relieve via the main track through Q.25.a.Central.

HANDING OVER   III   All S.O.S. grenades, S.A.A., spare bombs will be carefully handed over, and the receipts obtained forwarded to Battalion H.Q. after relief. All details of work done and work proposed will be carefully handed over.
All tools and 2 bombs per man will be carried out.

TRANSPORT   IV   One limber per Company and 1 for Battalion H.Q. will be at DOUCE CREME FARM at 10.30 p.m. to take Lewis Guns, kits, etc.

MOVE   V   On completion of relief the Battalion will move to billets in BUSHETTES. Guides and billeting parties will be arranged by the Quartermaster.

ACTION IN EVENT OF ATTACK   VI   In the event of an attack or preliminary bombardment developing the relief will not take place, or if commenced all troops of 12th Infantry Brigade South of the canal will occupy their battle positions under orders which will be issued by 12th Brigade. The troops of 12th Brigade North of the canal bank will occupy nearest trenches and place themselves under the orders of Battalion Commander of 11th Infantry Brigade, whose regiment theirs is relieving.

TOOLS   VII   Tools will not be handed over on relief but will be brought out of the line.
Companies will report to Orderly Room by 6.0 p.m. 12th inst.
(a) No of tools in possession
(b) If every man, less specialists, is in possession of a pick or shovel.
(c) Nos required to complete one per man, if any.

REPORT   VIII   Completion of relief will be reported by any sentence containing the code word "CUTLET".
IX   ACKNOWLEDGE
X.   All movement will be at an interval of 200 yards between platoons.

(sd) J. A. DAVISON, Captain
Issued at 4.30 p.m.   Adjutant 1st Batt THE RIFLE BRIGADE
11-5-18

DISTRIBUTION

Copy No 1 Commanding Officer : Copy No 7 Transport Officer
: 2 Adjutant : : : 8 Quartermaster
: 3 O.C. "A" Company : : : 9 1st Bn KINGS OWN Rt
: 4 : "B" : : : : 10 War Diary
: 5 : "C" : : : : 11 " "
: 6 : "I" : : : : 12 File

SECRET
OPERATION ORDER No 36
APP V

Ref Sheet 36 a S.E. Defence Scheme for Brigade in Divisional Reserve. Copy No. 1.

I. There appears to be some doubt as to the enemy's intentions with regard to an attack against the 4th Divisional Sector, but whilst the Battalion is in its present position it will be prepared to act as follows at 1¼ hours Notice:—

    I. "A" and "B" Companies on the Canal Bank will be under the tactical command of the O.C. 12th Inf. Brigade until the arrival of the 11th Inf. Brigade at V.12.b.3.7 when they will be notified. They will be relieved by 2 Companies 1st SOMERSET LIGHT INFANTRY. On relief:—

    "A" Coy will move to the Support line 2nd System in W.2.a and b.
    "B" " will move to Reserve line 2nd System in W.2.d and W.9.a.

    II. "C" Company will move 2 platoons to the Switch in W.8.a and b and 1 platoon to the front line 3rd System in W.8.a.

    III. "I" Company will move to front line 3rd System placing 2 platoons astride the road on front line 3rd System in W.8.b and W.9.c. and 1 platoon in support in the Orchard at LE CAUROY. Special attention will be paid to the right flank.

    IV. Battalion HQ will be at W.8.d.1.6.

    ROUTE Tracks 1 and 2.

II. The order for the above move will be "BATTLE POSITIONS". On receipt of this order O's C Companies will fall their Companies in and either report in person or send an officer to see the C.O. at Battalion HQ.

III. Haversack rations and full water bottles will be carried by all men.

IV. "C" and "I" Coys and Batt. HQ. will draw from Battn HQ the ammunition etc as shown below and will carry it up with them.

    "C" and "I" Coys each.
      10 tins of water
      5 (5 boxes) of Mills Rifle Grenades
      2 1 Box of rods and blanks
    The latter will be issued out among the Rifle Grenadiers of the Companies.

    Battn HQ
      10 tins of water
      1 box of S.O.S.
      1 box red ground flares
      1 box of 1" White Very lights.

"A" and "B" Coys will carry their water tins to their new positions.

II. Should a further supply of ammunition be required there are 3 dumps at the undermentioned places.
    (a) W.1.d.1.6. (near broken windmill).
    (b) W.1.a.6.8. (in barn)
    (c) P.3b.c.2.2. (in trench on W. side of road)

V. On arrival at Battle Positions each Company will send 1 runner to Battalion HQ.

ACKNOWLEDGE

J A Dawson
Captain

Issued at
12 noon
13.5.18.

Adjutant 1st Bn, THE RIFLE BRIGADE.

DISTRIBUTION

Copy No. 1	COMMANDING OFFICER	Copy No. 7	OC "A" COMPANY
" 2	ADJUTANT	" 8	" B "
" 3	A/ADJUTANT	" 9	" C "
" 4	2ND IN COMMAND	" 10	" I "
" 5	L.G. OFFICER	" 11	WAR DIARY
" 6	SIGNALLING OFFICER	" 12	" " "
	COPY No 13 - FILE.	" 13	

AMENDMENTS to OPERATION ORDER No 36

PRELIMINARY DEFENCE SCHEME
(for Brigade in Divisional Reserve)

Paragraph I - I Delete from "A" and "B" Companies" to "on relief".

Paragraph IV   "A" and "B" Companies will also carry the ammunition, stores, etc., laid down for "C" and "I" Companies.

ACKNOWLEDGE.

(sd) J. A. DAVISON   Capt & Adjt
1st Batt THE RIFLE BRIGADE

25-5-18

AMENDMENT No 2 to

OPERATION ORDER No 36
(Preliminary Defence Scheme)
----

1. Delete paragraphs I. I, II, and III, and substitute
   "On the order 'Battle Positions' being received
   Companies will move to the positions shown below:-
   I.   "A" Coy. to the front and support line, 2nd
        system, in W.3.c.70.95. to W.2.a.70.95.
   II. "C" Coy. in trench in W.1.b.2.6 to W.2.c.7.5.
        One platoon in support in switch W.1.b. and d.
   III. "B" Coy. in trench W.2.c.7.5. to W.9.a.4.7.
        One platoon in the switch W.8.b.
   IV. "I" Coy. in front line, 3rd system, from road
        W.8.b.9.4. to W.1.d.0.3.
        Special attention will be paid to the right flank.
   For "IV" read "V".

2.   Each Company will carry the stores mentioned in
   paragraph IV. These have been sent to Companies
   to-night. On receipt of the order to move they will
   be distributed as far as possible, but the move must
   in no way be delayed.

                              (sd) J. A. DAVISON Capt.
                           Adjt 1st Batt THE RIFLE BRIGADE

25th May, 1918

SECRET   OPERATION ORDER No.43   COPY NO

BY
LIEUT. COL. R.T. FELLOWES DSO, MC
COMMANDING 1st BATTALION THE RIFLE BRIGADE

Preliminary Defence Scheme for Centre Battalion
(RIEZ DU VINAGE SECTOR)

Ref Neuve Chapelle Sheet   27 May 1918

1. **DISPOSITIONS.**   Battalion HQ   Q.31.a.0.5.
One Company   Front line Q.20.d.6.7 to house Q.27.a.0.35 inclusive
Two Companies   Support line from road at Q.20.d.2.5 to road at Q.26.d.4.9
One Company   Reserve line from road at Q.25.b.9.4 to Q.26.c.3.5.

2. **ACTION IN CASE OF ATTACK.**
(1) Each line will be held to the last and there will be no withdrawal of any sort. Troops will remain and fight in the lines they occupy.
(2) Should the enemy succeed in piercing the front held by the troops on our right a defensive flank will be formed along the road running through RIEZ DU VINAGE from Q.27.a.3.5 to Q.26.c.2.0. by
   (a) the front line Company dropping posts back in echelon to join touch with the support line
   (b) the right support Company placing posts in echelon to join touch with the reserve line
Should a further penetration be made the Reserve Company is responsible for gaining touch with troops on the Canal bank by dropping posts back in echelon.
(3) Should a penetration be made on our left a defensive flank will be formed in the same manner.
(4) The word "RETIRE" will on no account be used. Anyone heard using it will be shot at once.

These orders will be explained thoroughly to all ranks and every man is to know what he has to do and how he has got to do it should different situations arise

    ACKNOWLEDGE

                     J A Davison
                         Captain
           Adjutant, 1st Bn The Rifle Brigade

DISTRIBUTION

Copy No. 1	OC "A" Company
" 2	B
" 3	C
" 4	I
" 5	Commanding Officer
" 6	Adjutant
" 7	Intelligence Officer
" 8	11 Infantry Brigade
" 9	War Diary No 1
" 10	" 2
" 11	File

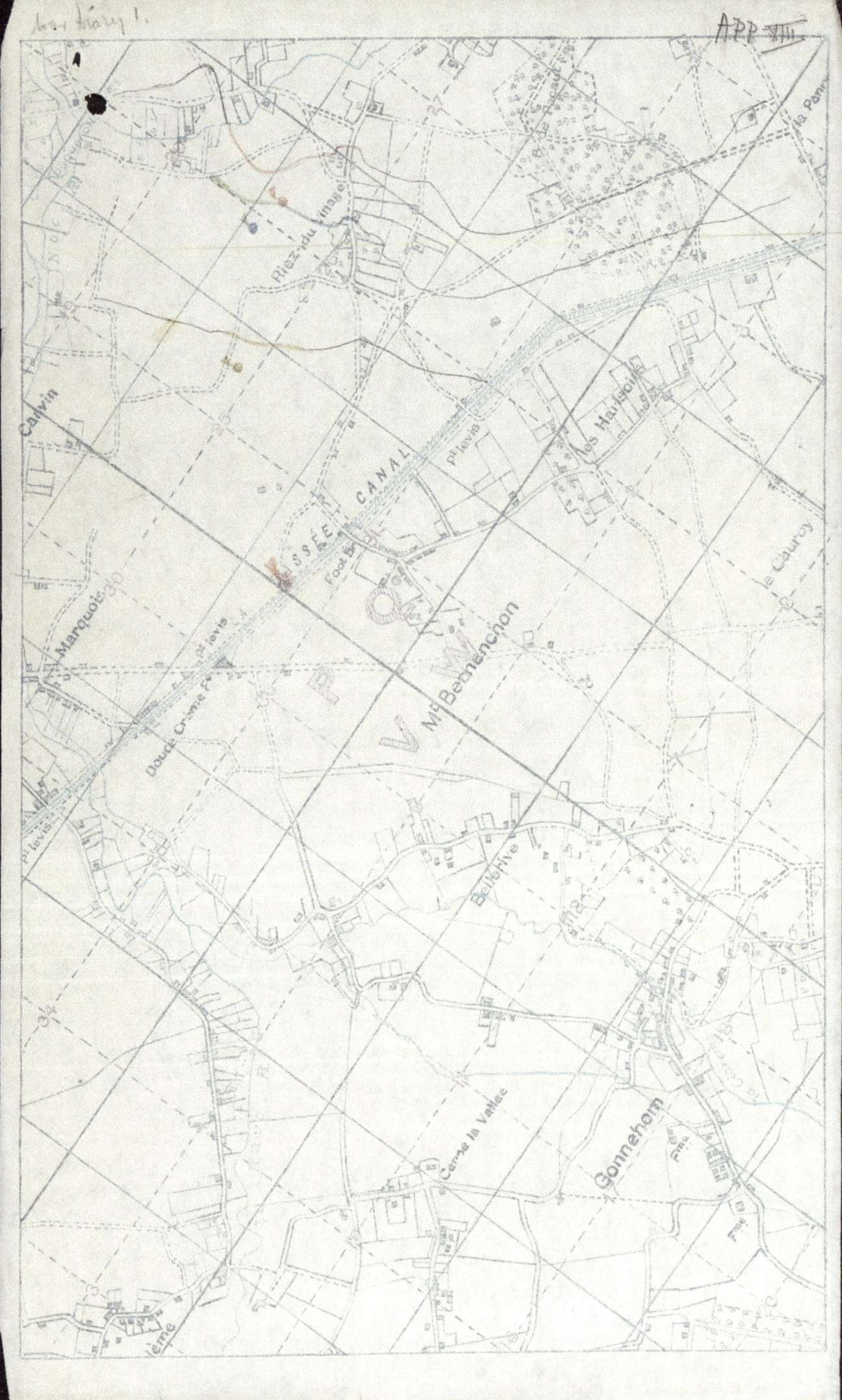

AMENDMENT No 1 to OPERATION ORDER No 40
----

1. Particular attention will be paid that all greatcoats tea packs, water tins, tools & salvage be brought out and loaded on the limbers.

2. In the event of an attack or preliminary bombardment developing the relief will not proceed and if commenced all troops of 12th Brigade S.W. of Support line of 2nd system will occupy battle positions of reserve Brigade. Troops of the Brigade North of this line will occupy the nearest trenches and place themselves under orders of Commander of Battalion whom they are relieving.

3. Cissie will hand over A.A. Lewis Gun positions.

         (sd) C.C. NAUMANN Lieut.
       A/Adjt 1st Bn THE RIFLE BRIGADE

22-5-1918

SECRET

Appendix I

OPERATION ORDER No 44
by
Lieut.Col. R.T. FELLOWES, D.S.O., M.C.
Commanding 1st Battalion THE RIFLE BRIGADE

Ref Sheet 36 A   Copy No

RELIEF: I   "I" Company will relieve "C" Company in the front line tomorrow night 2/3 inst. On relief "C" Coy. will move to the position vacated by "I" Coy. in Support.

         The relief will commence immediately after rations have been issued.

         All details of relief will be arranged between Os.C. Companies concerned.

TAKING OVER: II   All Trench stores will be carefully checked before being handed over, and receipts for same will be forwarded to Battalion H.Q.

ADVANCE PARTIES: III   O.C. "I" Company will arrange to send forward Officers and N.C.Os to reconnoitre the front line tonight.

RATIONS: IV   Rations will come up each night as usual.

REPORT: V   The completion of relief will be reported by wire by any sentence containing the code word "RUDDY".

ACTION IN CASE OF ATTACK: VI   In the event of a hostile bombardment or an attack developing the relief will not take place. All troops on the move will man the nearest trenches and place themselves under the orders of the Company Commander in whose area they are, reporting their position at the same time to Battalion H.Q.

LEWIS GUNS: VII   O.C. "A" Company will send 1 Lewis gun and team to report to O.C. "I" Coy. by 11 p.m., which will accompany "I" Company into the front line.

         O.C. "B" Company will arrange to relieve the team now in the front line tomorrow night.

                               (sd) J.A. DAVISON, Captain
                           Adjutant 1st Battn THE RIFLE BRIGADE

1-8-18

APPENDIX III

AMENDMENT No 2
to OPERATION ORDER No 46
PRELIMINARY DEFENCE SCHEME

(1) Amendment No 2, issued on the 11th June, will be altered to read "Amendment No 1".

(2) For the period that the Battalion, when in Divisional reserve, has two companies on the CANAL BANK the dispositions to be taken up in the event of the order "Battle Positions" being given, will be as follows:-
  (i) "A" Company will move to the front line, 2nd System North of the Canal in P.36.b. and P.30.
  (ii) The remaining three Companies will move to the CANAL BANK between P.35.b.9.9. inclusive and the bridge Q.32.c.6.9 exclusive
  (iii) "B" Company will be on the left: "C" Company will be in the centre and "I" Company will be on the right.
  (iv) Boundaries will be as follows:-
        "B" Coy. from P.35.b.9.9 inclusive to the point where the front line 2nd System meets the CANAL BANK exclusive.
        "C" Coy. where the front line 2nd System meets the CANAL BANK inclusive to the foot-bridge inclusive.
        "I" Coy. from the footbridge exclusive to the Bridge at Q.32.c.6.9. exclusive.
  (v) Position of Battalion Headquarters will be notified later.

  ROUTE For the two Companies in BUSNETTES through CENSE LA VALLEE-Route 3.

(3) Reference Para. 6, the material mentioned therein will only be carried by the two Companies in BUSNETTES.
  In the event of a move to Battle Positions the two Companies on the CANAL BANK will carry all their water tins, etc. with them.

(4) When this Battalion does not provide two Companies on the CANAL BANK the move to Battle Positions will be carried out as mentioned in Operation Order No 46.

  ACKNOWLEDGE.

                                            Captain
                        Adjt, 1st Battn. THE RIFLE BRIGADE
Issued to all recipients of Operation Order NO 46

SECRET OPERATION ORDER No 37 **APP VI**
by
LIEUT. COL. R.T. FELLOWES, DSO, MC
COMMANDING 1st BATTALION THE RIFLE BRIGADE

Ref. 1:10,000 136 SE COPY No 11

RELIEF I. "A" and "B" Companies will tonight relieve "C" and "A" Companies 1st SOMERSET L.I. respectively on the CANAL BANK.
"A" Company will be on the left and "B" Company on the right. The boundaries are:— On the left Bridge at P.35.b.9.9 inclusive; Coy HQ at P.36.a.9.5. On the right, PONT LEVIS at Q.32.c.6.9 inclusive; Coy HQ at Q.31.a.4.0. The inter-company boundary will be the grid line between squares P and Q.
The exact dispositions will be taken over.

COMMAND II. Captain J.R. TAYLOR will assume command of the 2 Companies which will come under the tactical command of the B.G.C. 12th Infantry Brigade. He will report arrival and name to 12" Inf. Brigade HQ through Batt. HQ at P.36.a.9.5. He will leave 2 runners at these HQ to convey messages from there to his own HQ.

GUIDES III. No guides will be provided. Companies will proceed with an interval of 100 yards between platoons direct to their respective HQ. Hereafter 1 guide per platoon will be provided.

ROUTE IV. 1 and 2 as far as V.11.a.9.7. thence VIA BELLERIVE - DOUCE CREME ROAD. Cross roads at V.5.C will not be crossed until 9.15 PM
All trench stores will be taken over.

RATIONS V. Rations for consumption on the 14th inst will be carried on the man. Water will arrive at DOUCE CREME FARM at 12.0 MN. Rations and water each succeeding night will arrive at 9.30 PM at DOUCE CREME FARM.

TRANSPORT VI. One Lewis gun limber will accompany each Company as far as P.36 central. The Transport Officer will collect Officers kits, blankets and packs at 6.30 PM.

REPORT VII. Completion of relief will be reported by BAB Code being addressed to 12th Brigade HQ and repeated to 11 Brigade HQ and this Office.

PRELIMINARY DEFENCE SCHEME VIII. The preliminary Defence Scheme is issued herewith
ACKNOWLEDGE

J A Davison
Captain
Adjutant 1st Bn The Rifle Brigade

Issued at
2.0 PM
13.5.18

SECRET   OPERATION ORDER No 38
BY
LIEUT COL. R.T. FELLOWES DSO, MC,
COMMANDING 1st BATTALION THE RIFLE BRIGADE

APP VII

Ref Sheet 36 A SE   COPY NO. 13

RELIEF I. The Battalion will relieve the 1st Bn Royal Warwick Regt in the front line tomorrow night.
"A" Coy R.B will relieve "A" Coy R.W. Regt in the front line from Q.33.d.80.55 to Q.34.d.0.1
"B" " " " "C" " " in the support line from Q.33.d.5.3 to W.4.a.4.4.
"C" " " " "B" " " on the CANAL BANK from W.3.b.1.7 to W.3.b.9.0
"I" " " " "D" " " in the front line 2" system from W.3.a/6.0 to W.3.d.3.4.
Battalion HQ will be at W.3.C.1.6.

GUIDES II. Unless further instructions are issued guides will be provided as follows:-
4 for "A" Coy and 4 for "B" Coy at W.3.a.7.9 at 9.45 PM.
4 for each "C" and "I" Coys and 2 for Battn HQ at V.12.b.8.5 at 9.30 PM
Order of relief A, B, C, I, Battalion HQ.
An interval of 200 yards will be kept between platoons.

ROUTE III. "A" and "B" Companies will move along the CANAL BANK.
Route for "C" and "I" Coys and Battalion HQ:- BUSNETTES - LA VALLEE - CENSE LA VALLEE - thence via Route 2, to V.12.b.8.5 where guides will be met.

RATIONS IV. Rations for consumption on the 16th for "C" and "I" Coys and Battn HQ will be carried on the man.
Rations and water for "A" and "B" Coys will arrive at W.3.C.1.6 at 12 midnight. OC "I" Coy will make necessary arrangements for drawing and delivering these rations.
On each successive night rations etc will be delivered at W.3.C.1.6 at a time to be notified later. OC "I" Coy will arrange to draw and deliver to the two forward companies (A and B) & OC "C" Coy will arrange to draw and deliver to I Coy and also to draw his own.

TRANSPORT V. One limber for each "C" and "I" Coys will be loaded by 8.0 PM and move to W.3.C.1.6 where they will be unloaded by the men detailed to accompany them. Lewis Guns, Water, Officers Kits etc will go on these limbers.
Battn HQ limber will be loaded by 8.30 PM and move to W.3.d.1.6.
Blankets will be rolled and Officers kits and surplus mess stores packed and dumped outside billets by 7.0 PM.
Transport Officer will arrange to collect.

GREAT COATS VI. Greatcoats will be rolled and carried strapped onto the back of the belt.

AID POST VII. Aid post will be at the farm W.2.a.8.2

TAKING OVER VIII. All SOS grenades SAA etc will be taken over. Duplicate receipts given will be forwarded to relieved Battalion HQ as soon as possible after completion of relief. All details of work in progress will be carefully taken over.

RELIEF IX. Relief complete will be reported by wire and confirmed by runner. the Code word of "GRANDPA" being used for the wire report.

ACKNOWLEDGE

14-5-18

J.C.W. Cumming
Lieut
Adjdt 1st Bn. The Rifle Brigade

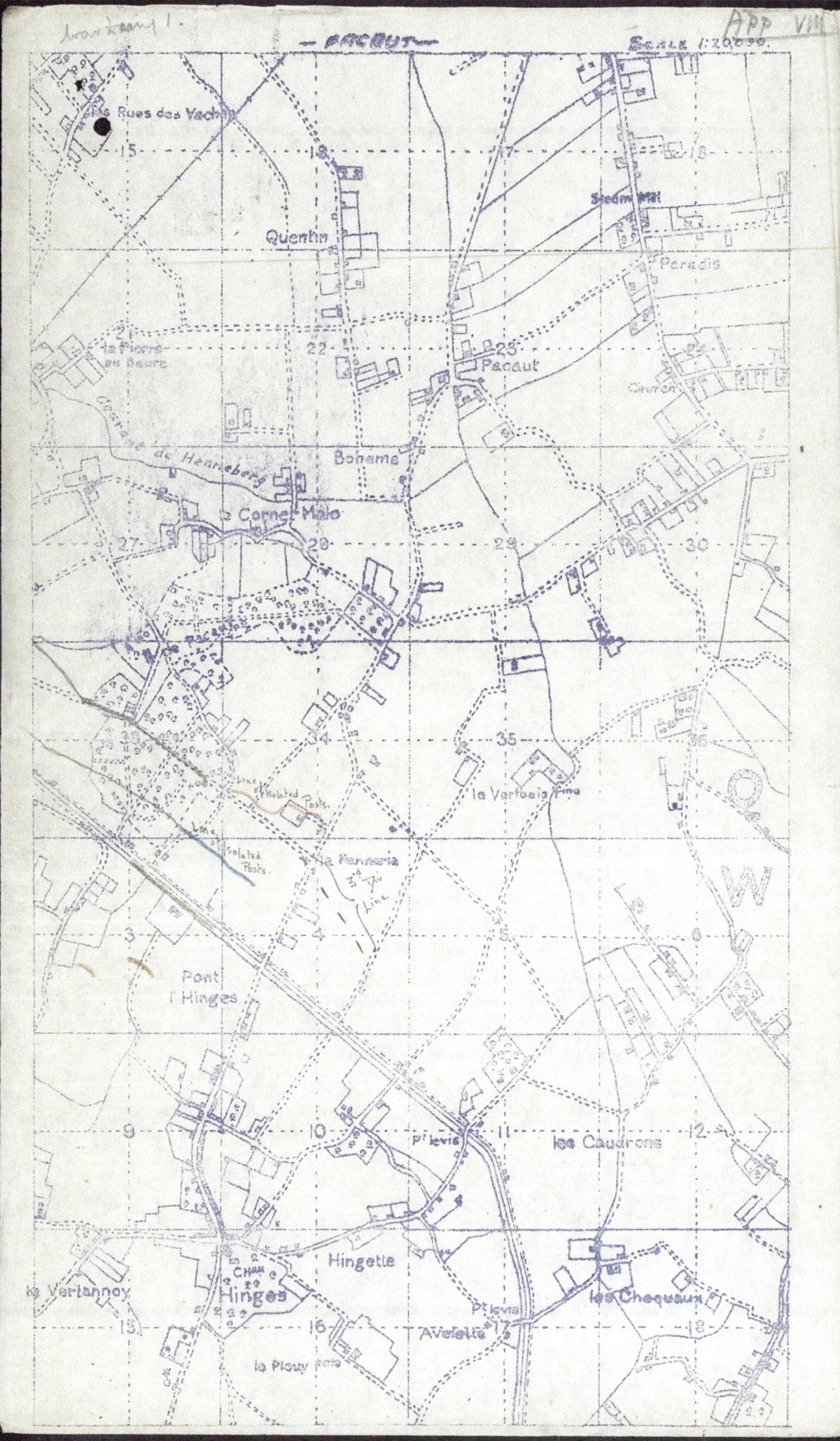

SECRET.

OPERATION ORDER No. 59.
by
Lieut.Col. R.T. FELLOWES, D.S.O., M.C.
Comdg. 1st Battalion, THE RIFLE BRIGADE.

(PRELIMINARY DEFENCE SCHEME, LA PANNERIE Sector.)
Ref. Sheet 20A. S.E.   14th MAY,1918.   Copy No. 9.

1. DISPOSITIONS: Battn.H.Q. at W.5.d.1.65.
    One Company- Front Line (Cross Roads, Q.31.c.0.45,
                 inclusive to LA PANNERIE, road junction
                 exclusive).
    One Company- Support line in W.5.b. and W.4.a.
    One Company- Along CANAL BANK in W.5.b.
    One Company- Front Line (2nd system in W.5.c and d.)

2. ACTION IN CASE OF ATTACK:
    (i)   Each line will be held at all costs, and there will be
no withdrawal of any sort from one line to another. Troops will
remain and fight in the lines they occupy.
    (ii) Should the enemy succeed in crossing the canal the
company in the front line (2nd system) will counter-attack immediately without waiting for orders and will drive him back over
over the Canal.
    (iii) Should the enemy succeed in forcing back the troops on
our flanks:
        (a) The Front Line Company will drop back posts in echelon
            to gain touch with the Support Company.
        (b) The Support Company will act in a similar manner to
            gain touch with the company along the CANAL BANK,and
            Defensive flanks will then be formed facing East/South-
            East in the event of an enemy penetration on our right,
            and North-West should he penetrate on our left.
    (iv) The word "Retire" will on no account be used. Anyone
heard using it will be shot at once.

3. RESPONSIBILITY FOR BRIDGES OVER THE CANAL:
    There is a footbridge at W.5.b.1.7. Two Sappers of the
475th (RENFREW) Field Company R.E. live on the CANAL BANK near the
bridge. They are responsible for the upkeep and repair of the bridge
and for swinging the bridge when necessary. The O.C. the Company
manning the CANAL BANK will get into touch with these men and make
himself known to them. He will be responsible for giving the order
when to destroy the Bridge. The Bridge will then be swung into

                            /our own bank and the barrels will

our own bank and the barrels will be perforated with rifle
fire. The order for demolition will be given should it appear
likely that the enemy is going to cross the Canal in force.

4. The above orders will be thoroughly explained to all ranks, and
every man should know what he has to do in the event of
different eventualities arising.

5. ACKNOWLEDGE.

                                                          Captain.
Adjutant, 1st Battalion, THE RIFLE BRIGADE.

DISTRIBUTION:-

Copy No. 1...O.C. "A" Company.
  "   "   2..: : "B"   :
  "   "   3..: : "C"   :
  "   "   4..: : "D"   :
  "   "   5...Commanding Officer.
  "   "   6...Adjutant.
  "   "   7...Intelligence Officer.
  "   "   8...11th Infantry Brigade.
  "   "   9...War Diary No.1.
  "   " 10..: : : " 2.
  "   " 11..File.

WORK TO BE DONE

APP X
1stR.B No L 35/554
15.5.18

1 WIRING. "C" Coys special party will wire the front line and "D" Coys special party will wire the support line each night under their own Special Officer. At least 3 hours actual wiring will be done each night. Wiring material will be drawn from Brigade Dump at Q.33.C.6.4 and taken up by the wiring parties each night.

In the first place fences will be erected to start with, which can be added to afterwards by the addition of coils of barbed concertina wire.

Wire will be put out at least 40 yards in advance of our lines.

The special wiring parties will not be used for any other work except carrying up the material and putting it out.

"A" and "B" Coys will be prepared to provide men to assist these special parties should it be necessary.

2. BARBED CONCERTINA COILS "C" Company will construct at least 20 coils of barbed concertina each day which they will arrange to send up to H.Q. of the front line company at night.

3 IMPROVEMENT OF THE LINE
(1) Posts to be joined up and line made continuous. Extra posts to be established where necessary.
(2) Parapets to be thickened and strengthened.
(3) Accommodation to be improved and made more comfortable.
(4) SANITARY CONDITIONS to be completed and improved.

4 PATROLS. Nightly by front line Company

5 OBSERVATION A proper system of observation will be organised and as much information sent back as possible

6 SALVAGE "A" Coy will clear the front line area.
"B" Coy will thoroughly search and clear the area up to the front line.
"C" Coy is allotted the area from the Canal Bank to the support line.
"D" Coy the area up to the Canal Bank
Salvage will be brought back to Company H.Q. and will be taken back by ration carrying parties to the limbers. Should the limbers have gone salvage will be dumped at the ration dump at W.B.C.1.6 and will be taken back next night.

Lists of salvage brought back each night will be rendered by each Company to Battalion H.Q. by 9.a.m. each day under the specified head of kinds of items salvaged.

P.T.O.

6. SALVAGE (Cont'd) Company Commanders will give this matter of salvage their very closest attention. All spare coils of barbed wire and other R.E. material will be collected. Such material collected from behind the Canal will be dumped at the Coy HQ on the Canal Bank. Material collected from in front of the Canal will be dumped at HQ of the front line Company.

The greatest care will be taken of picks & shovels; those of casualties and of men going sick will be collected and sent back with Salvage

Lieut. Col.
Commanding 1st Bn. G. Rifle Brigade.

SECRET

APP XI

OPERATION ORDER No 40
by
Lieut.Colonel R. T. FELLOWES, D.S.O., M.C.
Commanding 1st Battalion   THE RIFLE BRIGADE

R
Ref. Sheet 36 A, S.E.   22nd MAY, 1918   Copy No 10

RELIEF 1. The Battalion will be relieved by the 2nd Battalion
LANCASHIRE FUSILIERS tomorrow night, as follows:-
"C" Coy. L.F. will relieve "A" Coy. Rifle Brigade in the front line
"B"   :   :   :   :   :   "B"   :   :   :   :   support   :
"D"   :   :   :   :   :   "C"   :   :   :   :   on the Canal Bank
"A"   :   :   :   :   :   "I"   :   :   :   :   in Reserve.
ORDER of relief "A", "B", "C", "I", Battalion H.Q.

GUIDES II. Guides at the rate of 4 per Company (1 per platoon and 1 for
Company H.Q.) and 2 for Battalion H.Q. will meet the incoming
unit at Cross Roads W.7.b.95.78 at 10.30 p.m.   All Company
guides will rendezvous at Battalion H.Q. at 5.0 a.m. tomorrow
and remain there all day.

MOVE III. After completion of relief the Battalion will move back
to billets in BUSNETTES.   An interval of 200 yards between
platoons will be maintained.
     The Quartermaster will make all arrangements as to
billeting party and guides.

HANDING IV. All S.O.S. grenades, S.A.A. etc will be handed over and
OVER   receipts obtained, the latter being forwarded to Battalion H.Q.
as soon as possible after relief.   All details of work done and
proposed will be carefully handed over.   Tools will NOT be
handed over but will be taken out on the man.

TRANSPORT V. One limber per Company will be at the ration dump at 11.0
p.m.   One limber for Battalion H.Q. will be at W.8.d.1.6. at
9.45 p.m.

REPORT VI. Relief complete will be reported by any sentence containing
the code words "WILLIAM HENRY".

       VII. ACKNOWLEDGE.

                                        (sd)   C. C. NAUMANN, Lieut.
                                    A/Adjt 1st Bn. THE RIFLE BRIGADE

       Distribution
       Copy No 1   Commanding Officer
              2   Adjutant
              3   L.G. Offr. and Sig. Offr.
              4   O.C. "A" Coy
              5   :   "B" :
              6   :   "C" :
              7   :   "I" :
              8   Transport Officer
              9   Quartermaster
             10   War Diary
             11   :   :
             12   File

SECRET

APP XII

OPERATION ORDER No 42
by
Lieut.Colonel R.T.FELLOWES, D.S.O., R.C.
Commanding 1st Battalion THE RIFLE BRIGADE

Ref. Sheet 36 A S.E.   27th MAY, 1916   Copy No 13

RELIEF   I.   The Battalion will relieve the 2nd Battalion (Duke of Wellingtons) WEST RIDING REGT. to-day. On relief the Battalion will be the centre Battalion, Left sector.
"A" Coy. R.B. will relieve "C" Coy. Duke of Wellingtons in Reserve
"C" " "   "   "   "B" & "D" Coys   " "   " "   in front line
"I" & "B" Coys R.B.   "   "A"   "   " "   " "   in Support
"I" Company will be on left, and "B" Company on the right.
Battalion H.Q. will be at Q.31.a.6.4.
The Regimental Aid Post will be at P.36.d.2.9.

GUIDES   II.   Guides will be provided at the rate of 1 per Platoon, 4 for Company Headquarters and 2 for Battalion Headquarters. These guides will be at the PONT LEVIS (P.36.a.3.7.) at 11.0 ~~10.30~~ p.m.

MOVE   III.   The Battalion will move off in the under mentioned order with an interval of 100 yards between Platoons:-
"C", "I", "B", "A", Battalion H.Q.
The leading Platoon of "C" Company will move off at 8.45 p.m. but will not cross bridge at P.35.C.6.5., until 10.45 p.m.
ROUTE: L'ECLEME and Route 4.
The necessary reconnaissances will be carried out early to-day.
DRESS: Fighting order. Great coats will be carried rolled on the belt.

WIRING PARTIES   IV.   The special wiring parties of "C" and "I" Companies will move up with Battalion Headquarters. The Battalion Lewis Gun Officer will be responsible for accomodating these parties.
The same parties of "A" and "B" Companies (plus 10 men of "I" Company) will rejoin the Battalion on the night 28/29th inst. in accordance with this Battalion No M 23/360 issued to Companies last night.

TRANSPORT   V.   One Lewis Gun limber per Company, and one for Battalion Headquarters will report at the various Headquarters at 8.0 p.m., for Lewis Guns, trench kit, etc. These limbers will move off to DOUCE CREME FME at 8.30 p.m., via Cross roads in V.5.b. The personnel mentioned in R.B.6 will accompany these limbers and off load them at the above mentioned place.

KITS   VI.   Officers' kits, blankets, etc. will be collected at 3 p.m. and taken to 1st Line Transport. The Mess Cart will collect surplus Officers' Mess kit at 8.0 p.m.

TAKING OVER   VII.   All trench stores, maps, defence schemes, will be carefully taken over and receipts forwarded to Battalion Headquarters The programmes of work of the Battalion relieved will be adhered to until further instructions are received from the 2nd in Command.

DISPOSITIONS   VIII.   Detailed maps showing numbered posts will be forwarded to reach Battalion Headquarters by 4.0 a.m. tomorrow, 28th inst.

Cont on sheet 2

- 2 -

RATIONS: IX. Rations and water will come up each night, arriving for the four Companies at Q.25.b.0.5. at 10.30 p.m., for Battalion Headquarters at Q.31.a.4.8. at the same time.

Rations and water for the special wiring parties of "A", "B", "C" and "I" Companies will come up with those of Battalion Headquarters. The officers' servants of these parties will draw these rations.

Rations for consumption to-morrow, 28th inst., will be carried on the man. Water for to-morrow will be placed on the Lewis Gun limbers and carried by Companies and Headquarters from DOUCE CREME FME.

SUPPLY: X. "B" and "I" Companies will be responsible for drawing their own rations, etc. "A" Company will carry supplies for "C" Company. Receipts will be obtained by "A" Company, signed by an officer, for all stores, etc. carried to "C" Company. These receipts will be forwarded to Battalion H.Q.

BODIES: XI. All dead bodies and effects will be brought to Battalion H.Q. after dark.

STORES: XII. The ammunition, etc. which was issued to Companies on the 25th inst. to be carried up to the forward area in case of attack, will be returned to Battalion Headquarters by 3.0 p.m. to-day.

REPORT: XIII. Completion of relief will be forwarded to Battalion Headquarters by wire and runner. In the case of the former the code word "NELLIE" will be used.

XIV. ACKNOWLEDGE

(sd) J. A. DAVISON, Captain
Adjutant 1st Battalion THE RIFLE BRIGADE

Distribution.
Copy No 1 Commanding Officer
2 2nd in Command
3 Adjutant
4 A/Adjutant
5 Lewis Gun Officer
6 Transport Officer
7 Quartermaster
8 O.C. Duke of Wellingtons
9 O.C. "A" Company
10   "B"   :
11   "C"   :
12   "I"   :
13 War Diary
14   :   :
15 File

FRANCE.

SHEET 51c.

EDITION 2.

INDEX TO ADJOINING SHEETS.

SCALE $\frac{1}{40,000}$.

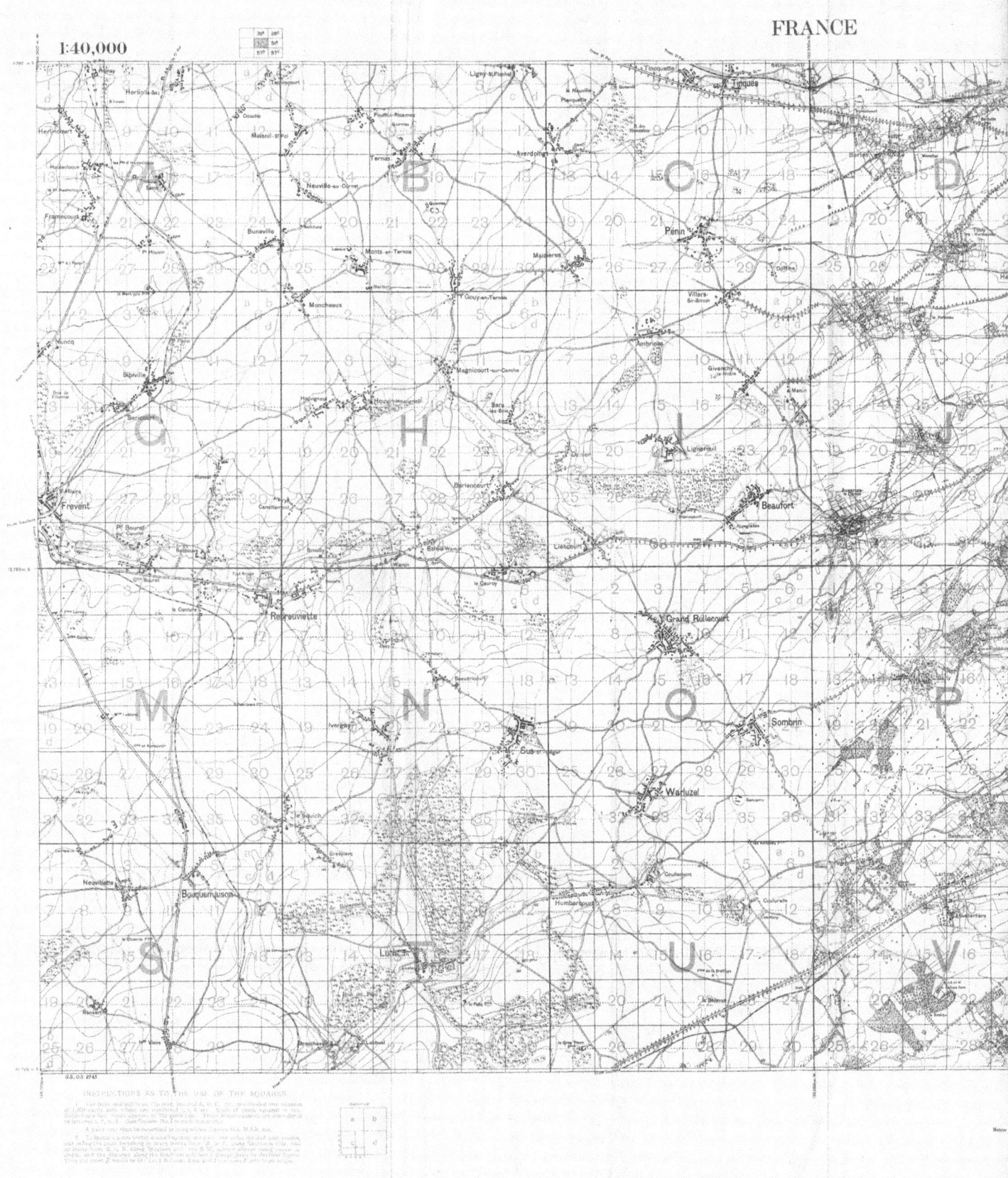

FRANCE

EDITION 2.

SHEET 51c

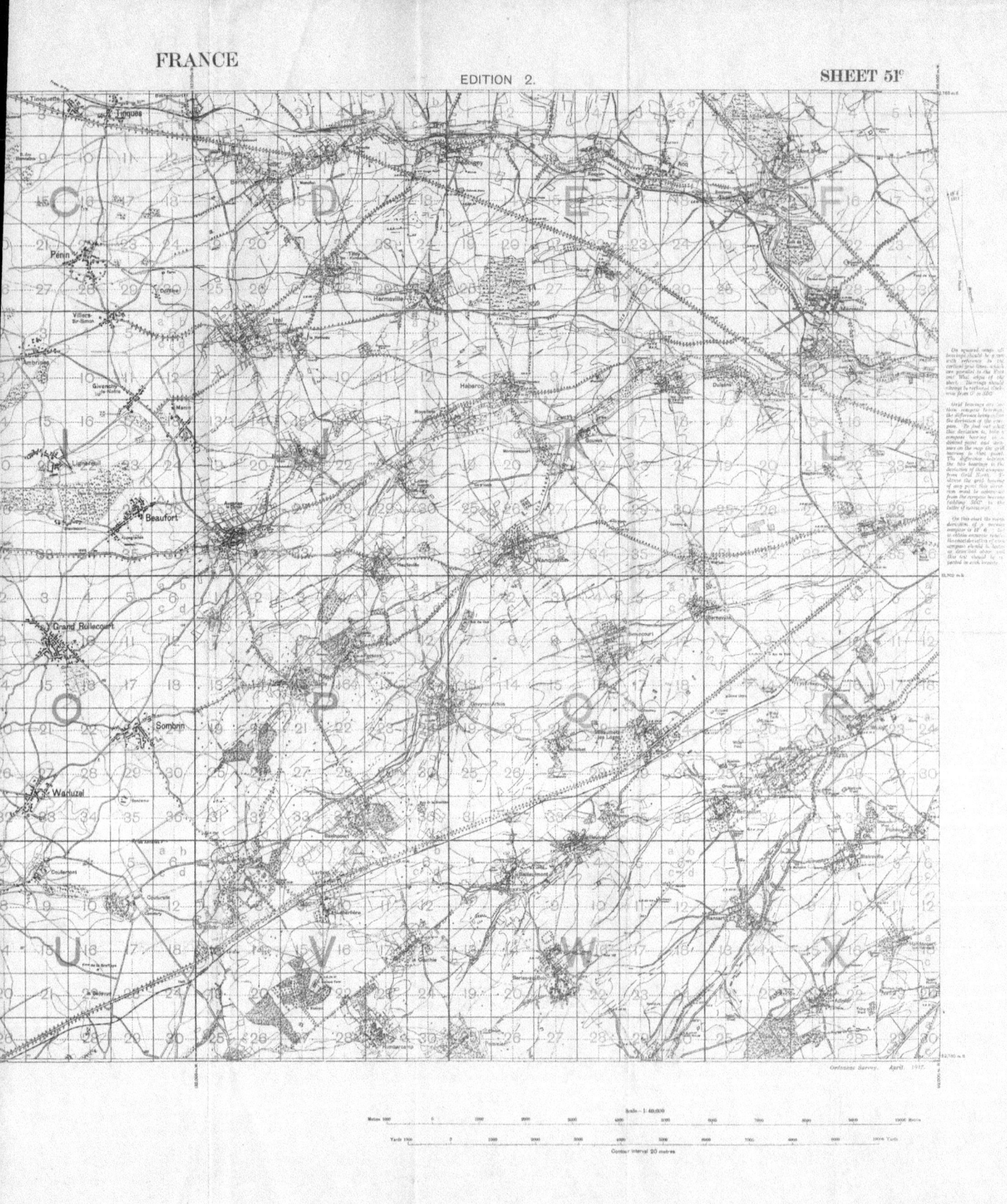

Scale 1:40,000
Contour interval 20 metres

Ordnance Survey. April 1917.

GLOSSARY.

Abbaye, Abb⁽ᵉ⁾	Abbey
Abreuvoir, Ab⁽ʳ⁾	Watering-place
Abri de douaniers	Custom-shelter
Aciérie	Steel works
Aiguilles	Points (Ry.)
Allée	Alley, Narrow road
Ancien, -ne, Anc⁽ⁿ⁾	Old
Aqueduc	Aqueduct
Arbre	Tree
,, éventail	fan-shaped
,, déchiré	bare
,, fourchu	forked
,, isolé	isolated
,, penché	leaning
Arbrisseau	Small tree
Arc	Arch
Ardoisière, Ard⁽ʳᵉ⁾	Slate quarry
Arrêt	Halt
Asile	Asylum
,, des aliénés	Lunatic asylum
,, de charité	Asylum
,, des pauvres de refuge	Asylum
Auberge, Aub⁽ᵍᵉ⁾	Inn
Aune	Alder-tree
Bac	Ferry
,, à traille	Ferry
Bains	Baths
Place aux bains	Bathing place
Balise	Boom, Beacon
Banc de sable	Sand-bank
,, ,, vase	Mud-bank
Baraque	Hut
Barrage	Dam
Barrière	Gate, Stile
(Machine à) Bascule	Weigh-bridge
Bassin	Dock, Pond
,, d'échouage	Tidal dock
Bassin de radoub	Dry dock
Bateau phare	Light-ship
Blanchisserie	Laundry
B.M. (borne militaire)	Mile stone
B⁽ᵉ⁾ (borne kilométrique)	
Boulangerie	
Fab⁽ʳ⁾ de boulons	Bolt Factory
Bouée	Buoy
Brasserie, Brass⁽ⁱᵉ⁾	Brewery
Briqueterie, Briq⁽ᵗᵉ⁾	Brickfield
Brise-lames	Breakwater
Bureau de poste	Post office
,, ,, de douane	Custom house
Butte	Butt, Mound
Cabane	Hut
Cabaret, Cab⁽ᵗ⁾	Inn
Câble sous-marin	Submarine cable
Calvaire, Cal⁽ᵛᵉ⁾	Calvary
Canal de dessèchement	Drainage canal
Canal d'irrigation	Irrigation canal
Fab⁽ʳ⁾ de caoutchouc	Rubber factory
Carrière, Carr⁽ᵉ⁾	Quarry
,, de gravier	Gravel-pit
Caserne	Barracks
Champ de courses	Race course
,, ,, manœuvres	Drill-ground
,, ,, tir	Rifle range
Chantier	Building yard
,, ,,	Ship yard
,, ,,	Dock yard
Chantier de construction	Slip-way
Chapelle, Ch⁽ᵖᵉ⁾	Chapel
Charbonnage	Colliery
Château d'eau	Water tower
Chaussée	Causeway, Highway
Chemin de fer	Railway
Cheminée, Ch⁽ᵉᵉ⁾	Chimney
Chêne	Oak tree
Cimetière, Cim⁽ᵗᵉ⁾	Cemetery
Clocher	Belfry
Clouterie	Nail factory
Colombier	Dove-cot
Coron	Workmen's dwellings
Cour des marchandises	Goods yard
Couvent	Convent
Crassier	Slag heap
Croix	Cross
Darse	Inner dock
Démoli, -e, Dét⁽ᵗ⁾	Destroyed
Déversoir	Weir
Digue	Dyke, causeway
Distillerie, Dist⁽ⁱᵉ⁾	Distillery
Douane	Custom-house
Bureau de douane	
Entrepôt de douane	Custom warehouse
Dynamitière, Dynam⁽ᵗᵉ⁾	Dynamite magazine
Dynamiterie	Dynamite factory
Écluse	Sluice, Lock
Écluette, Écl⁽ᵗᵉ⁾	Sluice
École	School
Écurie	Stable
Église	Church
Émaillerie	Enamel works
Embarcadère, Emb⁽ʳᵉ⁾	Landing-place
Estaminet, Estam⁽ᵗ⁾	Inn
Étang	Pond
Fabrique, Fab⁽ʳ⁾	Factory
Fab⁽ʳ⁾ de produits chimiques	Chemical works
Fab⁽ʳ⁾ de faïence	Pottery
Faïencerie	Pottery
Ferme, F⁽ᵐᵉ⁾	Farm
Filature, Fil⁽ʳᵉ⁾	Spinning mill
Fonderie, Fond⁽ⁱᵉ⁾	Foundry
Fontaine, Font⁽ⁿᵉ⁾	Spring, fountain
Forêt	Forest
Forme de radoub	Dry dock
Forge	Smithy
Fosse	Mine, Pit
Fossé	Moat, Ditch
Four	Kiln
,, à chaux	Lime-kiln
Four à coke	Coke oven
Ganterie	Glove Factory
Gare	Station
Garenne	Warren
Garnison	Garrison
Gazomètre	Gasometer
Glacerie	
Fab⁽ʳ⁾ de glaces	Mirror Factory
Glacière	Ice factory
Grue	Crane
Gué	Ford
Guérite	Sentry-box, Turret
,, à signaux	Signal-box (Ry.)
Halte	Halt
Hangar	Shed, Hangar
Hôpital	Hospital
Hôtel-de-Ville	Town hall
Houillère	Colliery
Huilerie	Oil factory
Imprimerie, Impr⁽ⁱᵉ⁾	Printing works
Jetée	Pier
Laminerie	Rolling mills
Ligne de haute marée	High water mark
Laisse de basse marée	Low water mark
Maison Forestière, M⁽ᵒⁿ⁾ F⁽ʳᵉ⁾	Forester's house
Malterie	Malt-house
Marbrerie	Marble works
Marais	Marsh
Marais salant	Saltern, Salt marsh
Marché	Market
Mare	Pool
Meule	Rick
Minière	Mine
Monastère	Monastery
Moulin, M⁽ⁿ⁾	Mill
,, à vapeur	Steam mill
Mur	Wall
,, crénelé	Loop-holed wall
Nacelle	Ferry
Orme	Elm
Orphelinat	Orphanage
Ossuaire	Osier-beds
Ouvrage	Fort
Ouvrages hydrauliques	Water works
Papeterie	Paper-mill
Parc	Park, yard
,, aérostatique	Aviation ground
,, à charbon	Coal yard
,, à pétrole	Petrol store
Passage à niveau P.N.	Level-crossing
Passerelle, Pass⁽ᵉ⁾	Foot-bridge
Pépinière	Nursery-garden
Peuplier	Poplar tree
Phare	Light-house
Pilier, Pil⁽ʳ⁾	Post
Plaine d'exercice	Drill ground
Pompe	Pump
Ponceau	Culvert
Pont	Bridge
,, levis	Drawbridge
Poste de garde-côte	Coast-guard
Station	Post
Poteau P⁽ᵘ⁾	Post
Poterie	Pottery
Poudrière, Poud⁽ʳᵉ⁾	Powder magazine
Magasin à poudre	
Prise d'eau	Water supply
Puits	Pit-hole, Shaft
,, artésien	Artesian well
,, d'orage	
,, ventilateur	Ventilating
,, de sondage	Boring
Quai	Quay, Platform
,, aux bestiaux	Cattle platform
,, aux marchandises	Goods platform
Raccordement	Junction
Raffinerie	Refinery
,, de sucre	Sugar refinery
Râperie	Beet-root factory

11th Brigade.
4th Division.

1st BATTALION

THE RIFLE BRIGADE

JUNE 1918

A ppendices attached:-
Operation Orders.

4th Division

11th Infantry Bde

1st Rifle Bde

April to June

1915

WAR DIARY
INTELLIGENCE SUMMARY
(Erase heading not required.)

1st Bn. THE RIFLE BRIGADE. JUNE 1918.

Army Form C. 2118.

Instructions regarding War Diaries and Intelligence Summaries are contained in F. S. Regs., Part II. and the Staff Manual respectively. Title pages will be prepared in manuscript.

Place	Date	Hour	Summary of Events and Information	Remarks and references to Appendices
VINAGE SECTOR	1st		Enemy artillery active during the afternoon to Q.26 central and Q.19.d. with 4.2's and 5.9's. During the night RIEZ–CARVIN road area Q.25. ROBECQ, the CANAL BANK were shelled with H.E. and Gas. Hostile M.G.s were active. Between 7p.m. and 9.p.m. E.A. being active over our lines. Our 6" Newton's and 3" Stokes' mortars fired to selected targets in Q.27.a. Lewis Guns and Rifle Grenadiers co-operated. 1 Patrol went out.	REF. MAP. ATTACHED (SKETCH SHEET.) APPENDIX I RELIEF ORDER
	2d		During the morning a few rounds H.E. and Shrapnel to Q.26.b. At night RIEZ–CARVIN Road and area Q.25. again shelled with H.E. and Gas (BLUE CROSS). Hostile M.G.s very quiet. E.A. flew from RIEZ to PIERRE-AU-BEURRE at 9.30 a.m. 2 Patrols went out. Casualties:– 3 O.Rs killed. Reinforcement:– 12. O.Rs	
	3d		RIEZ–AU–VINAGE shelled intermittently throughout the day all calibre up to 5.9. Being wood, Area Q.20.d. Q.26 and Q.19.d. shelled at intervals during the day. A few BLUE CROSS Gas shell being used. Quiet during the night. Sniping from M.G.s being done at night. Suffered machine-gun forward. Areas. After turning to tracks leading to the front line. Low flying E.A. attempted to our lines at intervals during the day but was driven off by A.A. fire. 2 Patrols went out. Casualties:– 1 O.R. wounded.	
	4th		8.20 a.m. to 8.100 a.m. RIEZ Q.19.b.d. Q.20 central railway tracks Q.26.b. and BAQUEROLLES FM. shelled with all calibre up to 8" this shoot was carried out with 2 E.A. flying low over our lines. Hostile M.G.s intermittently active on reserve line tracks. E.A. inactive. 1 Patrol went out. Casualties:– 2 O.Rs (1 killed, 1 wounded).	

WAR DIARY

INTELLIGENCE SUMMARY

(Erase heading not required.)

1st Rifle Brigade Army Form C. 2118.

June 1918

Place	Date	Hour	Summary of Events and Information	Remarks and references to Appendices
VINAGE SECTOR.	5th		Hostile artillery very quiet throughout the day & night. M.G. active harassing tracks. E.A. active morning & evening. 2 Patrols went out and a day and night standing patrol posted at the B.R.N. Q.27.a.2.8.	REF. MAP ATTACHED SKETCH SHEET
	6th		Our artillery fired concentrated shoots on hostile area from 11.40p.m. to 6.10.a.m and a barrage shoot on forward area on enemy night hostile retaliation was slight. M.G. less active than usual. E.A. active from 7.45p.m. to 8.45p.m. 1 Patrol went out, a standing patrol posted at B.20.d.8.4. to remain out all day. 1 Patrol went out.	APPENDIX I
	7th		SUPPORT LINE, Q.26.f. shelled at intervals during the day with all calibre to gas shells. Between 7.30.a.m and 9.a.m 2 rounds fired at BACQUEROLLES FM. M.G. unusual. Quiet. E.A. fairly active. Casualties :- 4. O.Rs. 1 killed, 3 wounded.	
	8th		The remainder of the RESERVE LINE and BN. H.Q. Shelled from 2.15a.m to 2.40a.m The BN. was relieved by the 1st/5th BN. (K.O) ROYAL LANCASTER REGT, during the relief the enemy attempted to raid the BN. overnight plant the P. sentries finding 6 our 2 night ports but were repulsed our casualties were very slight. Casualties:- 1. O.R. wounded. Reinforcements 5 B. O.R.S.	RELIEF ORDER APPENDIX II
BUSNETTES	9th to 13th		Resting, cleaning up and reorganisation. On the 10th A and B Companies have moved to the CANAL BANK joint P.36.a. and relieved 2 companies of the 12th Brigade. C and D Companies remained at BUSNETTES and carried out Certain training each day. On the evening of the 13th the Battalion moved	DEFENCE SCHEME APPENDIX III RELIEF ORDER APPEN IV

1st Rifle Brigade
June 1918.

WAR DIARY
or
INTELLIGENCE SUMMARY.
(Erase heading not required.)

Army Form C. 2118.

Place	Date	Hour	Summary of Events and Information	Remarks and references to Appendices
BUSNETTAR			up and relieved the 1st Bn THE ROYAL WARWICKSHIRE REGT in the right sector	O.O. 48 +Plan/Maps APPENDIX V
PACAUT Sector	May 14th to 25th		PACAUT WOOD. Troops on the right 1st/7th 1st GORDON HIGHLANDERS and on the left 1st HAMPSHIRE REGT. On the night of the 14/15th at 11.45 P.M. the right platoon of "A" Company co-operated with the attack of the 2nd Division on the right. At 6.0 A.M. on the 15th, 1 Sgt, 1 Cpl and 3 O.R. went out to the strong point at 8.34 c.6.7. here a M.G. shell burst upon that post, down to about 8.34 c.6.7. here a Machine Gun held the party up and one STR party was brutally wounded; they then returned to their own front line, bringing with them the wounded men; 18 unwounded and 2 wounded prisoners were captured and 2 light MGs were taken over 25 other's Inclusive some Officers were killed. The Canal was heavily shelled for the next three days and afterwards the enemy switched down Consistently. On the night of 17th - 17/15/18 the [?] on the CANAL BANK was relieved by C Coy; on the evening of 17th to 18th B Coy in support relieved A Coy in the front line, and two days later C Coy on the CANAL BANK turned up and released A Coy towards the end of the run in the support line was the occasion heavily shelled. Much work was done in the front line herring, deepening, making trenches and digging of new position of captured front line, switch line to 3rd Division and new communication trench. Much wiring was also done.	O.O. 49 APPENDIX VI O.O.50. Defence Scheme APPENDIX VII

1st Rifle Brigade
June 1918

WAR DIARY
or
INTELLIGENCE SUMMARY
(Erase heading not required.)

Army Form C. 2118.

Instructions regarding War Diaries and Intelligence Summaries are contained in F.S. Regs., Part II. and the Staff Manual respectively. Title pages will be prepared in manuscript.

Place	Date	Hour	Summary of Events and Information	Remarks and references to Appendices
PACHOT WOOD SECTOR	25th		The Battalion was relieved by the 2nd Bn THE LANCASHIRE FUSILIERS and move back to CHICK IN BUSNETTES.	O.O. 57 APPENDIX VIII O.O. 52 DEFENCE SCHEME IX
BUSNETTES	26th to 30		Bath, cleaning up, making up S.T. deficiencies, and reorganisation. Battle Position Practice and a General's Inspection took place on the 29th.	

Casualties:
2/Lt. J. H. Ansley. Killed 21-6-18
Other Ranks
Killed 24
Wounded 26
Wd. at Duty 4

Capt D.C. Scott (R.A.M.C.) to 10th Field Ambulance 26-6-18

Evacuated Sick
Other Ranks 87

Evacuated sick to England
2/Lieut F.C. Fillywhite 13-6-18

Officers joined Battn.
Lieut R. W. Holmes-a-Court 21-6-18
2/Lieut A.S. Ballel 21-6-18
Lieut B.Q. Buckept 25-6-18
" F.V. Corbet 27-6-18
" S.W. Aldridge (U.S.R, M.O.R.C.) 26-6-15

Other Ranks joined Battn: 124

E. Murray Major.
Comdg. 1st Bn The Rifle Brigade

1.7.18

Honours & Awards
Z. 1030 Sergt. J. WOODHEAD Awarded Victoria Cross
3300 Cpl. W. PRANGLE " Military Medal
301530 Pte. S. SYMONS "   "   "
17706 " H. SAMWELS "   "   "
283 Q.M.S. E. GODDEN " Meritorious Service Medal

AMENDMENT No 1
to OPERATION ORDER No 46
PRELIMINARY DEFENCE SCHEME

In the event of "BATTLE POSITIONS" being ordered

I   "A" and "B" Companies on the CANAL BANK will await relief by two Companies of the 1st SOMERSET LIGHT INFANTRY. On the arrival of these two Companies they will proceed at once to their Battle Positions.

II   Reference Para. VI. The material mentioned therein will only be carried by "C" and "I" Companies. "A" and "B" Companies will arrange to return their's to the Guard Room before moving off to-day.

In the event of a move to Battle Positions from the CANAL BANK, "A" and "B" Companies will carry with them their 18 water tins.

III   The move of "A" and "B" Companies to the CANAL BANK will in no way interfere with the cutting of crops in front of the Battle Positions.

ACKNOWLEDGE

[signature]

Captain
10th June, 1918   Adjutant 1st Battn THE RIFLE BRIGADE

Copies to all recipients of O.O. No 46

AMENDMENT No 2
To OPERATION ORDER No 46
PRELIMINARY DEFENCE SCHEME

1. The Right Brigade has at present 2 Companies in the front line 2nd System and these will be replaced as detailed in Para. III, Operation Order No 46.

When there are 3 Companies in the Front line 2nd System, and in the event of moving forward, "B" and "C" Companies will be ready to send up sufficient troops to occupy the area thus evacuated. "A" and "I" Companies will automatically send forward troops to occupy areas evacuated by "B" and "C" Companies.

All moves will be reported to Battalion H.Q. at once.

Officers Commanding "B" and "C" Companies will keep close liason with the Officers Commanding Companies in the front line 2nd System.

2. Special attention will be paid to the right flank.

Lieut.
A/Adjt 1st Batt THE RIFLE BRIGADE

11th June, 1916

Issued to all recipients of Operation Order No 46

Appendix II

SECRET   OPERATION ORDER No 45
by
Major I.C. MONTFORD
Commanding 1st Battalion THE RIFLE BRIGADE

Ref Sheet 36A S.E.   7 - 6 - 18   Copy No

RELIEF   1. The Battalion will be relieved in the front line tomorrow night 8/9th inst. by the 1st Battalion (K.O.) ROYAL LANCASTER Regt.
"I" Coy. RIFLE BRIGADE will be relieved by "C" Coy KINGS OWN
"B" "   "   "   "   "   "   "A" "   "   "
"C" "   "   "   "   "   "   "B" "   "   "
"A" "   "   "   "   "   "   "D" "   "   "

The order of relief will be as shown above, Battalion H.Q. being relieved last.

GUIDES   II. Guides at the rate of 1 per platoon and 1 for Company H.Q. will be provided. These guides will report at Battalion H.Q. before dawn tomorrow morning where they will remain. Each guide will bring with him a chit stating exactly what platoon he is to guide in.

ROUTE   III. The route of relief will be as follows:-
For "I" Coy. Track from PONT LEVIS P.36.a. - house at Q.31.b.8.9. - RIEZ-Battn. H.Q. road - Light Railway.
For "A", "B" and "C" Coys. Main track through Q.25.Central

TRANSPORT   IV. One Lewis Gun limber per Company will report at DOUCE CREME FME at 11.30 p.m. and 2 for Battn. H.Q. at 10.30 p.m.

TRENCH STORES   V. A list of all trench stores to be handed over will be forwarded to Battalion H.Q. before dawn to-morrow. These lists will be carefully checked. All aeroplane photographs, this Battalion Nos N14/165 and N14/182 regarding gas shoots, programmes of work and defence schemes, will be handed over. Also all trench maps and aeroplane photographs will be handed over. Receipts for the above will reach Battalion H.Q. by 12 noon on the 9th inst. Great care must be taken to bring out all tea packs, water tins and gas rattles.

MOVE   VI. On completion of relief the Battalion will move back to billets in BUSNETTES. The Quartermaster will arrange for the allotment of billets. Kits, cookers, etc. will be there on arrival of the Battalion
ROUTE. Track 4 - L'ECLEME
The special wiring parties will move from their present positions with Battalion H.Q.

RETURNS   VII. Companies will render to Battalion H.Q. with their receipts a return showing the numbers of picks and shovels
(a) in possession
(b) to complete to 1 tool per man.
A return showing the numbers of Lewis Gunners present with Companies will be rendered at the same time.
The forms R.B. 7 will be distributed in due course and will be rendered completed by 9 a.m. on the day after that on which the new draft joins. Any deficiency in bombs, S.A.A. etc. should be made good before leaving the trenches. This will be subtracted from the Trench Store lists submitted to Battalion H.Q.

ACTION IN CASE OF ATTACK   VIII In the event of a bombardment developing, the relief will not take place, or if commenced all troops of the KINGS OWN North of Canal will man man the nearest trenches and place themselves under the command of the Commanding Officer.

REPORT   IX. Completion of relief will be wired to Battalion H.Q. by any sentence containing the code word "PUISSLE".

P.T.O.

STORES at BUSNETTES   X   On arrival in BUSNETTES Companies will draw AT ONCE the material laid down in para IV of Operation Order No 36 (Preliminary Defence Scheme). The Provost Sergeant will arrange to have these stores divided up accordingly. The Transport Officer will arrange to dump 10 tins of water at each Company H.Q. These stores will on no account be used until the order "BATTLE POSITIONS" is given from Battalion H.Q.

     ACKNOWLEDGE

                       (sd) J. A. DAVISON   Captain
              Adjutant 1st Batt. THE RIFLE BRIGADE

SECRET   OPERATION ORDER No 45   Appendix II
                                by
                        Major I.C. MONTFORD
                Commanding 1st Battalion THE RIFLE BRIGADE
Ref Sheet 36A S.E.   7 - 6 - 18   Copy No

RELIEF   1. The Battalion will be relieved in the front line tomorrow
            night 8/9th inst. by the 1st Battalion (K.O.) ROYAL LANCASTER
            Regt.
                "I" Coy. RIFLE BRIGADE will be relieved by "C" Coy KINGS OWN
                "B"   "   "   "   "   "   " "A" "   "   "
                "C"   "   "   "   "   "   " "B" "   "   "
                "A"   "   "   "   "   "   " "D" "   "   "
                The order of relief will be as shown above, Battalion
            H.Q. being relieved last.

GUIDES   II. Guides at the rate of 1 per platoon and 1 for Company H.Q.
            will be provided. These guides will report at Battalion H.Q.
            before dawn tomorrow morning where they will remain. Each
            guide will bring with him a chit stating exactly what platoon
            he is to guide in.

ROUTE   III. The route of relief will be as follows:-
                    For "I" Coy. Track from PONT LEVIS P.36.a. - house at
                                   Q.31.b.8.9. - RIEZ-Battn. H.Q. road -
                                   Light Railway.
                    For "A", "B" and "C" Coys. Main track through
                                   Q.25.Central

TRANSPORT   IV. One Lewis Gun limber per Company will report at DOUCE
            CREME FME at 11.30 p.m. and 2 for Battn. H.Q. at 10.30 p.m.

TRENCH   V. A list of all trench stores to be handed over will be
STORES   forwarded to Battalion H.Q. before dawn to-morrow. These lists
            will be carefully checked. All aeroplane photographs, this
            Battalion Nos N14/165 and N14/182 regarding gas shoots, pro-
            grammes of work and defence schemes, will be handed over.
            Also all trench maps and aeroplane photographs will be handed
            over. Receipts for the above will reach Battalion H.Q. by
            12 noon on the 9th inst. Great care must be taken to bring
            out all tea packs, water tins and gas rattles.

MOVE   VI. On completion of relief the Battalion will move back to
            billets in BUSNETTES. The Quartermaster will arrange for the
            allotment of billets. Kits, cookers, etc. will be there on
            arrival of the Battalion
                ROUTE. Track 4 - L'ECLEME
            The special wiring parties will move from their present posi-
            tions with Battalion H.Q.

RETURNS   VII. Companies will render to Battalion H.Q. with their
            receipts a return showing the numbers of picks and shovels
                    (a) in possession
                    (b) to complete to 1 tool per man.
                A return showing the numbers of Lewis Gunners present
            with Companies will be rendered at the same time.
                The forms R.B. 7 will be distributed in due course and
            will be rendered completed by 9 a.m. on the day after that on
            which the new draft joins. Any deficiency in bombs, S.A.A.
            etc. should be made good before leaving the trenches. This
            will be subtracted from the Trench Store lists submitted to
            Battalion H.Q.

ACTION IN   VIII In the event of a bombardment developing, the relief
CASE OF   will not take place, or if commenced all troops of the KINGS
ATTACK   OWN North of Canal will man man the nearest trenches and
            place themselves under the command of the Commanding Officer.

REPORT   IX. Completion of relief will be wired to Battalion H.Q. by
            any sentence containing the code word "PUISSLE".

                                                              P.T.O.

STORES at BUSNETTES X On arrival in BUSNETTES Companies will draw <u>AT ONCE</u> the material laid down in para IV of Operation Order No 36 (Preliminary Defence Scheme). The Provost Sergeant will arrange to have these stores divided up accordingly. The Transport officer will arrange to dump 10 tins of water at each Company H.Q. These stores will on no account be used until the order "BATTLE POSITIONS" is given from Battalion H.Q.

ACKNOWLEDGE

(sd) J. A. DAVISON Captain
Adjutant 1st Batt. THE RIFLE BRIGADE

SECRET

OPERATION ORDER No 46
by
Major I.C.MONTFORD
Commanding 1st Battn. THE RIFLE BRIGADE
PRELIMINARY DEFENCE SCHEME for BRIGADE IN DIVISIONAL RESERVE

Ref Sheet 36A S.E.   8 - 6- 18   Copy No

I   This Battalion Operation Order No 36 and amendment is cancelled.
II In the event of "BATTLE POSITIONS" being ordered, the Battalion while
    in its present position will be prepared to move as follows at two
    and a half hours notice:-
    1. "C" Coy in trench in W.1.b.2.6. to W.2.c.7.5. with one platoon
       in support in Switch W.8.b. and d.
    2. "B" Coy. in trench W.2.c.7.5. to W.9.a.4.7. with one platoon in
       support in Switch in W.8.b.
    3. "D" Coy. in front line 3rd System from road W.8.b.9.4. to
       W.1.d.0.3.
    4. "A" Coy. in 2nd line 3rd System from W.8.c.5.0. to W.7.a.5.6.
       Battalion H.Q. to V.6.d.7.2.
       ROUTE - Tracks 1 and 2.
       O.C. "A" Coy. will arrange to reconnoitre his new position
       before 6 p.m. tomorrow 9th inst.
III   The right Brigade has 6 platoons in the front line 2nd System
    between W.3.d.15.90 and W.2.a.7.4.
          In the event of these troops moving forward "C" Coy. will
    automatically move forward to replace them. "D" Coy will then replace
    "C" Coy. and "A" Coy. will replace "D" Coy.
          These moves will take place automatically, Battalion H.Q. being
    notified AT ONCE.
          Special attention will be paid to the right flank.
IV   On the order "BATTLE POSITIONS" being received Companies will
    at once fall in and Os.C. either report in person or send a representa-
    tive to report to the Commanding officer at Battalion H.Q.
V   Haversack rations and full water bottles will be carried by
    all ranks.
VI   The material as shown below will be drawn by Companies as soon
    as possible after arrival in billets tonight.
          This material, except the water which will be carried in tins,
    will be issued ONLY if the order "BATTLE POSITIONS" is received.
          Each Company   10 tins water
                            15 boxes Mills rifle grenades, and 1 box
                               rods and blank.
          Battalion H.Q.   10 tins water
                            1 box S.O.S.
                            1 box red ground flares
                            1 box 1" white Very lights.
VII   Should a further supply of ammunition etc. be required there
    are dumps at the undermentioned places:-
              (a) W.1.d.1.6. (in broken windmill)
              (b) W.1.a.6.8. (in barn)
              (c) P.36.c.2.2.(in trench W. of road)
VIII   On arrival in Battle positions each Company will send a runner
    to Battalion H.Q.
IX   Each Company will arrange to cut the crops in front of its
    Battle Positions forthwith. Six reaping hooks per Company may be
    drawn on application to the Quartermaster. A field of fire of at
    least 400 yards will be obtained, all crops being cut to a height of
    not more than 1 foot. Those Companies that have not already pegged
    out their platoon frontages will do so at once.
X   ACKNOWLEDGE

                                                    Captain
                                        Adjutant 1st Batt THE RIFLE BRIGADE

SECRET   OPERATION ORDER No 46
                          by
                   Major I.C. MONTFORD
              Commanding 1st Battn. THE RIFLE BRIGADE
         PRELIMINARY DEFENCE SCHEME for BRIGADE IN DIVISIONAL RESERVE
Ref Sheet 36A S.E.   8 - 6 - 18   Copy No

I. This Battalion Operation Order No 36 and amendment is cancelled.

II. In the event of "BATTLE POSITIONS" being ordered, the Battalion while in its present position will be prepared to move as follows at two and a half hours notice:-
  1. "C" Coy in trench in W.1.b.2.6. to W.9.c.7.5. with one platoon in support in Switch W.8.b. and d.
  2. "B" Coy. in trench W.9.c.7.5. to W.9.a.4.71 with one platoon in support in Switch in W.8.b.
  3. "I" Coy. in front line 3rd System from road W.8.b.9.4. to W.1.d.0.3.
  4. "A" Coy. in 2nd line 3rd System from W.8.c.5.0. to W.7.a.5.6.
     Battalion H.Q. to V.6.d.7.2.
     ROUTE - Tracks 1 and 2.
     O.C. "A" Coy. will arrange to reconnoitre his new position before 6 p.m. tomorrow 9th inst.

III. The right Brigade has 6 platoons in the front line 2nd System between W.3.d.15.20 and W.9.a.7.4.
     In the event of these troops moving forward "C" Coy. will automatically move forward to replace them. "I" Coy will then replace "C" Coy. and "A" Coy. will replace I" Coy.
     These moves will take place automatically, Battalion H.Q. being notified AT ONCE.
     Special attention will be paid to the right flank.

IV. On the order "BATTLE POSITIONS" being received Companies will at once fall in and Os.C. either report in person or send a representative to report to the Commanding officer at Battalion H.Q.

V. Haversack rations and full water bottles will be carried by all ranks.

VI. The material as shown below will be drawn by Companies as soon as possible after arrival in billets tonight.
    This material, except the water which will be carried in tins, will be issued ONLY if the order "BATTLE POSITIONS" is received.
    Each Company   10 tins water
                     15 boxes Mills rifle grenades, and 1 box rods and blank.
    Battalion H.Q.   10 tins water
                     1 box S.O.S.
                     1 box red ground flares
                     1 box 1" white Very lights.

VII. Should a further supply of ammunition etc. be required there are dumps at the undermentioned places:-
    (a) W.1.d.1.6. (in broken windmill)
    (b) W.1.a.6.8. (in barn)
    (c) P.36.c.2.2. (in trench W. of road)

VIII. On arrival in Battle positions each Company will send a runner to Battalion H.Q.

IX. Each Company will arrange to cut the crops in front of its Battle Positions forthwith. Six reaping hooks per Company may be drawn on application to the Quartermaster. A field of fire of at least 400 yards will be obtained, all crops being cut to a height of not more than 1 foot. Those Companies that have not already pegged out their platoon frontages will do so at once.

X. ACKNOWLEDGE

                                                    Captain
                                   Adjutant 1st Batt THE RIFLE BRIGADE

AMENDMENT No 1
to OPERATION ORDER No 46
PRELIMINARY DEFENCE SCHEME

In the event of "BATTLE POSITIONS" being ordered

I   "A" and "B" Companies on the CANAL BANK will await relief by two Companies of the 1st SOMERSET LIGHT INFANTRY. On the arrival of these two Companies they will proceed at once to their Battle Positions.

II   Reference Para. VI. The material mentioned therein will only be carried by "C" and "I" Companies. "A" and "B" Companies will arrange to return their's to the Guard Room before moving off to-day.

In the event of a move to Battle Positions from the CANAL BANK, "A" and "B" Companies will carry with them their 18 water tins.

III   The move of "A" and "B" Companies to the CANAL BANK will in no way interfere with the cutting of crops in front of the Battle Positions.

ACKNOWLEDGE

[signature]

Captain
10th June, 1918   Adjutant 1st Battn THE RIFLE BRIGADE

Copies to all recipients of O.O. No 46

W.D.   Appendix III

AMENDMENT No 2
to OPERATION ORDER   No 46
PRELIMINARY DEFENCE SCHEME
----

1.   The Right Brigade has at present 2 Companies in the
front line 2nd System and these will be replaced as
detailed in Para. III, Operation Order No 46.
        When there are 2 Companies in the Front line 2nd
System, and in the event of moving forward, "B" and "C"
Companies will be ready to send up sufficient troops to
occupy the area thus evacuated. "A" and "I" Companies
will automatically send forward troops to occupy areas
evacuated by "B" and "C" Companies.
        All moves will be reported to Battalion H.Q. at
once.
        Officers Commanding "B" and "C" Companies will keep
close liason with the Officers Commanding Companies
in the front line 2nd System.

        Special attention will be paid to the right flank.

                                                    Lieut.
                A/Adjt. 1st Batt.   THE RIFLE BRIGADE

11th June, 1918

        Issued to all recipients of Operation Order No 46

AMENDMENT No 2
to OPERATION ORDER No 46
PRELIMINARY DEFENCE SCHEME
----

(1)   Amendment No 2, issued on the 11th June, will be altered to read "Amendment No 1".

(2)   For the period that the Battalion, when in Divisional reserve, has two companies on the CANAL BANK the dispositions to be taken up in the event of the order "Battle Positions" being given, will be as follows:-
   (i)   "A" Company will move to the front line, 2nd System North of the Canal in P.36.b. and P.30.
   (ii) The remaining three Companies will move to the CANAL BANK between P.35.b.9.9. inclusive and the bridge Q.32.c.6.9 exclusive
   (iii) "B" Company will be on the left: "C" Company will be in the centre and "I" Company will be on the right.
   (iv) Boundaries will be as follows:-
         "B" Coy. from P.35.b.0.0 inclusive to the point where the front line 2nd System meets the CANAL BANK exclusive.
         "C" Coy. where the front line 2nd System meets the CANAL BANK inclusive to the foot-bridge inclusive.
         "I" Coy. from the footbridge exclusive to the Bridge at Q.32.c.6.9. exclusive.
   (v)   Position of Battalion Headquarters will be notified later.

   ROUTE For the two Companies in BUSNETTES through CENSE LA VALLEE-Route 3.

(3)   Reference Para. 6, the material mentioned therein will only be carried by the two Companies in BUSNETTES.
   In the event of a move to Battle Positions the two Companies on the CANAL BANK will carry all their water tins, etc. with them.

(4)   When this Battalion does not provide two Companies on the CANAL BANK the move to Battle Positions will be carried out as mentioned in Operation Order No 46.

   ACKNOWLEDGE.

                                                    Captain
                              Adjt. 1st Battn. THE RIFLE BRIGADE

   Issued to all recipients of Operation Order NO 46

WD Appendix IV

OPERATION ORDER No 47
by
Major I. C. MONTFORD
Commanding 1st Battalion THE RIFLE BRIGADE

Ref Sheet 36 A S.E.   10th JUNE, 1918   Copy No 10

RELIEF I.   "A" and "B" Companies will to-night relieve two Companies of 2nd ESSEX REGT. and 2nd LANCASHIRE FUSILIERS respectively, on the CANAL LINE. "B" Company will be on the left and "A" Company on the right.
        The boundaries are as follows:-
            "B" Coy. P.35.b.9.0 - Q.32.Central
        The inter-company boundary will be the Grid line between Q.31.a. and b.
        The exact dispositions of the companies relieved will be taken over.

COMMAND II.   Capt. T. CARLYLE will assume command of the two Companies, which will come under the tactical command of the B.G.C. 12th Infantry Brigade. He will report arrival and name to H.Q. 12th Infantry Brigade through Battalion H.Q. at P.36.a.9.5. He will leave two runners at these Headquarters to convey messages from there to his own Headquarters.

GUIDES III.   No guides will be provided. Companies will proceed with an interval of 100 yards between platoons, "A" Company loading via L'ECLEME and Route 4.
        DRESS - Fighting Order.

TAKING OVER IV.   All trench stores, etc. will be carefully taken over and receipts forwarded to these Headquarters by not later than 12.0 noon to-morrow, 11th instant.

RATIONS V.   Rations for consumption on the 11th inst. will be carried on the man. For 12th inst. they will arrive at DOUCE CRAME at 10.0 p.m.

KITS VI.   One Lewis Gun limber will accompany each Company as far as P.36.Central. 12 tins of water per Company will also be placed on these limbers. The Transport Officer will collect all officers' kits, packs, etc. and return them to the 1st Line Transport at 5.0 p.m.

REPORT VII.   Completion of relief will be wired to 12th Brigade H.Q. and will be repeated to 11th Brigade H.Q. and Battalion H.Q. FIELD CIPHER WILL BE USED.

PRELIMINARY DEFENCE SCHEME VIII.   Amendments to Operation Order No 46 are issued herewith.

IX.   ACKNOWLEDGE.

J A Davison

Captain
Adjutant 1st Battn. THE RIFLE BRIGADE

DISTRIBUTION
Copy No 1 Adjutant   No 9 12th Brigade
         2 A/Adjt.   10 War Diary
         3 Transport Offr   11   "   "
         4 Quartermaster   12 File
         5 O.C. "A" Coy.   13. Commanding Officer
         6   " "B" "   14. 2/Lancs Fus
         7   " "C" "   15. 2/Essex Regt.
         8   " "D" "

APPENDIX IV

OPERATION ORDER No 47
by
Major I. C. MONTFORD
Commanding 1st Battalion THE RIFLE BRIGADE

Ref Sheet 36 A S.E.   10th JUNE, 1918   Copy No 11

RELIEF   I.   "A" and "B" Companies will to-night relieve two Companies of 2nd ESSEX REGT. and 2nd LANCASHIRE FUSILIERS respectively, on the CANAL BANK. "B" Company will be on the left and "A" Company on the right.
  The boundaries are as follows:-
    "B" Coy. P.35.b.9.0 - Q.32.Central
  The inter-company boundary will be the Grid line between Q.31.a. and b.
  The exact dispositions of the companies relieved will be taken over.

COMMAND   II.   Capt. T. CARLYLE will assume command of the two Companies, which will come under the tactical command of the B.G.C. 12th Infantry Brigade. He will report arrival and name to H.Q. 12th Infantry Brigade through Battalion H.Q. at P.36.a.9.5. He will leave two runners at these Headquarters to convey messages from there to his own Headquarters.

GUIDES   III.   No guides will be provided. Companies will proceed with an interval of 100 yards between platoons, "A" Company loading via L'ECLEME and Route 4.
  DRESS - Fighting Order.

TAKING OVER   IV.   All trench stores, etc. will be carefully taken over and receipts forwarded to these Headquarters by not later than 12.0 noon to-morrow, 11th instant.

RATIONS   V.   Rations for consumption on the 11th inst. will be carried on the man. For 12th inst. they will arrive at DOUCE CRÊME at 10.0 p.m.

KITS   VI.   One Lewis Gun limber will accompany each Company as far as P.36.Central. 12 tins of water per Company will also be placed on those limbers. The Transport Officer will collect all officers' kits, packs, etc. and return them to the 1st Line Transport at 5.0 p.m.

REPORT   VII.   Completion of relief will be wired to 12th Brigade H.Q. and will be repeated to 11th Brigade H.Q. and Battalion H.Q. FIELD CIPHER WILL BE USED.

PRELIMINARY DEFENCE SCHEME   VIII.   Amendments to Operation Order No 46 are issued herewith.

  IX.   ACKNOWLEDGE.

J A Davison

Captain
Adjutant 1st Battn. THE RIFLE BRIGADE

DISTRIBUTION
Copy No 1 Adjutant   No 9 12th Brigade
       2 A/Adjt.   10 War Diary
       3 Transport Offr   11   "   "
       4 Quartermaster   12 File
       5 O.C. "A" Coy.   13. Commanding Officer
       6   "B" "   14. 2/Lancs Fus.
       7   "C" "   15. 2/Essex Regt.
       8   "D" "

Dispositions - Right Battalion.

Front Line.

Support Line.

Reserve Line.

Reserve Coy.

Scale 1/6,000

24.vi.18

SECRET

Appendix IV

OPERATION ORDER No 48
by
Major I. C. MONTFORD
Commanding 1st Battalion, THE RIFLE BRIGADE

Ref. Sheet 36A S.E.   12th JUNE, 1918   Copy No 13

RELIEF 1. The Battalion will relieve the 1st Battalion ROYAL WARWICK-
SHIRE Regiment in the front line to-morrow night.
"A" Coy R.B. will relieve "D" Coy R.W.R. in the front line from
Q.34.c.0.5 to Q.34.d.0.4.
The two left hand posts at
Q.33.d.80.55 and Q.33.d.
90.45 will be taken over
by the 1st HAMPSHIRE Regt.
The garrison of these posts
will be kept in trenches
near BURKE'S FME. In view
of this each platoon will
sidestep two posts.

"B" Coy R.B. will relieve "C" Coy R.W.R. in the Support line from
Q.33.d.5.3 to W.4.a.4.4.
"I" Coy R.B.   "   "   "A"   "   "   on the CANAL BANK from
W.3.b.1.7 to W.3.b.2.0.
"C" Coy R.B.   "   "   "B"   "   "   in reserve in the front
line 2nd System from
W.3.a.6.0 to W.3.d.3.4.

Battalion Headquarters will be at W.8.d.1.6.
The Aid Post will be at W.2.a.7.1.
The two special wiring parties of "C" and "I" Companies
will go to the LE CAUROY SWITCH from W.8.b.30.65 to W.8.b.8.8.
The special wiring party of "B" Company will also be accommodated
in LE CAUROY SWITCH. The A/Adjutant will arrange to put them
in position.
The order of relief will be as follows:-
"A", "B", "I", "C", H.Q.

GUIDES 2. Guides will be provided as follows:-
Four for each "A" and "B" Coys at W.3.a.7.9 at 10.15 p.m., and
four for each "C" and "I" Coys at W.8.a.0.8. at 11.0 p.m.
The two special wiring parties of "C" and "I" Coys. will
march as one party in rear of Battalion H.Q., no guides being
provided.

MOVE 3. Companies will move off with an interval of 100 yards
between platoons, the leading platoon of "I" Coy. moving off at
9.30 p.m.
"A" and "B" Coys. will move off in time to meet their
guides at 10.15 p.m.
ROUTE for "C" and "I" Coys and H.Q. Cross Roads in
V.16.c. - road junction V.17.a., thence via Route 2.
for "A" and "B" Coys along CANAL BANK.
DRESS: Fighting order. Great coats will be carried rolled
on the belt.

RATIONS 4. Rations for consumption on the 14th for "C" and "I" Coys
and H.Q. will be carried on the man. Rations and water for
"A" and "B" Coys will arrive at W.3.c.1.6. at 12 midnight.
O.C. "C" Coy. will arrange to draw and deliver these rations.
On each successive night, rations, etc., will be delivered
at W.3.c.1.6., at 10.50 p.m. O.C. "C" Coy. will arrange to
draw and deliver to the two forward Companies ("A" and "B") and
will also draw their own. O.C. "I" Coy. will be responsible
for his own rations. "A" and "B" Companies will carry their
empty water tins, tea packs etc., to their new position returning
them to the ration dump by "C" Company's carrying party.

TRANSPORT 5. One Lewis gun limber for each "C" and "I" Coys and one for

P.T.O.

- 2 -

TRANSPORT cont.
Battalion H.Q. will be loaded and will move off at 8.30 p.m. The limbers of "C" and "I" Coys. will move off to W.3.c.1.6. and will be unloaded by the men detailed to accompany them. Lewis guns, 18 tins of water, and trench kits, etc. will be put on these limbers. These limbers will proceed independently. The Battalion H.Q. limber will go to W.8.d.1.6. Packs, Officers valises, and Mess stores will be ready packed and dumped outside billets by 6.0 p.m. Transport Officer will arrange to collect these and take them to 1st Line Transport.

DUMP 6. The Battalion ration dump is at W.3.c.1.6.
" " R. E. " " " W.3.b.8.2.

TAKING OVER 7. All defence schemes, aeroplane photographs, etc., all A.A. mountings ("C" and "I" Coys), all S.O.S. grenades, S.A.A. etc., will be carefully taken over. Duplicates of receipts will be forwarded to Battalion H.Q. as soon as possible after completion of relief. All details of work in progress and work proposed will also be taken over.

ATTACK 8. In the event of a preliminary bombardment or attack developing the relief will not take place, and all troops of the Battalion South West of Support Line 2nd System will occupy their Battle Positions. Troops North East of this line will occupy the nearest trenches and report their action to O.C. 1st ROYAL WARWICKSHIRE Regiment.

REPORT 9. Relief complete will be reported by wire and confirmed by runner, the code word "WIGAN" being used for the wire report.

ACKNOWLEDGE.

[signature]

Captain
Adjt. 1st Battn. THE RIFLE BRIGADE

DISTRIBUTION

Copy No 1 O.C. "A" Coy
     2   "B" "
     3   "C" "
     4   "I" "
     5 Commdg Officer
     6 Adjutant
     7 A/Adjt.
     8 Intell. Offr.
     9 Signalling Offr.
    10 Transport Offr.
    11 Quartermaster
    12 O.C. R. Warwickshire Rgt
    13 War Diary
    14 "
    15 File.

Dispositions of Battalion 13.VI.18 – 25.VI.18

War Diary I

Front Line.

BOURKES FM.

PACAUT WOOD

Support Line.

† A.A. by day.
L.G. by night.

LA BASSÉE CANAL

HATE FARM.

Reserve Line.

1½ platoons.

1½ platoons.

Reserve Coy.

Note. All posts not marked † (L.Gun) are Rifle men posts.

Grid.
Mag. Var 12°

Scale in Yards (Rough)

or

$\dfrac{1}{6,600}$ Roughly.

B.H.Q.
W 8 d 1.6.

Dispositions of Battalion. 13.VI.18 – 25.VI.18

War Diary II

Front Line.

BOURKE'S FM.

Grid.
Mag. Var
12°

RACAPUT WOOD

Support Line.

† A.A. by day.
L.G. by night.

LA BASSÉE CANAL

HATE FARM.

Reserve Line.

1½ platoons.

Reserve Coy.

1½ platoons.

Note: All posts not marked † (L gun) are Rifleman posts.

Scale in Yards
or
1/6,600 Roughly.
(Rough)

B.H.Q.
W.6.a.6.

SECRET

OPERATION ORDER No 49
by
Major I. C. MONTFORD
Commanding 1st Battn. THE RIFLE BRIGADE

Ref Sheet 36A S.E.   13th JUNE, 1918   Copy No 12

1. On the night of the 14th/15th the Battalion will work in co-operation with the 3rd Division in an attack they are making to establish their line well forward of the LA BASSEE CANAL.

"A" Company will establish three posts, A, B and C, to join up with the 1st GORDONs on the right.   See attached map.
"A" Post (Lewis gun)   2 and 11
"B"   " (Riflemen)   1 " 6
"C"   "   "   1 " 6

2. PRELIMINARY ARRANGEMENTS
On the night of the 13th/14th the following preparations will be made:-
(a) The Signalling Officer will run a line from present Front Line Company H.Q. to Post 1A.
He will also establish a visual station at or near Post 1A in connection with Front line Coy. H.Q.
(b) The Works Officer will arrange to have 30 coils concertina barbed wire and 60 Long screw pickets dumped near Post 1A.
(c) Posts 2 and 3 will be dug by "I" Company.
(d) N.C.Os concerned will be shewn by O.C. "A" Company exactly where these posts are.
(e) Sgt. COOKE will tape out line of advance from rendezvous (see 4 d) to A post, and if possible A post will be started on.

3. (a) The garrisons of A, B and C posts will remain in trench near 1A post during the day (14th). O.C. "A" Coy. will be responsible for shewing all ranks of these garrisons during daylight their future positions and the local line of advance, and objective of the 1st GORDONS.
(b) Four Lewis guns will be used for covering fire during the operation. "I" Coy. will send 2 guns and teams to "A" Coy. to assist in this. O.C. "A" Coy. is responsible that the N.C.Os in charge of these four teams are shewn their fields of fire during the day (14th).
For positions and fields of fire see attached map.
Lewis guns will take up positions in front of trench. These positions will be prepared on night 13th/14th.
(c) "B" Company special wiring party will be in front line trench on evening of 14th. They will put out the 30 coils concertina as soon as possible after the operation, to connect up with 1st GORDONS.
"I" Company will have 4 groups in front line to connect up A, B and C posts.
O.C. "A" Company will issue instructions when these two parties are to start work. He will provide the necessary covering party.

4. ZERO minus 30
(a) O.C. "A" Coy. will have established Advanced Report Centre in Post 1A.
(b) Garrison of C post will be in 1A post.
(c) "   "   B "   " " " ditch on left of road where track from BURKES FARM joins the LA PANNERIE Road.
(d) Garrison of A post will be in a ditch on right of road - leading man of post to be level with track mentioned above.
(e) The four Lewis guns will be in position.

5. Action at ZERO
The four Lewis guns will open fire.
The first magazine will be fired in 10 to 15 seconds.
Then rate of fire reduced to 1 magazine a minute.
After ZERO plus 8 these guns will keep up harassing fire on active hostile Machine guns and Trench Mortars

P. T. O.

- 2 -

6. **Action at ZERO plus 5**
    Garrisons of Posts B and C will move forward and occupy posts. They will each send back 1 man to Advanced Report Centre to report post established.
    Garrison of A post will move forward to post as soon as possible after ZERO plus 5. Every opportunity will be taken of lulls in machine gun fire. They will also report to Advanced Report Centre when established. They will push forward Lewis guns to act as covering party during consolidation.

7. A post will get in touch with 1st GORDONS as soon as possible and report same to Advanced Report Centre.

8. O.C. "A" Company will send to Battalion H.Q. by wire (or if wire broken by Visual) as follows:-
    A Post established .... Code O 1.
    B "   "   .... "   O 2
    C "   "   .... "   O 3
    In touch with 1st Gordons - Series of Q's.
    In the event of 1st GORDONS not reaching objective, O.C. "A" Company will be responsible for getting in touch with them; if necessary dropping posts at intervals of 40 to 50 yards to connect up with their left. These posts can be relieved later by 1st GORDONS, but O.C. "A" Company is responsible for finding left of 1st GORDONS, getting in touch, and connecting up.

9. No 1 post will remain in present position until further orders.

10. ZERO will be notified later.

11. An orderly will be sent round on evening of 14th to all concerned for the synchronisation of watches.

12. ACKNOWLEDGE.

/A Davison/

Captain
Adjt 1st Batt. THE RIFLE BRIGADE

DISTRIBUTION
Copy No 1 and 2   O.C. "A" Coy   with 2 Maps
         3   "B" "
         4   "C" "
         5   "I" "   with map
         6   Commanding Offr. "   "
         7   Adjutant
         8   Works Offr.
         9   Signalling Offr
        10   11th Brigade   "   "
        11   1st Gordons   "   "
        12   War Diary   "   "
        13   "   "   "   "
        14   File

SECRET

Appendix V

OPERATION ORDER No 48
by
Major I. C. MONTFORD
Commanding 1st Battalion, THE RIFLE BRIGADE

Ref. Sheet 38A S.E.   12th JUNE, 1916.   Copy No 14

RELIEF 1. The Battalion will relieve the 1st Battalion ROYAL WARWICK-SHIRE Regiment in the front line to-morrow night.
"A" Coy R.B. will relieve "D" Coy R.W.R. in the front line from Q.34.c.0.5. to Q.34.d.0.1. The two left hand posts at Q.33.d.80.55 and Q.33.d.90.45. will be taken over by the 1st HAMPSHIRE Regt. The garrison of these posts will be kept in trenches near BURKE'S FEE. In view of this each platoon will sidestep two posts.

"B" Coy R.B. will relieve "C" Coy R.W.R. in the Support line from Q.33.d.5.3 to W.4.a.414.
"I" Coy R.B.   "   "   "A"   "   "   on the CANAL BANK from W.3.b.2.7. to W.3.b.9.0.
"C" Coy R.B.   "   "   "B"   "   "   in reserve in the front line 2nd System from W.3.a.6.0 to W.3.d.3.4.

Battalion Headquarters will be at W.8.d.1.6.
The Aid Post will be at W.2.a.7.1.
The two special wiring parties of "C" and "I" Companies will go to the LE CAUROY SWITCH from W.8.b.20.65 to W.8.b.8.8. The special wiring party of "B" Company will also be accommodated in LE CAUROY SWITCH. The A/Adjutant will arrange to put them in position.
The order of relief will be as follows:-
"A", "B", "I", "C", H.Q.

GUIDES 2. Guides will be provided as follows:-
Four for each "A" and "B" Coys at W.3.a.7.9 at 10.15 p.m., and four for each "C" and "I" Coys at W.8.a.0.8. at 11.0 p.m.
The two special wiring parties of "C" and "I" Coys. will march as one party in rear of Battalion H.Q., no guides being provided.

MOVE 3. Companies will move off with an interval of 100 yards between platoons, the leading platoon of "I" Coy. moving off at 9.30 p.m.
"A" and "B" Coys. will move off in time to meet their guides at 10.15 p.m.
ROUTE for "C" and "I" Coys and H.Q. Cross Roads in V.16.c. - road junction V.17.a., thence via Route 2.
for "A" and "B" Coys along CANAL BANK.
DRESS: Fighting order. Great coats will be carried rolled on the belt.

RATIONS 4. Rations for consumption on the 14th for "C" and "I" Coys and H.Q. will be carried on the man. Rations and water for "A" and "B" Coys will arrive at W.3.c.1.6. at 12 midnight. O.C. "C" Coy. will arrange to draw and deliver these rations.
On each successive night, rations, etc., will be delivered at W.3.c.1.6., at 10.50 p.m. O.C. "C" Coy. will arrange to draw and deliver to the two forward Companies ("A" and "B") and will also draw their own. O.C. "I" Coy. will be responsible for his own rations. "A" and "B" Companies will carry their empty water tins, tea packs etc., to their new position returning them to the ration dump by "C" Company's carrying party.

TRANSPORT 5. One Lewis gun limber for each "C" and "I" Coys and one for

P.T.O.

TRANSPORT cont.
Battalion H.Q. will be loaded and will move off at 8.30 p.m. The limbers of "C" and "I" Coys. will move off to W.3.c.1.6. and will be unloaded by the men detailed to accompany them. Lewis guns, 18 tins of water, and trench kits, etc. will be put on these limbers. These limbers will proceed independently. The Battalion H.Q. limber will go to W.2.d.1.6. Packs, Officers valises, and Mess stores will be ready packed and dumped outside billets by 6.0 p.m. Transport Officer will arrange to collect these and take them to 1st Line Transport.

DUMP 6. The Battalion ration dump is at W.3.c.1.6.
" " R. E. " " " W.3.b.8.2.

TAKING OVER 7. All defence schemes, aeroplane photographs, etc., all A.A. mountings ("C" and "I" Coys), all S.O.S. grenades, S.A.A. etc., will be carefully taken over. Duplicates of receipts will be forwarded to Battalion H.Q. as soon as possible after completion of relief. All details of work in progress and work proposed will also be taken over.

ATTACK 8. In the event of a preliminary bombardment or attack developing the relief will not take place, and all troops of the Battalion South West of Support Line 2nd System will occupy their Battle Positions. Troops North East of this line will occupy the nearest trenches and report their action to O.C. 1st ROYAL WARWICKSHIRE Regiment.

REPORT 9. Relief complete will be reported by wire and confirmed by runner, the code word "WIGAN" being used for the wire report.

ACKNOWLEDGE.

J A Dawson

Captain
Adjt. 1st Battn. THE RIFLE BRIGADE

DISTRIBUTION

```
Copy No  1  O.C. "A" Coy
         2       "B"  "
         3       "C"  "
         4       "I"  "
         5  Comndg Officer
         6  Adjutant
         7  A/Adjt.
         8  Intell. Offr.
         9  Signalling Offr.
        10  Transport Offr.
        11  Quartermaster
        12  O.C. R. Warwickshire Rgt
        13  War Diary
        14   "    "
        15  File.
```

SECRET

OPERATION ORDER No 49
by
Major I. C. MONTFORD
Commanding 1st Battn. THE RIFLE BRIGADE

Ref Sheet 36A S.E. 13th JUNE, 1940 Copy No 13

1. On the night of the 14th/15th the Battalion will work in co-operation with the 3rd Division in an attack they are making to establish their line well forward of the LA BASSEE CANAL.

   "A" Company will establish three posts, A, B and C, to join up with the 1st GORDONs on the right. See attached map.

   "A" Post (Lewis gun) 2 and 11
   "B" "   (Riflemen)   1 " 6
   "C" "   "   1 " 6

2. PRELIMINARY ARRANGEMENTS

   On the night of the 13th/14th the following preparations will be made:-
   (a) The Signalling Officer will run a line from present Front Line Company H.Q. to Post 1A.
       He will also establish a visual station at or near Post 1A in connection with Front line Coy. H.Q.
   (b) The Works Officer will arrange to have 30 coils concertina barbed wire and 60 Long screw pickets dumped near Post 1A.
   (c) Posts 2 and 3 will be dug by "I" Company.
   (d) N.C.Os concerned will be shewn by O.C. "A" Company exactly where these posts are.
   (e) Sgt. COOKE will tape out line of advance from rendezvous (see 4 d) to A post, and if possible A post will be started on.

3. (a) The garrisons of A, B and C posts will remain in trench near 1A post during the day (14th). O.C. "A" Coy. will be responsible for shewing all ranks of these garrisons during daylight their future positions and the local line of advance, and objective of the 1st GORDONS.
   (b) Four Lewis guns will be used for covering fire during the operation. "I" Coy. will send 2 guns and teams to "A" Coy. to assist in this. O.C. "A" Coy. is responsible that the N.C.Os in charge of these four teams are shewn their fields of fire during the day (14th).
       For positions and fields of fire see attached map.
       Lewis guns will take up positions in front of trench. These positions will be prepared on night 13th/14th.
   (c) "B" Company special wiring party will be in front line trench on evening of 14th. They will put out the 30 coils concertina as soon as possible after the operation, to connect up with 1st GORDONS.
       "I" Company will have 4 groups in front line to connect up A, B and C posts.
       O.C. "A" Company will issue instructions when these two parties are to start work. He will provide the necessary covering party.

4. ZERO minus 30
   (a) O.C. "A" Coy. will have established Advanced Report Centre in Post 1A.
   (b) Garrison of C post will be in 1A post.
   (c)   "   " B "   " " " ditch on left of road where track from BURKES FARM joins the LA PANNERIE Road.
   (d) Garrison of A post will be in a ditch on right of road - leading man of post to be level with track mentioned above.
   (e) The four Lewis guns will be in position.

5. Action at ZERO
   The four Lewis guns will open fire.
   The first magazine will be fired in 10 to 15 seconds.
   Then rate of fire reduced to 1 magazine a minute.
   After ZERO plus 8 these guns will keep up harassing fire on active hostile Machine guns and Trench Mortars

P. T. O.

- 2 -

6. **Action at ZERO plus 5**
   Garrisons of Posts B and C will move forward and occupy posts. They will each send back 1 man to Advanced Report Centre to report post established.
   Garrison of A post will move forward to post as soon as possible after ZERO plus 5. Every opportunity will be taken of lulls in Machine gun fire. They will also report to Advanced Report Centre when established. They will push forward Lewis guns to act as covering party during consolidation.

7. A post will get in touch with 1st GORDONS as soon as possible and report same to Advanced Report Centre.

8. O.C. "A" Company will send to Battalion H.Q. by wire (or if wire broken by Visual) as follows:-
   A Post established .... Code Q 1.
   B   "   "   .... "   Q 2
   C   "   "   .... "   Q 3
   In touch with 1st Gordons   Series of Q s.
   In the event of 1st GORDONS not reaching objective, O.C. "A" Company will be responsible for getting in touch with them; if necessary dropping posts at intervals of 40 to 50 yards to connect up with their left. These posts can be relieved later by 1st GORDONS, but O.C. "A" Company is responsible for finding left of 1st GORDONS, getting in touch, and connecting up.

9. No 1 post will remain in present position until further orders.

10. ZERO will be notified later.

11. An orderly will be sent round on evening of 14th to all concerned for the synchronisation of watches.

12. ACKNOWLEDGE.

J A Davison

Captain
Adjt 1st Batt. THE RIFLE BRIGADE

DISTRIBUTION
Copy No 1 and 2 O.C. "A" Coy   with 2 Maps
         3   "B"   "
         4   "C"   "
         5   "I"   "   with map
         6   Commanding Offr. "   "
         7   Adjutant
         8   Works Offr.
         9   Signalling Offr
        10   11th Brigade   "   "
        11   1st Gordons   "   "
        12   War Diary   "   "
        13   "   "
        14   File

WD

Appendix VI

AMENDMENT No 1 to
OPERATION ORDER No 40

1. Reference Para. 2 (c) for "posts 2 and 3" read "posts B and C".

2. Reference the attached map, Lewis guns Nos 1 and 2 will now fire on shell holes marked (1); Lewis guns Nos 3 and 4 on shell holes marked (2). The shell holes marked (3) and (4) will be engaged by the remaining Lewis guns in the front line.

3. O.C. "C" Company will detail one Lewis gun team complete to be attached to "A" Company for this tour in the line.

   ACKNOWLEDGE.

(sd) J. A. DAVISON Captain
Comndg 1st Batt. THE RIFLE BRIGADE

13th June 1919.

Issued to all recipients of Operation Order No 40

AMENDMENT No 1 to
OPERATION ORDER No 49

Appendix VI

1. Reference Para. 2 (c) for "posts 2 and 3" read "posts B and C".

2. Reference the attached map, Lewis guns Nos 1 and 2 will now fire on shell holes marked (1); Lewis guns Nos 3 and 4 on shell holes marked (2). The shell holes marked (3) and (4) will be engaged by the remaining Lewis guns in the front line.

3. O.C. "C" Company will detail one Lewis gun team complete to be attached to "A" Company for this tour in the line.

ACKNOWLEDGE.

          (sd) J. A. DAVIDSON Captain
        Comndg 1st Batt THE RIFLE BRIGADE

13th June, 1918

Issued to all recipients of Operation Order No 49

SECRET

Appendix VII

OPERATION ORDER No 50
by
Major I. C. MONTFORD
Commanding 1st Battn. THE RIFLE BRIGADE

PRELIMINARY DEFENCE SCHEME for RIGHT BATTALION - PACAUT SECTOR

Ref. Sheet 36A S.E.   Copy No /2

DISPOSITIONS 1. Battalion H.Q. W.8.d.1.6.
- 1 Company Front Line Divisional Boundary Q.34.d.35.40 to Q.34.c.05.45
- 1 Company Support Line S.E. edge of PACAUT WOOD to extreme reserve line, right of support line.
- 1 Company CANAL BANK W.3.b.2.7. to W.4.a.0.0.
- 1 Company Front and Support lines and System, 1 platoon about W.3.c.5.8., 2 platoons about W.3.d.2.4.

ACTION IN CASE OF ATTACK 2.

(i) Each line will be held to the last and there will be no withdrawal of any sort. Troops will remain and fight in the lines they occupy.

(ii) Should the enemy penetrate the front and the Support Company Commander decides to counter attack at least 1 platoon will be left in the Support line as a garrison of that trench.

(iii) Should the enemy succeed in penetrating the front held by the troops on our right a defensive flank will be formed behind LA PANNERIE - PONT L'HINGES road behind the wire. The echelon posts will be used.

(iv) Should the enemy appear to be approaching the Canal the Reserve Company Commander will dribble up 2 platoons to reinforce the Company on the Canal Bank on his own initiative. The remaining platoon will await the arrival of the Company of the reserve Brigade before moving. In the event of this happening the nearest Company of Reserve Brigade, Brigade H.Q. and Battalion H.Q. will be notified immediately. Care will be taken to keep touch with the troops on the right.

(v) It should be impossible for the enemy to make a frontal attack on that portion of PACAUT WOOD that we hold

The garrison in PACAUT WOOD is therefore to give all possible assistance to the troops on the flanks should they be driven back. The wood is on no account to be given up. This covering fire afforded will assist in the counter attack.

(vi) The word retire will on no account be used. Anyone heard using it will be shot at once.

RESPONSIBILITY FOR BRIDGES OVER CANAL 3. There is a footbridge at W.3.b.1.7. Two Sappers of the 406th Field Coy. R.E. live on the Canal Bank near the bridge who are responsible for the upkeep and repair of the bridge and for swinging it when necessary. The Company Commander on the Canal Bank will get into touch with these men and make himself known to them. He will be responsible for giving the order to destroy the bridge. The bridge will then be swung into our own bank and the barrels will be perforated with rifle fire. The order for the demolition will be given should it appear likely that the enemy is going to cross the Canal in force.

WORKING PARTIES 4. In case of attack all Working parties N. of the Canal Bank will occupy the nearest trenches placing themselves under the nearest Company Commander. They will at once notify Battalion H.Q. of their action. This does not apply to the CANAL BANK Company who will make their way at once to the South side of the Canal Bank.

5. The above order will be thoroughly explained to all ranks.
ACKNOWLEDGE

(sd) M.A.DAVISON   Capt.
Adjt 1st Batt THE RIFLE BRIGADE

15-6-18

SECRET   Appendix VII

OPERATION ORDER No 50
by
Major I. C. MONTFORD
Commanding 1st Battn. THE RIFLE BRIGADE
PRELIMINARY DEFENCE SCHEME for RIGHT BATTALION - PACAUT SECTOR

Ref. Sheet 36A S.E.   Copy No 13

DISPOSITIONS 1. Battalion H.Q. W.8.d.1.8.
1 Company Front Line Divisional Boundary Q.34.d.55.40 to Q.34.c.05.45
1 Company Support Line S.E. edge of PACAUT WOOD to extreme reserve line, right of support line.
1 Company CANAL BANK W.3.b.2.7. to W.4.a.0.0.
1 Company Front and Support lines and System, 1 platoon about W.3.c.5.8., 2 platoons about W.3.d.2.4.

ACTION IN CASE OF ATTACK 2. (i) Each line will be held to the last and there will be no withdrawal of any sort. Troops will remain and fight in the lines they occupy.
(ii) Should the enemy penetrate the front and the Support Company Commander decides to counter attack at least 1 platoon will be left in the Support line as a garrison of that trench.
(iii) Should the enemy succeed in penetrating the front held by the troops on our right a defensive flank will be formed behind LA PANNERIE - PONT L'HINGES road behind the wire. The echelon posts will be used.
(iv) Should the enemy appear to be approaching the Canal the Reserve Company Commander will dribble up 2 platoons to reinforce the Company on the Canal Bank on his own initiative. The remaining platoon will await the arrival of the Company of the reserve Brigade before moving. In the event of this happening the nearest Company of Reserve Brigade, Brigade H.Q. and Battalion H.Q. will be notified immediately. Care will be taken to keep touch with the troops on the right.
(v) It should be impossible for the enemy to make a frontal attack on that portion of PACAUT WOOD that we hold
The garrison in PACAUT WOOD is therefore to give all possible assistance to the troops on the flanks should they be driven back. The wood is on no account to be given up. This covering fire afforded will assist in the counter attack.
(vi) The word retire will on no account be used. Anyone heard using it will be shot at once.

RESPONSIBILITY FOR BRIDGES OVER CANAL 3. There is a footbridge at W.3.b.1.7. Two Sappers of the 406th Field Coy. R.E. live on the Canal Bank near the bridge who are responsible for the upkeep and repair of the bridge and for swinging it when necessary. The Company Commander on the Canal Bank will get into touch with these men and make himself known to them. He will be responsible for giving the order to destroy the bridge. The bridge will then be swung into our own bank and the barrels will be perforated with rifle fire. The order for the demolition will be given should it appear likely that the enemy is going to cross the Canal in force.

WORKING PARTIES 4. In case of attack all Working Parties N. of the Canal Bank will occupy the nearest trenches placing themselves under the nearest Company Commander. They will at once notify Battalion H.Q. of their action. This does not apply to the CANAL BANK Company who will make their way at once to the South side of the Canal Bank.
5. The above order will be thoroughly explained to all ranks.
ACKNOWLEDGE

(sd) H.A. DAVISON Capt.
15-6-18   Adjt 1st Batt THE RIFLE BRIGADE

Operation Order No 51
by
Major J C Montford
Commanding
1st Bn The Rifle Brigade.

Ref: Sheet
36 A.S.E.

Appendix VIII

Copy No ---- 14

25. 6. 18

RELIEF I The Battalion will be relieved by the 2nd Bn Lancashire Fusiliers in the front line, tonight:—
A Coy R.B. will be relieved by "A" Coy. L.F.s
B "   "   "   "   " B "
C "   "   "   "   " C "
D "   "   "   "   " D "

The order of relief will be as follows:— B, C, A, D, Bn HQ.

GUIDES II Guides at the rate of 2 per platoon + 1 for Coy H.Q. will be provided. These will report at Bn H.Q. at 10.0 pm, each bearing a slip stating exactly the location of his platoon. The Signalling officer will arrange to take these Guides to the Crossroads W.8.a.0.8.

ROUTE III The route of relief will be as follows:—
For the front line:— Bridge at W.3.a.9.9.
For the support line:— Bridge at W.3.b.70.25
No definite route is laid down for the remaining Coys.

HANDING IV All trench stores, Defence schemes, L.G. A.A. positions
OVER aeroplane photographs, maps etc will be carefully handed over and receipt obtained. These will be forwarded to each Bn H.Q. by not later than 12.0 noon on the 26th inst. All gas rattles, tin packs, empty water tins etc will be brought out. Companies will complete all deficiencies in S.A.A. before leaving the trenches.
The signalling officer will make arrangements that no Coy signal station is handed over to the Signallers of the incoming Unit until the wire stating that the relief is complete has been despatched to Battalion H.Q.

MOVE V On completion of the relief the Battalion will move to billets in BUSNETTES where the Q.M. & T.O. will arrange accomodation.

INTERVAL VI. All movement will be carried out with an interval of 100ˣ between platoons.

LEWIS GUNS etc VII. One Lewis Gun limber per company will be at the ration dump from 12 midnight onwards. 2 limbers will be at Battalion H.Q. at 11.30 p.m. These limbers will take all Lewis Guns, trench kit etc back to billets.

ATTACK. VIII. In the event of an attack or a preliminary bombardment developing the relief will not take place. All troops of the relieving unit North of the support line 2nd System will man the nearest trenches & place themselves under the orders of the C.O. All troops South of this line will occupy their Battle positions.

DEFENCE SCHEME. IX. On arrival in billets each Coy will draw the material laid down to be carried in operation order No. 46; the provost-serjeant will arrange to have this ready sorted out by the time they arrive. Steps will be taken to warn all ranks that the Battalion will at all times be ready to move at 1½ hours notice.

REPORT X. The completion of the relief will be reported by wire by any sentence containing the code word "AUDREY". O's C Coys should call in at Battalion H.Q. if they happen to pass it.

ACKNOWLEDGE.

J A Davison Captain
Adjutant
1st Bn. The Rifle Brigade.

Distribution :-
Copy No 1 C.O.
" 2 Capt Letts
" 3 Adjt
" 4 9/Adjt
" 5 Intelligence Officer
" 6 Signalling Officer
" 7 Transport Officer
" 8 Quartermaster
" 9 O.C. S/L an tus.
10 O.C. A Coy
11 " B "
12 " C "
13 " I "
14 & 15 War Diary
16 File.

Operation Order No 51
by
Major J C Montford
Commanding
1st Bn The Rifle Brigade.

Ref: Sheet
36 A. S.E.

Appendix VIII

Copy No ——

25. 6. 18

RELIEF **I** The Battalion will be relieved by the 2nd Bn Lancashire Fusiliers in the front line, tonight:—
    A Coy R B will be relieved by A Coy L F.s
    B " " " " B "
    C " " " " C "
    I " " " " D "
The order of relief will be as follows:— B, C, A, I, Bn H.Q.

GUIDES **II** Guides at the rate of 2 per platoon + 1 for Coy H.Q. will be provided. These will report at Bn H.Q. at 10.0 p.m., each bearing a slip stating exactly the location of his platoon. The signalling officer will arrange to take these guides to the crossroads W.8.a.0.8.

ROUTE **III** The route of relief will be as follows:—
    For the front line:— Bridge at W.3.a.9.9.
    For the support line:— Bridge at W.3.A.70.25.
No definite route is laid down for the relieving Coys.

HANDING OVER **IV** All trench stores, Defence schemes, S.O.S. A.A. positions, aeroplane photographs, maps etc will be carefully handed and receipt obtained. These will be forwarded to each Bn H.Q. by not later than 12.0 noon on the 26th inst. All gas rattles, tea packs empty, water tins etc will be brought out. Companies will complete all deficiencies in S.A.A. before leaving the trenches.

     The signalling officer will make arrangements that no Coy signal station is handed over to the signallers of the incoming Unit until the wire stating that the relief is complete has been despatched to Battalion H.Q.

MOVE **V** On completion of the relief the Battalion will move to billets in Busnettes. The Brigade transport will pick up equipment as shown.

INTERVAL VI All movement will be carried out with an interval of 100x between platoons.

LEWIS GUNS etc VII One Lewis Gun limber per Company will be at the ration dump from 12 midnight onwards. 2 limbers will be at Battalion H.Q. at 11.30 p.m. These limbers will take all Lewis Guns, trench kit etc back to billets.

ATTACK. VIII In the event of an attack or a preliminary bombardment developing the relief will not take place. All troops of the relieving unit north of the support line 2nd system will man the nearest trenches & place themselves under the orders of the C.O. All troops south of this line will occupy their Battle positions.

DEFENCE SCHEME. IX On arrival in billets each Coy will draw the material laid down to be carried, in Operation order no 46; the provost-sergeant will arrange to have this ready sorted out by the time they arrive. Steps will be taken to warn all ranks that the Battalion will at all times be ready to move at 1½ hours notice.

REPORT X The completion of the relief will be reported by wire by any sentence containing the code word "AUDREY". O.C. Coys should call in at Battalion H.Q. if they happen to pass it.

ACKNOWLEDGE.

JA Dawson Captain
Adjutant
1st Bn. The Rifle Brigade.

Distribution :- 1
Copy no 1 CO   10 O.C. A Coy
"   2 Capt Letts   11 " B "
"   3 Adjt   12 " C "
"   4 9/Capt   13 " Z "
"   5 Intelligence Officer 14 & 15 War Diary
"   6 Signalling Officer   16 File
"   7 Transport Officer
"   8 Quartermaster
"   9 O.C. 2/Lam Guns

SECRET
Operation Order No. 12
Copy No. 12

Commanding Officer, No. Rifle Brigade.
Preliminary Defence Scheme for Brigade in Divisional Reserve.
Ref: Sheet 36A.S.E.   26.6.16.

I. Operation Order No. 46 and Amendment are cancelled.

II. In the event of "BATTLE POSITIONS" being ordered, the Battalion will be prepared to move as follows at 12 hours notice:—
   a. "C" Coy to trench W.1.b.26.— W.2.c.9.5, with one platoon to support Switch W.1.b and d.
   b. "B" Coy to trench W.2.c.9.5 — W.1.a.4.7, with one platoon in Support to Switch W.8.b.
   c. "D" Coy to Front Line 3rd System from W.8.b.9.2 — W.1.d.6.2.
   d. "A" Coy to 2nd Line 3rd System from W.8.a.5.0 — W.7.a.9.4
   e. Battalion H.Q. to V.6.d.7.2.
      Route: Road through V.6.c.d.a.b., tracks Y.2 & Y.e.
      Dress: Fighting order. Greatcoats will be carried in rolls on the belt. Haversack rations, full water bottles will be carried.

III. On the order "BATTLE POSITIONS" being received, O.C. Coys will at once fall their coys in & either report in person or send a representative to report to the C.O. at Battalion H.Q. where they will receive further instructions.

IV. Ten full battle dues with bandoliers at each Coy H.Q. tomorrow 26th (?) instant in case of a move these will be carried up.
   There is a certain amount of S.A.A. (bandoliers & B rolls) at present in each position. Each Coy H.Q. will take steps to count the exact amount in their respective trenches, & state amount so taken each Battalion H.Q. by NOT LATER THAN 6.0 A.M. on the 29th inst.

V. On arrival at the BATTLE POSITIONS each Company will send a runner to Battalion H.Q.

VI. The action of the Battalion in any future will be to counter attack towards the enemy over the CANAL.
   The Light Brigade has at present 2 Coys in the front line 3rd system & these will be replaced as follows by this Battalion:— As each platoon etc of the above 2 Coys move forward so it will be replaced by a similar officer of Batt. Coys whichever happens to be immediately behind them. Thus D Coy will replace B Coy as they move forward & A Coy will replace C Coy. Close liaison between commanders con cerned must be main-tained. All moves must be reported to Battalion H.Q. AT ONCE.

VII. ACKNOWLEDGE.

J.A. Dawson Capt. and Adjutant
. Bn. The Rifle Brigade.

War Diary

SECRET

Operation Order No 60
Major [illegible]
Commanding 12th Batt. Rifle Brigade.

Preliminary Defence Scheme for Brigade in Divisional Reserve.
Ref: Sheet 36 A.S.E.   23.6.18

I. Operation Order No 46 and amendment are cancelled.

II. In the event of "BATTLE POSITIONS" being ordered, the Battalion will be prepared to move as follows at 1½ hours notice:—
   a. "C" Coy to trench W1d.2.6 — W2c.7.5, with one platoon in Support in Sunken W1d and d.
   b. "B" Coy to trench W2c.7.5 — W9a.4.7, with one platoon in Support in Sunken W.8.d.
   c. "D" Coy to Front Line 3rd System from W.8.d.9.2 — W.1.d.0.2
   d. "A" Coy to 2nd Line 3rd System from W.8.c.5.0 — W.7.c.9.4
   e. Battalion H.Q. to W.6.d.7.2.
      Route: Road through W.16.c.d and b, tracks Y2 and Y3.
      Dress Fighting order, Greatcoats will be carried rolled on the belt. Haversack rations & full water bottle will also be carried.

III. On the order "BATTLE POSITIONS" being received, O.C. Coys will at once fall their Coys in & either report in person or send a representative to the Adjutant or the O.C. at Battalion H.Q. to receive beyond receive further instructions.

IV. Ten full water tins will be distributed at each Coy H.Q. tomorrow 24th inst in case of a move these will be carried up.
   There is a certain amount of S.A.A. (Bandoliers & Bundles) at present in each position. Each Coy Officer will take steps to count the exact amount in their respective trenches, & start moving them to each Battalion H.Q. by NOT LATER THAN 6.0 P.M. on the 29th inst.

V. On arrival at the BATTLE POSITIONS each Company will send a runner to Battalion H.Q.

VI. The action of the Battalion when ordered will be to counter attack should the enemy overrun our lines.
   The Right Brigade has a further 2 Coys in the Front Line 3rd System & these will be replaced as follows by this Battalion:— As each platoon etc of the above 2 Coys moves forward so it will be replaced by a similar lot of men of our Coy whose are happen to be immediately behind them. Thus "D" Coy will replace "B" Coy as they move forward & "A" Coy will replace "C" Coy. Close liaison between commanders concerned must be maintained. All moves must be reported to Battalion H.Q. AT ONCE.

VII. ACKNOWLEDGE

J.A. Davison Capt and Adjutant
12 Bn The Rifle Brigade.

W. Craig

Dispositions of Eight Battalion.

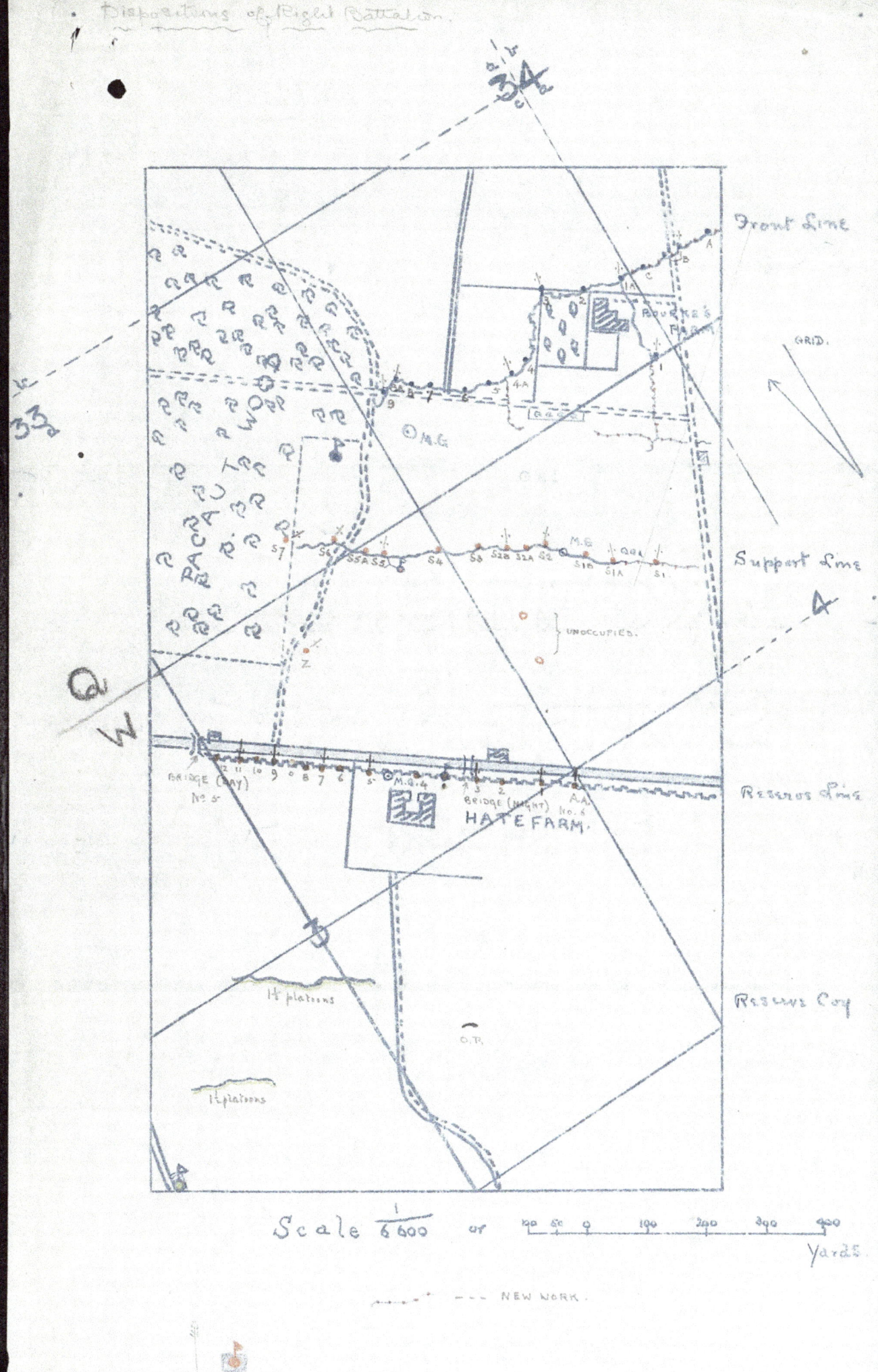

Scale 1/8600

--- NEW WORK.

24.vi.18.

AMENDMENT No 1 to OPERATION ORDER No 52
by -
Major I. C. MONTFORD
Commanding 1st Battalion THE RIFLE BRIGADE
Preliminary Defence Scheme for Brigade in Divisional Reserve

Reference Operation Order No 52, Companies will not counter attack without orders from Battalion H.Q., and will be disposed in the first instance with a view to defence. They must, however, be prepared to counter-attack at short notice.

(sd) C. C. NAUMANN Lieut.
A/Adjt
28th June, 1918   1st Batt. THE RIFLE BRIGADE

Issued to all recipients of O.O. 52

AMENDMENT No 1 to OPERATION ORDER No 52
by
Major I. C. MONTFORD
Commanding 1st Battalion THE RIFLE BRIGADE

Preliminary Defence Scheme for Brigade in Divisional Reserve

Reference Operation Order No 52, Companies will not counter attack without orders from Battalion H.Q., and will be disposed in the first instance with a view to defence. They must, however, be prepared to counter-attack at short notice.

(sd) C. C. NAUMANN Lieut.
A/Adjt
28th June, 1918 1st Batt. THE RIFLE BRIGADE

Issued to all recipients of O.O. 52

Appendix IX

O/1/191

```
!Issued to all!
!recipients of!
! Operation   !
! Orders No 52!
```

    The following establishment of S.A.A. will be maintained in Battle positions:-
        Each Company ... 12 boxes
        Battalion H.Q. ... 3 "

    The Transport Officer will deliver ammunition as shown below tomorrow afternoon:-

Company	Time	No of boxes	Place
"A"	3.0 p.m.	9	W.7.a.2.4.
"B"	3.0 p.m.	3	W.7.a.2.4.

    O.C. "A" and "B" Companies will arrange to have the necessary carrying parties there to place the ammunition in some central place in their Battle positions.
    O.C. "D" Coy. will arrange to carry 2 boxes, and O.C. "C" Coy. 1 box to Battalion H.Q. at V.6.d.8.2. at the same time.

                           (sd) J. A. DAVIDSON   Capt & Adjt
                              1st Batt THE RIFLE BRIGADE

29-6-16

Appendix IX   O/2/191

```
!Issued to all!
!recipients of!
! Operation   !
! Orders No 52!
```

The following establishment of S.A.A. will be maintained in Battle positions:-
    Each Company   ...   12 boxes
    Battalion H.Q. ...   3   "

The Transport Officer will deliver ammunition as shown below tomorrow afternoon:-

Company	Time	No of boxes	Place
"A"	3.0 p.m.	9	W.7.a.8.4.
"B"	3.0 p.m.	3	W.7.a.8.4.

O.C. "A" and "B" Companies will arrange to have the necessary carrying parties there to place the ammunition in some central place in their Battle positions.

O.C. "I" Coy. will arrange to carry 2 boxes, and O.C. "C" Coy. 1 box to Battalion H.Q. at V.6.d.8.8. at the same time.

(sd) J. A. DAVISON   Capt & Adjt
1st Batt THE RIFLE BRIGADE

4th Division

11th Infantry Bde.

1st Rifle Bde.

July to September

1915

11th Brigade.
4th Division.

1st BATTALION

THE RIFLE BRIGADE.

JULY 1918

Appendices attached:-

    Operation Orders.
    Casualties & Reinforcements.

Army Form C. 2118.

1st Bn. Rifle Brigade
July 1918 Vol 38

WAR DIARY
or
INTELLIGENCE SUMMARY.
(Erase heading not required.)

Instructions regarding War Diaries and Intelligence Summaries are contained in F. S. Regs., Part II. and the Staff Manual respectively. Title pages will be prepared in manuscript.

Place	Date	Hour	Summary of Events and Information	Remarks and references to Appendices
FRONT LINE VINAGE SECTOR	JULY. 1918		The Bn. relieved the 2nd Bn. Duke of Wellington's (West Riding) Regt. in the VINAGE sector as Centre front line Bn on the night of the 1st/2nd July. (Ref. O.O. No. 53, and Disposition Map attached) Defence Scheme was issued for the sector on the 2nd July. Ref. O.O. 54. On the 3rd Armoured Defence Scheme was issued cancelling O.O. 54. Ref. O.O. 55. From the 2nd to the 7th July the enemy was very quiet by day; hostile aeroplanes were very active during this, though very few ventured very far over the line: at night hostile artillery and machine guns were usually active, being especially so before 5 – 7. Hostile guns fire being very accurate along the tracks and roads. Enemy artillery harassing fire on the following targets, Rue du VINAGE road in Q.26, right of support line, CANAL BANK, P.36.6, and MOUNT BERNENCHON. Six patrols went out and much valuable information obtained: to PANN Q.27.a.29. Enemy visits seem high and found unoccupied; a L.G. post was established Q.27.c.7.55 C.Coy. by night activities occupied it by day. During the night of the 13th enemy artillery reached T Copse the Front Line. Ref. O.O. 56. from the 5th to 12th M.G. were somewhat active, but no snipers assist M.G. were observant, the weather E.A. have active, especially at night. During the inclemency of the weather E.A. were inactive. Six patrols went out, and an attempt was made to obtain an identity in the evening of the 12th; this however was unsuccessful. On the night of the 13th/14th the Bn. was relieved by the 15th Bn Kings' OWN LANCASTER REGT, A T.B. Corps remaining on the CANAL BANK and C of Coys an S.B.N. Sgt. having Ref. O.O. 57. Back to which the BUSMETTES. Ref. O.O. 56. Defence Scheme issued. The 15th Bn Hampshire Regt was in rear. During the tour the 1st Bn Somerset Light Infantry on our right, and the 1st Bn.	SHEET 36A.N.E. & Trench Plan & Maps attached to O.O.s APPENDIX I O.O. 53 O.O 53 APPENDIX II O.O 55 APPENDIX III O.O. 56 APPENDIX IV O.O. 57 APPENDIX V O.O. 57 APPENDIX VI
	to 13th			

1st Bn. Rifle Brigade
Army Form C. 2118.
July 1918.

WAR DIARY or INTELLIGENCE SUMMARY.
(Erase heading not required.)

Place	Date	Hour	Summary of Events and Information	Remarks and references to Appendices
FRONT LINE VINAGE SECTOR	July 1st to 13th		The following work was done:— Few trenches dug between Posts 53 and 57 in the FRONT LINE and Posts 550 and 557 in the SUPPORT LINE, about 1,000× BERM cleared, 300× parapet/parados lengthened thickened where required. SUPPORT LINE made ready to hinch boards, 600× double apron wire put out and general improvement in places of trenches. 982 hours of I.N.C.O + 8 men were also supplied for work under the O.C. 9th Field Coy R.E. and PIONEERS.	REF. SKETCH MAP.
BUSNETTES	14th to 20th		The first day was spent in cleaning up the billets. During the rest of the time training consisted of Platoon drill, Saluting, P.T. and games. R.S.M. M.O's, N.C.O's nightly, Lewis gun Classes paraded under the R.S.M. M.O's, N.C.O's nightly signed Subalterns. All Ranks enjoyed Cinema of 2nd Army Field Cinema Coy. The Lake & cafe, officers, cookers, shooting competitions and Foot Ball competitions for O.R's were carried out.	APPENDIX V O.O. 59 A
FRONT LINE VACANT WOOD SECTOR	20th to 31st		On 20th relieved the 1st Bn. ROYAL WARWICKSHIRE REGT in the front line on night of 13th Bn 20/21 July (Ref. O.O. 69 + Amendment No.1. During the tour the Bn. at the VACANT WOOD SECTOR. O.O. 50 + Amendment NO. 1. Defence Scheme. Enemy was fairly Quiet. Through the CANAL BANK, HATE FARM and the Pens A Coy. Continually received attention. EA were but very active and very few crossed the lines. On the 27th the B Coy Rd were A Coy and I Coy Rd Rd Rd S.D. 60. On the 30th at 8.20 pm. a patrol 1st Officer and 8 O.R's tried out to obtain an identification from a post at 93.c.6.6. previously reconnoitres. 5 prisoners were captured and brought in. C. Parker parker in all what went out and much valuable information was gained. Prisoners in Trenches were of 2nd Bn Suffolk Regt and on the [illeg] attention requested.	O.O. 59 APPENDIX VII O.O. 50 + Amendment APPENDIX IX O.O. 60. APPENDIX X

SECRET

APPENDIX I

OPERATION ORDER No 53
by
Major I. C. MONTFORD
Commanding 1st Batt. THE RIFLE BRIGADE

Ref. Sheet 36 A SE   30th JUNE, 1918   Copy No 15

RELIEF   I.   The Battalion will relieve the 2nd Batt. (DUKE OF WELLINGTONS) WEST RIDING REGT. in the front line to-morrow night the 1/2 July.
"I" Coy. R.B. will relieve "D" Coy. DUKES in the Front line
"C"   "   "   "   "   "B"   "   "   in the Support line.
"A"   "   "   "   "   "A"   "   "   in the Reserve line on the Left with 1 Platoon in the ROBECQ SWITCH
"B"   "   "   "   "   "C"   "   "   in the Reserve line on the right.

The relief will be carried out in the above order.
Battalion Headquarters will relieve last.
Battalion Headquarters will be at P.36.b.4.5. on the South side of the Canal.
The Regt. AID POST will be at P.36.d.2.9. There will be one squad of Battalion H.Q. Stretcher bearers at BRASS HAT FARM.

ADVANCE PARTIES   II.   The four Company Commanders will proceed in advance of their Companies. They will report at Battalion H.Q. 2nd DUKE OF WELLINGTONS Regt. at 8.30 p.m.

GUIDES   III.   Guides at the rate of 1 per platoon and one for Company H.Q. will be at P.36.a.9.7. at 10.30 p.m.

MOVE   IV.   The Battalion will move off in the above mentioned order with an interval of 100 yards between platoons, the leading platoon of "I" Coy. starting at 9.30 p.m.
     ROUTE: L'ECLEME and Route 4.
     DRESS: Fighting Order. Great Coats will be carried tied on the belt.

WIRING PARTIES   V.   2/Lieut. A. R. BURRIDGE will be in charge of the special wiring parties of "A" and "B" Coys. The Battalion Works Officer (Lieut. G.J. COLE, MC) will arrange to accomodate these parties in the vicinity of the CANAL BANK. They will move off with Battn. H.Q.

TRANSPORT   VI   One Lewis gun limber per Company and 2 for Battalion H.Q. will report at the various Headquarters at 8.0 p.m. to take trench kits, Lewis guns, etc. The limbers will move off to DOUCE CREME at 8.30 p.m. The personnel mentioned in R.B. 3 will accompany these limbers and off-load them at the above mentioned place.

KITS.   VII   Officers' kits, blankets, etc. will be collected at 5 p.m. and taken to the 1st Line Transport. The Mess cart will collect surplus Officers' mess kit at 9. p.m.

TAKING OVER   VIII   All trench stores, maps, defence schemes will be carefully taken over and receipts forwarded to Battalion H.Q. The programmes of work of the battalion relieved will be adhered to until further orders are issued by the works officer.

DISPOSITIONS   IX   Detailed maps showing numbered posts will be forwarded to reach Battalion H.Q. by 6.30 a.m. on the 2nd inst.

RATIONS   X   Rations and water will come up each night, arriving for the four companies at Q.28.b.9.5. at 11 p.m., for Battalion H.Q. at Q.31.a.6.6. at 10.30 p.m. Rations for "A" and "B" Companies' special wiring parties will come up with those of Battalion H.Q.
Rations for consumption on the 2nd inst. will be carried on the man, water for the same date being placed on the Lewis gun limbers.

P.T.O.

- 2 -

SUPPLY   XI.   "A", "B" and "C" Companies will be responsible for their own carrying. "B" Coy. will also carry supplies, rations, etc. for "I" Coy.

BODIES   XII.   All dead bodies and effects will be sent to Battalion H.Q. after dark.

REPORT   XIII   Completion of the relief will be reported by wire and runner in the case of the former by any sentence containing the code word "AUDREY"

ATTACK   XIV   In the event of an attack or preliminary bombardment developing the relief will not take place, or if commenced all troops of the Battalion South of the Canal will occupy their Battle positions.

         The troops of the Battalion North of the Canal will occupy the nearest trenches, reporting immediately to O.C. 2nd WEST RIDING REGT.

     ACKNOWLEDGE

J A Dawson

Captain
Adjt 1st Batt   THE RIFLE BRIGADE

DISTRIBUTION
Copy No 1 Commanding Officer
        2 2nd in Command
        3 Adjutant
        4 Asst Adjt
        5 Intelligence Offr
        6 Signalling Offr.
        7 Works Offr.
        8 O.C. "A" Coy
        9   "B" "
       10   "C" "
       11   "I" "
       12 Transport Offr
       13 Quartermaster
       14 Duke of Wellingtons
       15 War Diary No 1
       16 " ")
       17 File

APPENDIX II

(Preliminary Defence Scheme - RIEZ DU VINAGE Sector)
OPERATION ORDER No 54
by
Major I. C. MONTFORD
Commanding 1st Battalion THE RIFLE BRIGADE
1st JULY, 1918

REF Sheet 36 A SE   Copy No 13

DISPOSITIONS I. Battalion Headquarters P.36.b.4.5,
One Company, Front Line in Q.20.d.6.7. to house
Q.27.a.00.35. inclusive.
One Company, Support Line
Two Companies, Reserve Line.
(An amendment stating the exact Battalion boundaries
will be issued later)

ACTION IN CASE OF ATTACK II. (1) Each line will be held to the last. There will be no withdrawal of any sort. Troops will remain and fight in the lines they occupy.
(2) Should the enemy succeed in piercing the line held by the troops on our right a defensive flank will be formed along the road running through RIEZ DU VINAGE, from Q.27.a.3.5. to Q.26.c.2.0.
by (a) The front line Coy. Dropping posts back in echelon to gain touch with the support line.
(b) The support Company placing posts in echelon to gain touch with the reserve line.
Should a further penetration be made the reserve Companies are responsible for gaining touch with the troops on Canal Bank, by dropping posts back in echelon.
(3) Should a penetration be made on our left a defensive flank will be formed in the same way.
(4) The word "retire" will on no account be used. Any one heard using it will be shot at once.

WORKING PARTIES III In the event of an attack, all working parties will at once man the nearest trench, and will come under the Company Commander in whose area they are. They will notify Battalion H.Q. of their exact positon at the same time.

GAS SHELLING IV. In the event of Yellow Cross Gas shelling the following particulars will be wired PRIORITY to Battalion H.Q.
a. The area affected.
b. The degree of intensity of the shelling
c. The suspected location of the active batteries.

V. These orders will be explained to all ranks, and every man is to know what he has to do and how he is to do it should the different situations arise.

ACKNOWLEDGE

/ADavison
Captain
Adjt 1st Battn. THE RIFLE BRIGADE

Distribution:-
Copy No 1 Commanding Officer
2 2nd in Command
3 Adjutant
4 Asst/Adjt   10 O.C. "B" Coy
5 Works Offr.   11   "   "C" "
6 Intelligence Offr.   12   "   "D" "
7 Signalling Offr.   13 War Diary
8 Transport Offr & Quartermaster   14   "   "
9 O.C. "A" Coy.   15 File

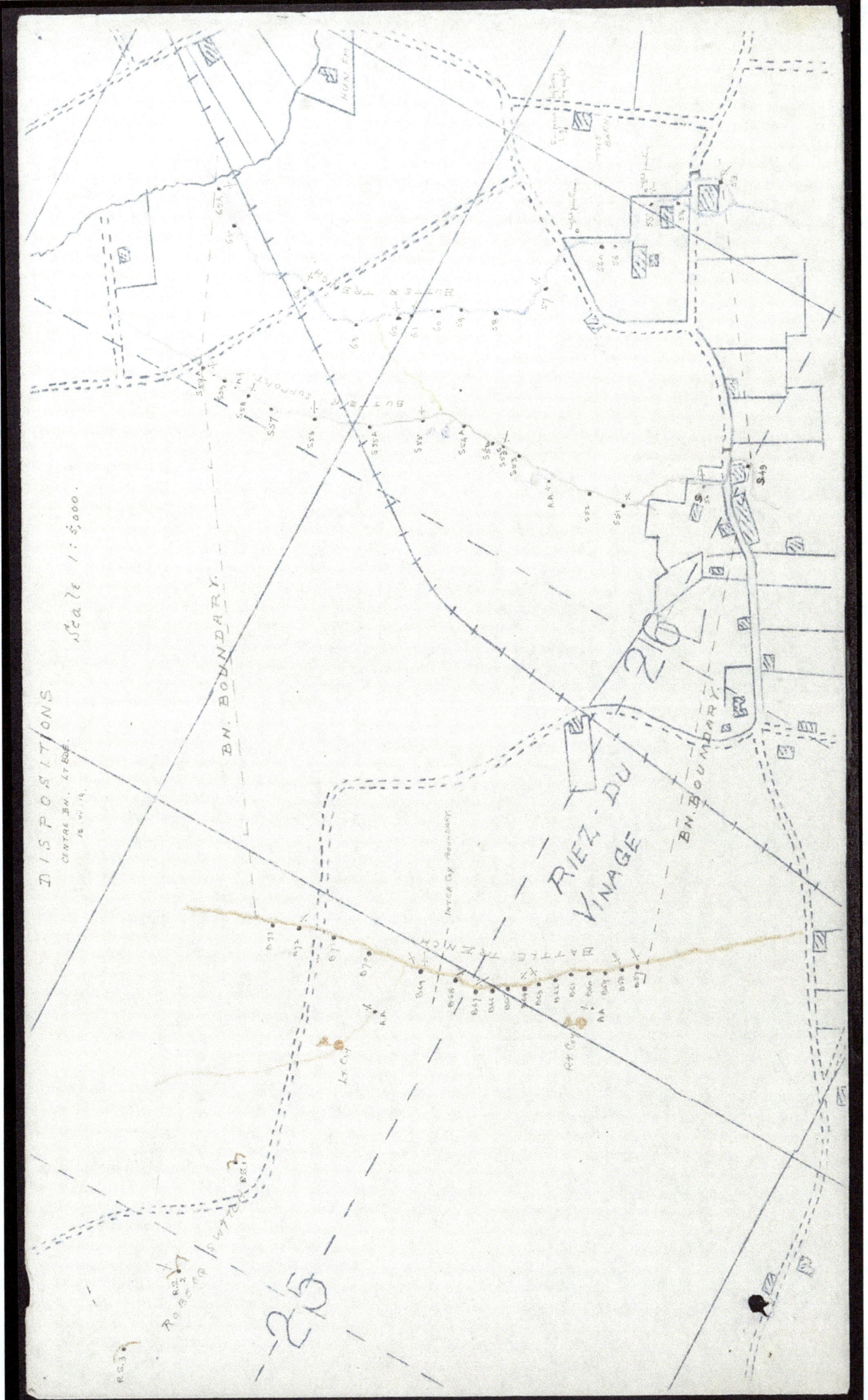

Operation Order No 55
by
Captain CFC Letts
Commanding
1st Bn. The Rifle Brigade

Ref Sheet (Preliminary Defence Scheme — VINTAGE SECTOR)
36cSE   3rd July 1918   Copy No. 11

I   Operation Order No 54 is cancelled

II DISPOSITIONS   Bn HQ. P.36.b.4.5.
    One Coy in Front Line in C.20.d.6c.68 to C.27.2.2.5/
    One Coy in the Support Line in C.20.d.2.5 to C.26.d.60.98 inclusive
    Two Coys in the Reserve line from C.25.d.88.62 to C.26.c.20.70
    The inter company boundary being C.25.b.90.15. One
    platoon of the Left Reserve Coy in ROBEC@ SWITCH

III GENERAL INSTRUCTIONS a) The main line of resistance throughout the
    ACTION IN CASE OF DIVISION will be the Reserve line First System which
    ATTACK   will be maintained at all costs.

    b) The Front and Support Lines will be considered the Outposts
       of the Battalion.

    c) The garrison of both lines will hold their positions until
       the last. There will be no withdrawal of any sort. It is to
       be made perfectly clear to all ranks that if forced
       out of any line by superior numbers they must not
       merely withdraw to the next line but that they
       must take advantage of every shell hole and fight
       every inch of the ground

    d) Troops in the Support line are the Battalion Reserves
       and troops in the Reserve line are the Brigade Reserve.
       In the case of the former should the Support Company
       Commander consider that a local counter-attack is likely
       to have a good effect he will act on his own initiative
       informing Battalion HQ of what he has done. The
       latter will not be used for a counter attack unless
       the enemy break into or through the Reserve line.
       In the latter case the local commander will
       counter attack immediately reporting his action direct
       to Brigade HQ repeating the information to Battalion
       HQ

    e) Not more than 50 per cent of the garrison of any line should
       be used for counter attacks unless relieved by troops from the
                                                              rear.

III (cont'd) f.) If an attack is delivered in great strength and the outpost line is penetrated such portions of the outpost line as have succeeded in holding their ground will hold on at all costs and drop posts in echelon to form a defensive flank, the idea being to hold on until a general counter attack can be delivered.

g.) The Bn HQ and one platoon of each of the 2 Reserve Coys will live in the works in rear of the Reserve line when completed. They will reinforce this line in case of attack. These works will ultimately be improved to form a line of supporting points behind the Reserve line or main line of resistance from the Left Divisional boundary to the CANAL BANK.

h.) Should the enemy pierce the line held by the troops on our right, a defensive flank will be formed along the road running through RIEZ du VINAGE from C.27.a.3.5. to C.26.c.2.0. by:

    a. The front line Coy dropping posts back in echelon to gain touch with the Support line

    b. The Support Coy placing posts in echelon to gain touch with the Reserve line.

    Similarly, should a further penetration be made the Reserve line Coys are responsible for gaining touch on the CANAL BANK.

k.) Should the enemy pierce the line held by the troops on our left, the same plan will be adopted, the defensive flank running along the railway as far as the Support line, then through the lunette at about C.26.b.0.9. to the Reserve line, then along the ROBECQ SWITCH.

l.) RAILWAY ALLEY will be used as a support line for defence to either flank.

m.) The word RETIRE will on no account be used. Anyone heard using it will be shot at once.

IV MACHINE GUNS. Machine guns are distributed in depth and are under the immediate tactical command of the Infantry Commander on the spot. Except in the case of urgent necessity the positions will not be moved without reference to the Machine Gun Battalion Commander.

V WORKING PARTIES In the event of an attack all working parties will at once man the nearest trench & will come under the Company Commander in whose area they are. They will notify Battalion HQ of their exact position at the same time.

VI REPORTS. OsC Coys are reminded of the immense importance of sending back early and accurate information to Battalion HQ not only if the attack has developed but during any preliminary bombardment at frequent intervals. Negative information is as valuable as positive. Visual signalling will at once be resorted to when the lines are cut.

After a bombardment has started a rough estimate of casualties must be sent in on every message sent. It must be remembered that each report of estimated casualties is understood to be a total & that each estimate cancels any previous report.

VII GAS SHELLING In the event of any yellow cross gas shelling the following particulars will be wired PRIORITY to Battalion H.Q.
    a. Area affected
    b. Degree of intensity of shelling
    c. Suspected location of batteries active

VIII These orders will be thoroughly explained to all ranks & every man should know exactly what he has to do & how he has to do it should any of the different situations arise

ACKNOWLEDGE

J M Davson Capt
Adjt
1st Bn The Rifle Brigade

Issued at
9 P.M.

Distribution :-
Copy No 1 OC A Coy   9. Signalling Officer
    2 " B "   10 M.O. Infy Bde
    3 " C "   11 OC War Diary
    4 " D "   12 File
    5 C.O.
    6 Adjt
    7 Lewis Gun Officer
    8 Intelligence Officer

SECRET   OPERATION ORDER No 56   APPENDIX IV
by
Captain C F C Sells
Comdg
Ref. Sheet   1st Bucks Rifle Brigade.
36A. SE   6th July 1918   Copy No. 9

RELIEF   I. "C" Company will relieve "I" Company in the front line tomorrow night 7th/8th inst.

II. All details will be arranged between Company Commanders concerned.

III. O.sC. A & B Coys will arrange to relieve their Lewis gun teams at present attached to I Company.

IV. All trench stores, defence schemes, aeroplane photos, papers concerning gas shoots and the establishment of ammunition etc will be carefully handed over. Receipts will be forwarded to reach Battalion HQ by not later than 6.30 PM on the 8th inst.

V. The Works Officer will arrange that work in progress is as little interfered with as possible.

VI. The Company Commanders concerned are reminded that the names of the platoon commanders on the flanks should reach Battalion HQ as soon as possible after the completion of the relief.

VII. Completion of the relief will be wired to Battn HQ by any sentence containing the codeword "TWINS."

VIII.   ACKNOWLEDGE

Issued at   J A Dawson
----- pm   Capt
                                  Adjutant
Distribution: 1st Bucks Rifle Brigade
Copy No 1   "A" Coy   Copy No 6   Adjt
"   2   B   "   7   Sig Officer
"   3   C   "   8   L.G.
"   4   D   "   9 & 10   War Diary
"   5   CO   "   11   File

Amendment No 1   APPENDIX III
to OPERATION ORDER No 55
by Captain C.F.L. LETTS
Commdg 1st Batt. THE RIFLE BRIGADE
(Preliminary Defence Scheme - VINAGE SECTOR)

The garrison of the ROBECQ SWITCH will on no account be used for a counter attack.

3/7/18
Issued to all recipients
of O.O. No 55

(sd) J.A. Durcan   Capt
                   Adjt
1st Batt. The Rifle Brigade

Secret   APPENDIX VI

Operation Order 57
by
Lieut-Col R. F. Meiklejohn D.S.O., M.C.
Comdg
1st Bn The Rifle Brigade
PRELIMINARY DEFENCE SCHEME whilst in Divisional Reserve

Ref:-   Copy No
Sheet 36 a S.E.   12th July 1918.   13

I. Operation Order No 52 and amendments will not come into force until 6.0 a.m. on the 17th inst when A & B Companies on the CANAL BANK will have been relieved by 2 Companies of the 1st Hampshire Regt. Until the above time the Battalion will take up the positions mentioned below, in the event of "BATTLE POSITIONS" being ordered, being ready to move at 1½ hours notice:-

   i. A & B Coys will remain in their positions on the CANAL BANK the boundaries being as follows:-
      a) B Coy from P.29.c.7.2.(exclusive) to where the front line 2nd System joins CANAL BANK in P.36.b.4.5.(excl)
      b) A Coy from P.36.b.4.5.(inclusive) to Q.32.c.6.9.(incl)

   ii. C Coy will move to the front and support lines 2nd System from W.2.a.40.95 to CANAL BANK P.36.b.4.5.

   iii. I Coy will move to Reserve Line 2nd System from W.16.2.6. through Q.31.c.5.2. to P.36.d.6.0

   iv. Battalion H.Q. will move to W.1.a.25.75.

   v. The position of the Regt Aid Post will be notified later.

II. On the order "BATTLE POSITIONS" being received C & I Coys will at once fall in, and the Company Commanders will either send a representative or report in person to the Commanding Officer at Battalion H.Q. On receiving the order, C & I Coys will move off via CENSE LA VALLEE, the leading troops will not pass through this village until the 1st Som LI are clear.

   Dress. Fighting order, Great coats will be carried rolled on the belt. Haversack rations & full water bottles will also be carried.

III. Ten full water tins will be delivered to C & I Coys on the 13th inst. These will be carried up by the Companies concerned.

IV. On arrival at BATTLE POSITIONS C & I Coys will send a runner to Battalion H.Q. stating that they are in position.

V. The positions mentioned in para I are primarily for defence but C & I Coys will hold themselves in readiness to counter-attack should the enemy cross the CANAL, on receipt of orders from Battalion H.Q.

VI. The establishment of S.A.A. in each position is 18 boxes. Indents to complete should be submitted as soon as possible.

VII. Each of A & B Coys will be responsible for the defence of the bridges in their respective areas. Definite parties will be detailed for this purpose. There is a party of sappers detailed for the repair of each bridge and the Company Comdr. will get into touch with the N.C.Os in charge. The Company Commander on the spot is responsible for giving the order to destroy the bridges, should it appear likely that a large number of the enemy are preparing to rush them. All bridges should first be swung into the side and then sunk by perforating the barrels with rifle fire.

VIII. A & B Coys will be responsible for cutting the crops etc in front of the Battle Positions of I & C Coys respectively during the three days on the CANAL BANK.

IX. Should more ammunition be required there are dumps at the following places:—
    WINDMILL W.1.d.1.2.
    HOUSE at V.12 d.5.5.
    DOUVE FARM P.36 a.9.5.

X. The above orders will have effect, up to 6.0 A.M. on the 17th inst at which time Operation Order No 52 and amendments will again come into force.

XI. ACKNOWLEDGE

Issued at 11.50 p.m.

J.A. Dawson Captain
Adjutant
1st Bn The Rifle Brigade.

A map is attached (to Coys only) showing the positions affected by these orders and also by O.O. No. 52.

Distribution:— Copy No 1 C.O.   Copy No 8 11th Brigade.
                    "   2 Adjt.   "   9 O.C. A Coy
                    "   3 M.O.   "   10 " B "
                    "   4   "   11 " C "
                                         "   12 " I "
                                         "   13 & 14 War Diary
                                              etc.

SECRET   Operation Order No 58   APPENDIX V
by
Lieut-Col R. T. Fellowes D.S.O. M.C.
Commanding
1st Bn The Rifle Brigade

Ref Sheet:- 36^a NE   13th July 1918.   Copy No. 15

RELIEF I. The Battalion will be relieved in the front line tonight 13th/14th inst by the 1st Bn (K.O.) Royal Lancaster Regt.

    C Coy R.B. will be relieved by D Coy K.Lings.Own.
    I   "   "   B   "   " .
    A   "   "   C   "   " .
    B   "   "   A   "   " .

The order of relief will be as shown above, Bn. H.Q. will be relieved last.

GUIDES II. Guides, at the rate of 1 per platoon (3 platoons per Coy) & 1 for Coy H.Q. will be provided. They will report to the Signalling Officer at Bn. H.Q. at 8.30 pm tonight. Each guide will bring with him a chit stating the exact platoon he has to guide in. The Signalling Officer will arrange to have these guides at BLACKFRIARS BRIDGE at 10.0 pm.

ROUTE III OF RELIEF The route of relief will be as follows:- For C Coy; the track from BLACKFRIARS BRIDGE, P 36 a, - house, G 31 b 8.9. - MEZ - Bn HQ road - light railway.

           For A, B & I Coys, the main track through G 20 central.

TRENCH IV STORES A list of all trench stores to be handed over will be forwarded to Bn. H.Q. by 11.0 am today. These lists will be carefully checked. All work, defence schemes, trench maps & aeroplane photos will be handed over. All receipts will be forwarded to reach Battalion H.Q. by 12.0 noon 14th inst. Care will be taken to see that all water tins, empty S.A.A. packs, gas rattles etc are taken out. C & I Coys will make up all deficiencies in S.A.A. etc before leaving their present positions.

MOVE V. On completion of the relief:- 1. a) A & B Coys will move to the CANAL BANK. They will occupy the positions vacated by 2 Coys 2nd Lancs Fus. between C.29.c.6.9. - and P. 29.c.7.2. (exclusive); A Coy will be on the right and B Coy will be on the left; the inter company boundary being P 36 b 4.5.; inclusive to B Coy.

V.i (Contd) b) On arrival, Capt T.W. Carlyle will assume command of these 2 Coys & will report both his name and the hour of arrival to the 12th Infantry Brigade through Bn H.Q. at DOUCE CREME FME; in the case of the latter the code-word "AQUATIC" will be used. (This wire will be repeated to H.Q. 11th Inf Bde & Bn H.Q.)

c) He will arrange to keep 2 orderlies at the C/m Bn H.Q. to carry any messages addressed to him, which will be sent through these H.Q.

d) On arrival A & B Coys will come under the tactical command of the B.G.C. 12th Inf Bde unless & until the Reserve Bde mans their Battle Positions.

ii. C & I Coys will move back to billets in BUSNETTES. The Quartermaster will make all preliminary arrangements.

TRANSPORT VI. The T.O. will arrange to have one Lewis gun limber for each C & I Coys and 2 for Battalion H.Q. at their respective ration dumps at 11 p.m.

RATIONS VII. The Quartermaster will arrange to send up to A & B Coys
etc   their rations & water. These will arrive each night at DOUCE CREME FME at 11.0 p.m. Tonight, 13/14th inst, they will arrive at 12.30 a.m.

ATTACK VIII. In the event of a hostile bombardment or attack developing, the relief will not take place. All troops of the 1st Kings Own, North East of the CANAL BANK will man the nearest trenches, placing themselves at the disposal of the C.O. All troops South of the CANAL will man their Battle Positions.

RETURN IX. The following returns will be submitted by Coys to reach Bn M.Q. by not later than 12 o noon on the 14th inst:-
a) Total no of picks & shovels in possession.
b) If every man has spare clothes to complete.
c) No if any required to complete.
Attention is called to the fact that picks must be shown separately from shovels.

PRELIMINARY X. (Operation Order No 6 - (R.B.) Peace Scheme for Brigade
DEFENCE in Brigade Reserve) is attached herewith.
SCHEME.
REPORT. XI. Completion of the relief will be reported by visual and by wire. The wire will be followed by any sentence containing the code word "DEEP".

XII. ACKNOWLEDGE   Davison Capt & Adjt
Issued at 2.30 p.m.   The Rifle Brigade.

SECRET

OPERATION ORDER No 5 9
by
Lieut.Colonel R.T.FELLOWES, DSO, MC
Commanding 1st Battalion THE RIFLE BRIGADE

APPENDIX VIII

Sheet.36 A S.E.   19th JULY, 1918   Copy No 13

RELIEF I. The Battalion will relieve the 1st Battalion ROYAL WARWICK-
SHIRE REGIMENT in the Front Line to-morrow night, 20th inst.
"A" Coy. R.B. will relieve "C" Coy. R.W.Regt. in the front line
"B" " " " " " " " in the support line.
"C" " " " " " "D" " " on Canal Bank.
"I" " " " " " "A" " " in the front line,
                                                                    2nd System.
  Battalion Headquarters W.2.d.1.6.
  The position of the Aid Post will be notified later.
  The two special wiring parties of "C" and "I" Coys. under
2/Lieut. J. HARVEY and 2/Lieut. W.J.WOODSIDE,MM, will be accomo-
dated in the BETHUNE-HINGES LINE from W.2.b.20.65 to W.8.b.2.8.
The Lewis gun officer will arrange to place these parties in
position.
  the ORDER OF RELIEF will be as follows:-
    "A", "B", "C", "I", H.Q.-

ADVANCE II. The four Company Commanders will proceed in advance of
PARTIES   their Companies. They will report at the respective
Company H.Qs of the 1st Batt ROYAL WARWICKSHIRE Regt. at 8.0
p.m. for taking over.

GUIDES III. Guides will be provided as follows.
  At the rate of 1 per Platoon and 1 for Company H.Q. at
W.8.a.0.8. at 11.0 p.m.
  The two special wiring parties of "C" and "I" Coys. will
march in rear of Battalion H.Q., no guides being provided.

MOVE IV. Companies will move off with an interval of 100 yards
between Platoons, the leading Platoon of "A" Coy. moving off at
9.30 p.m.
  ROUTE:- Cross roads in V.16.b. - road junction V.17.a. -
thence via route 2.
  DRESS:- Fighting order: great coats will be carried
rolled on the belt.

RATIONS V. Rations for consumption on the 21st inst. will be carried
on the man. On each successive night, rations etc. will be
delivered at W.3.c.1.6. at 10.30 p.m.
  O.C. "I" Coy. will arrange to draw and deliver to the
two forward Companies ("A" and "B"). He will also draw his own.
  O.C. "C" Company will be responsible for his own rations

TRANSPORT VI. One Lewis gun limber per Company and 2 for Battalion H.Q.
  will be loaded and will move off at 8.30 p.m. to
W.3.c.1.6., where they will be unloaded by the men detailed to
accompany them. The Lewis guns, 30 tins of water per Company,
Trench kits, etc. will be placed on these limbers, which will
proceed independently to the ration dumps.
  Packs, Officers' valises, Mess stores, will be packed
and dumped outside billets by 6.0 p.m. The Transport Officer
will arrange to collect these and take them back to the 1st Line
Transport.
  Officers Commanding Companies are reminded that caps will
on no account be taken into the forward area.

TAKING VII. All Defence schemes, Aeroplane photographs, Lewis gun
OVER   and Anti-Aircraft positions, Trench stores, etc. will be carefully
taken over. Duplicates of receipts will be forwarded to Battalion
H.Q. as soon as possible after completion of relief. All details
of work in progress, and work proposed, will also be taken over.

P. T. O.

- 2 -

DISPOSITION VIII. Detailed maps showing the number of posts will be forwarded to reach Battalion H.Q. by 6.30 a.m. on the 21st inst.

ATTACK IX. In the event of attack or preliminary bombardment developing relief will not proceed; and if commenced all troops south-west of the support line, 2nd system, will occupy their Battle Positions as detailed in Operation Order No 52. Troops of the Battalion north of this line will occupy the nearest trenches and place themselves at the disposal of the Officer Commanding the 1st Batt ROYAL WARWICKSHIRE Regt.

REPORT X. Completion of the relief will be reported by wire AND VISUAL. In the case of the former by any sentence containing the code word "TROPHIE".

XI. ACKNOWLEDGE.

JA Dawson
Captain
Adjutant
1st Battn. THE RIFLE BRIGADE

Distribution
Copy No 1 Commanding Officer
2 2nd in Command
3 Adjutant
4 Lewis gun officer
5 Signalling officer
6 O.C. "A" Coy
7 "B"
8 "C"
9 "I"
10 Transport officer
11 Quartermaster
12 O.C. 1st Bn Royal Warwicks
13 War Diary
14 " "
15 File

APPENDIX VII

SECRET

OPERATION ORDER No 59 A.
by
Lieut.Colonel R.T.FELLOWES, D.S.O., M.C.
Commanding 1st Battalion THE RIFLE BRIGADE
16th JULY, 1918

Ref Sheet 36 A S.E.   Copy No 11

RELIEF   I.   "A" and "B" Companies will be relieved on the CANAL BANK tonight, 16th inst., by two Companies 1st HAMPSHIRE REGT.

GUIDES   II. Guides at the rate of 2 per platoon and 1 for Company H.Q. will be provided: these will rendezvous at DOUCE CREME at 10.45 p.m.

TRANSPORT III. One Lewis Gun limber per Coy. will be at DOUCE CREME FME at 10.45 p.m. to bring back Lewis Guns, trench kits, etc., to billets. All empty water tins, gas rattles, etc. will be brought out.

BILLETS   IV. The Quartermaster will arrange the necessary billeting parties and will also arrange to have rations for the 17th inst. in billets.

TRENCH   V.   All trench stores, defence schemes, etc. will be carefully
STORES   handed over, and the receipts obtained will be forwarded to Battalion H.Q. after completion of the relief.

REPORT   VI. Completion of the relief will be reported by wire direct to 11th Infantry Brigade H.Q. through the Battalion H.Q. at DOUCE CREME FME, B.A.B. code being used. This wire will be repeated to Battalion Headquarters.

(sd) G. J. COLE   Lieut,
Act. Adjt 1st Batt THE RIFLE BRIGADE

DISTRIBUTION
O.C. "A" Company	Copy 1
"B" "	2
1st HAMPSHIRE REGT	3
Commanding Officer	4
2nd in Command	5
Adjutant	6
Act. Adjuant	7
Signalling Officer	8
Transport Offr.	9
Quartermaster	10
War Diary	11 & 12
File	13

SECRET   OPERATION ORDER No 50   APPENDIX IX
                                    by
                          Major I. C. MONTFORD
                    Commanding 1st Battalion, THE RIFLE BRIGADE
                 Preliminary Defence Scheme for RIGHT BATTALION - PACAUT Sector

Ref Sheet 36A S.E.   15th JUNE, 1918   Copy No 13
_____

DISPOSITIONS 1.   Battalion H.Q. W.8.d.4.0.
                    One Company Front line Divisional boundary Q.34.D.55.40.
                        to Q.34.c.00.45.
                    One Company Support line South East edge of PACAUT WOOD
                        to extreme reserve line, right of Support line
                    One Company CANAL BANK W.3.b.3.7. to W.4.a.0.0.
                    One Company Front and Support lines 2nd System. One
                        platoon about W.3.c.5.8. two platoons about
                        W.3.d.2.4.

ACTION IN CASE OF
ATTACK   2.   (1.) Each line will be held to the last and there will
                         be no withdrawal of any sort. Troops will remain
                    and fight in the lines they occupy.
                    (2) Should the enemy penetrate the Front, and the
                         Support Company Commander decide to counter attack
                    at least one platoon will be left in the support line, as a
                    garrison of that trench.
                    (3) Should the enemy succeed in penetrating the front
                         held by the troops on our right a defensive flank
                    will be formed behind the PANNERIE - PONT L'HINGES road behind
                    the wire. The echelon posts will be used.
                    (4) Should the enemy appear to be approaching the CANAL
                         the Reserve Company COMMANDER will dribble up two
                    platoons to reinforce the Company on the CANAL BANK on his own
                    initiative. The remaining platoon will await the arrival of
                    the Company of the reserve Brigade before moving. In the
                    event of this happening the nearest Company of Reserve Brigade,
                    Brigade H.Q. and Battalion H.Q. will be notified immediately.
                    Care will be taken to keep touch with the troops on the right.
                    (5) It should be impossible for the enemy to make a
                         frontal attack on that portion of PACAUT WOOD that
                    we hold.
                         The garrison in PACAUT WOOD is therefore to give all
                    possible assistance to the troops on the flanks should they be
                    driven back. The wood is on no account to be given up. The
                    covering fire afforded will assist in the counter attack.
                    (6) The word "Retire" will on no account be used. Any-
                    one heard using it will be shot at once.

RESPONSIBILITY 3.   There is a footbridge at W.3.b.3.7. Two Sappers of the
FOR BRIDGES   406 Field Coy. R.E. live on the CANAL BANK near the bridge
OVER CANAL   who are responsible for the upkeep and repair of the bridge,
                    and for swinging it when necessary. The Company Commander
                    on the CANAL BANK will get into touch with these men and make
                    himself known to them. He will be responsible for giving the
                    order to destroy the bridge. The Bridge will then be swung
                    into our own bank, and the barrels will be perforated with
                    rifle fire. The order for the demolition will be given
                    should it appear likely that the enemy is going to cross the
                    Canal in force.

WORKING   4.   In case of attack all working parties North of the Canal
PARTIES   Bank will occupy the nearest trenches, placing themselves
                    under the nearest Company Commander. They will at once
                    notify Battalion H.Q. of their action. This does not apply
                    to the Canal Bank Company who will make their way at once to
                    the South side of the Canal Bank.

              5.   The above order will be thoroughly explained to all ranks
                    ACKNOWLEDGE

AMENDMENT No 1
to
OPERATION ORDER No 50
by
Lieut. Col. R.T.FELLOWES DSO, MC.
Commdg 1st Battalion, THE RIFLE BRIGADE

1. / DISPOSITION of Support Company should read:- S.E. corner of PACAUT WOOD to Divisional Boundary W.4.a.4.4."

2. ACTION IN CASE OF ATTACK.
  (1) Should any part of our line be entered, troops on the flanks of the portion entered will immediately take steps to prevent the enemy extending his gains, and will also counter-attack him vigorously with all weapons, both from the flanks in the trenches and above ground.
  (2) Should the enemy succeed in forcing back the troops on our right and a defensive flank has to be formed, the front line Company will drop posts back in echelon South of 1A post to touch up in the first instance, with the original front line of the 3rd Division on our right, at about W.4.a.25.20. Should a deeper penetration take place further posts will be established along the new communication trench to touch up with the Support line.
      If necessary the Support Company Commander will drop posts back in echelon to touch up with the CANAL BANK.
  (3) Front and Support line Company Commanders will reconnoitre and ear-mark at once certain places along, and in front of, the South East corner of PACAUT WOOD which will be occupied by Lewis guns from their Companies in the event of the entire front or support line garrisons being forced out of their trenches. Lewis guns in their selected positions must be able to fire towards the North East, East and South East.
  (4) Every inch of ground, every shell hole, depression in the ground, etc. between the Front line and Support line, and between the Support line and the Canal Bank, will be defended to the last. There will be no complete withdrawal from one line of defence to the next organised line in rear.
  (5) Reference para. 2 (iv) of O.O No 50
      (a) For "2 Platoons" read "his Company" and delete from "The remaining platoon" to "Before moving". The 3rd platoon will NOT be left behind, but care will be taken to let the nearest Company of "A" Battn. of the Reserve Brigade know that the Reserve Company has moved forward to the Canal Bank.
      (b) Add at end of last sentence "Who will be informed that the Reserve Company is going to move forward". At all times the right post of the reserve Company will be in touch on the Divisional boundary with the Battalion on our right".
  (6) Should it appear likely to the Company Commander on the Canal Bank that the enemy would reach the Canal Bank, he will fire two white Very Lights in quick succession as a signal to the Trench Mortars to bring back their S.O.S. line on to the North East bank of the CANAL. This signal will only be used BY DAY.

(sd) J. A. DAVISON   Capt.
                    Adjt
21st July, 1918   1st Battn. THE RIFLE BRIGADE

Issued to all recipients of O.O. No 50

SECRET

Operation Order No 66
by
Lieut Colonel R.T. Fellowes D.S.O. M.C.
Commanding
1st Bn The Rifle Brigade

Ref
Sheet 36a SE.   27th July 1918   Copy No. 10

1. a) B. Coy will relieve A Coy in the front line. The relief will be carried in daylight & will be complete by 3.0 pm Friday.
b) L Coy will relieve C Coy on the CANAL BANK. The relief will be complete by 3.0 AM tomorrow the 28th inst.

II. All details of the reliefs will be arranged between the Company Commanders concerned.

III. The work in progress will be as little interfered with as possible.

IV. All details of work, Defence schemes, Aeroplane photographs, instructions regarding concentration & Gas shoots, trench stores etc will be carefully handed over. Receipts will be forwarded to Bn HQ by 6.30 am on the 28th inst.

V. In the event of an attack or preliminary bombardment developing the relief will not take place. All troops on the move will man the nearest trenches. The officer or N.C.O. in charge, reporting to the Company Commander in whose area he is, the action he has taken. Such information will at once be notified to Bn HQ.

VI. The completion of the relief will be wired to Bn HQ by the use of any sentence containing the code word "KOSHER". Such messages will also be sent by visual.

ACKNOWLEDGE.

Issued at
AM.

J.A. Duncan Capt & Adjt
1st Bn The Rifle Brigade

APPENDIX IX

11th Brigade.
4th Division.

1st BATTALION

THE RIFLE BRIGADE.

AUGUST 1 9 1 8

Appendices attached :-
Operation Orders & Maps.

Army Form C. 2118.

WAR DIARY
of
INTELLIGENCE SUMMARY.

1st Bn. The Rifle Brigade.

August 1918.

(Erase heading not required.)

Instructions regarding War Diaries and Intelligence Summaries are contained in F. S. Regs., Part II. and the Staff Manual respectively. Title pages will be prepared in manuscript.

Place	Date	Hour	Summary of Events and Information	Remarks and references to Appendices
PACAUT SECTOR	1st – 2nd		Rules unmet & remaining fine, especially active in vicinity of LE CAUROY and CANAL BANK near HATE FM. Hostile machine gun snipers, Trench mortars & aircraft inactive. Battalion was relieved by the 2nd Bn. The Lancashire Fusiliers & moved back to billets in BUSNETTES.	Ref. O.O. N° 61 Appendix 1.
	3rd		BUSNETTES.– The first three days were spent in cleaning up and reorganising. ORGANISATION. During the period, Divn. Inter Platoon demonstration by special platoon in open order, C.O.'s inspection and platoon demonstration & BCOL. At 2. p.m. on the 7th Battalion moved up to battle positions nine to the withdrawal of the enemy in this sector. At 7 p.m. order was received to return to BUSNETTES. Casualties – Officers, NIL. O. Rs. NIL.	Ref. O.O. 62 Appendix 2.
VINAGE SECTOR	9th		Battalion relieved in the front (outpost) Coy. B the 2nd Bn. the Seaforth Highlanders, the 2nd Bn. C Wiltshire Regt., & the 1st Royal Innskilling Regiment in the VINAGE SECTOR. Strength of the Battalion 20 officers 607 O.Rs. Support of a 2nd Gordon Regt. on the right, 14th Royal Highlanders on the left.	Ref. O.O. 63 Appendix 3. 1:10,000 Trench map.
	10th		Patrols were established post E. of the TURBEAUTÉ, but were afterwards driven in to the line of the river. Enemy artillery continuously active all day and night, m.guns and snipers were also very active. Late in the day patrols were established along the NINJE'S ROAD to the S. of PACAUT and near BOHEME. The enemy did not show much sign of withdrawing further, and was extremely alert when attempts to advance were made.	Ref. O. 0564,65 and MAP Appendix #3.

WAR DIARY
INTELLIGENCE SUMMARY
(Erase heading not required.)

Army Form C. 2118.

Instructions regarding War Diaries and Intelligence Summaries are contained in F. S. Regs., Part II. and the Staff Manual respectively. Title pages will be prepared in manuscript.

1st Bn. The Rifle Brigade

Place	Date	Hour	Summary of Events and Information	Remarks and references to Appendices
	11th		Posts were established E. of the River TURBEAUTE, 200x depth; nearly the whole line of the HINGES ROAD was also occupied. In the early morning the enemy attacked our left posts with about 60 men; they were driven off and about a dozen casualties inflicted & one prisoner captured, valuable information being obtained. During the night the Right Coy extended to relieve the Heavy Artillery on the right; sending a Coy in support to the whole line of the HINGES ROAD at PACAUT; S. of the River PACAUT. Reconnaissances were maintained into the enemy's lines. Bombardments were very active. Hostile machine guns & snipers were still very active.	Ref. 0.05.64.65 & MAP Appendix 3.
	12th		In the evening the Bn. was relieved by the 1st Somersets Light Infantry and went to left support Bn posts; A Coy in its old front line, B Coy in Support + C + D in Support Bn reserve.	Ref. 0.05.66.67 & MAP Appendix 4.
LEFT SUPPORT VINAGE SECTOR			Casualties – OFFICERS. 3. Lt. C.J.C. SCHUSTER Killed. Major C.G.C. LETTS. Wounded. 2/Lt. S.H. BURCH " OTHER RANKS. 33. Killed 7. Wounded 20. Wounded at duty 5. Accidentally Wounded 1.	

Army Form C. 2118.

WAR DIARY
or
INTELLIGENCE SUMMARY.
(Erase heading not required.)

Instructions regarding War Diaries and Intelligence Summaries are contained in F. S. Regs., Part II. and the Staff Manual respectively. Title pages will be prepared in manuscript.

1st. Bn. The Rifle Brigade

Place	Date	Hour	Summary of Events and Information	Remarks and references to Appendices
LEFT SUPPORT VIMAGE SECTOR	13th – 18th		During the period very little shelling was experienced except for some mortars for shelling of the old front line in the early morning of the 13th. A considerable amount of platoon training was carried out, including patrol practice, attack + artillery formations, and continuous digging. Organised salvage parties were sent out from the front line, and large quantities of salvage were collected. One medium T.M. and two rocket mortars were brought back, having fallen into our hands during the advance of the previous 3 days. Work was done on the new line in front of the old front line on new breastworks. During the evening of the 16th Battalion Commander visited the B Coy in the old front line, and A Coy moved back to the new line in the Support Line. Shortly after the relief had been carried out the Army Commander visited the new front line. Casualties: OFFICERS – 2. 2/Lt. E. C. GARTON Wounded Gas. 2/Lt. E. J. FREEAR " " OTHER RANKS. – 37 Killed – 1. Wounded – 36.	Ref. S.R.N.12 wef Appendix 4.
VIMAGE SECTOR	18th –		On the night of the 18th the Bn. relieved the 1st Bn. the Hampshire Regt. on outpost Pn. Our troops on the right were with the 1st Hampshires, + on the left the 24th Welch Regiment. Enemy was very active with M.G. and snipers in the early morning. At 7 a.m. patrols pushed forward and established themselves 150° W. of PARADISE ROAD: The	Ref. O.O. 68/69 Appendix 5. (see sketch map)
	19 –			

Army Form C. 2118.

WAR DIARY
INTELLIGENCE SUMMARY.
(Erase heading not required.)

Instructions regarding War Diaries and Intelligence Summaries are contained in F. S. Regs., Part II. and the Staff Manual respectively. Title pages will be prepared in manuscript.

Summary of Events and Information 1st Bn. The Rifle Brigade

Place	Date	Hour	Summary of Events and Information	Remarks and references to Appendices
RIGHT SUPPORT VINAGE SECTOR.	20th		Bn. then moved forwards and after establishing this time moved across the PARADISE ROAD and that the approximate dispositions were as follows: - Picquets 200° E of PARADISE ROAD and support about 200° W. of two road. Bn. enemy shelled the vicinity of PARADIS very heavily at intervals during the day and night. Bn. H.Q. moved at 12.30 p.m. to three rifle pits between QUENTIN and the TURBEAUTÉ. Patrols were pushed out early from the start were maintained. On advance of about 900° in depth was made along the Bn. the day before. Sunk, and the same mentioned inside the lines in the vicinity of during the morning. Bn. enemy continued to shell the PARADISE ROAD and the vicinity very heavily, especially in front of ABBEY ROAD. Machine guns & snipers were more active than the day before, supplied from posts and an advance by the 1st Somersetshire Light Infantry In the evening, the Bn. was relieved by the 1st Somersetshire Light Infantry and had an night outpost Bn. Casualties - OFFICERS 2. CAPT. V.J. WHEELER wounded 19th - 20th. 2/Lt R.P. WINSLOE " OTHER RANKS 21. Killed - 6 Wounded - 13 Missing - 2	Ref. Sketch Map. see Appendix 5. Ref. O.O.70. Appendix 6 (see sketch map.)
	21st		Very Quiet. Bn. rested.	

Army Form C.2118.

WAR DIARY
or
INTELLIGENCE SUMMARY.
(Erase heading not required.)

Summary of Events and Information 1st Bn. The Rifle Brigade

Place	Date	Hour	Summary of Events and Information	Remarks and references to Appendices
	22nd		In the afternoon the Bn. was relieved by the 1st Warwicks advancing its own left, and the 1st Suffolks to their right, and moved to BUSNETTES at 3 p.m.	Ref. O.O.71 Appendix 6.
	23rd		The Bn. marched back to FAUCQUEMBERGUES, Bn. H.Q. moving off at 7.30 a.m. on arrival the troops were dismissed to their various billets, the remainder of the day being spent in reorganising the Bn.	Ref. O.O.72 Appendix 7.
	24th		During the morning Company and platoon training was carried out; in the afternoon orders were received for a further move and Transport moved off between 7 & 8 p.m.	
	25th		Bn. moved off at 7 a.m. to LILLERS where it entrained. On arrival at BRYAS it detrained and marched to FOUFFLIN-RICAMETZ, commencing about 4 p.m.	Ref. O.O.73 Appendix 8.
	26th		Company and platoon training carried out during the morning. Orders for Ltt. VILLERS AU BOIS were received at 2.30 p.m., and Bn. marched off at 5.20 p.m. Advance was reached at 1 a.m. on 27th, and Bn. was billeted in huts.	
	27th		Bn. rested; preparations for further moves were made.	
	28th		Bn. moved from VILLERS AU BOIS at 2 p.m. and advanced, after detraining at road junction S. of BLANGY took the Bn. moved up to the old front system and relieved Germans (front and support lines) S.E. of MONCHY. Dispositions:- T Coy on right of Light Railway and A Coy on the left in the old German System C Coy on the right and B Coy on the left in the old British System. Strength of Bn. 20 officers 650 O.R.s.	Ref. O.O.74 Appendix 9.

Army Form C. 2118.

WAR DIARY
or
INTELLIGENCE SUMMARY.
(Erase heading not required.)

Summary of Events and Information 1st. Bn. The Rifle Brigade

Instructions regarding War Diaries and Intelligence Summaries are contained in F. S. Regs., Part II. and the Staff Manual respectively. Title pages will be prepared in manuscript.

Place	Date	Hour	Summary of Events and Information	Remarks and references to Appendices
	29/9		In the morning the Bn moved forward and relieved a portion of the 1st Bn.	Ref. O.O. 73 + map. Appendix 10.
SENSÉE RIVER	30th		Scenced P.S. on the SENSÉE RIVER J. W. of ETERPIGNY. The attack tonight on the day was thoroughly heavy and very heavy casualties were suffered in consequence. At 4 p.m. the Bn attacked the village of ETERPIGNY and the wood, soon after ZERO; prisoners captured about 35 and 3 machine guns. The Bn then went on to continue attack.	Ref. O.O. 76 Appendix 11
ETERPIGNY			Enemy M.G. and artillery fire was very heavy and its advance through the village was very difficult owing to its mud and river growth. Early in the morning the 1st HAMPSHIRE REGT. was ordered to relieve by dawn : part of I. C. and B Coy. were relieved, but A Coy. was unable to be relieved. The enemy artillery fire was very heavy again but slackened down towards the latter part of the day. During the night the Bn was relieved by the 2nd LANCASHIRE FUSILIERS and moved back to the western end of SEVENTY RIDGE.	Ref. to be in Appendix 12.
ETERPIGNY	31st			

WAR DIARY
INTELLIGENCE SUMMARY.
(Erase heading not required.)

Army Form C. 2118.

Summary of Events and Information 1st Bn. The Rifle Brigade

Casualties 28th & 29th (inclusive)

OFFICERS — 11.

Lt. C.A. Pearse — Killed
Capt. H.J. Cowie — Died of Wounds
Lt. G.W. Glover R.S.O. — " " "
2/Lt. J.C. Strobridge — Wounded
      J. Stanley — "
2/Lt. A.B. South — "
2/Lt. W.G.J. Smith — "
Lt. R.W. St Stephens i/c — Wounded (Gas)
Capt. A.W.M. Pryor — Wounded at duty
2/Lt. H.V. Woolcock — "
Lt. P.G. Batten — "

OTHER RANKS — 232

Killed 9.
Wounded 214 } this number can only
Missing 9   } approximate as full details
             } are not yet to hand

BPGrant ?/Lt
O.C. 1st Bn. The Rifle Brigade

Army Form C. 2118.

WAR DIARY
or
INTELLIGENCE SUMMARY.
(Erase heading not required.)

Instructions regarding War Diaries and Intelligence Summaries are contained in F. S. Regs., Part II. and the Staff Manual respectively. Title pages will be prepared in manuscript.

1st. Bn. The Rifle Brigade

Place	Date	Hour	Summary of Events and Information	Remarks and references to Appendices
REINFORCEMENTS.				
	AUG 20th		2nd Lieut. F. S. WILSON	
	22nd		" " W. G. T. TUSTIN	
	"		" " P. ROMNEY	
	23rd		" " E. J. PODBURY	
	"		" " J. H. DAVIES	
	24th		Lieut. O. A. PICKERING	
	30th		2nd Lieut. E. J. FREEAR	
	"		" " E. C. GARTON	
			OTHER RANKS 251	

Army Form C.2118.

WAR DIARY
or
INTELLIGENCE SUMMARY.
(Erase heading not required.)

Summary of Events and Information: 1st. Bn. The Rifle Brigade

Place	Date	Hour	Summary of Events and Information	Remarks and references to Appendices
CASUALTIES	AUG 10th		Major C. F. G. LETTS — Wounded	
			2nd Lieut. C.J.C.SCHUSTER — Killed	overlay updates
	13th		" " S. H. BURGH — Wounded	
			" " E. J. FREEAR — do (gas)	
			" " E. C. GARTON — do	
	19th		Capt. V. J. WHEELER — do	
			2nd Lieut. R. D. WINSLOE — do	
	29th		" " J. C. SHOOBRIDGE — do	
	30th		Capt. W. H. CORRIS — do	
			Lieut. G. W. GLOVER, DSO — Died of wounds 31-8-18	
			— Wounded 31-8-18	
			2nd Lieut. J. HARVEY — Died of wounds	
			" " A. E. SALTER — Wounded	
			" " W.G.J.TUSTIN — do	
			Lieut. C. A. PICKERING — do	
			Capt. A.W.M.RISSIK — Killed	
			2nd Lieut. H.V.MORLOCK — Wounded: Remaining at duty	
			Lieut. B. G. BAKER — do - ditto -	
			Lieut. R.W.H.HOLMES A'COURT — do - ditto -	
	31st		— Wounded (gas)	
	24th		2nd Lieut. H. L. ROUTH — Hospital sick	
			OTHER RANKS	
			Killed 19	
			Wounded 244	
			Missing 11	
			Hospital (N.Y.D. Gas) ... 51	
			do sick ... 41	

Army Form C. 2118.

WAR DIARY
or
INTELLIGENCE SUMMARY.
(Erase heading not required.)

Summary of Events and Information 1st. Bn. The Rifle Brigade

Instructions regarding War Diaries and Intelligence Summaries are contained in F. S. Regs., Part II. and the Staff Manual respectively. Title pages will be prepared in manuscript.

Place	Date	Hour		Remarks and references to Appendices
	AUG 20th		HONOURS & AWARDS	
			3011 Rfn. ERNEST G. MORRISH MILITARY MEDAL	
			5197 " GEORGE WRATTEN – do –	
			10928 " ALBERT R. LAIRD – do –	
			80910 Cpl. ALFRED CORNWELL – do –	
			46376 Rfn. ERIC GIBSON – do –	
	31st		B/200755 Cpl. WILLIAM ISON – do –	

DISTRIBUTION

A. Proceeded to the Line

	OTHER RANKS
Lt.Col. R.T. FELLOWES, DSO, MC	
Capt. J. A. DAVISON, MC	
Lieut. U. C. NAUMANN	650
" A. WAUDBY, DCM	
Capt. A.S.B. HERBERT, MC	
Lieut. G.H. PICKERING	
2/Lieut. A. E. SALTER	
" W. G. J. TUSTIN	
Lieut. B. G. BAKER	
2nd Lieut. J. HARVEY	
" " J. C. SHOOBRIDGE	
Capt. A. W. M. RISSIK	
Lieut. R.W.H. HOLMES A COURT	
2nd Lieut. A. R. BURRIDGE	
" " P. ROMNEY	
Capt. W. H. CORRIS	
2nd Lieut. H. V. HORLOCK	
" " W. J. WOODSIDE, MM	
" " F. S. WILSON	
1/Lieut. J. W. ALDRIDGE, A.A.M.C.	

B. With S.S. 135 Details

Capt. T. CARLYLE	
: J. A. TAYLOR	
Lieut. N. R. HARVEY	115
: G. BLAND	
2/Lieut. C. B. CRAVEN	
" E. J. PODBURY	
" J. A. DAVIES	
" H. K. SHORT	

C. With 1st Line Transport

Lieut. G. W. GLOVER, DSO	92
: G. J. COLE, MC	
T/Lieut & Q.M. C. MORGAN	

D Otherwise Employed

Lieut. W.F. SHOOBERT 5th Army School
2/Lieut. H.L. ROUTH G.H.Q., P&B.T Sch.
  :   A. O. HUNTING 5th Army Sch.
  :   F. R. M. LEE 13th Corps Sch.
  :   R. C. LOVELL Hospital
  :   W. G. WAYMOUTH 4th Div. H.Q.
  :   F. W. RAY   11th T.M.B.
  :   T. R. LECKIE   do

Other ranks

11th Inf. Brigade	14
3 Sect. 4th Signal Coy	9
11th T.M.B.	8
4th Division H.Q.	5
" " Signal Coy	5
3rd Echelon	1
4th Division Recep. Camp	2
Army Rest Camp	3
Escort duty	2
Hospital	5
	54

SECRET   Appendix No 1.

OPERATION ORDER No 1.
BY
LIEUT. COL. R.T. FELLOWES DSO, MC
COMMANDING 1st BATTALION THE RIFLE BRIGADE.

Ref. Sheet 36A SE.   3-8-18.   COPY No. 10

RELIEF 1. The Battalion will be relieved in the front line tonight by the 2nd Battn. LANCASHIRE FUSILIERS as follows:—
"A" Coy Rifle Brigade will be relieved by "C" Coy Lancs. Fus.
"B" "   "   "   "   "   "   " "B" "   "   "
"C" "   "   "   "   "   "   " "A" "   "   "
"D" "   "   "   "   "   "   " "D" "   "   "
The order of relief will be as follows — "B" "A" "D" "C" Bn HQ.

GUIDES 2. Guides at the rate of 2 per platoon (i.e. 3 per Coy) and 2 for Company HQ will be provided. These will report to the Signalling Officer at Battalion HQ at 10.0 p.m. Each bearing a chit stating exactly the location of his platoon. The Signalling Officer will take these guides to the Cross Roads W.8.a.0.8. to be there at 10.40 p.m.

ROUTE 3. The route of relief will be as follows:—
For the front line Company bridge at W.3.b.7.2.
  "   " Support   "   "   "   " W.8.b.1.6.
No definite route is laid down for the remaining Companies — the area between TWIN FMES and Battalion HQ will be avoided as far as possible.

BRIDGES The bridges shown below are allotted to this Battalion only and will be used exclusively as stated. IC HQ troops will post a Regtl. policeman on each bridge to see that no crowding etc takes place.
AT W.3.b.7.2 } for IN traffic proceeding N.E. ONLY
" W.3.b.1.6 }
" W.3.b.4.5 for OUT - "   -   " - S.W. ONLY

HANDING OVER 4. All trench stores, Defence Schemes L.G. A.A. positions aeroplane photographs maps etc will be carefully handed over and receipts obtained. These will be forwarded to reach Battalion HQ. by not later than 12 noon on 4th inst. All gas rattles tea packs empty water tins etc will be brought out. Companies will complete all deficiencies in S.A.A. before leaving the trenches.
The Signalling Officer will make arrangements that no Company signal station is handed over to the signallers of the incoming Unit until the wire stating that the relief is complete has been despatched to Battalion HQ.

MOVE 5. On completion of the relief the Battalion will move to billets in BUSNETTES where the Quartermaster will arrange accommodation.

INTERVAL 6. All movement will be carried out with an interval of 100' between platoons.

(Contd on SHEET 2.)

SHEET 2.

LEWIS GUNS 7. One Lewis gun limber per Company will be at the Ration Dump from 12 midnight onwards. 2 limbers will be at Battalion HQ at 11.0 PM. These limbers will take all Lewis guns, trench kit etc back to billets.

RETURN 8. A return will be rendered to Orderly Room by 5.0 pm on the 5th inst showing
(a) No. of picks and shovels in possession. (to be rendered also by QM)
(b) If every man less specialists is complete.
(c) Number if any required to complete.

ATTACK 9. In the event of an attack or a preliminary bombardment developing the relief will not take place. All troops of the relieving unit North of the Support Line 2nd System will man the nearest trenches and place themselves under the orders of the C.O. All troops South of this line will occupy their Battle Positions.

DEFENCE SCHEME 10. On arrival in billets each Company will draw the material laid down to be carried in Operation Order No. 52. The T.O. will arrange to deliver 10 tins of water to each Company and Battalion HQ.

Steps will be taken to warn all ranks that the Battalion will at all times be ready to move at 1½ hours notice.

REPORT 11. The Completion of the relief will be reported by wire and by visual. In the case of the former any sentence containing the code word "STEAL" will be used.

OsC Companies should call in at Battalion HQ if they happen to pass it.

ACKNOWLEDGE

3.8.18

W Wauchy 2/Lieut for
Captain
Adjutant 1st Bn. The Rifle Brigade

DISTRIBUTION

COPY No 1:	ADJUTANT	COPY No 7	O.C. "I" COY
" 2	LEWIS GUN OFFR	" 8	T.O and QM
" 3	SIGNALLING OFFR.	" 9	OC 2nd James Fusiliers
" 4	O.C. "A" COY.	" 10	WAR DIARY
" 5	" "B" "	" 11	" "
" 6	" "C" "	" 12	FILE

AMENDMENT No 1 to
OPERATION ORDER No 61
by
Lt.Col. R. T. FELLOWES, DSO, MC
Commdg 1st Battn. THE RIFLE BRIGADE

I. GUIDES
(i) Ref. para II "(i.e. 3 per Company)" read "(i.e. 6 per Company)".
(ii) They will report to the Signalling officer at 9.0 p.m. at "I" Coys H.Q. and not as stated therein. They will be shown the bridges to be used and their approaches.
(iii) They will also be shown the cross country track from W.3.c.1.6. to W.8.a.0.8.
(iv) For Bridge W.8.b.1.6. read W.3.b.1.6.

II. Care will be taken to see that all tools, gas rattles, etc. are brought out of the line.

III. Ref. para. 10, delete from "On arrival in billets ....Operation Order No 52"

(sd) J. A. DAVISON, Capt.
Adjt.
1st Battn. THE RIFLE BRIGADE

3-8-18

SECRET

OPERATION ORDER No 63
by
Lieut.Colonel R.T.FELLOWES, D.S.O., M.C.
Commanding 1st Battalion THE RIFLE BRIGADE

Appendix No 2

Ref. Sheet 36A,S.E.   6th AUGUST, 1918   Copy No 8

I. There will be a practise manning of the Battle Positions in accordance with Operation Order No 53 to-morrow afternoon, 7th inst.

II. Three officers per Company (this will include all officers who have not hitherto participated), 75% of N.C.Os, Runners and Signallers, and one man per Rifle section and one man per Lewis gun section, will take part.

III. Companies will parade and will move off in the following order, "B" Company starting at 3.0 p.m.
"B", "C", "I", "A", Battalion H.Q.
DRESS: Great coats and haversack rations will not be carried.
Tools will be carried.
Lewis guns and the ten tins of water per Company and H.Q. will not be taken.

IV. Signal communication will be practised. For this purpose the Signalling officer will arrange to take a Fullerphone.
All runners will make themselves thoroughly acquainted with the Headquarters to which they would run in case of necessity.

V. Any officers and N.C.Os who have not previously reconnoitred the routes up to the Battle Positions and the gaps in the wire in the forward area will do so to-day. Any such officers at Details have been ordered to report at their Company H.Q. at 1.30 p.m. to-day for this purpose.

VI. The time that Companies arrive in their Battle Positions and the position of Companies, will be reported by visual and runner to Battalion H.Q. directly after arrival of the Battalion in Battle Positions.

VII. ACKNOWLEDGE

Captain
Adjutant
1st Battalion THE RIFLE BRIGADE

Distribution

Copy No 1   Adjutant
        2   Signalling Officer
        3   Lewis gun Officer
        4   O.C. "A" Coy.
        5   "B" "
        6   "C" "
        7   "I" "
        8   War Diary
        9   "   "
       10   File

Appendix No 3

OPERATION ORDER No 63
by
Lieut.Colonel R. T. FELLOWES, DSO, MC.
Commanding 1st Battalion THE RIFLE BRIGADE.

Ref. Sheet 36A S.E.   9th AUGUST, 1916.   Copy No 11

RELIEF.	1. The Battalion will relieve the 2 outpost Companies of each Battalion in the 10th Brigade to-night.
	On relief the Battalion will become the outpost Battalion of the 14th Infantry Brigade.
	Companies will be disposed as follows:-
	  "C" Coy. Left Front.
	  "I" " Right Front.
	  "A" " Left Support.
	  "B" " Right Support.
	Boundaries will be as follows:-
	  Left Battalion boundary:- Q.30.b.2.7. - Q.14.d.9.7. - thence due East.
	  Right Battalion boundary:- Q.27.c.1.0. - Q.28.a.8.8. - Q.23.d.0.5.
	The inter-company boundary will be the existing boundary between the 2nd W.Riding Regt and 1st Royal Warwick Regt.
	Battalion Headquarters will be Q.26.b.2.8.
	The position of the Aid Post will be at Q.26.b.5.1.

MOVE	2. The Battalion will move off from here in the following order, and at the following times:-
	  Bn H.Q., "C", "I", "A", "B".
	Battalion H.Q. will move off at 6.0 p.m.
	The 4 Companies will move off with an interval of 200 yards between platoons, the leading platoon of "C" Coy. moving off at 6.45 p.m.
	  ROUTE:- CENSE LA VALLEE - Cross Roads V.5.b.5.2. - BLACKFRIARS BRIDGE - NOSE CAP Road - Rendezvous of the guides.
	  DRESS:- Fighting order: great coats will NOT be carried.

GUIDES	3. Guides for Battalion H.Q. will be at NOBBY FARM at 8.0 p.m Guides for "C" and "A" Companies will be at Q.30.d.5.3. at 9.0 p.m. Guides for "B" and "I" Companies will be at Q.27.a.50.50., where the old front line crosses NORTH Road at 9.0 p.m. Guides will be provided at the rate of 1 per platoon and 1 for Company H.Q.
TRANSPORT	4. (a) One Lewis gun limber per Company and one for Battalion H.Q. will be at the respective H.Q. in BUSNETTES at 5.0 p.m. to take the Lewis guns and 18 tins of water per Coy. etc. These limbers will move off independently to NOBBY FARM, where they will be off loaded at 8.30 p.m. All Lewis guns, ammunition water tins, etc. will be carried from here. The limber for H.Q. will accompany H.Q. troops, moving off at 6.0 p.m. (b) The Transport Officer will collect Officers' kits, packs, etc at 5.0 p.m. and will take them back to 1st Line Transport

STORES	5. The following material will be issued to each "C" and "I" Companies:- 2 S.O.S. Grenades,
	  Half a box of red ground flares,
	  6 O Very lights.
	These will be distributed among the 2 Companies, care being taken to see that they are kept dry.

TRENCH STORES	6. Any trench stores, S.A.A. etc. will be carefully taken over. An accurate list is urgently required and will be rendered to Battalion H.Q. as soon as possible after relief.

P. T. O.

- 2 -

BILLETS   7. All billets will be left scrupulously clean and a certificate to this effect rendered to Orderly Room before moving off.

BODIES   8. Bodies of all dead will be brought back to the Regtl. Aid Post.

REPORT   9. Completion of relief will be reported by wire if possible, in which case the code word "WINKLE" will be used. Companies will also send 2 runners to Battalion H.Q. bearing confirmation of this message.

ATTACK.   10. In the event of a preliminary bombardment or an attack developing all troops of the Battalion South of the old front line, 2nd System, will man their Battle Positions, as laid down in Operation Order No 52, with the following exception: "A" Company will man HARRISON'S Trench, and not the 2nd line 3rd System as laid down therein.

         All troops North of the front line 2nd System will man the nearest trenches and place themselves under the orders of the Battalion Commander in whose area they are, at the same time notifying Battalion H.Q. of their action.

         11. ACKNOWLEDGE

J A Dawson
Captain
Adjutant
1st Batt THE RIFLE BRIGADE

```
Distribution
Copy No 1   O.C. "A" Coy
        2        "B"  "
        3        "C"  "
        4        "I"  "
        5   Commanding Officer
        6   2nd in Command
        7   Adjutant
        8   A/Adjt.
        9   R. Sig. O.
       10   T.O. and Q.M.
       11   War Diary
       12    "    "
       13   File
```

Tracing from 36 A S.E.
1:20,000

Battle Positions

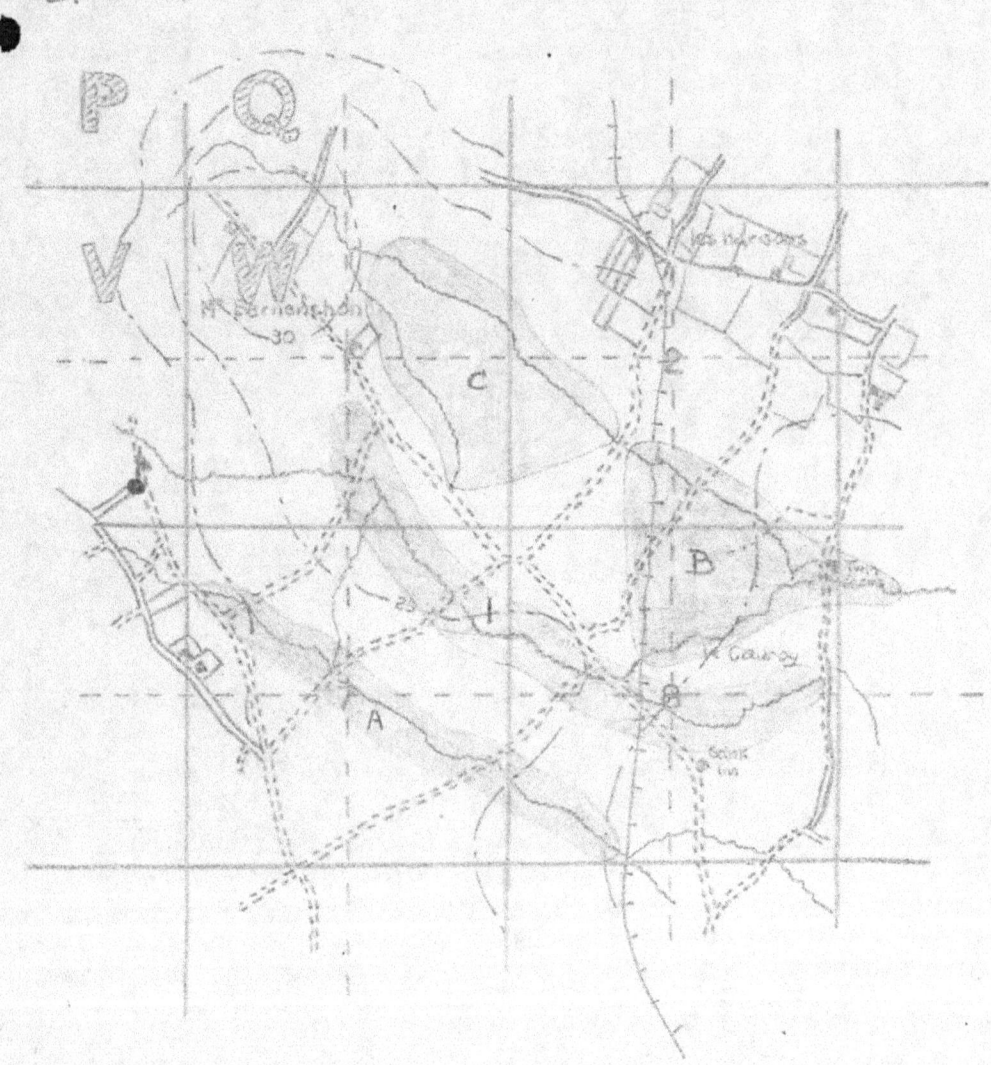

SECRET } OPERATION ORDER No 64   Copy No
by
Lieut. Colonel R. T. FELLOWES, DSO, MC.
Commanding 1st Battalion THE RIFLE BRIGADE

REF. Sheet 36A.S.E. Ed 8a 1/20,000   9th August 1918

1. The enemy is withdrawing opposite this front so as to shorten his line or to place himself in a more suitable defensive position.
   The Battalion will keep in touch with the enemy and follow him up as his posts withdraw. Slight opposition will be overcome.

2. The Battalion will act as Advanced Guard from night of 9th inst, and will also provide the outposts when halted, and will work on the basis of two Coys. in Front, "I" on Right and "C" on Left, and two in Support, "B" on Right and "A" on Left.
   The remaining two Battalions of the Brigade will be retained in present first system.

3. Battalion Boundaries are as follows:-
   Left boundary:-   Q.20.b.2.7. - Q.11.d.9.7. thence due East to main road at H.6.d.5.5. Sheet 36

   Right boundary:-   Q.27.c.1.0. - Q.28.a.8.8. - Q.23.d.0.3. -
                      Q.24.a.65.30. - R.20.a.3.6. - R.21.b.15.30.-
                      4.24.a.9.2.

   Inter-Coy. boundary:- Road junction Q.22.b.3.3. - Q.17.c.5.0. -
                         Q.18.a.5.1.

4. The next line to be made good by patrols willbe Q.24.a.65.20 along the PARADIS Road to Q.11.d.85.75.
   This will be known as first Green line.
   Touch will be established with Brigades on flank at Q.2 4.a.65.20 by "I" Coy and Q.11.d.85.75 by "C" Coy.

5. SUBSIDIARY WEAPONS. The following will be at direct disposal of Advanced Guard Commander:-
   (a) 137th Battery (18 pdr) at Q.20.b.9.4.
       An Artillery Liaison Officer will be attached to Battalion H.Q.
   (b) 4 Mobile Vickers Guns.
   (c) 4 L. Trench Mortars.

6. PRECAUTIONS must be taken to guard against ambushes, road mines and booby traps installed by the enemy.
   Dugouts and houses should not be entered until they have been inspected by the R.E. A small party of R.E. will be attached to the Advanced Guard Battalion
   The possible destruction of roads and bridges in rear of our advancing troops by means of charges provided with delay action fuzes must be considered.
   No water should be drunk from wells or other sources until it has been proved fit for drinking purposes.

7. At 5.30 a.m. and 7 p.m. a contact patrol will fly over our lines daily. Advanced Guard Battalion will arrange for foremost troops to light red flares at these times when the aeroplane appears overhead.

8. "C" and "I" Coys will report position of foremost posts every one and a half hours.

9. Battalion H.Q. will be at Q.26.b.2.8. to begin with.
10. ACKNOWLEDGE

                                    (sd) C. C. NAUMANN Lieut,
9-8-18   A/Adjt. 1st Battalion. THE RIFLE BRIGADE

AMENDMENT No 1 to
OPERATION ORDER No 64
by Lt.Col. R. T. FELLOWES, DSO,MC
Commdg 1st Battn. THE RIFLE BRIGADE

Ref. para. 3, the last two map references of the inter-Company boundary should read Q.23.d.5.7. - Q.18.c.5.9. and not as stated before.

(sd) E. C. NAUMANN   Lieut.
Act/Adjt. 1st Batt THE RIFLE BRIGADE

9-8-18

SECRET

OPERATION ORDER No 65
by
Lieut.Col. R. T. FELLOWES, DSO, MC
Commanding 1st Battn. THE RIFLE BRIGADE
9th August, 1918

Ref Sheet 36A S.E.

1. The following moves will take place after relief tonight, 9th inst.
   (a) "B" Coy. will extend its left to BUTTER LANE
   (b) "A" Coy's right will rest on BUTTER LANE and will get touch will "B" Coy. Its left will rest on the railway in Q.15.d.

2. As soon as the necessary reconnaissances have taken place the following moves will take place:-
   (a) "C" Coy will move forward and occupy the line of the TURBEAUTE.
   (b) "I" Coy. will move forward and occupy the line of the HINGES Road from Q.24.a.4.4. to the Battalion boundary on the right; when this is done "I" Company's right will move forward and occupy the line of the TURBEAUTE in Q.23.c.
      Officers Commanding "C" and "I" Companies will take care to keep all concerned informed of their moves forward.

3. As soon as the moves mentioned in para. 2 have been completed
   (a) "A" Coy. less 1 platoon will move forward and occupy the line of the road running through Q.16.c. thus coming up in line with "B" Coy.
   (b) The platoon of "A" Coy. in close support to "C" Coy. will move forward and occupy part of the line evacuated by "C" Coy. about Q.16.d.Central.
   (c) "C" and "I" Coys will re-arrange their right and left flanks respectively so that they are in touch on the inter-Company boundary at Q.23.a.45.65. Arrangements to be made between Company Commanders concerned.

4. The First Green Line mentioned in para. 4 of Operation Order No 64 will be made in two bounds. The intermediate line will run approximately from the left Battalion boundary - along the HINGES Road to Q.17.b. and d. Patrols will be sent forward to make good this line first of all. "C" and "I" Coys will then move forward and occupy this line. The same procedure will be adopted till the First Green Line is reached.

5. It is essential that close touch be maintained with the enemy and that he does not succeed in giving us the slip. Patrols will act with boldness and every effort made to surround and capture isolated enemy posts that may be delaying the advance.

6. Movement in the outpost line - except by patrols, by officers and N.C.Os doing their necessary visits to the posts along their front, will be reduced to a minimum.

7. The two support companies will arrange to send visiting patrols along the fronts of the front Company they are supporting.

8. Any change of Company H.Q. is to be reported immediately. "C" and "I" Coys will as soon as possible select and occupy a common H.Q.

9. Two 3" T.Ms are allotted to each of "C" and "I" Coys. These guns will be used to assist patrols should they be hung up, to bombard and assist in the capture of any enemy posts that are hanging out and to harrass the enemy generally.

10. Information is of the utmost importance and will be transmitted by all means available.

(sd) R. T. FELLOWES, DSO,MC.
1st Battn. THE RIFLE BRIGADE

Appendix No 4

OPERATION ORDER No 66
by
Lt.Colonel R. T. FELLOWES, DSO, MC
Commanding 1st Battalion, THE RIFLE BRIGADE
11th AUGUST, 1918

RELIEF 1. The Battalion will be relieved by the 1st Battn SOMERSET L.I. to-morrow night and will move back to the old 1st System as left Support Battalion.

DISPOSITIONS 2. Dispositions as support Battalion will be:-
"A" Coy in front line from left Divisional Boundary to Q.26.b.7.3., Post 59 exclusive.
"B" Coy. in support line from left Divisional Boundary to Q.26.b.3.6., Post B53 exclusive.
"C" Coy. in the reserve line from left Divisional Boundary to Q.26.a.0.0., Post B 62 exclusive.
"I" Coy: two platoons in ROEECQ Switch and two platoons in the Battle Positions behind.
Battalion H.Q. and Aid Post at POMPADOUR FARM.

GUIDES. 3. (a) Found by the Battalion.
4 from "A" Coy., 3 from "B" Coy., 6 from "C" Coy. and 7 from "I" Coy, (i.e. for platoons attached or detached, as the case may be) will report to Battalion H.Q. at 5 a.m. tomorrow morning, bringing their own rations.
Time and place for guides to meet incoming unit will be at junction of original front line and road Q.20.d.5.3. at 9.0 p.m.
(b) Found by 1st Batt Somerset L.I.
10 guides (5 for "C" and 5 for "I") at Lancashire Farm from 12 midnight onwards.
No guides will be found for "A" and "B" Coys but Officers Commanding these Companies will send either an officer or C.S.M. to reconnoitre their new positions.
No guides will be found for Battalion H.Q.

HANDING OVER 4. All ammunition, S.O.S, Red Flares, and all that is known of the enemy, will be carefully handed over,

TAKING OVER 5. "C" and "I" Coys will each send 1 responsible N.C.O. to be at Battalion H.Q. by 7 a.m. tomorrow morning. They will take over Trench stores and dispositions of the Company being relieved, taking particular note of platoon boundaries and will then return to their Coy. H.Q. in the line, each handing over all information gained to his Coy Commander.
The Officer or C.S.M. of "A" and "B" Coys sent forward to reconnoitre (see para 3 (b) will do as detailed above for the N.C.Os of "C" and "I" Coys.
Empty Water tins, Salvage, etc. will be carried back by Coys to their new positions. Receipts for stores, etc. handed and taken over will be forwarded to reach Batt. H.Q. by not later than 12 noon, 13th inst.

RATIONS 6. Rations will be sent up to arrive at the under mentioned places at midnight:-
"A" and "B" Coys at road junction Q.20.a.6.4.
"C" Coy at Q.19.d.40.20.
"I" " at Q.19.c.85.20.
Battalion H.Q. at POMPADOUR FARM.
On arrival at new positions Coys will immediately draw their rations as above mentioned.
C.Q.M.Ss will be responsible for looking after their Companies' rations until drawn.

GREATCOATS 7. Greatcoats will be sent up for the Battalion to Battn. H.Q. by 11.30 a.m. 13th inst.
Coys will detail an adequate party to arrive at Battn.

Greatcoats cont.
        H.Q. at the following times
            "I" Coy ... 11.30 a.m.
            "C" " ... 12.0 noon
            "B" " ... 12.30 p.m.
            "A" " ... 1.0 p.m.
These parties will being down with them to Battalion H.Q. the empty water tins and salvage brought out of the line. These will be loaded on the vehicles after the greatcoats have been off loaded.

ACTION IN CASE 8. In the event of an attack or preliminary bombardment
OF ATTACK the relief will not take place.
        If the troops are already west of a line running N. and S. through the second T in HUTTER LANE, Sheet 36A S.E. the relief will carry on and Coys. will get into their positions as detailed a s soon as possible.

REPORT   On relief complete the code word TURBOT will be wired to Battn. H.Q. and confirmed by runner.
        On occupying the new positions Coys. will wire the code word SALMON and confirm this by runner.

ACKNOWLEDGE.

                      (sd) C. C. NAUMANN   Lieut,
                      A/Adjt 1st Batt THE RIFLE BRIGADE

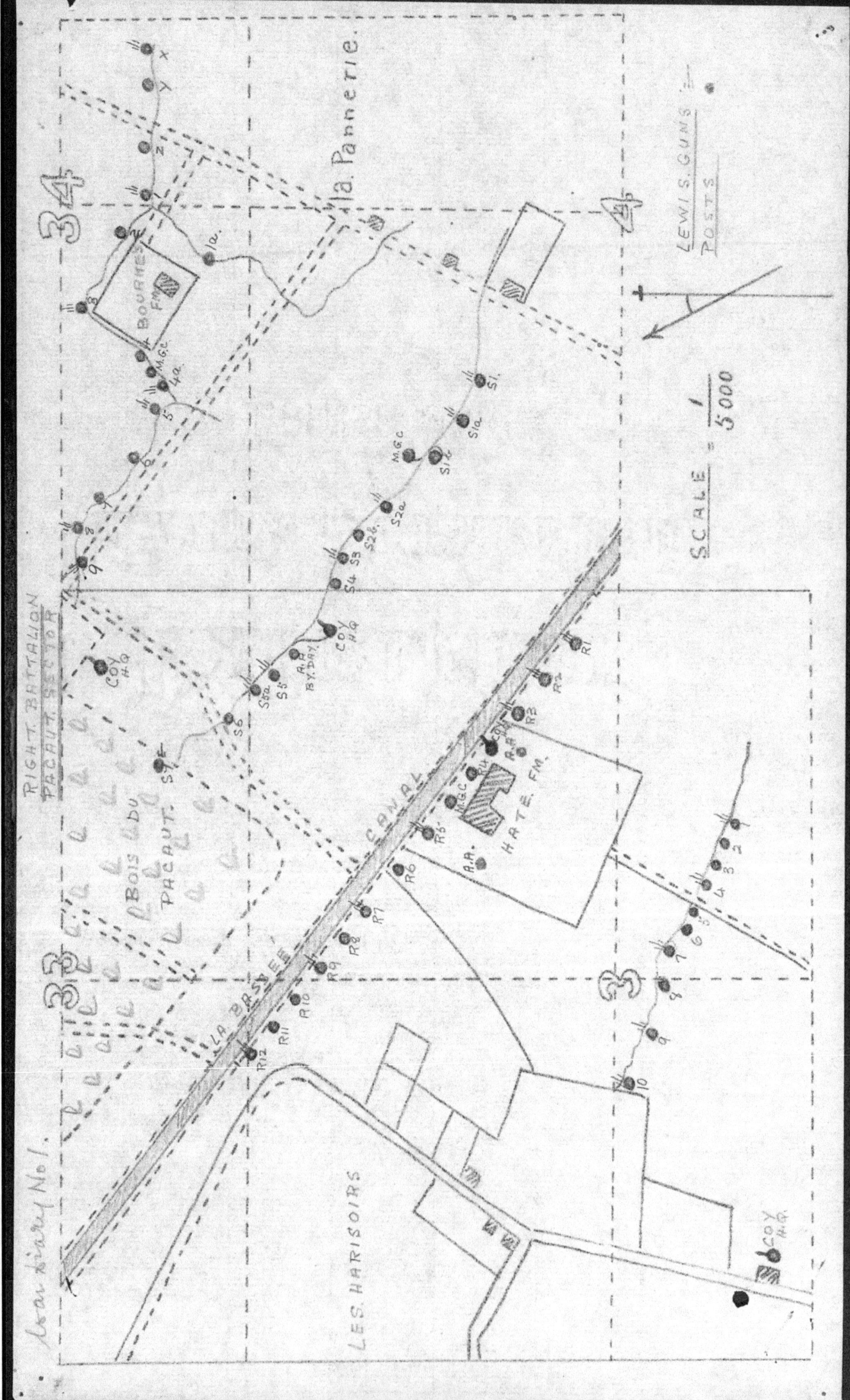

00s
63, 64, 65, 66.

SECRET

OPERATION ORDER No 67
by
Lt.Colonel R.T.FELLOWES, DSO,MC
Commanding 1st Battn. THE RIFLE BRIGADE
PRELIMINARY DEFENCE SCHEME - LEFT SUPPORT BATTALION

Ref. Sheet 36A S.E. Ed 2   17-8-18   Copy No 9

1. All previous Defence Orders for the Left Brigade (VINAGE Sector) are hereby cancelled.

2. DISPOSITIONS   1 Company in Front line
2 Companies in Reserve line, including Supporting Posts to BATTLE TRENCH ("C" Coy in Battalion Reserve)
1 Company ROBECQ SWITCH
Battalion H.Q. F.24.d.60.55.

3. The area at present occupied by the Battalion will be known as the First System of the Battle Zone.

4. BOUNDARIES
Left. F.29.c.7.2. (bridge exclusive - F.30.a.7.0. - Q.20.b.2.7. - Q.11.d.9.7. thence due East to main road M.8.d.5.5.
Right. Q.25.b.95.40. - Q.26.b.3.3. - Q.26.b.7.9.

5. ACTION IN CASE OF ATTACK.
The outpost Battalion, if the enemy attack is in great force, will fall back fighting and will reoccupy the front trench of the 1st System of the Battle Zone. In the event of a hostile attack in force the First System Battle Zone is the ground on which the battle will be fought and within this system the enemy will be fought to the last. There will be no withdrawal from the front line of the First System.
The reserve line of the First System will be the line of of the Battle Zone and on no account will the enemy be allowed to enter or pass this line.
Should the enemy reach the Battle Zone and succeed in getting a footing in any portion of the front and support lines of the First System, Battalion Reserves as shown in para 2 will if necessary, drive the enemy out by immediate local counter attacks. Should the enemy penetrate the front and support lines of the First System on a scale too large for counter attack to be successful effective, Battalion will hold the reserve line of this system. Any portions of the front and support lines not penetrated will hold on at all costs, making defensive flanks in echelon, where possible.
The Company in the ROBECQ SWITCH detailed for the defence of this line and the Companies in the reserve line (other than Battalion Reserves) will not on any account move forward unless relieved from the rear.

6. CONTACT AEROPLANE
A contact aeroplane will in case of attack be sent out to fly over the enemy's lines, and will indicate the movement of the enemy's infantry by dropping smoke bombs.

7. COMMUNICATIONS
The front line Company will keep one orderly at the BARN; he will be given copies of all visual messages received to ensure that the front line Coy. Commander is promptly advised of changes in the situation in the event of telephone wires being broken.

8. ACKNOWLEDGE

(sd) C. C. NAUMANN Lieut.
A/Adjt 1st Batt THE RIFLE BRIGADE

17-8-18

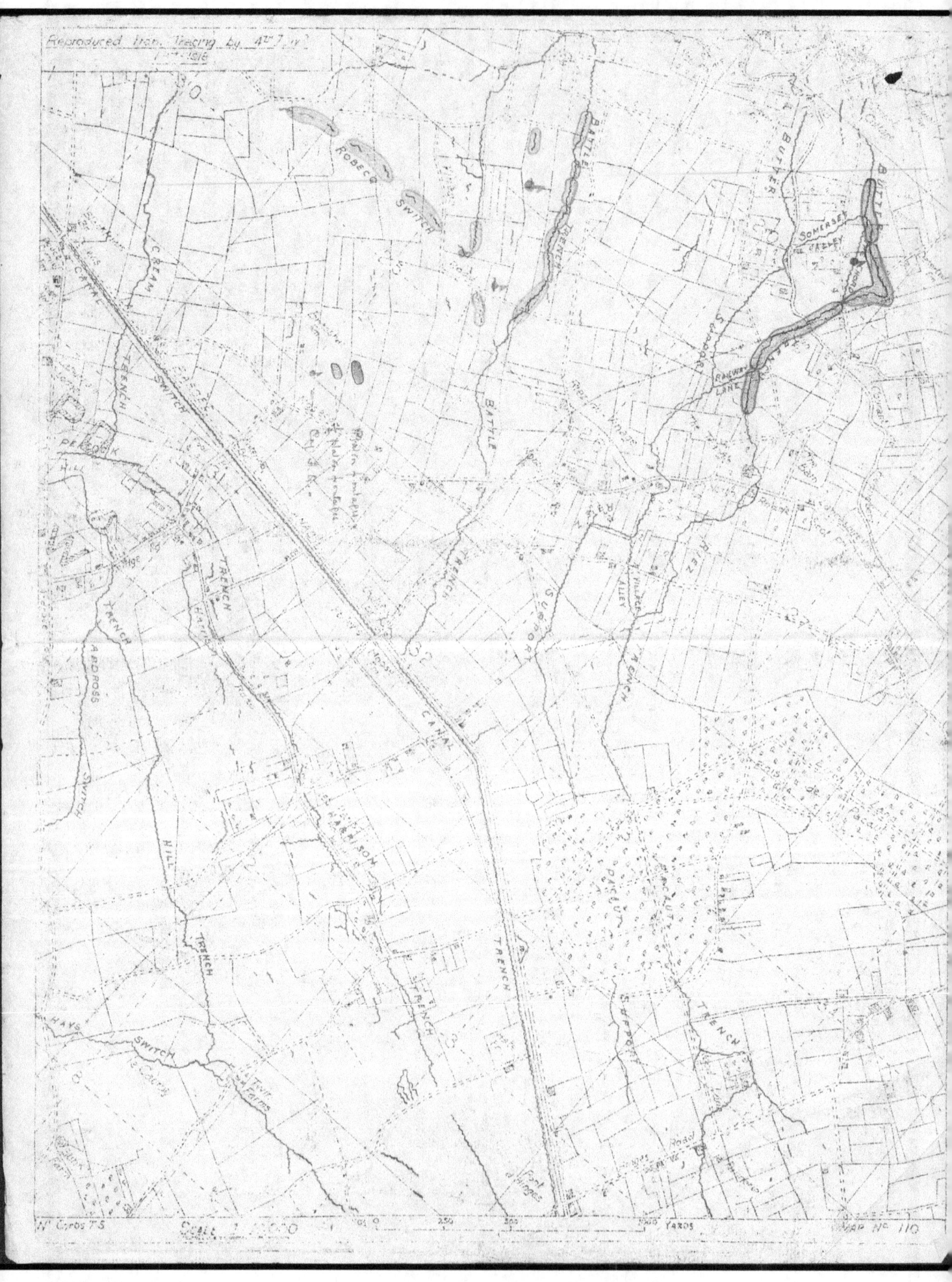

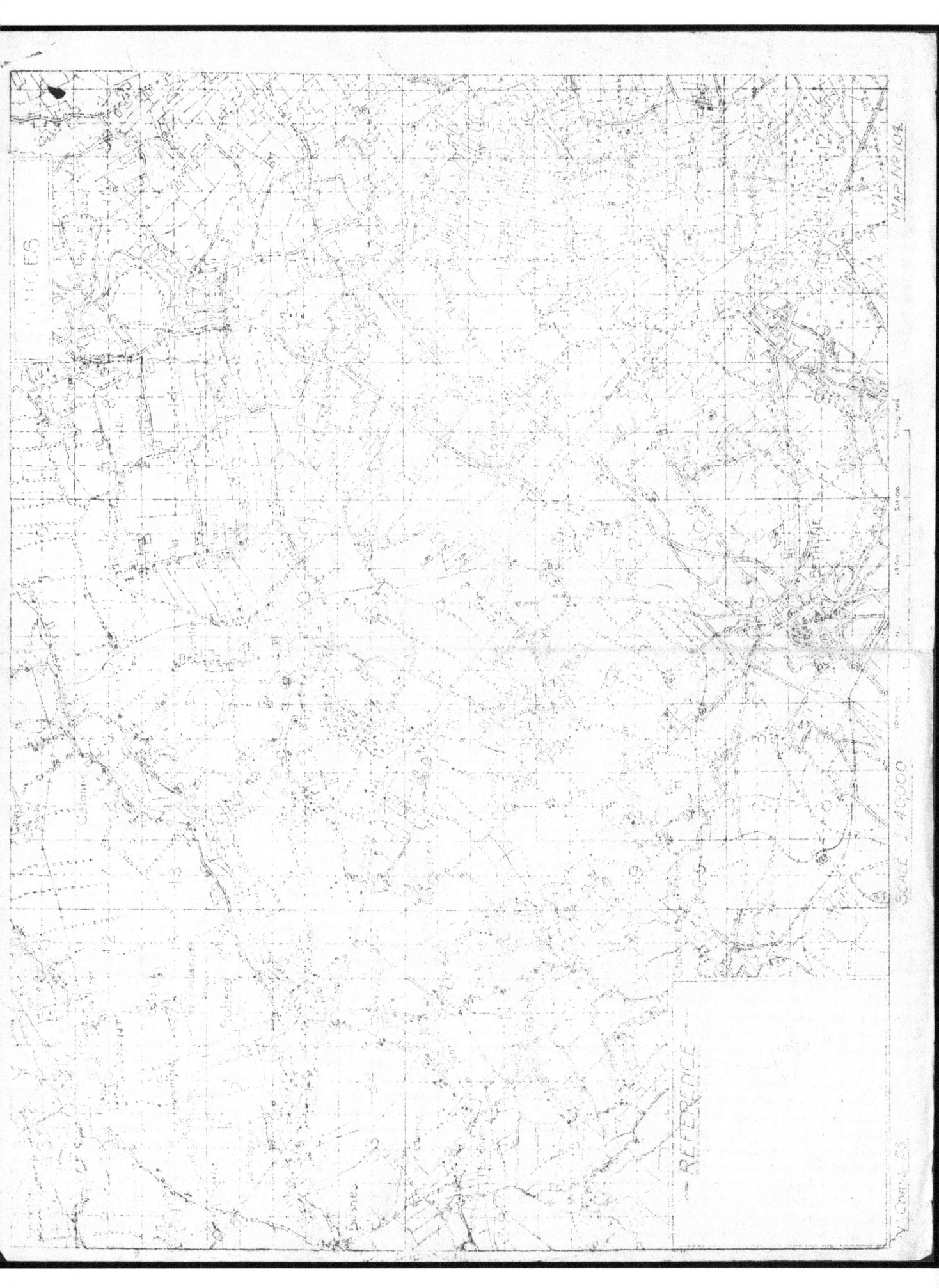

OPERATION ORDER No 68
by
Lieut.Colonel R.T.FELLOWES, DSO., MC.
Commanding 1st Battalion THE RIFLE BRIGADE
DEFENCE SCHEME for OUTPOST BATTALION - LEFT BRIGADE

Ref. Sheet 36a S.E. Edition 8a

Copy No 14

1. All previous Defence Orders for the Left Brigade (VINAGE Sector) are hereby cancelled.

2. The area occupied by the Battalion will be known as the Outpost Zone and will include the area E. and exclusive of the old British Front line (Front line, First system, Battle Zone).

3. DISPOSITIONS:
   All four Companies in line, not more than 5 O% being in the line of picquets. The picquet posts and outpost supports will be disposed chequerwise in depth, mutually covering each other with fire.
   The Outpost Supports will be from 300-500 yards behind the picquet posts.
   Company H.Q. will be about 500 yards behind the picquet posts.
   Whenever possible each post will have an alternative position to which the garrison can move if shelled.
   Battalion H.Q. will be at Q.22.a.2.0.

4. BOUNDARIES
   (a) Battalion
       Left:- P.29.c.7.2. (Bridge exclusive), P.30.a.7.0., Q.30.b.3.7., Q.11.d.9.7., thence due East to main road M.3.d.5.5.
       Right:- Q.32.c.6.9. (Bridge exclusive) Q.27.c.1.0., Q.28.a.8.8., Q.25.d.0.3., Q.34.a.65.80., R.20.a.2.8., R.21.b.15.30., R.24.a.9.2.
   (b) Inter-Company
       (1) Q.18.c.4.2. - House Q.23.a.4.5.(exclusive to right Coy.) - Q.22.d.50.95.
       (2) Q.16.a.3.4. - Q.17.c.40.23. - Q.22.b.30.85.
       (3) Q.12.c.45.00 - Q.47.a.95.10. - House Q.16.d.2.2. (inclusive to left Company).

5. ACTION IN CASE OF ATTACK.
   In the event of a hostile attack in force the role of the Battalion will be as follows:-
   (a) Give the alarm.
   (b) Harass, delay and inflict casualties on the enemy and so disorganize and check his advance before it reaches the First System of the Battle Zone.
   (c) Give time for all troops in rear to man their Battle Positions and reserves to be moved forward. The line of resistance is the line of the supporting platoons and all ranks must thoroughly understand that it is their duty to repel raids and minor enterprises undertaken by the enemy into our outpost Zone, and no withdrawal beyond the line of resistance in the Outpost Zone is to be contemplated unless it is clear that the enemy have launched an attack in force, in which case the outpost troops will withdraw fighting, first to the Outpost line of resistance, thence to the First system of the Battle Zone, carrying out the role assigned to them in (a), (b) and (c) of this paragraph.

   Any withdrawal will be carried out systematically - troops being sent back to definite lines in rear which have previously been pointed out, and an officer or senior N.C.O. sent back to meet troops as they withdraw, and to put them in their positions. Whole Companies will not withdraw at the same time. Certain platoons and sections will remain behind to cover the withdrawal. When troops in rear are in position those in front will gradually withdraw in good order to their new positions.

   Every foot of ground will be contested and there will be no withdrawal from any position unless the enemy attack is in force. Local enemy patrols and detachments who are merely feeling their way forward will be driven off by fire.

   Touch will be maintained with troops on the flanks.
   The following approximate lines of defence will be taken up successively should a withdrawal be forced on us:-
   (1) E. edge of Orchards and enclosures E. of the QUENTIN Road.

Para. 5. cont.
    (2) Line of lunettes in Q.46.c. and Q.28.a. (450 yards West of Road) thence along road from LE CORNET MALO to the Q of QUENTIN.
    (3) Old German trench in Q.15.d., Q.21.b. to houses at Q.22.c.4.8.
    (4) A N. and S. line running through LA PIERRE AU BEURE to the HENNEBECQ and thence along the HENNEBECQ
    (5) From Q.15.c.2.0. to the HENNEBECQ at Q.21.c.5.5. along the stream and thence to houses in Q.27.b.
    (6) DESERTED FARM - E. of HUN FARM - E. of SCOT and LANCASHIRE FARMS - Q.27.Central.

On reaching the Battle Zone they will occupy the front trench of the First System augmenting the existing garrison of this trench. From this line there will be no further withdrawal. In the event of the Battalion retiring to the First System, Battalion H.Q. will be established at Q.26.b.2.0.

6.   ARTILLERY, MACHINE GUNS and TRENCH MORTARS
    (a) An artillery S.O.S. barrage has been arranged to cover the Picquet line.
    (b) 4 Machine Guns are at the disposal of the Battalion.
    (c) 6 Trench mortars : : : : : : :
    In the event of a withdrawal all 4 Machine Guns will **not** be on the move at the same time.
    The same applies to the Trench Mortars.
    Machine guns and Trench mortars will assist the infantry in holding back the enemy's advance, and prevent him debouching from houses, orchards, enclosures, etc. - particularly those along the QUENTIN ROAD.

7.   CONTACT AEROPLANE.
    A contact aeroplane will in case of attack be sent out to fly over the enemy's lines and will indicate the movement of the enemy's infantry by dropping smoke bombs.

8.   ACKNOWLEDGE.

                            (sd) C. C. NAUMANN   Lieut.
17-8-18   Act/Adjt 1st Batt THE RIFLE BRIGADE

    DISTRIBUTION

Copy No				
1	O.C. "A" Coy		No 9	14th Inf. Bde.
2	"B" "		10	4th Bn M.G. Coy.
3	"C" "		11	11th T.M.B.
4	"D" "		12	Outpost Bn. Right Bde 74 Div.
5	Commanding Offr.		13	" " " " 4 Div.
6	Adjutant		14	War Diary.
7	Int. Offr.		15	" "
8	Sig. Offr.		16	File

-:-:-:-:-:-:-:-:-:-:-:-

Appendix No 5

SECRET

OPERATION ORDER No 69
by
Lt.Colonel R.T.FELLOWES, DSO,MC
Commanding 1st Battn. THE RIFLE BRIGADE
17 AUGUST, 1918

Ref. Sheet 36A S.E.   Copy No 11

RELIEF   1.   The Battalion will relieve the 1st Batt. THE HAMPSHIRE Regt. as Outpost Battalion tomorrow night.
"B" Coy R.B. will relieve "B" Coy 1st HAMPSHIRE Regt on the right
"I" " " " " "A" " " " " on the right centre
"A" " " " " "D" " " " " on the left centre
"C" " " " " "C" " " " " on the left.

       Battalion H.Q. will be at Q.22.a.2.0.
       Regtl Aid Post will be at Q.26.B.5.1.

GUIDES   2.   GUIDES will be provided by the 1st HAMPSHIRE Regt as follows
5 for "B","C" and "I" Coys (1 per platoon and 1 per Coy. H.Q.)
4 " "A" Company (1 per platoon and 1 for Company H.Q.)
1 " Battalion H.Q.
at Road Junction Q.21.c.20.15 at 8.45 p.m.

MOVE   3.   ORDER of MARCH will be:- "B", "A", "C", "I" Batt H.Q.; the leading platoon of "B" Coy. will reach the rendezvous for Guides at 8.45 p.m.
       Interval of 200 yards will be kept between platoons.

LEWIS GUNS   4.   LEWIS GUNS, magazines, etc. will be carried from the present positions.

RATIONS   5.   RATIONS and Water for consumption on the 19th will be carried up to the new positions.
       Rations for the 20th and 21st will come up by limber to Road Junction Q.21.b.80.25. Each Company will be responsible for drawing its own rations; limbers will arrive at an interval of quarter of an hour: "A" Coy. at 9.45 p.m., "B" Coy. at 10.0 p.m., "C" Coy at 10.15 p.m. and "I" Coy. at 10.30 p.m. Great care will be taken to see that all water tins and salvage are loaded on to the returning limbers.

GREATCOATS   6.   GREATCOATS will not be taken up but will be dumped by Companies at their rations dumps by 12 noon tomorrow. The Transport Officer will arrange to collect.

TRENCH STORES   7.   ALL TRENCH STORES, S.O.S., S.A.A., Very lights, Ground flares will be carefully taken over and receipts forwarded to Battalion H.Q. by 12 noon on the 19th.

HANDING OVER   8.   REPRESENTATIVES of the 1st HAMPSHIRE Regt. will report to Company H.Q. to take over Trench Stores and Company dispositions some time tomorrow morning. All lists of stores handed over will be forwarded to Battalion H.Q. by 12 noon on the 19th inst.

CONTACT AEROPLANE   9.   AT 5.30 a.m. and 7.0 p.m. daily a contact patrol aeroplane will fly over our lines. When the aeroplane calls the foremost troops of Companies will use the signalling flaps fitted to the Box Respirator to show what position they are holding. Should posts not have these flaps they will light the Red flares as previously.

DISPOSITION MAPS   10.   Os.C. Companies will forward an accurate map or sketch of their dispositions to Battalion H.Q. by 12 noon on the 19th inst.

REPORT   11.   Completion of relief will be reported by wire by the code word "LORRY" and will be confirmed by runner.

       12.   ACKNOWLEDGE

                         (sd) C. C. NAUMANN   Lieut,
                         Act/Adjt 1st Bn THE RIFLE BRIGADE

DISTRIBUTION
Copy No 1 O.C. "A" Coy.   7 Commdg Offr.
     2   "B" "   8 Adjutant
     3   "C" "   9 A/Adjt.
     4   "I" "   10 Sig. Offr.
     5 1st Hants Regt.   11 War Diary
     6 Transport Offr   12 " "
                13 File.

'Line as taken over'   18.viii.18. .... •
Line as at 9.0 p.m.   19.viii.18. .... •
Line as at 9.0 p.m.   20.viii.18. .... •
Support platoon positions. .... ⬭
Company Headquarters. .... ♩

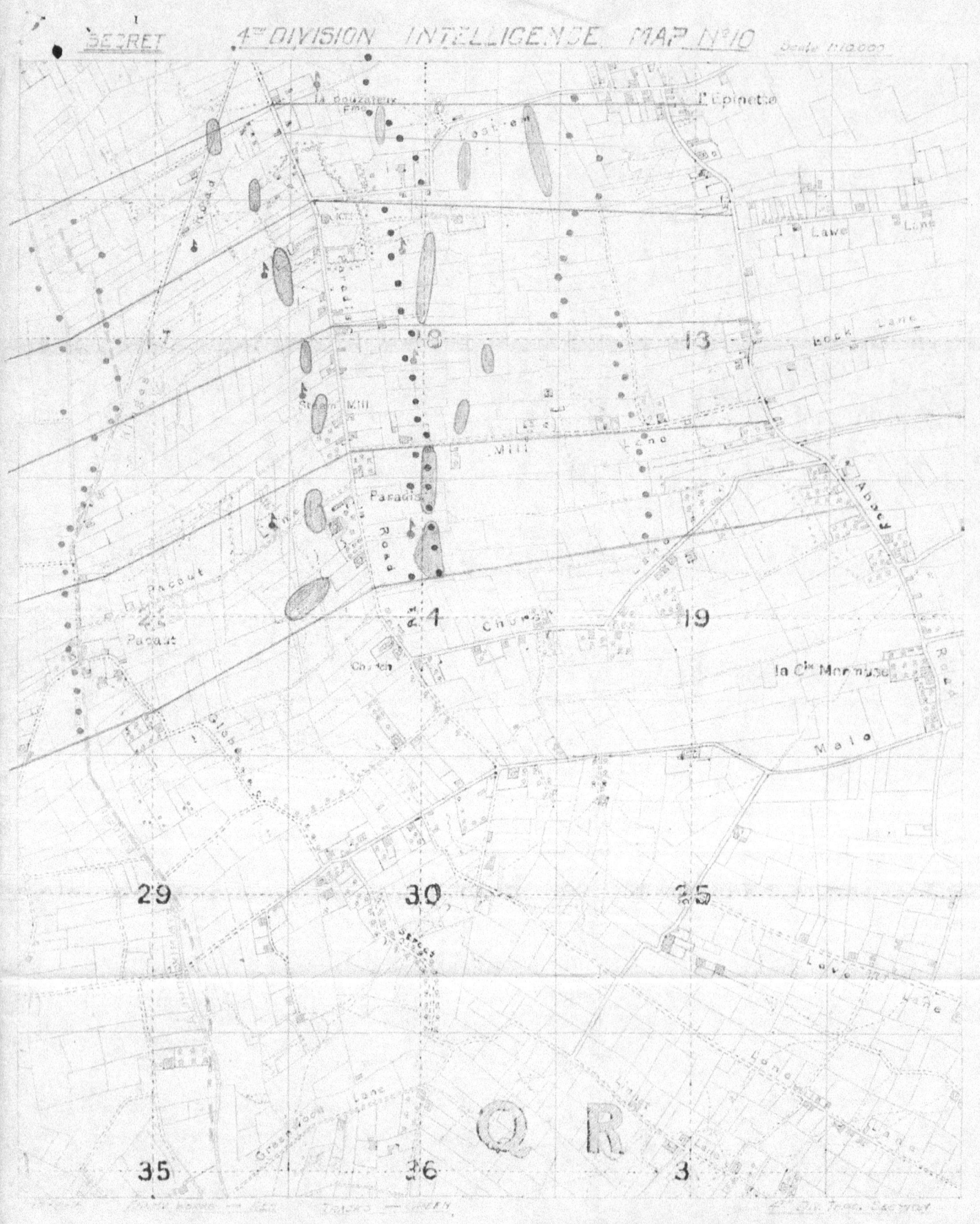

SECRET   OPERATION ORDER No 70
by
Lieut.Colonel R.T.FELLOWES, DSO, MC
Commanding 1st Battn. THE RIFLE BRIGADE

REF Sheet 36A S.E.   30-8-18   Copy No 11

RELIEF   1.   The Battalion will be relieved to-night by the 1st Batt SOMERSET L.I. and will move back as right support Battalion with 1 Company in the original front line and 3 Companies in the reserve line.

DISPOSITIONS   2.   "C" Coy. will be in the front line from RAILWAY LANE inclusive to Q.27.c.1.0.
         "B" Coy. will be on the right in reserve with 2 platoons in the reserve trench and 2 in Battle positions behind.
         "A" Coy. will be in the centre with 2 platoons in the reserve trench and 2 in Battle Positions behind
         "I" Coy. will be on the left with 2 platoons in the reserve trench and 2 in the Battle positions behind.
         The reserve line will be occupied from Q.32.a.8.3. to Q.26.a.0.4.
         Battalion H.Q. ROSE HOUSE, P.36.b.2.3.
         Aid Post LABURNUM LODGE   P.36.d.45.85.

GUIDES   3.   (a)   Guides, 5 per Coy. will report to Batt. H.Q. by 9.0 p.m. to-night without fail. They will meet 1st SOMERSET L.I. at road junction Q.22.b.30.25 at 9.30 p.m. under arrangements to be made by the Signalling Officer.
     (b)   Battalion H.Q. will provide 1 guide for each Company at THE BARN Q.27.a.2.9. who will direct platoons as they pass.

RATIONS   4.   Rations will be dumped as follows:-
         For "A", "B" and "I" Coys at point where NOSECAP ROAD crosses reserve line Q.26.c.55.25.
         For "C" Coy. at Q.26.b.5.1.
         For Battalion H.Q. ROSE HOUSE.
         Companies will draw rations as soon as they arrive at their new positions.

TRANSPORT   5.   One limber per Company and one for Battalion H.Q. will be at road junction Q.21.b.60.25. from 10.30 p.m. onwards for conveyance of Lewis Guns, magazines, Officers' kits etc.

REPORT   6.   Relief complete will be wired to Battalion H.Q. by the code word "DOUBTFUL" and confirmed by runner.

         7.   ACKNOWLEDGE.

                                  (sd)   C. C. NAUMANN, Lieut.
                                  Act/Adjt 1st Bn   THE RIFLE BRIGADE

DISTRIBUTION
Copy No 1   O.C. "A" Coy   7   Adjutant
       2   "B"   "   8   A/Adjt
       3   "C"   "   9   Sig. Offr.
       4   "I"   10   T.O and Q.M.
       5   1st Som.L.I.   11   War Diary
       6   Commdg Officer   12   "   "
                             13   File

SECRET

OPERATION ORDER No 71
by
Lt.Col. R. T. FELLOWES, D.S.O., M.C.
Commanding 1st Battn. THE RIFLE BRIGADE

Ref. Sheet 36A, S.E. 22-8-1918   Copy No 11

Appendix D.6

RELIEF 1. The Battalion will be relieved to-day 22nd inst. and will move back to billets in BUSNETTES. The relief will be carried out as follows:-
(a) All troops in the front line 1st System from Q.27.c.1.0 to Q.26.d.90.95 will be relieved by the 1st ROYAL WARWICKSHIRE Regt. at 2.15 p.m.
All troops in the Reserve Line between Q.32.a.90.10. and Q.26.c.30.53. will be relieved by the 1st ROYAL WARWICKSHIRE Regt. at 2.30 p.m.
(b) Remainder of Front Line Company will move from the front line 1st System back to BUSNETTES At 2.45 p.m.
(c) Remainder of troops in the Reserve Line will be relieved by a Company of the 15th SUFFOLK Regt. at 3.0 p.m. and move back to billets after handing over to the incoming unit.

On relief units (platoons or sections as relieved) will move back independently to billets in BUSNETTES, an interval of 200 yards being kept between parties.

ROUTE 2. WATERLOO BRIDGE- CENSE LA VALLEE - LA VALLEE - BUSNETTES.

HANDING OVER 3. ALL TRENCHES whether handed over or vacated will be left scrupulously clean.

TRENCH STORES 4. ALL TRENCH STORES will be handed over as far as possible, receipts obtained and forwarded to Battn. H.Q. by 6p.m. tonight.

TOOLS 5. PICKS and SHOVELS will NOT be handed over, but will be brought out of the line. Os.C. Companies will see that all deficiencies as regards tools are made up before relief.

TRANSPORT 6. ALL GREATCOATS of "C" Company will be dumped at NOBBY FARM at 11 a.m. - those of "A", "B" and "I" Companies at Q.28.C. 55.20 at 11 a.m. - those of Battn. H.Q. at ROSE HOUSE at 11.15 a.m. Transport Officer will arrange to collect these before 12 noon and convey them to BUSNETTES, handing them over to C.Q.M.Ss.

The Transport Officer will arrange to have limbers at the following places at the undermentioned times for conveyance of Water tins, Salvage, Lewis guns, magazines, etc.
One for "C" Coy at NOBBY FARM AT 2.30 p.m.
Three at Q.26.C.55.20 at 3.0 p.m.
One at Battalion H.Q. at 2.30 p.m.

BILLETING 7. Quartermaster will detail the usual Billeting party to report to Town Major, BUSNETTES, at 10 a.m. to take over Billets for the Battalion.

REPORT 8. Completion of relief will be reported to Battalion H.Q. by telephone, the code word "IVANHOE" being used.

BILLETS 9. Billets in BUSNETTES will be thoroughly cleaned this evening as an early start to the AMES area is to be expected on the morning of the 23rd inst.

10. ACKNOWLEDGE.

(sd) C. C. NAUMANN, Lieut.
22-8-18   Act/Adjt 1st Battn. THE RIFLE BRIGADE

DISTRIBUTION
Copy No 1 "A" Coy.   7 A/Adjt.
       2 "B" "   8 Int. and Sig. Offrs
       3 "C" "   9 T.O. and Q.M.
       4 "I" "   10 O.C. 1st R. Warwicks
       5 Commdg Offr 11 War Diary
       6 Adjutant   12 "   "
                    13 File.

SECRET

OPERATION ORDER No 72
by
Lieut.Colonel R.T.FELLOWES, DSO,MC
Commdg 1st Battalion THE RIFLE BRIGADE
22nd August,1918

Copy No /2

---

1. MOVE:
   The Battalion will proceed to-morrow by march Route to billets in FAUQUENCHEM.

2. ORDER OF MARCH:
   H.Q., "B", "A", "C", "I". The head of the H.Q. unit will be at the Cross roads Q.14.d.2.6, and will move off at 7.30 a.m.
   An interval of 100 yards will be kept between Companies throughout the march. There will be a halt 10 minutes to every clock hour.
   DRESS:- Fighting Order, less tools
   ROUTE:- BAS RIEUX - LILLERS - HURIONVILLE - FAUQUENHEM.
   Buglers will march first with "B" Coy., then with each Company after each successive halt.

3. DISCIPLINE:
   Strict march discipline will be kept and no one will be allowed to fall out without written permission from his platoon Commander.
   Sticks will not be carried except by officers.
   O.C. "I" Coy. will detail one platoon to march in rear of the Transport proceeding with the Battalion, to act as Baggage Guard, and pick up all stragglers: the officer commanding this platoon will be mounted.
   The transport accompanying the Battalion will move 100 yards in rear of the third platoon of "I" Company.

4. TRANSPORT:
   All officers' kits, mess stores, etc. will be packed and dumped outside billets by 6.30 a.m. The Transport Officer will arrange to collect.
   Lewis guns limbers will be left ready loaded tonight.
   Two lorries will report at BUSNETTES CHURCH at 7.0 a.m: all packs, picks and shovels, will be dumped by Companies at BUSNETTES CHURCH by 6.30 a.m. These lorries will be loaded by the platoon of "A" Company mentioned in para 6 (a) Two men per Company will travel on these lorries.
   The remainder of the Transport starting from the Transport Lines will move under orders of the Brigade Transport Officer.

5. SICK:
   The 11th Field Ambulance will be located at AMETTES, and will call at Regimental Aid Posts daily.

6. BILLETS:
   (a) All billets will be left scrupulously clean, and great care will be taken to see that all latrines, grease-traps, urine buckets, etc., vicinity of cookhouses, etc., are left in a thoroughly clean condition.
   Capt. J. A. TAYLOR will detail one platoon of "A" Company to remain behind to clean up anything that has been overlooked: he will himself inspect all billets etc., in company with the Town Major, obtaining a certificate of cleanliness afterwards.
   (b) As the Battalion Transport lines will not be taken over, the Transport Officer will see that the area occupied is

6. BILLETS: cont.
   left thoroughly clean.
          All Officers Commanding Companies, O.C. Headquarters, and Transport Officer, will render all above mentioned certificates of cleanliness to Orderly Room by 4 p.m. to-morrow.

7. PACKS & TOOLS:
          On arrival at FAUQUENHEM Companies will send for packs and tools, great care being taken that every man is in possession of either a pick or a shovel, as soon after getting settled in as possible.

8. READINESS:
          Whilst the Battalion is in FAUQUENHEM, it will be ready to move at 24 hours' notice.

9. REPORT:
          O.C. Companies will report to Orderly Room by 4.0 p.m. tomorrow the number of men (a) who did not march in with Battalion, (b) who marched in with rear platoon of "I" Company, (c) who came in after the Battalion.

10. ACKNOWLEDGE

                                    (sd) C. C. NAUMANN   Lieut.
                                    Act/Adjt 1st Batt. THE RIFLE BRIGADE

DISTRIBUTION
   Copy No 1   O.C. "A" Coy.   8 Signal. Offr
          2   "B" "   9 Intell. Offr.
          3   "C" "   10 Transport Offr
          4   "I" "   11 Quartermaster
          5   Commanding Officer   12 War Diary
          6   Act./Adjutant   13   "   "
          7   Lewis Gun Offr   14 File

Appendix No 7.

AMENDMENT No 1 to
OPERATION ORDER No 79

22 August, 1918

Ref. Para 2 DRESS will be Shirtsleeves, Fighting Order less tools. Tunics will be neatly and carefully folded and rolled on the back of the belt.

Ref. Para 3 DISCIPLINE: Add N.C.Os and men must not carry on the march anything extra to their arms and equipment.

(sd) C. C. NAUMANN Lieut.
Act/Adjt 1st Batt THE RIFLE BRIGADE

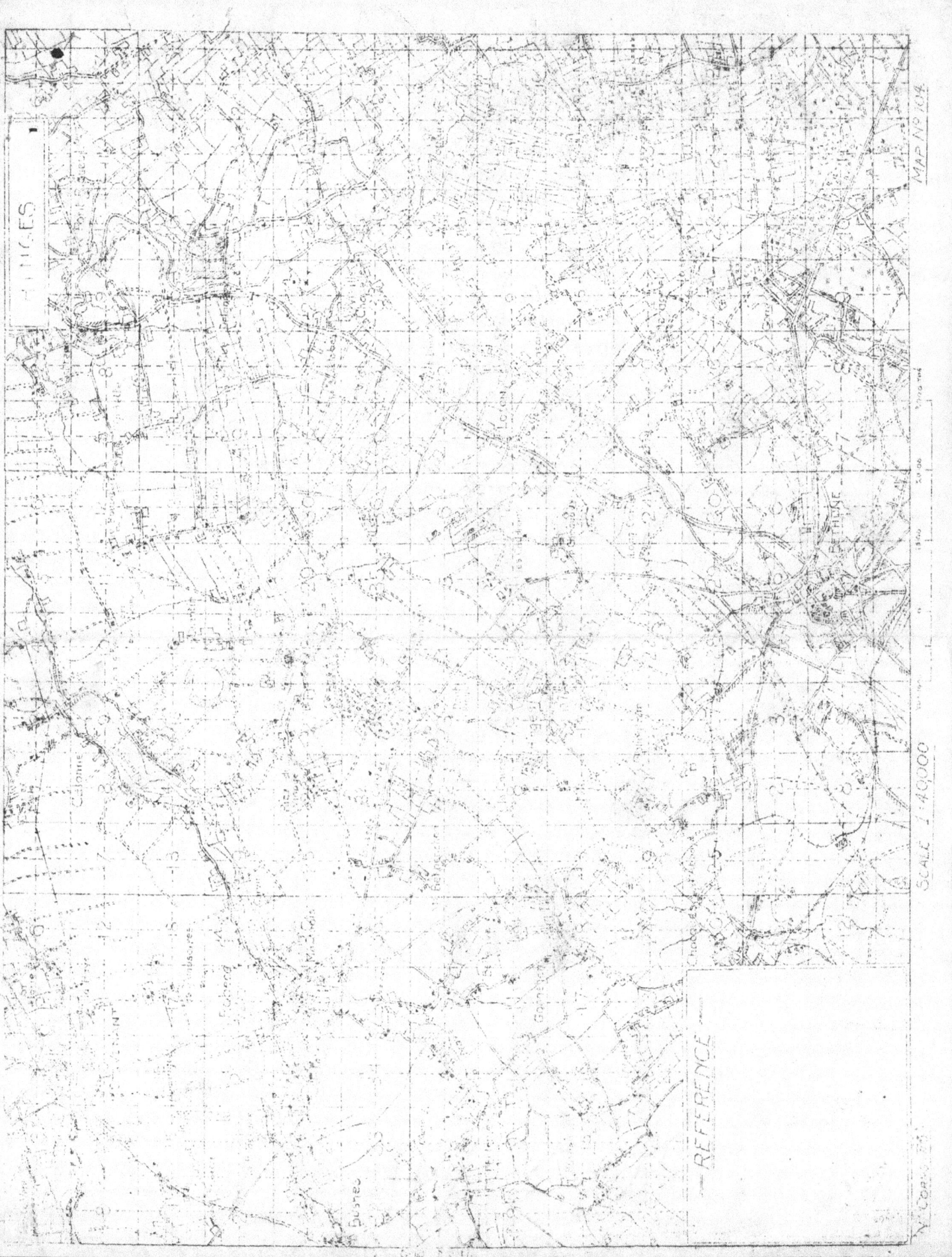

SECRET.   WARNING ORDER   24th AUG. 1918

MOVE   1.   The Battalion will be prepared to move at 4.30 a.m. to-
                 morrow and march to LILLERS.
                     DRESS:-. Full Marching Order. Greatcoats will be carried
                 in packs.   Tools will be carried.
                     ORDER OF MARCH:- H.Q. "B", "C", "D", "A".   100 yards inter
             val will be kept between Companies.
                     O.C. "A" Coy. will detail 1 platoon as baggage guard.

TRANSPORT   2.   Officers' kits, surplus mess stores and Q.M. Stores will
                 be packed ready on transport by 8.45 p.m. this evening. The
                 Transport Officer will arrange to collect Officers' kits which
                 will be dumped outside billets by 8 p.m.   One Lorry will report
                 at Q.M. Stores this afternoon to take surplus stores to the new
                 area.   All stores which cannot be moved will be taken to billet
                 No 59 PERNES by the transport some time to-day.
                     The following transport will accompany the Battalion
                 to-morrow:-
                         3 Lewis gun limbers
                         5 Cookers
                         2 Water carts
                 The remainder will move at 9 p.m. tonight.
                     Transport stages St.POL.

BILLETS   3.   All billets will be thoroughly clear by 7.30 p.m. tonight
                 and a certificate to this effect will be rendered to Orderly Room
                 by 8 p.m.

LEWIS GUNS   4.   Two Lewis guns per Company will be loaded on 1 limber going
                 with the Transport tonight ; also the 4 Anti Aircraft Lewis guns
                 will go with the Transport to-night.   The remaining 6 Lewis guns
                 per Coy. will be loaded on the limbers proceeding with the Batta-
                 lion to-morrow.

RATIONS   5.   Rations for to-morrow's consumption will be carried on the
                 man.

             6.   ACKNOWLEDGE

                                                                   Lieut.
                                        Ast/Adjt. 1st Batt THE RIFLE BRIGADE

SECRET

Appendix No 8

OPERATION ORDER No 73
by
Lt.Colonel R.T.FELLOWES, DSO, MC.
Commdg 1st Battalion THE RIFLE BRIGADE
25 August, 1918

Ref. Sheets 36A, 36B, and LENS 11.   Copy No

MOVE   1.   The Battalion will move by march route and train to the ST. MICHEL sub area to-day. The Battalion will march to and entrain at LILLERS: it will detrain at BRYAS and march to the ST MICHEZ sub area.

ORDER OF MARCH   2.   H.Q., "B", "C", "I", "A".
      The head of H.Q. troops will pass the road junction T.24.b.1.6 at 7.0 a.m. Companies will follow on in the above mentioned order, an interval of 100 yards being kept between Companies.
      DRESS: Full marching order - Greatcoats in packs; tools will be carried.
      ROUTE to LILLERS STATION:- Road junction T.24.b.1.6. - T.24.b.5.3. - thence by track to U.19.a.6.3. - U.19.b.8.5. - HURIONVILLE U.20.d.6.4. - LILLERS STATION U.16.b.6.8.

DISCIPLINE   3.   Strict march discipline will be observed: any N.C.O. or man found carrying a stick on the line of march will be tried by Court Martial.

BILLETS   4.   Each Company and H.Q. will obtain a certificate of cleanliness for their billets from the billet Warden, and these certificates will be forwarded to Orderly Room as soon after arrival in new area as possible.

BILLETING PARTY   5.   2nd Lieut. C. B. CRAVEN and 2 N.C.Os already detailed will proceed on bicycles at 5.45 a.m. today and report to the Staff Captain at ST MICHEZ Church at 9.0 a.m.

ENTRAINMENT   6.   (i) On arrival at LILLERS Station each Company and H.Q. will detail 1 officer to report to the entraining officer, Major H.P. HUDSON, 1st HAMPSHIRE Regt. taking the entraining states of their Companies with them.
      (ii) All doors of covered trucks on the right hand side of the train on the main line will be kept closed throughout the journey.
      (iii) O.C. "A" Coy. will detail 1 platoon to act as picquet at all stops to prevent troops from leaving the train.
      (iv) No N.C.O. or man will be allowed in the brake vans at each end of the train or on the roofs of trucks.
      (v) All rifles will be placed in the corners of carriages, and not leant up against the doors.

RATIONS   7.   Rations for to-day will be carried on the man.

DESTINATION   8.   Destination in ST. MICHEZ area - FOUFFLIN-RICAMETZ.

      9.   ACKNOWLEDGE.

                                            (sd) C. C. NAUMANN Lieut.
                                Act/Adjt. 1st Batt THE RIFLE BRIGADE

Issued
2.15 a.m.
25-8-18

SECRET

Appendix 9.

OPERATION ORDER No 74
by
Lieut.Colonel R.T.FELLOWES, DSO,MC
Commdg 1st Battalion, THE RIFLE BRIGADE
28th August, 1918

REF. LENS 11 1/100,000: 51B N.W. & S.W. 1/100,000

MOVE 1. The Battalion will proceed by busses to positions of assembly East of ARRAS, as follows, to-day.
The Battalion will move from Camp in the following order:-
H.Q., "A", "I", "B", "C".
H.Q. will move off in time to allow the last platoon of "C" Coy. to reach the embussing point at 1.10 p.m.

EMBUSSING 2. The busses will be drawn up on the CHATEAU DE LA HAIE - VILLERS AU BOIS Road, facing S.E. The head of the Bus convoy will be 50 yards N.W. of the Cross Roads in VILLERS AU BOIS.
The following busses are allotted to the Battalion:-
1 to 26 inclusive.
Care will be taken to see that the road is kept clear, the Battalion being drawn up on the south side of the road. Parties of 25 will be told off immediately on arrival at the embussing point.
DEBUSSING point 50 yards West of the Cross Roads H.31.b.4.0.
On arrival at the debussing point troops will move well clear of the road.

ASSEMBLY 3. From the debussing point the Battalion will move to an
POSITION assembly position in H.20.c. and H.26.a.
"A" Coy. will be on the left front, "I" Coy. on the right front, in TILLOY Trench. Battalion H.Q. in TUBE ALLEY. "B" Coy. in the left rear, "C" Coy. in the right rear in TILLOY Support.
On arrival in the assembly positions Companies will each send one runner to Battalion H.Q.

DRESS etc. 4. DRESS:- Fighting Order.
LEWIS GUNS and 24 drums per gun will be taken into the Busses
AMMUNITION:- 170 rounds per man: FLARES 2 per man: RIFLE
GRENADES 36 per platoon: S.O.S. and ALL CLEAR
SIGNALS 9 per Coy: VERY LIGHTS 24 per Coy.

DETAILS 5. The party proceeding to details will parade under Capt. CARLYLE in the camp at 11.45 a.m. They will proceed to the field just south of the Railway Crossing on the CHATEAU DE LA HAIE road.
They will parade with the remainder of Brigade details in the field under Major P.H.HUDSON of 1st HAMPSHIRE REGT. They will move off from here in time to arrive at the above place by 12.25 p.m
ROUTE:- via Track N.E. of the CHATEAU DE LA HAIE Road.
Brigade details will move to the embussing point in rear of Brigade H.Q.

DINNERS 6. Dinners for the Battalion will be at 11.45 a.m. with the exception of details who will have their's at 11.0 a.m.

RATIONS 7. Rations for consumption on the 29th inst. will be carried on the man. Each Coy. will take 10 tins of water with them. These will be carried from the debussing point to the place of assembly.

TRANSPORT 8. All Transport will move off in time to pass the starting point at the road junction S.W. of VILLERS AU BOIS, and immediately North of the N in LE PENDU at 2.25 p.m. They will proceed to the transport lines in the vicinity of ARRAS.

cont on sheet 2

- 2 -

TRANSPORT 8 cont.

The Transport Officer will make his own arrangements to collect officers' kits, Orderly room boxes, etc.

All packs and surplus baggage not carried on the transport will be stored in SCHRAMM BARRACKS, ARRAS. Each Company will detail one old man to take charge of these stores. Two lorries have been allotted to the Battalion to take all such surplus stores.

WATER. 9. Care will be taken to see that all water bottles are filled before starting.

The following water points are available East of ARRAS:- H.20.d.5.0., H.26.b.10.10., FEUCHY CHAPEL Cross Roads N.3.b.8.1. Full advantage should br taken of these water points for filling water bottles during the halt at the position of assembly.

10. O.C. "B" Coy. will detail one man with a good knowledge of detaonating of grenades to report at Chapel dump at N.3.b.7.3. at 4 p.m. to-day. This man will proceed with the Battalion as far as the Debussing point. He will be rationed on and after the 30th inst. under Divisional arrangements.

11. ACKNOWLEDGE.

(sd) J. A. DAVISON, Capt.
Adjt
1st Battn. THE RIFLE BRIGADE

SECRET   OPERATION ORDER N0 75   Appendix 10
                             by
               Lieut.Colonel R.T.FELLOWES, DSO., MC.
               Commdg 1st Battalion, THE RIFLE BRIGADE
                     29th AUGUST, 1918

RELIEF   1.   The Battalion will relieve a portion of the 1st Batt. SOMERSET L.I. on the SENSEE River from P.7.c.8.4. to p.13.a.00.05 tonight.

            Battalion Boundaries   LEFT   P.7.c.8.4. - P.14.a.4.9 to P.15.b.75.40
                                  RIGHT   P.15.a.00.05 - P.13.d.7.6. -
                                           P.13.d.6.0. then E.

DISPOSITIONS   2.   "A" Coy. will be on the left on the SENSEE River.
                     "I" "   will be on the right on the SENSEE River.
                     "B" "   will be in support to "A" Coy.
                     "C" "   "   "   "   "I"   "

            Inter-Coy. Boundary   P.13.a.4.8. to p.14.a.05.00 -
            P.15.d.8.7.
            BATTALION H.Q. will be at 0.10.c.4.6.
            AID POST   0.9.b.85.00

MOVE   3.   Companies will move off in the order "I", "A", "C", "B" in order to reach the place of assembly: Area South of LONG WOOD P.12.c. by 10 p.m. Route will be as reconnoitred by Coy. Commanders beforehand. The line of the SENSEE River will be occupied as soon after dark as possible and steps will immediately be taken to occupy the following line, P.14.a.4.9. round the E. outskirt of ETERPIGNY to P.13.d.65.00, the following procedure being adopted:-
As soon as the moon rises patrols will be sent out to try and establish the above mentioned line; should resistance be encountered patrols will return and further patrols will be sent out at dawn and again at 7.0 a.m.
Should patrols encounter no resistance they will remain on the above mentioned line and each will send back a man to report the fact.

         O.C. "A" and "I" Coys. will forward a definite report by 12 noon to Battalion H.Q. stating whether they have been able to establish this line or not; if not artillery support will be arranged and the line will be established under cover of this.

         This line **must** be established by 12 midnight on the night of 30/31st inst.

         Consolidation will be carried out with lunettes in Artillery formation so as to facilitate any further advance which may be contemplated.

RATIONS   4.   Rations for to-morrow's consumption will be drawn by Coys at the point where the old front line crosses STIRRUP LANE at 5.45 p.m. and will be carried on the man when the move is made. Care will be taken to see that all petrol tins and salvage are sent back, and also that parties are kept in the trench when awaiting the arrival of the limbers.

REPORT   5.   When Coys. are in position report will be made by runner to Battalion H.Q.

         ACKNOWLEDGE.

                                                      (sd)   J.A.DAVISON,   Capt.
                                                        for O.C. 1st Bn THE RIFLE BRIGADE

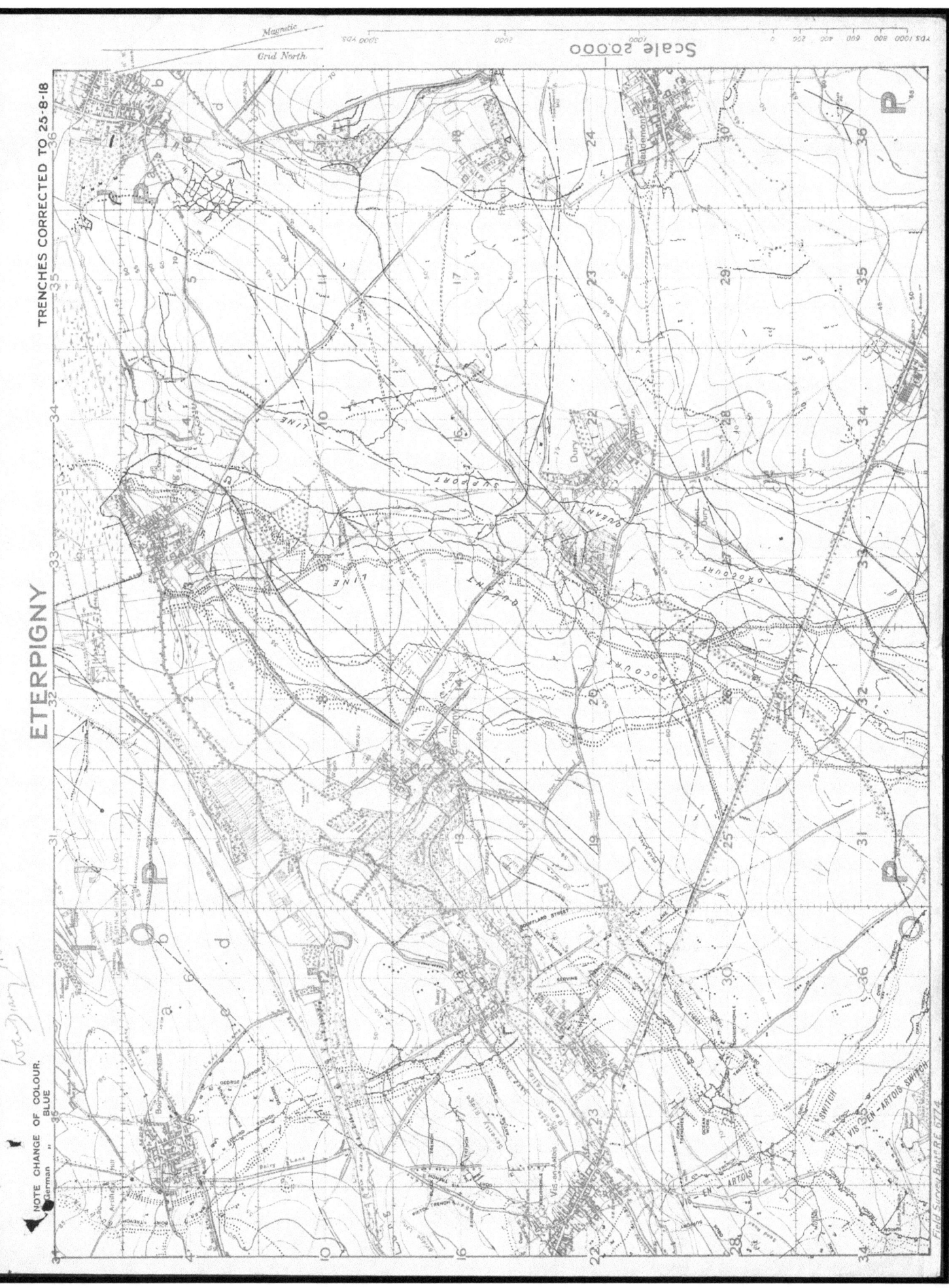

Reference Sketch on back.

To

1. My {Platoon / Company} has reached

 (Mark position on map or give map reference).

 and is consolidating.
 has consolidated.
 is ready to advance.

2. I am (not) in touch with   on right

 and (not) with   on left.

3. I am held up at   {by wire.
                                            by M.G. fire.
                                            by rifle fire.

4. Enemy's artillery is firing on

 from

5. I have sent forward patrols to

6. I estimate {my casualties at
               my strength at

7. I need   boxes S.A.A.
             Lewis gun drums
             Bombs
             Rifle Grenades
             Stokes Shells
             Very Lights   (at once)
             Ground Flares   (to-night)
             Stakes
             Coils wire
             Tins water
             Rations

8. I intend to

9. (General remarks on position and strength of enemy. Number of prisoners taken and identifications, if known).

Time	Name	Rank
Date	Platoon	Coy
	Battalion	

Strike out all that is not applicable and forward at once to Bn. H.Q.

SECRET   OPERATION ORDER No 76
                       by
            Lt.Colonel R. T. FELLOWES, DSO, MC
            Commanding 1st Battn. THE RIFLE BRIGADE
                   30th AUGUST, 1918
----

1.   The Battalion will to-day capture and establish the line
P.14.a.4.9. - round the Eastern outskirts of ETERPIGNY to E. of
Sunken Road in P.13.d. to P.13.d.85.00.

2.   Zero hour will be at 4 p.m.   Barrage table will be issued
later.

3.   Boundaries as laid down in O.O. 75.

4.   Support Companies will move 300 yards in rear of Front Companies
(Disposition of Battalion as laid down in O.O. No 75), and will be
prepared to form defensive flanks if necessary to maintain touch with
troops on flanks.   Definite platoons willbe told off for this work.

5.   (i) Information is of the utmost importance, especially as
regards positions occupied by Companies.
        (ii) Coy. Signallers will be used as extra runners.
        (iii)   There will be an Advanced Report Centre at the Artillery
Bridge over the COTEUL RIVER at the Western end of LONG WOOD
to which place all messages will be sent.
        (iv)   Dispositions of Companies and Company H.Q. will be sent
as soon as possible after reaching the final objective, and any
change will be notified immediately.
        (v)   The timing of messages is most important.

6.   For consolidation see O.O.75 last sub-para, Para 3.

7.   ACKNOWLEDGE.

                                   (sd) J. A. DAVISON,   Capt.
                                                          Adjt.
                                   1st Battn. THE RIFLE BRIGADE

30:8:18
1.15 p.m.

AMENDMENT No 1
to OPERATION ORDER No 76

Appendix "D"

I. <u>Artillery Programme</u> 3.45 p.m. a destructive shoot on ETERPIGNY Wood and village.

   4.0 p.m. barrage will come down on a line 150 yards East of the SENSEE (all troops will be withdrawn to a line 70 yards East of the SENSEE.

   4.02 p.m. barrage will move forward by 50 yard lifts at the rate of 50 yards every 2 minutes to final objective.

   After reaching final objective a protective barrage at slow rate will come down on line 300 yards in front of final objective.

II. "I" Coy. is responsible for keeping touch with troops of 10th Brigade who are attacking on our right, but "C" Coy. will detail a special platoon to fill any gaps that may occur.

III. Men must keep as close behind the bursting shells of our barrage as possible.

IV. ACKNOWLEDGE.

30th AUGUST, 1918   (sd) J. A. DAVISON, Capt.
1.55 p.m.   Adjt
                                              1st Batt THE RIFLE BRIGADE

HAMBLAIN-LES-PRES. Ed. 5^E.
SPECIAL SHEET. Scale 1 : 20,000.
Parts of 51^B N.W. N.E. S.W. & S.E.

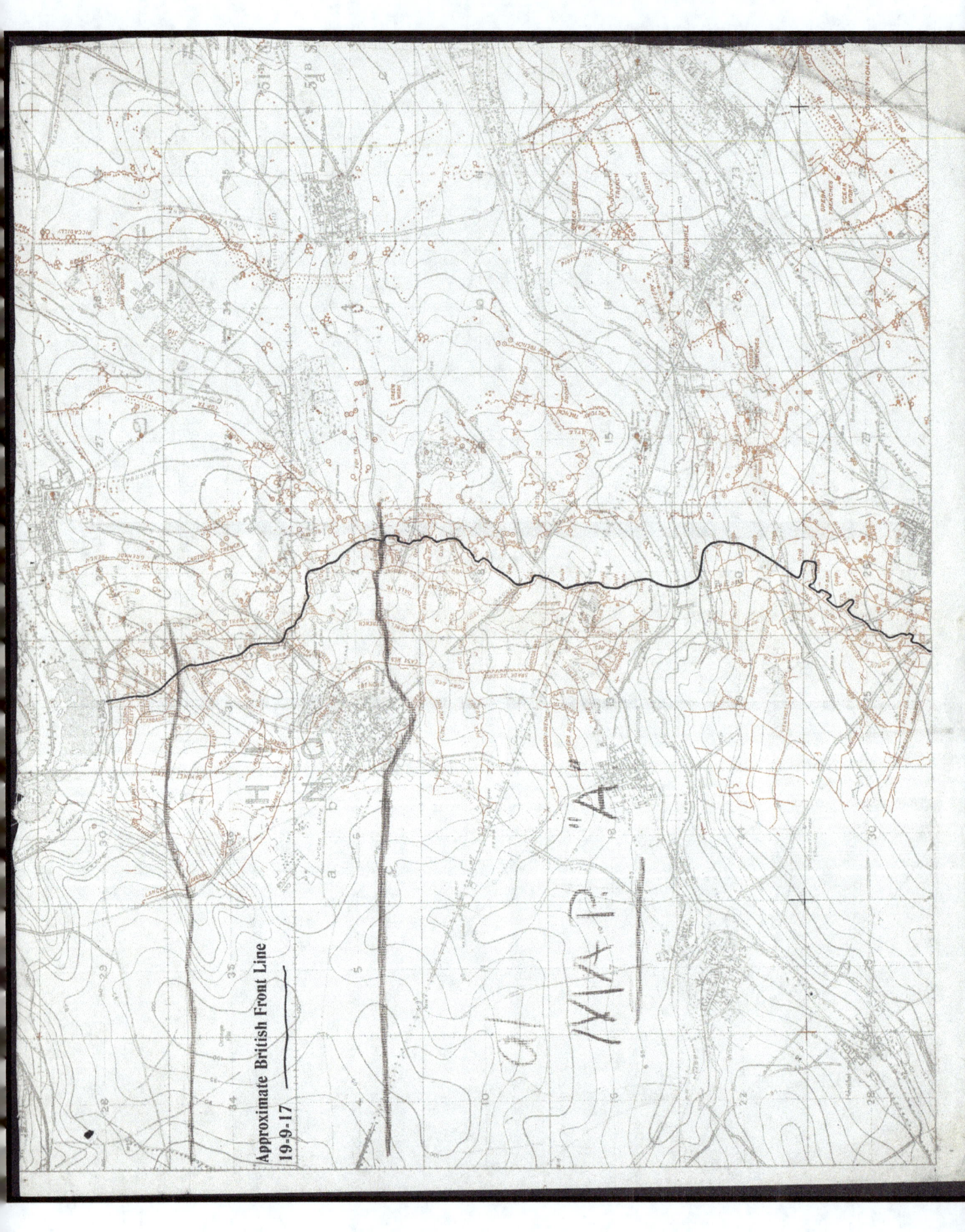

MAP "A"

Approximate British Front Line
19-9-17

WAR DIARY
or
INTELLIGENCE SUMMARY

Army Form C. 2118.

1st Bn. THE RIFLE BRIGADE

SEPTEMBER 1918.

Place	Date	Hour	Summary of Events and Information	Remarks and references to Appendices
ETERPIGNY	1st		The Bn remained in the old German trenches on SEVENTY RIDGE during the day. At 11.0 p.m. moved to the assembly position South of the SENSÉE RIVER and West of ETERPIGNY, ready for the attack on the DROCOURT-QUEANT LINE, the Brigade being in SUPPORT to the 12th Brigade.	REF. ETERPIGNY MAP. AND O.O.No 78 APPENDIX I.
	2nd		The barrage commenced at 5 a.m. and the Bn moved forward at 5.30 a.m. A half-hour's march should have been made W. of the main DROCOURT-QUEANT LINE but the Bn pressed on too quickly they found it to close to the advancing troops crossing the DROCOURT-QUEANT line (SUPPORT) soon after the 12th Brigade had reached it. After crossing the 2 right Coys lost direction going off to the right leaving touch with the left Coys and becoming mixed up in the 4th CANADIAN DIVISION on our Right. The left Coys came under a terrific M.G. barrage & were compelled to withdraw to the SUPPORT LINE again sustaining many casualties in doing so. The right Coys attempted to get back to the SUPPORT LINE & gain touch with the left Coys but were unable to do so until evening owing to terrific M.G. fire. Situation quiet during the night. Bn strength left Bn. H.Q. was two hundred & five.	REF. ETERPIGNY MAP APPENDIX I.
	3rd		Orders were received at 2 a.m. to attack at 5 a.m. the objective being RECOURT WOOD. At 3 a.m. the attack was cancelled. It was just possible to skip Coys who were forming up, in waiting for the barrage to open. The situation was very quiet. A patrol was sent out to reconnoitre & opened 1 Officer, 4 O.R. and 6 Machine Guns.	

13th Bn The Rifle Brigade

Army Form C. 2118.

September 1918

WAR DIARY
INTELLIGENCE SUMMARY

(Erase heading not required.)

Place	Date	Hour	Summary of Events and Information	Remarks and references to Appendices
	3rd contd.		Information from these prisoners showed that the enemy had withdrawn to the N. of the SENSEE RIVER. The Bn received orders to move forward. The line of the trench P.10.d. and P.16.b. was first found, from there to the sunken road P.11.c. and P.17.b. finally RECOURT WOOD. The sunken road N. of the wood was held by us. Patrols pushed forward. At 6 p.m. orders were received to move back to an area between MONCHY and the ARRAS-CAMBRAI R.D.	REF:— ETERPIGNY MAP. APPENDIX I. REF:— O.O. No 79 APPENDIX II. REF:— O.O. No 80 APPENDIX III.
FREVILLERS	4th 5th		The Bn moved by tunic to billets in FREVILLERS (CAUCOURT Sub area) Orders received that training would not commence until the 8th inst.	
	to		Till then, time spent resting, cleaning up, and reorganizing. Training consisted of Musketry on the Range, half an hour's close order drill daily, "The Platoon & Company in the attack", Patrolling, Scouting, Lewis Gun & Signalling classes held. Instruction given in the No 36 Grenade. 2 Bn Schemes were carried out.	
	18th		Baths at CAUCOURT were attended to by the 13Bn. On the 17th 13 Bn Sports were successfully carried out, also during the period inter-Coy football matches were played. The following reinforcements arrived on dates mentioned. 5th O.Rs 135 : 6th O.Rs 104 : 7th Major G.W. LIDDELL D.S.O to command the Bn. 8th O.Rs 33.	

D.D. & L., London, E.C.
(A8001) Wt. W1771/M7031 750,000 5/17 Sch. 32 Forms/C.2118/24

WAR DIARY

INTELLIGENCE SUMMARY.

(Erase heading not required.)

1st Bn. The Rifle Brigade — **September 1918**

Place	Date	Hour	Summary of Events and Information	Remarks and references to Appendices
	19th		Bn. moved from FREVILLERS at 6.10 a.m. marched to the CAUCOURT – MINGOVAL road where it entrained for the MENCHY area arriving at 12 noon. at the detraining point on the FEUCHY – FEUCHY CHAPEL Roads at H.33.d. "proceeded to area N.5/a. At 5 p.m. the Bn proceeded to the front line HAMBLAIN-LES-PRES sector relieved the 7th Bn. South Staffordshire Regt. 11th Brigade. The Bn. went into the line with 14 Officers and 650 O.Rs. Relief was complete at 9.30 p.m. the 1st Bn Hampshire Regt. being on my right the 5th Bn. west Yorks to my left. During the night the 5th Bn west Yorks relieved the 6th Bn. to our left.	REF. O.O. No 81 APPENDIX IV. REF. O.O. No 82 and MAP VALLEY WOOD APPENDIX VI
HAMBLAIN-LES-PRES	20th		On the 20.9.18. the area TIGSAW WOOD. and VICTORIA COPSE was heavily shelled with Yellow Cross Gas. during the bombardle activity was exceptionally quiet occasional shell harassing fire in QUARRY WOOD, VICTORIA COPSE, Road I.27.d the vicinity of Bn. TRENCH being the only activity. Right-Coy H.Q. & the reserve Platoon were forced to evacuate their position owing to the gas from TIGSAW WOOD area being blown across by favourable wind. Another platoon being taken up higher up PICCADILLY TRENCH. Ten casualties resulted from the gas. Patrols were sent out to find crossings or bridges across the river but none were discovered. close touch with the enemy was impossible owing to his having flooded the intervening area by damming the SCARPE RIVER	
	24.		On the 24th the Bn. was relieved by the 2nd Bn. The Lancashire Fusiliers moved to ORANGE HILL area, following Brigade in Reserve. The Brigade	REF. O.O. No 83 APPENDIX V

Army Form C. 2118.

WAR DIARY
of
INTELLIGENCE SUMMARY.
(Erase heading not required.)

1st Bn. the Rifle Brigade

September 1918

Place	Date	Hour	Summary of Events and Information	Remarks and references to Appendices
ORANGE HILL AREA.	25th		Companies at the disposal of Coy. Commanders for cleaning up and reorganising.	
	26th		Coys conveyed by lorries to ST CATHARINE for baths.	
	27th		Training consisted of Chas. Arm drill, Platoon tactical scheme, and rifle Lewis Rifle and the No 36 'Grenade, also musketry in the range. In the afternoon orders were received that the Bn would be prepared to move at short notice in case of a hostile withdrawal by the enemy. Officers reconnoitred the route to the Defence Scheme for the area, and the new Sector.	REF. WARNING ORDER APPENDIX VIA REF. O.O. No 84 APPENDIX VII
	28th		Cleaning Orders were received for the Bn to be ready to move at half an hours notice to the FALFUEL area. This was cancelled next day & with orders received that the normal relief would take place in the evg 29/30/1st during the stay in this area a miniature range was built. Accommodation improved.	REF. WARNING ORDER APPENDIX VIIA
	29th		Training continued as above.	
E. HOULETTE	30th	2.30 pm	Bn moved off at 2.30 p.m. arrived at FOSSE FM at 3.45 p.m. Tea was served after which it rained detraining at VIS-EN-ARTOIS. At 6.10 p.m the Bn moved off to relieve the 2nd Bn. Seaforth Highlanders in the front line LECLUSE SECTOR. Guides being met at ST SERVINS FM and Sketch Map Relief completed at 11.10 p.m. the 1st Somerset Light Infantry being on our right. the Brigade 1st Hampshire Regt on our left. Bn. Strength in coming out is with 18 Officers and 640 O.R's.	REF. O.O. No 85 APPENDIX VIII

O.C. 1st Bn. R.B.

REINFORCEMENTS

2nd Lieut. W. E. G. LEGHORN, MC		1/9/18
" " R. C. LOVELL		5/9/18
Lt.Col. G. W. LIDDELL, DSO		7/9/18
2nd Lieut. H. L. ROUTH		11/9/18
Major C. F. C. LETTS		23/9/18
Capt. W. H. P. SWAINE		26/9/18
2nd Lieut. A. E. BOYLAND		26/9/18
Lieut. W. H. GOSNEY		27/9/18
" G. T. KERSWELL		29/9/18
2nd Lieut. J. S. TIDBALL		do
" " R. WILSON		do
" " C. KNOWLES		do
" " G. A. LUKER		do
" " L. WATSON		do
" " W. G. KING		do
" " C. BALDWIN		do

OTHER RANKS   416

[signature] for
O.C. 1st Bn. The Rifle Brigade

CASUALTIES

Lt.Col. R. T. FELLOWES, DSO, MC	Wounded	2/9/18
Capt. A. S. S. HERBERT, MC	Wounded	do
Lieut. B. G. BAKER	Wounded	do
Capt. A.W.M.RISSIK	Missing believed prisoner	do
2nd Lieut. E. J. FREEAR	Wounded	do
" " E. C. GARTON	Wounded	do
" " P. ROMNEY	Died of wounds	2/9/18
	Wounded	2/9/18
2nd Lieut. F. S. WILSON	To Hospital	1/9/18
" " W. E. G. LEGHORN	" "	13/9/18
Capt. J. A. DAVISON, MC	To England (Home duty 6 months)	28/9/18

OTHER RANKS Killed   24
             Wounded   99
             Missing   14
             Hospital 25

G.J. Cole Lt. for
O.C. 1st Bn. The Rifle Brigade

DISTRIBUTION of BATTALION 30/9/18

OFFICERS	OTHER RANKS

A Proceeded into the line
Lieut.Col. G. W. LIDDELL, D.S.O.
Major C.F.S. LETTS
Lieut. C. C. NAUMANN
  "   A. WAUDBY, DCM
2nd Lieut. C. B. CRAVEN
Capt. J. A. TAYLOR   640
2nd Lieut. R. C. LOVELL
  "   "   J. H. PODBURY
Lieut. W. H. SHOOBERT
Lieut. H. L. ROUTH
2nd Lieut. A. E. BOYLAND
Capt. N. C. HARVEY
2nd Lieut. A. R. BURRIDGE
  "   "   J. H. LAVIES
Capt. W. H. P. SWAINE
2nd Lieut. H. K. SHORT
  "   "   W. J. WOODSIDE, MM

1st Lieut. J. W. ALDRIDGE, A.A.M.C.

B AT 1st Line Transport
Capt. G. BLAND
Lieut. & Q.M. C. MORGAN   95
  "   G. J. COLE, MC

C At S.S. 135 Details
Lieut. H. H. GOSNEY
2nd Lieut. A. O. HUNTING   78
  "   "   F. R. M. LEE
Lieut. G. T. KERSWELL
2nd Lieut. J. S. TIDBALL
  "   "   R. WILSON
  "   "   C. KNOWLES
  "   "   G. A. LUKER
  "   "   L. WATSON
  "   "   W. G. KING
  "   "   C. BALDWIN

D Otherwise employed
Capt. T. CARLYLE   Leave   11th T.M.B.   6
2/Lieut. W.G.WAYMOUTH   4th Div H.Q.   3 Sec 4 Sig Coy   9
  "   T. R. LECKIE   11th T.M.B.   11th Inf Bde   10
  "   F. W. RAY   do   4th Div. H.Q.   7
  "   W.E.G.LEGHORN   Hospital   "   " Sig Co   6
  "   H. V. MORLOCK   1st Army Sch.   "   " Train   1
                                           3rd Echelon   1
                                           Escort & prisoner   3
                                           Absent without leave 1
                                           Hospital   10
                                           Leave U.K.   60
                                             "   France   2
                                           1st Army Rest Cp   3
                                           On courses   9
                                           Boulogne duty   1
                                                               129

G. Cole Lt for
O.C. 1st Bn The Rifle Brigade

OPERATION ORDER No 77
by
Lieut.Col. R.T.FELLOWES, DSO, MC
Comndg 1st Batt THE RIFLE BRIGADE
1st SEPTEMBER, 1918

SECRET

APPENDIX. I

Ref. Map 51B, S.E. or S.W.   Copy No 7

GENERAL 1. The DROCOURT-QUEANT Line will be attacked tomorrow, and the advance continued in a N.E. direction to the SENSEE River.
2. The Battalion will be the Right Battn of the 4th British Division. The 10th Canadian Infantry Brigade of the 4th Canadian Division will be on our right.

BOUNDARY 3. RIGHT: Grid line running W to E. between square P.13 and P.19 as far E. as P.13.d.0.0. thence in a straight line through Q.7.Central.

OBJECTIVE 4. As marked on the maps copied by Coy. Commanders. The RED Line will be captured by the 12th British Inf. Brigade. The GREEN and BLUE Lines by the 11th British Inf. Brigade which will also be prepared to press home the attack of the 12th British Inf. Brigade, should it fail to secure the RED Line.

ASSEMBLY 5. The Battalion will be assembled in the triangle formed by the following points by 1.0 a.m. 2-9-18:- P.13.c.5.6.
P.13.c.15.50
P.13.c.4.1.

"B" Coy. will be left front Company
"C" "   "   " right   "   "
"I" "   "   " Right support Coy.
"A" "   "   " Left

The 1st HAMPSHIRE Regt. will be on our left and the 2nd SEAFORTH HIGHLANDERS behind us.

ACTION FROM ZERO 6. (1) At ZERO plus 30 minutes the Battalion will move forward. The two leading Coys. will halt 150 yards E. of Sunken Road in P.13.d. The two support Coys. will halt 100 yards of same road.
(2) The Battalion will move forward again in sufficient time to cross the RED Line at ZERO plus 3 hours.
(3) The Battalion will make for the BOIS DE RECOURT which it will capture together with the 1st HAMPSHIRE Regt. The advance will then be continued over the high ground in square P.12 and the Crossings over the SENSEE River will be seized and held.
(4) Touch will be maintained and liason established with the 10th Canadian Inf. Brigade at the following points:- P.16.c.15.00 (only if the Battalion has to attack the DROCOURT-QUEANT line) P.17.b.85.45: P.12.d.60.30. "C" Coy. are responsible for establishing posts of 3 men at these points.

DIRECTION OF ADVANCE 7. The general direction of the advance as far as the RED Line is on a Magnetic bearing of 102. After passing the RED Line the general direction is on a magnetic bearing of 74. Coy. Commanders will carefully check the direction taken and be prepared to lead by compass through the smoke.
Cpl BIDLAKE and 2 men to be detailed by O.C. "I" Coy. will march on the right flank of the Battn and will form a special Compass party. This party will fly a blue flag and will also check the direction of the advance.

ARTILLERY 8. After the capture of the RED Line.
6 6" Hows will bombard RECOURT
3 8" "   "   "   Cross Roads P.11.c.
The hour at which these will lift will be notified later.
Fire will then be directed on to the crossings over the SENSEE River - particularly the bridge at LECLUSE.

TANKS 9. Eight Tanks will be used for the capture of the DROCOURT-QUEANT Line.
Two of these Tanks will put down a smoke screen.
The smoke, though evil smelling, is in no way dangerous.
All ranks will be instructed of this and also that on no account are they to wait for the Tanks.

cont. on sheet 2

BATTALION   From 1.0 a.m, 9-9-18 at P.13.c.1.5.
H.Q.   When the Battalion moves forward from the Sunken Road in P.13.O Head-Quarters will follow in rear of the centre of the 2 support Coys. and will establish a station at the E. end of the railway triangle in P.15.D.

The Report Centre of the 11th British Inf. Brigade will also be established at this point and will accept all messages sent there even if the Battalion station has moved.

At all stages of the advance Companies must keep in communication with a signal station that will follow in rear of the centre of the 2 support Companies

(sd) R. T. FELLOWES, Lieut.Colonel
Commdg 1st Battn. THE RIFLE BRIGADE

Issued at 8.50 p.m.

Distribution

Copy No 1   O.C. "A" Coy.
        2   "B" "
        3   "C" "
        4   "D" "
        5   Commanding offr.
        6   Adjutant
        7   War Diary
        8   "   "
        9   File

Reference Sketch on back.

To

1. My {Platoon / Company} has reached

                  (Mark position on map or give map reference).

   and is consolidating.
     has consolidated.
     is ready to advance.

2. I am (not) in touch with   on right

   and (not) with   on left.

3. I am held up at   { by wire. / by M.G. fire. / by rifle fire.

4. Enemy's artillery is firing on

        from

5. I have sent forward patrols to

6. I estimate { my casualties at / my strength at

7. I need   boxes S.A.A.
             Lewis gun drums
             Bombs
             Rifle Grenades
             Stokes Shells   (at once)
             Very Lights
             Ground Flares   (to-night)
             Stakes
             Coils wire
             Tins water
             Rations

8. I intend to

9. (General remarks on position and strength of enemy. Number of prisoners taken and identifications, if known).

Time   Name   Rank

Date   Platoon   Coy

                 Battalion

Strike out all that is not applicable and **forward at once to Bn. H.Q.**

SECRET

OPERATION ORDER No 78
by
Lieut.Col. R.T.FELLOWES, DSO, MC
Commdg 1st Batt THE RIFLE BRIGADE
1st SEPTEMBER, 1918

APPENDIX I

Ref. Map 51B, S.E. or S.W. Copy No 8

GENERAL 1. The DROCOURT-QUEANT Line will be attacked tomorrow, and the advance continued in a N.E. direction to the SENSEE River.
2. The Battalion will be the Right Battn of the 4th British Division. The 10th Canadian Infantry Brigade of the 4th Canadian Division will be on our right.

BOUNDARY 3. RIGHT: Grid line running W to E. between square P.13 and P.19 as far E. as P.16.d.0.0. thence in a straight line through Q.7.Central.

OBJECTIVE 4. As marked on the maps copied by Coy. Commanders. The RED Line will be captured by the 12th British Inf. Brigade. The GREEN and BLUE Lines by the 11th British Inf. Brigade which will also be prepared to press home the attack of the 12th British Inf. Brigade, should it fail to secure the RED Line.

ASSEMBLY 5. The Battalion will be assembled in the triangle formed by the following points by 1.0 a.m. 2-9-18:- P.13.c.5.6.
P.13.c.15.50
P.13.c.4.1.

"B" Coy. will be left front Company
"C" "   " " right   "   "
"I" "   " " Right support Coy.
"A" "   " " Left   "   "

The 1st HAMPSHIRE Regt. will be on our left and the 2nd SEAFORTH HIGHLANDERS behind us.

ACTION FROM ZERO 6. (1) At ZERO plus 30 minutes the Battalion will move forward. The two leading Coys. will halt 150 yards E. of Sunken Road in P.13.d. The two support Coys. will halt 100 yards of same road.
(2) The Battalion will move forward again in sufficient time to cross the RED Line at ZERO plus 3 hours.
(3) The Battalion will make for the BOIS DE RECOURT which it will capture together with the 1st HAMPSHIRE Regt. The advance will then be continued over the high ground in square P.12 and the Crossings over the SENSEE River will be seized and held.
(4) Touch will be maintained and liason established with the 10th Canadian Inf. Brigade at the following points:- P.16.c.15.00 (only if the Battalion has to attack the DROCOURT-QUEANT line) P.17.b.85.45: P.19.d.60.30. "C" Coy. are responsible for establishing posts of 3 men at these points.

DIRECTION OF ADVANCE 7. The general direction of the advance as far as the RED Line is on a Magnetic bearing of 102. After passing the RED Line the general direction is on a magnetic bearing of 74. Coy. Commanders will carefully check the direction taken and be prepared to lead by compass through the smoke.
Cpl BIDLAKE and 2 men to be detailed by O.C. "I" Coy. will march on the right flank of the Battn and will form a special Compass party. This party will fly a blue flag and will also check the direction of the advance.

ARTILLERY 8. After the capture of the RED Line.
6 6" Hows will bombard RECOURT
3 6" "   "   "   Cross roads P.11.c.
The hour at which these will lift will be notified later.
Fire will then be directed on to the crossings over the SENSEE River - particularly the bridge at LECLUSE.

TANKS 9. Eight Tanks will be used for the capture of the DROCOURT-QUEANT Line.
Two of these Tanks will put down a smoke screen.
The smoke, though evil smelling, is in no way dangerous. All ranks will be instructed of this and also that on no account are they to wait for the Tanks.

cont. on sheet 2

BATTALION From 1.0 a.m, 2-9-18 at P.13.c.1.5.
H.Q.
When the Battalion moves forward from the Sunken Road in P.13.O Head-Quarters will follow in rear of the centre of the 2 support Coys. and will establish a station at the E. end of the railway triangle in P.15.D.

The Report Centre of the 11th British Inf. Brigade will also be established at this point and will accept all messages sent there even if the Battalion station has moved.

At all stages of the advance Companies must keep in communication with a signal station that will follow in rear of the centre of the 2 support Companies

(sd) R. T. FELLOWES, Lieut.Colonel
Commdg 1st Battn. THE RIFLE BRIGADE

Issued at 8.50 p.m.

Distribution

Copy No 1   O.C. "A" Coy.
         2   "B" "
         3   "C" "
         4   "D" "
         5   Commanding Offr.
         6   Adjutant
         7   War Diary
         8   "   "
         9   File

APPENDIX II

OPERATION ORDER No 79
by
Capt. J. A. DAVISON, MC
Comndg 1st Battalion, THE RIFLE BRIGADE
3rd SEPTEMBER, 1918

----

1. The Battalion will move back to the MONCHY AREA at once. Each Company and Battn. H.Q. will move independently. The move across the area West of RECOURT WOOD will be carried out in artillery formation with large intervals.
    ROUTE:- Coys. will pass through DROCOURT-QUEANT Line by the TANK P.16.a.95.95.
    By this time Battn. H.Q. will have moved there and two guides per Company will be provided to guide Companies to the new area.

2. ACCOMODATION:
    The Battn. will be accomodated in the old British Front System between SADDLE LANE and the CAMBRAI ROAD.
    Battalion H.Q. probably in HOE SUPPORT.

3. LEWIS GUNS, etc.
    All Companies on passing the QUARRY in p.15.c.7.3. will dump their Lewis guns, ammunition, etc., leaving them in charge of a suitable guard. Lewis gun limbers will call for them at about 9 p.m.

4. RATIONS.
    The Quartermaster will arrange to have rations in the new area on arrival of the Battalion. Companies will draw rations, water, etc. and will be guided to their accomodation by their C.Q.M.Ss.

5. ACKNOWLEDGE

                                (sd) C. C. NAUMANN   Lieut.
                                                      Act/Adjt
3-9-18   1st Battn. THE RIFLE BRIGADE

APPENDIX "II"

OPERATION ORDER No 79
by
Capt. J. A. DAVISON, MC
Commdg 1st Battalion, THE RIFLE BRIGADE
3rd SEPTEMBER, 1918

1. The Battalion will move back to the MONCHY AREA at once. Each Company and Battn. H.Q. will move independently. The move across the area West of RECOURT WOOD will be carried out in artillery formation with large intervals.
ROUTE:- Coys. will pass through DROCOURT-QUEANT Line by the TANK P.16.a.25.25.
By this time Battn. H.Q. will have moved there and two guides per Company will be provided to guide Companies to the new area.

2. ACCOMODATION:
The Battn. will be accomodated in the old British Front System between SADDLE LANE and the CAMBRAI ROAD.
Battalion H.Q. probably in HOE SUPPORT.

3. LEWIS GUNS, etc.
All Companies on passing the QUARRY in p.15.c.7.3. will dump their Lewis guns, ammunition, etc., leaving them in charge of a suitable guard. Lewis gun limbers will call for them at about 9 p.m.

4. RATIONS.
The Quartermaster will arrange to have rations in the new area on arrival of the Battalion. Companies will draw rations, water, etc. and will be guided to their accomodation by their C.Q.M.Ss.

5. ACKNOWLEDGE

(sd) C. C. NAUMANN   Lieut.
Act/Adjt
3-9-18   1st Battn. THE RIFLE BRIGADE

R.B. No T 1/185

11th Infantry Brigade

Account of Operations at ARRAS

AUGUST 28th - SEPTEMBER 2nd, 1918

On the night of August 28th the Battalion proceeded to the old front line East of MONCHY where we remained until the evening of the 29th when we proceeded to take over the front from the MOULIN DU ROI - P.7.c.8.4. on the SENSEE River. The relief this night was only completed at 5.0 a.m. on the 30th on account of gas shellings and the darkness, and also of the fact that the country was to a great extent unknown. That day orders were issued for Companies to push on to a line 400 yards East of the SENSEE River, and at 1.0 p.m. they reported that they were unable to do this on account of machine gun and artillery fire.

The attack on ETERPIGNY was to come off at 4.0 p.m. but at the last minute the barrage line was brought back to a point 150 yards East of the SENSEE River, instead of 400 yards. At 4.0 p.m. the barrage came down and unfortunately the two leading Companies were a little too far forward and a number of casualties were inflicted by our own barrage. The barrage itself was extraordinarily accurate, and on the whole was well followed up. The objective was gained at all points except on the immediate right of the village where a sunken road was mistaken for the one which was the objective. The road, however, was made good the same night.

On the night of the 30th/31st the Battalion was relieved by the 1st HAMPSHIRE Regt., the last Company being relieved at about 10.0 a.m. on the 31st. The lateness of the relief was due to the incessant shell fire on the BOIS SOUFFLARD, there being only two bridges which could be crossed at all, and both these were subjected to heavy shelling and machine gun fire.

The Battalion was relieved on the western slopes of "SEVENTY" Ridge on the night of the 31st/1st by the 2nd Battn. LANCASHIRE FUSILIERS. This relief was complete by 4.0 a.m., and was delayed on account of the fact that the relieving battalion did not know the ground at all. The whole of the 1st inst. the Battalion was situated in communication trenches running East and West on "SEVENTY" Ridge, and practically continuous shell fire was directed on to this area during the day.

At 10.0 p.m. that night the Battalion moved off through REMY to the assembly position 200 yards in rear of the front line on the right of ETERPIGNY. It was the first star-light night we had had, and Companies and Headquarters were all in position by 1.0 a.m. on 2nd September. There was very little shelling on our rear, and at about 3.0 a.m. the Tanks took up a position about 150 yards in rear of Battalion H.Q. They made a considerable noise as they approached, and it would have been quite possible for the enemy to have heard them, being only 350 yards away.

At 5.0 a.m. that morning (2nd Sept.) the barrage dropped. The enemy barrage was weak and scattered. His machine guns, however, were extremely accurate. The pace of our barrage was very slow and the Battalion perhaps got slightly in advance of where it should have been. However, orders were issued for a halt of one hour just behind the DROCOURT-QUEANT front line. This was carried out, but a little too soon the two right Companies moved onwards and were caught in the most terrific machine gun fire. There were also two batteries of 7.7 m.m. guns firing point blank at them. The two Company Commanders were not heard of for some time, though one managed to rejoin after having been captured by two German machine gunners. The Colonel was wounded at about 7.30 a.m. At 8.0 a.m. the two left Companies tried to move forward, with the 1st HAMPSHIRE Regt. but as soon as they left the DROCOURT-QUEANT SUPPORT the most terrific and accurate machine gun

cont. on sheet 2.

was opened on them and they were quite unable to move in the face of it. The Tanks by this time had halted on DROCOURT-QUEANT SUPPORT. These two Companies, with one Company of the HAMPSHIRE Regt. tried hard to get forward, but it was utterly impossible. Severe casualties were inflicted, and the two Companies withdrew to DROCOURT-QUEANT SUPPORT (150 yards) where they reorganized and consolidated. After a long time the Battalion was collected together and reorganized in one trench, and there was no further incident until warning was passed down the trench to say that the Germans were massing for a counter attack on DURY. By this time every man had a fire position and was ready for the heavy counter attack of which we had been previously warned. No counter attack, however, was delivered.

At 2.0 a.m. on the morning of the 3rd inst. verbal orders were received for the Battalion to attack the trench line in front behind a barrage, at 5.0 a.m. The four Company Commanders came to Battalion H.Q. and were allotted their frontages, and "moppers-up" for the dug-outs, etc. were detailed off. However, at zero, no barrage dropped, so the four Companies were ordered to proceed in front of the front line (DROCOURT-QUEANT SUPPORT) where they would be under better control if necessary, but at zero plus 4 minutes word was received that the attack was cancelled. Patrols were at once sent out, and it was found that the Germans had gone. Orders were at once issued that the trench line in front, through P.16.b. and d. should be made good: after this the line of the road through p.11.a. and b. This line was to be held until the patrols had made good the ridge East of the BOIS DE RECOURT. By 12 noon, however, the four Companies were holding the sunken road East of the BOIS DE RECOURT, with the 1st SOMERSET L.I. on the left and the CANADIANS on the right. During the afternoon Battalion H.Q. moved to the BOIS DE RECOURT.

As the 2nd SEAFORTH HIGHLANDERS had been ordered up to support the Battalion, which was by this time extremely weak, to simplify the relief the Battalion pulled out in daylight and moved back to the MONCHY AREA

------ O.C. 1st Bn. The Rifle Brigade

OPERATION ORDER No 80
by
Capt. J. A. DAVISON, MC
Comndg 1st Battalion, THE RIFLE BRIGADE
4th SEPTEMBER, 1918

APPENDIX III

MOVE 1. The Battalion will move to-day by bus to the CAUCOURT Sub Area. Destination will be notified later.

LORRIES 2. A Lorry convoy will be drawn up facing W. on the ARRAS-CAMBRAI Road at 4.0 p.m., with head of column just N. of TILLOY LES MOFFLAINES.
Debussing point on road between MINGOVAL and CAUCOURT.

ORDER of MARCH 3. Order of march, Battalion H.Q., "B", "A", "C", "I".
An interval of 200 yards will be kept between Companies.
Battalion H.Q. will move off at 1.20 p.m.
ROUTE to embussing point - ARRAS-CAMBRAI Road
On arrival at embussing point Companies will be drawn up on the N. side and clear of the road.

EMBUSSING 4. Lieut. A. WAUDBY, DCM, will report to Capt. FLINT at the head of column at 3.0 p.m. taking with him embussing strength of Battalion.

BILLETING 5. A Billeting party of all C.Q.M.Ss and one N.C.O. of Battalion H.Q. will report to Sub Area Commandant CAUCOURT at once.

RETURN 6. All Companies and Battalion H.Q. will forward total number of officers and other ranks to Battalion H.Q. immediately on receipt of these orders.

ACKNOWLEDGE

(sd) C. C. NAUMANN Lieut.
Adjt. 1st Battn. THE RIFLE BRIGADE

APPENDIX III

OPERATION ORDER No 80
by
Capt. J. A. DAVISON, MC
Commdg 1st Battalion, THE RIFLE BRIGADE
4th SEPTEMBER, 1918

MOVE 1. The Battalion will move to-day by bus to the CAUCOURT Sub Area. Destination will be notified later.

LORRIES 2. A Lorry convoy will be drawn up facing W. on the ARRAS-CAMBRAI Road at 4.0 p.m., with head of column just N. of TILLOY LES MOFFLAINES.
Debussing point on road between MINGOVAL and CAUCOURT.

ORDER of MARCH 3. Order of march, Battalion H.Q., "B", "A", "C", "I".
An interval of 200 yards will be kept between Companies.
Battalion H.Q. will move off at 1.20 p.m.
ROUTE to embussing point - ARRAS-CAMBRAI Road
On arrival at embussing point Companies will be drawn up on the N. side and clear of the road.

EMBUSSING 4. Lieut. A. WAUDBY, DCM, will report to Capt. FLINT at the head of column at 3.0 p.m. taking with him embussing strength of Battalion.

BILLETING 5. A Billeting party of all C.Q.M.Ss and one N.C.O. of Battalion H.Q. will report to Sub Area Commandant CAUCOURT at once.

RETURN 6. All Companies and Battalion H.Q. will forward total number of officers and other ranks to Battalion H.Q. immediately on receipt of these orders.

ACKNOWLEDGE

(sd) C. C. NAUMANN Lieut.
Adjt. 1st Battn. THE RIFLE BRIGADE

SECRET

APPENDIX IV

OPERATION ORDER No 84
by
Major G. W. LIDDELL, D.S.O.
Commanding 1st Battalion THE RIFLE BRIGADE

COPY NO 12:

REF. Sheets 36B: 51 B N.W. & S.W.   18th SEPT. 1918

MOVE 1. The Battalion will move to the vicinity of MONCHY LE PREUX by bus to-morrow preparatory to taking over a sub sector of the front line to-morrow night (vide Operation Order No 82)

ORDER 2. The Battn will be formed up in column of route facing S.E. in the following order, at 6.10 a.m: H.Q., "B", "A", "C", "I".
Head of the column outside the Orderly Room.
DRESS: Fighting order. Packs and great coats will be carried.
ROUTE: via BETHONSART

EMBUSSING 3. The Battn will embuss on the CAUCOURT-HINGOVAL Road facing South in square H.17.d. All troops will get clear of the road on the right hand side. Parties of 25 will be told off from front to rear of the column on arrival. The Battalion will move in accordance with S.S. 724.
2nd Lieut. C. B. CRAVEN will report to Major P.H.HUDSON at the embussing point with the strength of the Battn. at 7.15 a.m.

DETAILS 4. S.S. 135 Details will proceed to LOUEZ under Capt. CARLYLE in accordance with instructions to be issued later. They will probably embus with the Battalion.

DEBUSSING 5. The Battalion will debuss on the FEUCHY-FEUCHY CHAPEL Road in square H.28. and will proceed to the area N.5.a. South of SWORD LANE.

MEALS 6. Companies and Headquarters will make their own arrangements to keep back a certain number of camp kettles for breakfasts. These will be carried to the embussing point by parties who will move off at 6.0 a.m.
Dinners and teas will be in N.5.a.

COOKERS etc. 7. The cookers, water carts, Lewis gun limbers, Mess cart etc. will proceed in advance to reach the area N.5.a. by dinner time to-morrow, 19th inst.

TRANSPORT 8. Officers' kits, Orderly Room boxes, etc. will be collected at 5.30 a.m. to-morrow. The remainder of the Transport not mentioned in para. 7. will proceed to the new Transport lines, near FEUCHY, under orders issued direct to the Transport Officer.

BILLETS 9. Officers commanding Companies will ensure that their billets are left scrupulously clean. Certificates to this effect will reach Orderly Room by 5.30 a.m. tomorrow.

ACKNOWLEDGE

J. A. Davison
Capt.
Adjt
1st Battn. THE RIFLE BRIGADE

DISTRIBUTION

Copy No 1 O.C. "A" Coy   8 L. G. Offr
         2   "B" "   9 Int. & Sig. Offr
         3   "C" "   10 Transport Offr
         4   "I" "   11 Quartermaster
         5 Commanding Offr   12 War Diary
         6 Adjutant   13   do
         7 A/Adjt   14 File

APPENDIX IV

OPERATION ORDER No. 84   COPY NO 13
by
Major G. W. LIDDELL, D.S.O.
Commanding 1st Battalion THE RIFLE BRIGADE

REF. Sheets 36B: 51 B N.W. & S.W.   18th SEPT. 1918

MOVE 1. The Battalion will move to the vicinity of MONCHY LE PREUX by bus to-morrow preparatory to taking over a sub sector of the front line to-morrow night (vide Operation Order No 82)

ORDER 2. The Battn will be formed up in column of route facing S.E. in the following order, at 6.10 a.m: H.Q., "B", "A", "C", "I".
Head of the column outside the Orderly Room.
DRESS: Fighting order. Packs and great coats will be carried.
ROUTE: via BETHONSART

EMBUS-SING 3. The Battn will embuss on the CAUCOURT-MINGOVAL Road facing South in square H.17.d. All troops will get clear of the road on the right hand side. Parties of 25 will be told off from front to rear of the column on arrival. The Battalion will move in accordance with S.S. 724.
2nd Lieut. C. B. CRAVEN will report to Major P.H. HUDSON at the embussing point with the strength of the Battn. at 7.15 a.m.

DETAILS 4 S.S. 135 Details will proceed to LOUEZ under Capt. CARLYLE in accordance with instructions to be issued later. They will probably embus with the Battalion.

DEBUS-SING 5. The Battalion will debuss on the FEUCHY-FEUCHY CHAPEL Road in square H.28. and will proceed to the area N.5.a. South of SWORD LANE.

MEALS 6. Companies and Headquarters will make their own arrangements to keep back a certain number of camp kettles for breakfasts. These will be carried to the embussing point by parties who will move off at 6.0 a.m.
Dinners and teas will be in N.5.a.

COOKERS etc. 7. The cookers, water carts, Lewis gun limbers, Mess cart etc. will proceed in advance to reach the area N.5.a. by dinner time to-morrow, 19th inst.

TRANSPORT 8. Officers' kits, Orderly Room boxes, etc. will be collected at 5.30 a.m. to-morrow. The remainder of the Transport not mentioned in para. 7. will proceed to the new Transport lines, near FEUCHY, under orders issued direct to the Transport Officer.

BILLETS 9 Officers commanding Companies will ensure that their billets are left scrupulously clean. Certificates to this effect will reach Orderly Room by 5.30 a.m. tomorrow.

ACKNOWLEDGE

Capt.
Adjt
1st Battn. THE RIFLE BRIGADE

DISTRIBUTION

Copy No 1 O.C. "A" Coy   8 L. G. Offr
     2   "B" "   9 Int. & Sig. Offr
     3   "C" "   10 Transport Offr
     4   "I" "   11 Quartermaster
     5 Commanding Offr. 12 War Diary
     6 Adjutant   13   do
     7 A/Adjt   14 File

AMENDMENT No 1.
to OPERATION ORDER No 81
18th September, 1916

I. Ref. Para 3 for "H.17.d." read V.17.d.

II. Ref. Para. 4   The details will proceed to ST. AUBIN by march route. They will be drawn up by the Church ready to move off at 1.0 p.m.   They join the Brigade details at the starting point at Cross roads W.14.d.7.5. where they will form up in rear of the Trench Mortar Battery.
DRESS: Full marching order.

III. The Quarter Master will detail one cooker and one water cart to accompany the party.

IV. packs will be loaded on a lorry at the above starting point

(sd) J. A. DAVISON   Capt.
Adjt
1st Battn. THE RIFLE BRIGADE

Issued to all recipients of Operation Order No 81

AMENDMENT No 1
to OPERATION ORDER No 21
18th September, 1916

I. Ref. Para. 3 for "W.17.d." read V.-17.d.

II. Ref. Para. 4. The details will proceed to ST. AUBIN by march route. They will be drawn up by the Church ready to move off at 1.0 p.m. They join the Brigade details at the starting point at Cross roads W.44.d.7.5. where they will form up in rear of the Trench Mortar Battery.
DRESS: Full marching order.

III. The Quarter Master will detail one cooker and one water cart to accompany the party.

IV. Packs will be loaded on a lorry at the above starting point

(sd) J. A. DAVISON   Capt.
                     Adjt
1st Battn. THE RIFLE BRIGADE

Issued to all recipients of Operation Order No 21

SECRET OPERATION ORDER No.

by

Major G. W. LIDDELL, D.S.O.

Commdg 1st Battalion THE RIFLE BRIGADE

APPENDIX V

R.M.F. Sheets 51B N.W. & S.W.   18th SEPT. 1918   COPY No 13

RELIEF 1. The Battalion will relieve the 7th Battn S. STAFFORDSHIRE Regt. in the front line to-morrow night, 19th inst.
"A" Coy. RIFLE BRIGADE will be the Left Front Coy.
"B" "   "   "   "   "   "   in support
"C" "   "   "   "   "   "   the Right Front Coy.
"I" "   "   "   "   "   "   in reserve.
Battalion Hd Qrs will be at O.3.a.3.9. The position of the Regtl. AID POST will be notified later.

ADVANCE PARTY 2. An advance party consisting of the 4 Company Commanders and 1 N.C.O. per Coy. will meet guides at I.25.d.7.9. at 10 a.m.

MOVE 3. The Battalion will move off in the following order from area N.5.a: "A", "C", "B", "I" H.Q. in time to meet guides at O.7.b.4.9. at 6.0 p.m.
Companies will move with an interval of 200 yards between platoons, the leading platoon of "A" Coy. moving off at 5.15 p.m.

RATIONS WATER 4. Rations for the 19th inst will be carried. All water bottles will be filled before leaving area N.5.a. as water in tins will not arrive before 1.0 a.m. on 20th inst. This water will be supplied under arrangements to be notified later.

SUPPLIES 5. The Reserve Company will be responsible for supplying the two front line Coys. and the Support Coy. will supply itself.

HAVERSACKS & TOOLS 6. All haversacks, picks and shovels, will be dumped in area N.5.a before the Battalion moves off. Each Company and Headquarters will detail one old man to look after these until they are collected by the Transport Officer.

REPORTS 7. Reports, returns, etc. will be rendered by Companies in accordance with the table already in their possession.

MOVEMENT 8. All movement in daylight will be restricted as far as possible. Therefore, if necessary, runners must leave Company H.Q. in time to return from Battalion H.Q. before daylight.

9. The attention of Company Commanders is directed to 4th Divisional Trench Orders and Battalion "NOTES".

DIS. MAPS 10. Complete maps showing dispositions of Companies will reach Battalion H.Q. by 5 a.m. on the 20th.

11. Completion of relief will be reported by runner (and visual if possible), by any sentence containing the code word "SUNSHINE".

12. ACKNOWLEDGE

Capt.
Adjt.
1st Battn. THE RIFLE BRIGADE

DISTRIBUTION.

No 1 O.C. "A" Coy   8 L.G. Offr
   2   "B" "   9 Int: & Sig Offr
   3   "C" "   10 Transport Offr
   4   "I" "   11 Quartermaster
   5 Commanding Offr   12 War Diary
   6 Adjutant   13 do
   7 A/Adjt.   14 File

SECRET   OPERATION ORDER No 68   APPENDIX V
by
Major G. W. LIDDELL, D.S.O.
Commdg 1st Battalion THE RIFLE BRIGADE

REF Sheets 51B N.W. & S.W.   18th SEPT. 1916   COPY No 12

RELIEF 1. The Battalion will relieve the 7th Battn S. STAFFORDSHIRE Regt. in the front line to-morrow night, 19th inst.
"A" Coy. RIFLE BRIGADE will be the Left Front Coy.
"B" " " " " in support
"C" " " " " the Right Front Coy.
"I" " " " " in reserve.
Battalion Hd Qrs will be at O.3.a.3.9. The position of the Regtl. AID POST will be notified later.

ADVANCE PARTY 2. An advance party consisting of the 4 Company Commanders and 1 N.C.O. per Coy. will meet guides at I.25.d.7.9. at 10 a.m.

MOVE 3. The Battalion will move off in the following order from area N.5.a: "A", "C", "B", "I" H.Q. in time to meet guides at O.7.b.4.9. at 6.0 p.m.
Companies will move with an interval of 200 yards between platoons, the leading platoon of "A" Coy. moving off at 5.15 p.m.

RATIONS WATER 4. Rations for the 19th inst willbe carried. All water bottles will be filled before leaving area N.5.a. as water in tins will not arrive before 1.0 a.m. on 20th inst. This water will be supplied under arrangements to be notified later.

SUPPLIES 5. The Reserve Company will be responsible for supplying the two front line Coys. and the Support Coy. will supply itself.

HAVERSACKS & TOOLS 6. All haversacks, picks and shovels, will be dumped in area N.5.a before the Battalion moves off. Each Company and Headquarters will detail one old man to look after these until they are collected by the Transport Officer.

REPORTS 7. Reports, returns, etc. will be rendered by Companies in accordance with the table already in their possession.

MOVEMENT 8. All movement in daylight will be restricted as far as possible. Therefore, if necessary, runners must leave Company H.Q. in time to return from Battalion H.Q. before daylight.

9. The attention of Company Commanders is directed to 4th Divisional Trench Orders and Battalion "NOTES".

DIS. MAPS 10. Complete maps showing dispositions of Companies will reach Battalion H.Q. by 5 a.m. on the 20th.

11. Completion of relief will be reported by runner (and visual if possible), by any sentence containing the code word "SUNSHINE".

12. ACKNOWLEDGE

[signature]
Capt.
Adjt.
1st Battn. THE RIFLE BRIGADE

DISTRIBUTION.

No 1 O.C. "A" Coy   8 L.G. Offr
   2   " "B" "   9 Int. & Sig Offr
   3   " "C" "   10 Transport Offr
   4   " "I" "   11 Quartermaster
   5 Commanding Offr   12 War Diary
   6 Adjutant   13 do
   7 A/Adjt.   14 File

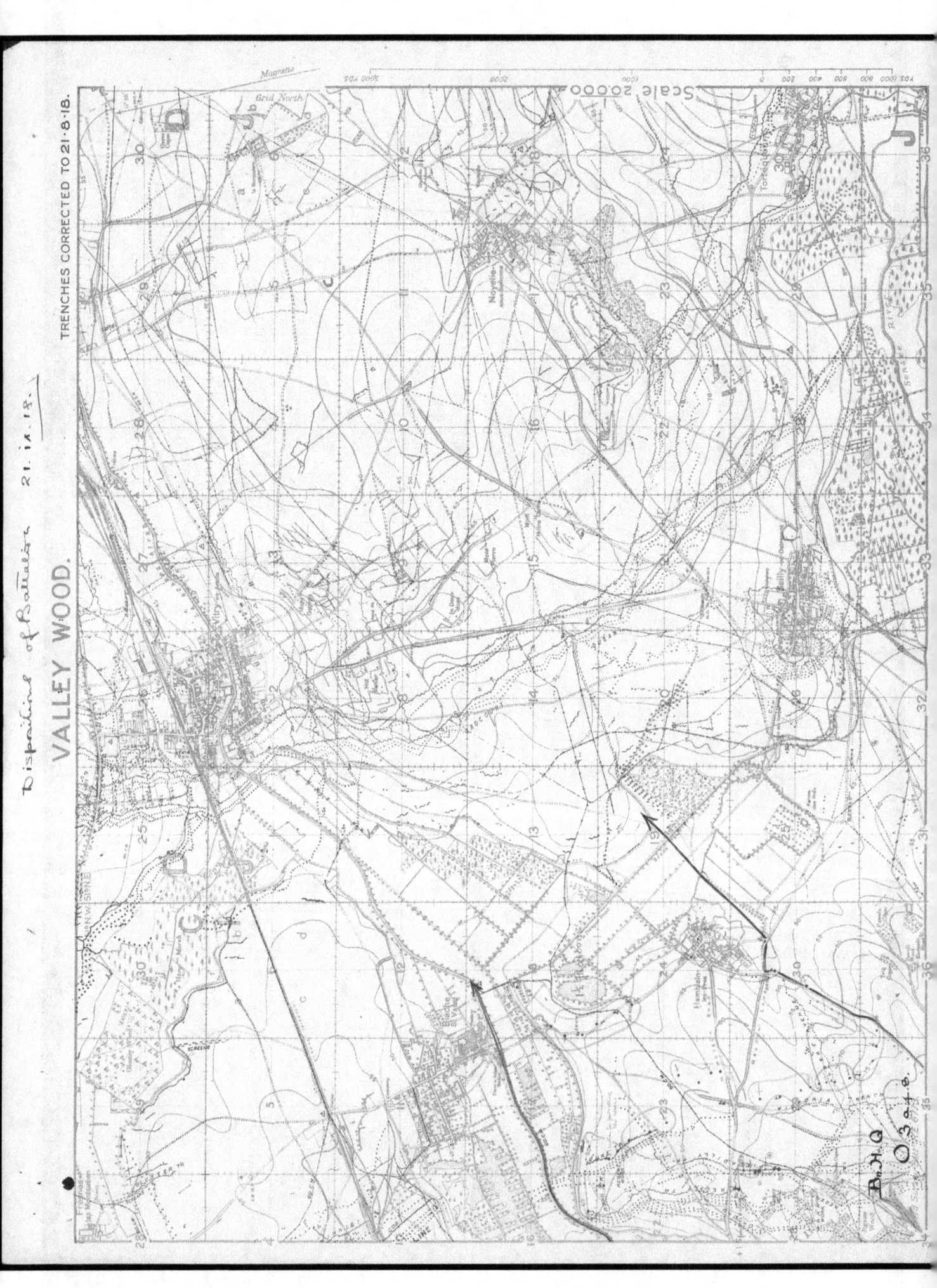

APPENDIX V

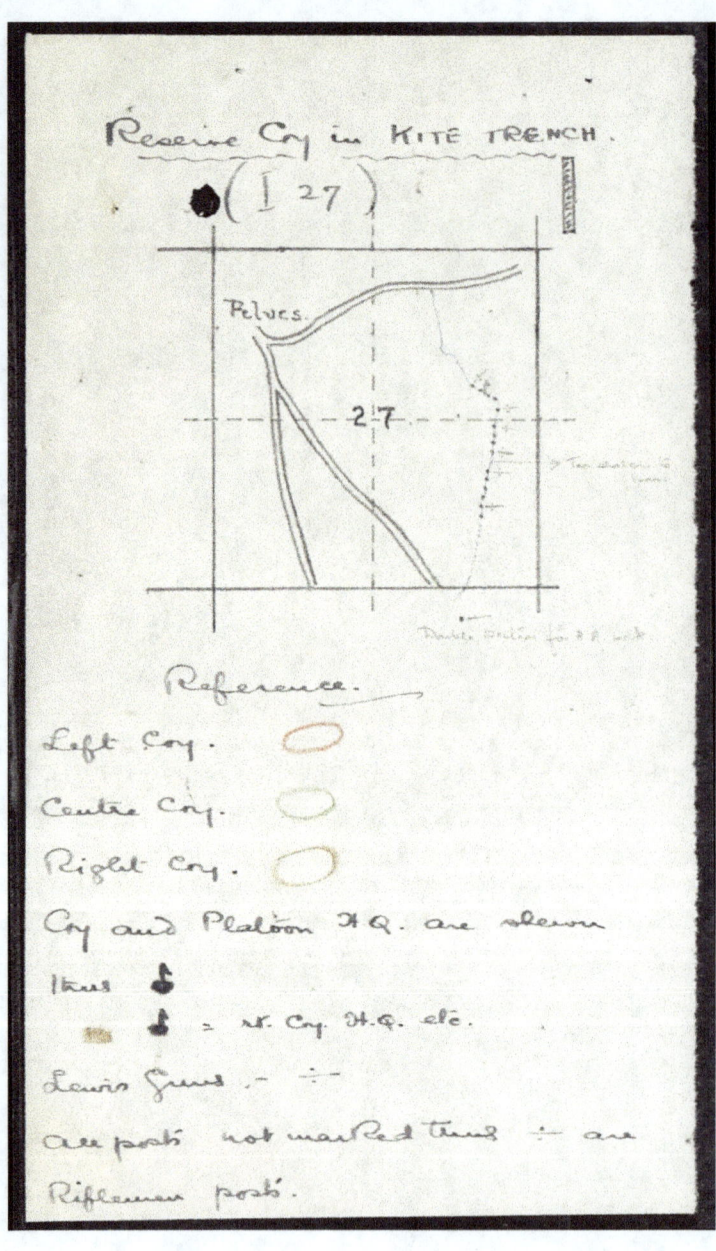

Reserve Coy in KITE TRENCH.
(I 27)

Reference.
Left Coy. 🔴
Centre Coy. 🟡
Right Coy. 🟢

Coy and Platoon H.Q. are shewn thus ♪

♪ = Rt. Coy. H.Q. etc.

Lewis Guns. — ÷

All posts not marked thus ÷ are Riflemen posts.

Reserve Coy in KITE TRENCH.
(I 27.)

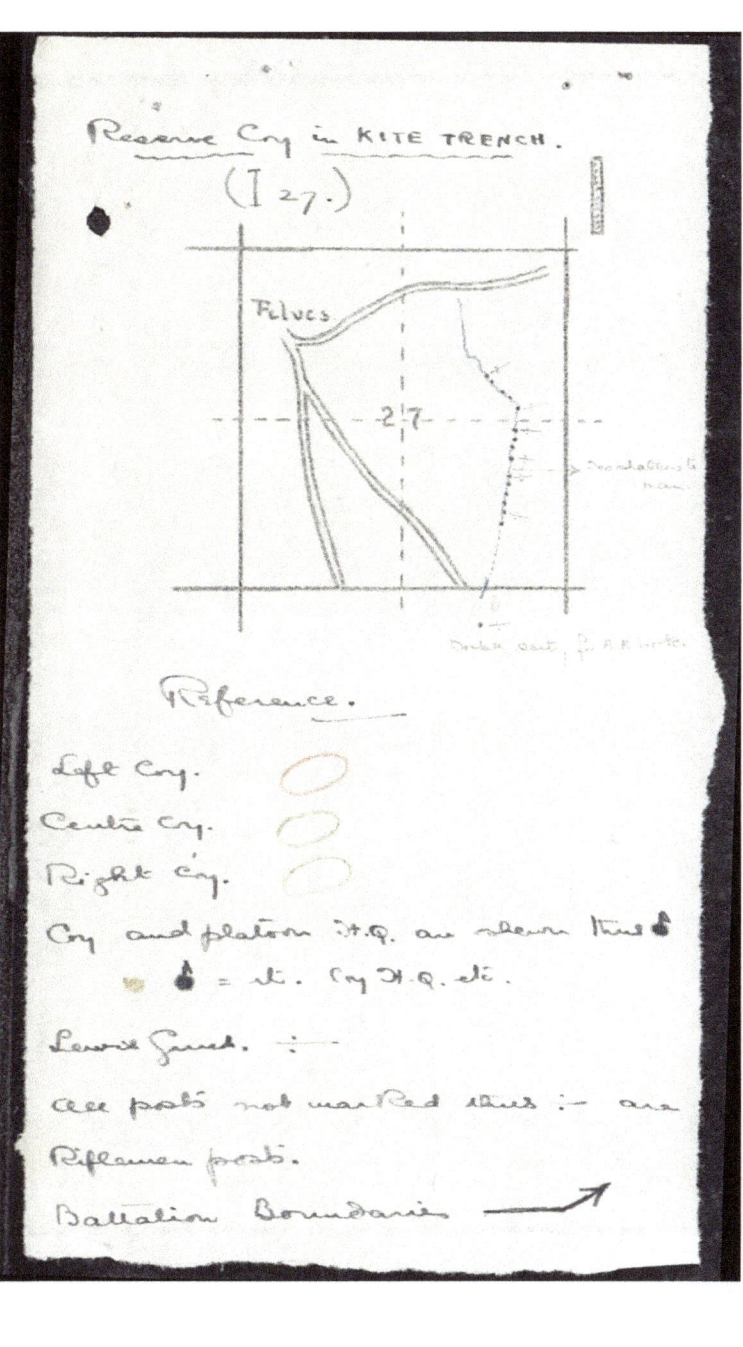

Reference.

Left Coy.   ⭕
Centre Coy.   ⭕
Right Coy.   ⭕

Coy and platoon H.Q. are shown thus ♠
♠ = Bn. Coy H.Q. etc.

Lewis Guns. :–

All posts not marked thus :– are
Riflemen posts.

Battalion Boundaries ⟶

AMENDMENT No 1
to OPERATION ORDER No 82
18th September, 1918

I.   Ref. para 4, for "19th inst" read 20th inst.

II. All maps, defence schemes, aeroplane photos, trench stores, etc. will be taken over and duplicate receipts forwarded to reach Battalion H.Q. with the morning reports on the 20th inst.

                                (sd) J. A. DAVISON   Capt.
                                                     Adjt
                                1st Battn. THE RIFLE BRIGADE

Issued to all recipients of Operation Order No 82

AMENDMENT No 1
to OPERATION ORDER No 83
18th September, 1918

I. Ref. para 4, for "19th inst" read 20th inst.

II. All maps, defence schemes, aeroplane photos, trench stores, etc. will be taken over and duplicate receipts forwarded to reach Battalion H.Q. with the morning reports on the 20th inst.

(sd) J. A. DAVISON   Capt.
                      Adjt
1st Battn. THE RIFLE BRIGADE

Issued to all recipients of Operation Order No 83

SECRET   OPERATION ORDER No 83
                                by
                      Lieut. Col. G. W. LIDDELL, DSO.
                   Commdg 1st Battalion, THE RIFLE BRIGADE

23-9-18   Copy No 8

RELIEF   I.   The Battalion will be relieved in the front line tomorrow
                  night by the 2nd Battalion LANCASHIRE FUSILIERS.
                  "A" Coy. RIFLE BRIGADE will be relieved by "A" Coy. LANCS FUSLRS.
                  "B"   "   "   "   "   "   " "B" "   "   "
                  "C"   "   "   "   "   "   " "C" "   "   "
                  "I"   "   "   "   "   "   " "D" "   "   "

GUIDES   II.   Guides at the rte of two per platoon and two for Company
                  and Battalion Hd Qrs will be provided. They will reconnoitre
                  the routes of relief forward of Battalion Hd Qrs and will report
                  at Battalion Hd Qrs before dawn tomorrow morning. The Intelli-
                  gence Officer will conduct these guides to arrive at road junctin
                  O.7.b.4.9. at 6.0 p.m.

ORDER OF   III. The order and route of relief will be as follows;-
RELIEF.   ORDER: "A", "C", "B", "I", H.Q.
                ROUTE: The shortest way via Battalion Hd Qrs for all Com-
                         panies. These guides will on no account pass the
                  line BOIRY I.27.b.8.3. before 7.30 p.m.

MOVE   IV.   On completion of relief the Battalion will move with an
                  interval of 200 yards between platoons to the FEUCHY or ORANGE
                  HILL area. All preliminary arrangements will be made by the
                  Quartermaster. The exact area, time and place of guides
                  will be notified later.

HANDING   V.   All defence schemes, aeroplane photos, etc. and all trench
OVER   stores, etc. will be handed over. Lists of these will reach
                  Battalion Hd.Qrs by 6.30 a.m. tomorrow. Receipts for same will
                  be forwarded to reach Battalion Hd Qrs as soon as possible after
                  relief. At present there is a great shortage of petrol tins.
                  Company Commanders will ensure that all their's are brought out
                  and as many more salved as possible.

TRANSPORT   VI.   One lewis gun limber per Company and two for Battalion H.Q.
                  will be at the respective ration dumps from 9.15 p.m. onwards.

REPORT   VII. Completion of relief will be reported to Battalion Hd Qrs.
                  by wire and runner. In the case of the former by any sentence
                  containing the code word "WOPLAES"

                        ACKNOWLEDGE

                                          (sd) J. A. DAVISON   Capt.
                                                                Adjt.
                                         1st Battn. THE RIFLE BRIGADE

SECRET OPERATION ORDER No 23 APPENDIX VI
by
Lieut.Col. G.W.LIDDELL, DSO.
Commdg 1st Battalion, THE RIFLE BRIGADE

23-9-18   Copy No 9

RELIEF   I.   The Battalion will be relieved in the front line tomorrow
                    night by the 2nd Battalion LANCASHIRE FUSILIERS.
                    "A" Coy. RIFLE BRIGADE will be relieved by "A" Coy. LANCS FUSLRS.
                    "B"   "   "   "   "   "   "   "B"   "   "   "
                    "C"   "   "   "   "   "   "   "C"   "   "   "
                    "I"   "   "   "   "   "   "   "D"   "   "   "

GUIDES   II.   Guides at the rte of two per platoon and two for Company
                    and Battalion Hd Qrs will be provided. They will reconnoitre
                    the routes of relief forward of Battalion Hd Qrs and will report
                    at Battalion Hd Qrs before dawn tomorrow morning. The Intelli-
                    gence Officer will conduct these guides to arrive at road junctin
                    O.7.b.4.9. at 6.0 p.m.

ORDER OF   III.   The order and route of relief will be as follows:-
RELIEF.   ORDER: "A", "C", "B", "I", H.Q.
                ROUTE: The shortest way via Battalion Hd Qrs for all Com-
                         panies.   These guides will on no account pass the
                    Line BOIRY I.27.b.8.3. before 7.30 p.m.

MOVE   IV.   On completion of relief the Battalion will move with an
                    interval of 200 yards between platoons to the FEUCHY or ORANGE
                    HILL area. All preliminary arrangements will be made by the
                    Quartermaster. The exact area, time and place of guides
                    will be notified later.

HANDING   V.   All defence schemes, aeroplane photos, etc. and all trench
OVER   stores, etc. will be handed over. Lists of these will reach
                    Battalion Hd.Qrs by 6.30 a.m. tomorrow. Receipts for same will
                    be forwarded to reach Battalion Hd Qrs as soon as possible after
                    relief. At present there is a great shortage of petrol tins.
                    Company Commanders will ensure that all their's are brought out
                    and as many more salved as possible.

TRANSPORT   VI.   One lewis gun limber per Company and two for Battalion H.Q.
                    will be at the respective ration dumps from 9.15 p.m. onwards.

REPORT   VII.   Completion of relief will be reported to Battalion Hd Qrs.
                    by wire and runner. In the case of the former by any sentence
                    containing the code word "WOPLAES"

            ACKNOWLEDGE

                                    (sd) J. A. DAVISON   Capt.
                                                          Adjt.
                                    1st Battn. THE RIFLE BRIGADE

- 2 -

6. **MOVE:** No move will be made by any Company without orders from Battalion H.Q. "C" Company will be prepared to counter-attack, and the ground forward of their area will be reconnoitred in preparation for this.
"A" Company will not move up to "C" Company's position should the latter move forward.

7. ACKNOWLEDGE

(sd) G. G. NAUMANN, Lieut.
Adjt 1st Batt. THE RIFLE BRIGADE

APPENDIX VIA

WARNING ORDER
in the event of an enemy withdrawal
27th SEPTEMBER, 1918

MOVE   1.   From 6 p.m. today, 27th onwards, the Battalion will be prepared to move forward at one hour's notice in full fighting order.

TRANSPORT   2.   The Transport Officer will be responsible that the limbers (1 per Coy and 1 for H.Q.) bringing rations up to-day remain at their respective Hd.Qrs., and will be loaded up immediately with Lewis guns, ammunition, etc. In the event of a move these limbers will accompany the Battalion.

KITS   3.   Officers' kits, surplus mess stores, haversacks, etc. will be packed and blankets rolled in bundles of ten and labelled by 6 p.m. Should the Battalion move forward the Transport Officer will make arrangements to have the above mentioned collected and conveyed to the Transport Lines. One man will also be detailed by each Company to remain with his Company's kits, etc. and accompany them to transport.

TOOLS   4.   Companies will send out salvage parties at once to collect sufficient picks and shovels.

RATIONS   5.   In the event of a move rations for the 28th instant will be carried on the man: the Quartermaster will make the necessary arrangements.

WATER   6.   All water bottles will be filled by 6 p.m. to-day and will be kept full.

(sd) C. C. NAUMANN Lieut.
A/Adjt 1st Bn THE RIFLE BRIGADE

AMENDMENT No 1
to OPERATION ORDER No 83

24th September, 1918

I. On completion of relief the Battalion will move as laid down to the area H.35.b., H.36.a. and c.
Battalion Hd Qrs will be at H.36.a.3.2.

II. The Quartermaster will arrange to have guides at O.7.b.&.9 from 10. p.m. onwards to guide the troops relieved to their bivouac areas.

III. Hot tea will be provided on arrival.

IV. In order that the changing over of Details may be carried out as soon as possible, the form R.B. 19/2 will be rendered to reach orderly room by not later than 6.0 p.m. to-morrow 25th inst.

V. Each Company will hand over 20 petrol tins to the incoming unit, also all trench maps.

VI. Picks and shovels will be handed over.

(sd) J. A. DAVISON, Capt.
Adjt
1st Battn. THE RIFLE BRIGADE

AMENDMENT No 1
to OPERATION ORDER No 83

24th September, 1918

I. On completion of relief the Battalion will move as laid down to the area H.35.b., H.36.a. and c.
Battalion Hd Qrs will be at H.36.a.3.2.

II. The Quartermaster will arrange to have guides at O.7.b.&.9 from 10. p.m. onwards to guide the troops relieved to their bivouac areas.

III. Hot tea will be provided on arrival.

IV. In order that the changing over of Details may be carried out as soon as possible, the form R.B. 10/2 will be rendered to reach orderly room by not later than 6.0 p.m. to-morrow 25th inst.

V. Each Company will hand over 20 petrol tins to the incoming unit, also all trench maps.

VI. Picks and shovels will be handed over.

(sd) J. A. DAVISON, Capt.
Adjt
1st Battn. THE RIFLE BRIGADE

SECRET   OPERATION ORDER No 84   APPENDIX VII
by
Lieut.Col. G. W. LIDDELL, D.S.O.
Commdg 1st Battalion THE RIFLE BRIGADE
CENTRE BATTALION of RESERVE BRIGADE

Ref. Sheet 51B   26 SEPTEMBER, 1918

1. **DESCRIPTION:** (i) The whole front of the Division is covered by a flooded area. The only possible crossing places, except by boat, appear to be in the vicinity of LECLUSE, SAILLY-en-OSTREVENT and BIACHE.
(ii) If these crossing places are carefully watched and firmly held, any surprise operation on the enemy's part should be impossible, and a hostile attack should only be able to develop slowly.
(iii) The forward slopes of the ridge South of the flooded area form a natural OUTPOST LINE OF RESISTANCE. Behind this line the area up to DROCOURT-QUEANT Line in the right (LECLUSE) sector, and the FRESNES-ROUVROY Line in the left (HAMBLAIN) Sector is suitable for the main defensive zone.

2. **BOUNDARIES:** Left Battalion Boundary:- O.2.d.8.9. - N.W. Edge of BOIS du SART - I.34.a.3.6.
Right Battalion Boundary:- O.9.a.8.0. to O.4.b.3.0.
Inter-Company Boundary for two forward Companies:- O.3. Central to I.34.a.0.4.

3. **GENERAL PRINCIPLES OF DEFENCE** The area will be divided into two zones as follows:-
(a) THE OUTPOST ZONE
This will comprise the ground East of and excluding the main line of resistance.
(b) THE BATTLE ZONE
This will comprise the ground West of and including the main line of resistance.

4. **ACTION IN CASE OF HOSTILE ATTACK** In case of a hostile attack the Battalion will move at once to the line BOIS du VERT - BOIS du SART.
DISPOSITIONS of the Battalion will be:-
"B" and "I" Coys in front, "B" on the left and "I" on the right, "C" Coy. in close support and "A" Coy. in reserve.
"B" and "I" Coys will be on the high ground N.E. and E. of the BOIS DU SART.
"C" Coy. S.W. of the BOIS DU SART
"A" Coy. in reserve in the area round the mound O.2.d. and O.3.c.
Location of Battalion H.Q. will be notified later.
ROUTE to Battle Positions:- North of MONCHY.
Positions as laid down above will be thoroughly reconnoitred by O.C. Companies as soon as possible, and the location of their Company H.Q. will be forwarded to Battalion H.Q. before 12.0 noon to-morrow.

5. **FLANKS:** In the event of Companies having to take up these positions special attention will be paid to getting t.. on the flanks. The 1st Somerset L.I. will be on left and the 1st Hampshire Regt. on the right.

cont

6. MOVE: No move will be made by any Company without orders from Battalion H.Q. "C" Company will be prepared to counter-attack, and the ground forward of their area will be reconnoitred in preparation for this.
    "A" Company will not move up to "C" Company's position should the latter move forward.

7.   ACKNOWLEDGE

                              (sd) C. G. NAUMANN, Lieut.
                           Adjt 1st Batt, THE RIFLE BRIGADE

SECRET   OPERATION ORDER No 34
by
Lieut.Col. G. W. LIDDELL, D.S.O.
Commdg 1st Battalion THE RIFLE BRIGADE
CENTRE BATTALION of RESERVE BRIGADE

APPENDIX VII

Ref. Sheet 51B   26 SEPTEMBER, 1918

1. **DESCRIPTION:** (i) The whole front of the Division is covered by a flooded area. The only possible crossing places, except by boat, appear to be in the vicinity of LECLUSE, SAILLY-en-OSTREVENT and BIACHE.
(ii) If these crossing places are carefully watched and firmly held, any surprise operation on the enemy's part should be impossible, and a hostile attack should only be able to develop slowly.
(iii) The forward slopes of the ridge South of the flooded area form a natural OUTPOST LINE OF RESISTANCE. Behind this line the area up to DROCOURT-QUEANT Line in the right (LECLUSE) sector, and the FRESNES-ROUVROY Line in the left (HAMBLAIN) Sector is suitable for the main defensive zone.

2. **BOUNDARIES:** Left Battalion Boundary:- O.3.d.8.9. - N.W. Edge of BOIS du SART - I.34.a.3.0.
Right Battalion Boundary:- O.2.a.2.0. to O.4.b.3.0.
Inter-Company Boundary for two forward Companies:- O.3. Central to I.34.a.0.4.

3. **GENERAL PRINCIPLES OF DEFENCE** The area will be divided into two zones as follows:-
   (a) THE OUTPOST ZONE
       This will comprise the ground East of and excluding the main line of resistance.
   (b) THE BATTLE ZONE
       This will comprise the ground West of and including the main line of resistance.

4. **ACTION IN CASE OF HOSTILE ATTACK** In case of a hostile attack the Battalion will move at once to the line BOIS du VERT - BOIS du SART.
DISPOSITIONS of the Battalion will be:-
"B" and "I" Coys in front, "B" on the left and "I" on the right, "C" Coy. in close support and "A" Coy. in reserve.
"B" and "I" Coys will be on the high ground N.E. and E. of the BOIS DU SART.
"C" Coy. S.W. of the BOIS DU SART
"A" Coy. in reserve in the area round the mound O.9.d. and O.3.c.
Location of Battalion H.Q. will be notified later.
ROUTE to Battle Positions:- North of MONCHY.
Positions as laid down above will be thoroughly reconnoitred by O.C. Companies as soon as possible, and the location of their Company H.Q. will be forwarded to Battalion H.Q. before 12.0 noon to-morrow.

5. **FLANKS:** In the event of Companies having to take up these positions special attention will be paid to getting touch on the flanks. The 1st Somerset L.I. will be on the left and the 1st Hampshire Regt. on the right.

cont on sheet 2

WARNING ORDER

APPENDIX VII.A

1. The Battalion will be prepared to relieve the 2nd Battn SEAFORTH HIGHLANDERS in the Centre of the Right Brigade front to-morrow night (30/1st).

2. All arrangements as regards guides, move, rations, conveyance of Lewis guns, etc. will be notified later.

3. All Officers' kits, surplus mess stores, haversacks, will be dumped near Battalion H.Q. by 10 a.m. tomorrow. Blankets will be rolled in bundles of ten, labelled and dumped at the same place by the same time.
   Transport Officer will arrange to collect these and carry them to the Transport Lines.

(sd) C. C. NAUMANN Lieut
                     Adjt
1st Battn THE RIFLE BRIGADE

29th Sept. 1918

APPENDIX VIA

WARNING ORDER
in the event of an enemy withdrawal
27th SEPTEMBER, 1918

MOVE   1.   From 6 p.m. today, 27th onwards, the Battalion will be prepared to move forward at one hour's notice in full fighting order.

TRANSPORT   2.   The Transport Officer will be responsible that the limbers (1 per Coy and 1 for H.Q.) bringing rations up to-day remain at their respective Hd.Qrs., and will be loaded up immediately with Lewis guns, ammunition, etc. In the event of a move these limbers will accompany the Battalion.

KITS   3.   Officers' kits, surplus mess stores, haversacks, etc. will be packed and blankets rolled in bundles of ten and labelled by 6 p.m. Should the Battalion move forward the Transport Officer will make arrangements to have the above mentioned collected and conveyed to the Transport Lines. One man will also be detailed by each Company to remain with his Company's kits, etc. and accompany them to transport.

TOOLS   4.   Companies will send out salvage parties at once to collect sufficient picks and shovels.

RATIONS   5.   In the event of a move rations for the 28th instant will be carried on the man: the Quartermaster will make the necessary arrangements.

WATER   6.   All water bottles will be filled by 6 p.m. to-day and will be kept full.

                                     (sd) C. C. NAUMANN Lieut.
                                A/Adjt 1st Bn THE RIFLE BRIGADE

SECRET

OPERATION ORDER No 85
by Lt.Colonel G. W. LIDDELL, D.S.O.
Commdg 1st Battalion, THE RIFLE BRIGADE

APPENDIX VIII

Ref. Sheet 51B   30th SEPTEMBER, 1918   Copy No

RELIEF   1. The Battalion will relieve the 2nd Battalion THE SEAFORTH HIGHLANDERS in the front line as Centre Battalion of the right Brigade to-night 30 Sept/1 Oct.

DISPOSITIONS   2. Dispositions will be as follows:-
"I" Coy Rifle Brigade will relieve "B" Coy Seaforths as right Front Coy.
"B" " " " " " "D" " " as Left Front Coy.
"C" " " " " " "A" " " as Support Coy.
"A" " " " " " "C" " " as Reserve Coy.

Battalion H.Q. will be at P.16.b.2.8.
Aid Post as P.16.b.2.8.

GUIDES   3. Guides, one per platoon, 1 for Coy. H.Q. and 2 for Battalion H.Q., will meet Companies at P.16.c.3.9. at 6.30 p.m.

MOVE   4. The Battalion will probably embuss on the FEUCHY-FEUCHY CHAPEL Road about 4.30 p.m. Exact time and place will be notified later. In the above case the Battalion will move off from this area by platoons at 100 yards interval.
Order of March:- Battn H.Q., "I", "B", "C", "A".
Probable route to embussing point:-
Lancer Lane, PELVES Lane on to the FEUCHY-FEUCHY CHAPEL Road.
Probable time of leaving area:- 3.30 p.m.
Debussing point about VIS-en-ARTOIS.
The Battalion will have teas at the Embussing point about 3.45 p.m. The Transport Officer will arrange to have Cookers at the Embussing point to provide teas by the above mentioned time. Companies will tell off in parties of 25 before teas are drawn and will be ready to embuss at a quarter of an hour's notice.
Dress:- Fighting order, with packs and greatcoats.
Battle ammunition and tools will be carried into the line.
Order of march after debussing:- "I", "B", "C", "A" Battn. H.Q.

BOUNDARIES   5. Right Battalion Boundary Q.2.a.0.0. - Q.1.d.1.1. to P.6.b.9.1. to Cross Roads P.11.c.7.4. to P.15.Central, thence due West.
Left Battalion Boundary, Road junction P.4.b.70.45 - DROCOURT QUEANT Support Line P.4.d.65.90, thence a trench P.10.b.15.9P - P.15.Central.
Inter Company Front Company Boundary:- J.36.d.0.5. - P.1.a.0.0.

TRANSPORT   6. The Transport Officer will arrange to have one limber for each Company and one for Battalion H.Q. at their respective H.Qrs. by 1.30 p.m. for carrying Lewis guns, Officers' trench kit and mess stores, etc.
These limbers will meet the Battalion at P.16.c.3.9. at 6.15 p.m. Each Company's limber will follow in rear of the front platoon of each Company and will be loaded at the various Coy. Ration dumps, vide Para. 3.

Cont on sheet 2

- 2 -

KITS 7. Officers' kits, surplus mess stores, haversacks, will be packed and blankets rolled and dumped near Battalion H.Qrs by 10 a.m.
    Transport Officer will arrange to collect and convey to Transport Lines.
    Cookers will return to Transport Lines after the Battalion has had teas.

RATIONS 8. Rations and water will be brought up each night to the following places:-

    "I" Coy   P.11.b.7.3.
    "B" "   P.10.b.2.9.
    "C" "   P.11.c.3.5.
    "A" "   P.16.b.8.5.
    Battn. H.Q.   P.10.d.1.0.

    Rations and water will be delivered at the above mentioned dumps to-night at 12 midnight: each successive night at 8.0 p.m.
    Companies will be responsible for drawing their own rations and water.

BODIES 9. All dead bodies will be brought back to Battalion H.Q. if possible.

TAKING OVER 10. All trench stores, ammunition, defence schemes, aeroplane photographs, etc. will be carefully taken over. Receipts will be forwarded to Battalion H.Q. by 6 a.m. on the 1st Oct. with indents etc.

MAPS 11. Maps showing posts and platoon areas will be forwarded to reach Battalion H.Q. by 12 noon 1st Oct.

REPORT 12. Relief complete will be reported to Battalion H.Q. by wire and confirmed by runner, the code word "BUBBLY" being used in the former case.

13. ACKNOWLEDGE.

(sd) C. C. NAUMANN   Lieut.
Adjt 1st Battn THE RIFLE BRIGADE

SECRET   OPERATION ORDER No 85   APPENDIX VIII
                   by Lt.Colonel G. W. LIDDELL, D.S.O.
                   Commdg 1st Battalion, THE RIFLE BRIGADE

Ref. Sheet 51B   30th SEPTEMBER, 1918   Copy No

RELIEF   1.   The Battalion will relieve the 2nd Battalion THE
               SEAFORTH HIGHLANDERS in the front line as Centre Battalion
               of the right Brigade to-night 30 Sept/1 Oct.

DISPOSITIONS   2.   Dispositions will be as follows:-
               "I" Coy Rifle Brigade will relieve "B" Coy Seaforths as right
                                                                Front Coy.
               "B" "   "   "   "   "   "D" "   "   as Left
                                                                Front Coy.
               "C" "   "   "   "   "   "A" "   "   as Support
                                                                Coy.
               "A" "   "   "   "   "   "C" "   "   as Reserve
                                                                Coy.
               Battalion H.Q. will be at P.16.b.2.8.
               Aid Post as P.16.b.2.8.

GUIDES   3.   Guides, one per platoon, 1 for Coy. H.Q. and 2 for
               Battalion H.Q., will meet Companies at P.16.c.3.9. at 6.30 p.m.

MOVE   4.   The Battalion will probably embuss on the FEUCHY-
               FEUCHY CHAPEL Road about 4.30 p.m.   Exact time and place
               will be notified later.   In the above case the Battalion
               will move off from this area by platoons at 100 yards interval.
               Order of March:-   Battn H.Q., "I", "B", "C", "A".
                    Probable route to embussing point:-
               Lancer Lane, PELVES Lane on to the FEUCHY-FEUCHY CHAPEL Road.
                    Probable time of leaving area:- 2.30 p.m.
                    Debussing point about VIS-en-ARTOIS.
                    The Battalion will have teas at the Embussing point
               about 3.45 p.m.   The Transport Officer will arrange to have
               Cookers at the Embussing point to provide teas by the above
               mentioned time.   Companies will tell off in parties of 25
               before teas are drawn and will be ready to embuss at a
               quarter of an hour's notice.
                    Dress:- Fighting order, with packs and greatcoats.
               Battle ammunition and tools will be carried into the line.
                    Order of march after debussing:- "I", "B", "C", "A"
               Battn. H.Q.

BOUNDARIES   5.   Right Battalion Boundary Q.2.a.0.0. - Q.1.d.1.1. to
               P.6.b.9.1. to Cross Roads P.11.c.7.4. to P.15.Central, thence
               due West.
                    Left Battalion Boundary, Road junction P.4.b.70.45 -
               DROCOURT QUEANT Support Line P.4.d.65.99, thence a trench
               P.10.b.15.9P - P.15.Central.
                    Inter Company Front Company Boundary:- J.36.d.0.5. -
               P.1.a.0.0.

TRANSPORT   6.   The Transport Officer will arrange to have one limber
               for each Company and one for Battalion H.Q. at their respec-
               tive H.Qrs. by 1.30 p.m. for carrying Lewis guns, Officers'
               trench kit and mess stores, etc.
                    These limbers will meet the Battalion at P.16.c.3.9.
               at 6.15 p.m.   Each Company's limber will follow in rear of
               the front platoon of each Company and will be loaded at the
               various Coy. Ration dumps, vide Para. 8.

                                                       Cont on sheet 2

- 2 -

KITS 7. Officers' kits, surplus mess stores, haversacks, will be packed and blankets rolled and dumped near Battalion H.Qrs by 10 a.m.
    Transport Officer will arrange to collect and convey to Transport Lines.
    Cookers will return to Transport Lines after the Battalion has had teas.

RATIONS 8. Rations and water will be brought up each night to the following places:-
"I" Coy   P.11.b.7.3.
"B" "   P.10.b.2.9.
"C" "   P.11.c.3.5.
"A" "   P.16.b.8.5.
Battn. H.Q.   P.10.d.1.0.
    Rations and water will be delivered at the above mentioned dumps to-night at 12 midnight: each successive night at 8.0 p.m.
    Companies will be responsible for drawing their own rations and water.

BODIES 9. All dead bodies will be brought back to Battalion H.Q. if possible,

TAKING OVER 10. All trench stores, ammunition, defence schemes, aeroplane photographs, etc. will be carefully taken over. Receipts will be forwarded to Battalion H.Q. by 6 a.m. on the 1st Oct. with indents etc.

MAPS 11. Maps showing posts and platoon areas will be forwarded to reach Battalion H.Q. by 12 noon 1st Oct.

REPORT 12. Relief complete will be reported to Battalion H.Q. by wire and confirmed by runner, the code word "BUBBLY" being used in the former case.

13. ACKNOWLEDGE.

(sd) C. C. NAUMANN   Lieut.
Adjt 1st Battn THE RIFLE BRIGADE

AMENDMENT No 1
to OPERATION ORDER No 85

1. Ref. Para. 5 Delete from "The Battalion will probably embuss" to probable time of leacing area: 2.30 p.m." and insert:-
    The Battalion will embuss on the main ARRAS-CAMBRAI Road at 4 p.m: the head of the lorry convoy at FOSSE FARM facing E. The Battan will move off from this area at 2.30 p.m.
    Order of march, "A", "C", "B", "I", Battalion H.Q.
    Route to embussing point:- LANCER LANE - MONCHY B HUSSAR LANE - ARRAS-CAMBRAI Road.
    100 yards intervals will be kept between platoons.
    On arrival at Embussing point companies will close up and will be drawn up S. of the road.
    2nd Lieut. C. B. CRAVEN will act as Battalion Embussing Officer and will report to Brigade Embussing Officer at 4 p.m. at FOSSE FARM.

2. Ref. para 4 and 6 for "P.16.c.3.9." read p.19.c.3.9.

(sd) C. C. NAUMANN Lieut
Adjt 1st Battn THE RIFLE BRIGADE

30-9-18

AMENDMENT No 1
to OPERATION ORDER No 85

1. Ref. Para. 5 Delete from "The Battalion will probably embuss" to probable time of leaving area: 2.30 p.m." and insert:-

    The Battalion will embuss on the main ARRAS-CAMBRAI Road at 4 p.m: the head of the lorry convoy at FOSSE FARM facing E. The Battan will move off from this area at 2.30 p.m. Order of march, "A", "C", "B", "I", Battalion H.Q.
    Route to embussing point:- LANCER LANE - MONCHY B HUSSAR LANE - ARRAS-CAMBRAI Road.
    100 yards intervals will be kept between platoons.
    On arrival at Embussing point companies will close up and will be drawn up S. of the road.
    2nd Lieut. C. B. CRAVEN will act as Battalion Embussing Officer and will report to Brigade Embussing Officer at 4 p.m. at FOSSE FARM.

2. Ref. Para 4 and 6 for "p.16.c.3.9." read p.19.c.3.9.

(sd) C. C. NAUMANN Lieut
Adjt 1st Battn THE RIFLE BRIGADE

30-9-18

SKETCH MAP
SHOWING
DISPOSITIONS OF CENTRE BN. 1.X.18.

References

Right Front Coy ————
Left " " ————
Support ————
Reserve ————
Lewis Gun Post
Coy H.Q.
Bn. H.Q.

Reference.

——— ... Div. Boundary.

——— ... Bn. Boundary.

— — — ... Inter Coy Boundary

——— ... Line as taken over 29.viii.18.

——— ... Line after capture of ETERPIGNY
                             30.viii.18.

——— ...⎱ Objective 28. Ref. O.O. 77.
——— ...⎰ 2.ix.18.

——— ...⎱ Successive positions during
——— ...⎰ 2.ix.18.

——— ... Area occupied 1.ix.18.

4th Division
11th Infantry Bde
1st Rifle Bde

October to December
1918

WAR DIARY or INTELLIGENCE SUMMARY

Army Form C. 2118.

October 1918 1/4 1st Bn. K.O.Y.L.I. 64th Bde. 21st Div.

Place	Date	Hour	Summary of Events and Information	Remarks and references to Appendices
Front Line (L'ÉCLUSE Sector)	18–19	6/15	The line was extraordinarily quiet; there was very little shelling and the retirement stands on the Eastern side of the SENSÉE river made it very difficult for our troops to use the river. The only places where the river could be crossed were the L'ÉCLUSE – TORTEQUENNE Road and a foot bridge in Q.1.b. During the night a total of four patrols went out. On the evening of the 19th the following moves took place :— (i) 'A' Company relieved the left company of the 12th/13th SOMERSET L.I. and the three right posts of I Company (right front company) this evening night front company of the Bn. (ii) I Company took over the two posts of 'B' Company to and were the left front company. (iii) Remainder of 'B' Company was relieved by the 1st Bn. THE HAMPSHIRE REGT. and moved back into 'A' Company's old position in reserve. (iv) At 8 a.m. of the 4th 'C' Company relieved I Company, which moved back into 'C' Company's old position in support. On the night of the 6/7/7th the Bn. was relieved by the 7/8th Canadian Infantry Bn. and on completion of the relief moved back into the ORANGE HILL area.	O.O. 86 Appendix 1 O.O. 88 Appendix 3 O.O. 89 Appendix 4

Army Form C. 2118.

WAR DIARY
or
INTELLIGENCE SUMMARY.
(Erase heading not required.)

1 Bn the Kings (Liverpool)

October 1918

Place	Date	Hour	Summary of Events and Information	Remarks and references to Appendices
Front line (L'ECEULT SE[C])	1st – 6th		Strength of Bn. OFFICERS 17 O.R. 630 Casualties OFFICERS Nil O.R. Killed 1 Wounded (gas) 7 Wounded 1 (S.T.W.) 1	
BERNÉVILLE	7th	10.55	From the ORANGE HILL area the Bn. moved back by march route to BERNÉVILLE. Order of march H.Q., B, C, D, A. H.Q. started at 10.55 hours & the 7th. The Bn. halted for dinner near DARNVILLE and arrived at BERNÉVILLE about 16.30 hours. The 8th and 9th Companies were at the disposal of Company Commanders for cleaning up, reorganization and training. In the afternoon the 8th the B.G.C. inspected the officers and men of the Brigade and in the evening the G.O.C. spoke to all officers of the Brigade in the KINEMA HUT. On the 10th a Battalion attack scheme was carried out in cooperation with artillery and Stokes Mortars.	O.O. 90 Appendix 5
LIGAUDOEUVRES	11th – 16th		The Battalion left BERNÉVILLE, entraining at 11.30 hours on the ARRAS – DOULLENS road, in Company with the Remainder of the Brigade and detraining about 16.30 hours on the BAPAUME – CAMBRAI road just S.E. of BOURLON WOOD (F.24.c and d sheet 57c) The Bn. then marched to an area in F.10.a where it arrived shortly before dark.	O.O. 91 Appendix 6

WAR DIARY or **INTELLIGENCE SUMMARY.**
(Erase heading not required.)

Army Form C. 2118.

2/Bn. The Rifle Bde.
October 1918

Place	Date	Hour	Summary of Events and Information	Remarks and references to Appendices
ESCAUDOEUVRES	11th – 16th		The following day was spent in improving the shelters which the troops had built the previous night. On the 13th the Bn. marched to ESCAUDOEUVRES arriving about 13.00 hours and spent the remainder of the day cleaning up billets. For the two next days companies worked under their own arrangements devoting most of the time to training in the use of the attacking tool and the method of attacking isolated machine gun positions. The 16th was spent in moving into fresh billets, those which we were occupying being taken over by the XXII Corps headquarters.	O.O. 92 Appendix 7
HASPRES area	17th – 25th		On the 17th the Bn. proceeded by the dry march route, relieving the 4th Bn. of the York and Lancaster Regt. in a support position in front of AVESNE-LE-SEC. The position, as taken over, provided insufficient accommodation for the Bn., so that on arrival B and C Coys dug themselves in in new positions while A and I companies took over those vacated by the outgoing Bn. The Bn. went into the line on the 17th/18th. Enemy shelling was fairly heavy and very scattered. During the night of the 17th/18th 20 Officers (including the M.O.) and 650 O.R.	O.O. 94 Appendix 9

WAR DIARY
or
INTELLIGENCE SUMMARY.

Army Form C. 2118.

1st Bn. the Rifle Brigade
October 1918

Place	Date	Hour	Summary of Events and Information	Remarks and references to Appendices
HASPRES area	17th	- 25th	During 18th a thick mist which lasted throughout the day of the 18th. Companies were able to work all day improving their positions. Soon after dark B Company relieved the left company of the 1st Bn. THE HAMPSHIRE REGT. preparatory to the operations which were to take place on the night of the 19th/20th. During the night enemy shelling was very heavy and scattered, some shells fell in the Bn's area.	
			The 19th was quiet throughout. After dark the Bn. moved up into assembly positions. B and I Companies became front line, C and A Support. Shortly after Bn. H.Q. had been established in AVESNES-LE-SEC, the proposed attack of the 11th INFANTRY BDE. was cancelled whereupon A and C Companies returned to their original positions. B & I remaining forward.	O.O. 95 Appendix 10
			Next day, the 20th the Bn. followed the 1st Bn. SOMERSET L.I. and 15th HAMPSHIRE REGT. through the village of HASPRES. A and C companies passing through A and I on the approximate line O.24.a.80.90 — O.24.a.90.65 and then proceeded establishing a line in front of the Railway Embankment (vide map attached.) B and I billetted in cellars in HASPRES.	Map attached Appendix 10
			On the 21st the Bn. rested until the evening when it relieved the 1st Bn. SOMERSET L.I. in the front line. Patrols were immediately pushed out and met with heavy resistance from snipers and machine guns.	

WAR DIARY
INTELLIGENCE SUMMARY.
(Erase heading not required.)

1st Bn. The Hampshire Regt.
October 1918

Place	Date	Hour	Summary of Events and Information	Remarks and references to Appendices
HASPRES area	17th – 25th		Enemy artillery was also fairly active, paying special attention to the valley in P.9.c. and the road in P.7.d. On the morning of the 22nd our patrols succeeded in capturing a German machine gun post near the FERME DE BOUVENEUL. This capture, of 9 men, one light machine gun and one automatic rifle afforded a very valuable identification resulting in the clearing of the wood in P.4.c. Thus slightly advancing the right of our line. On the 23rd patrolling activity was Enemy artillery was active as usual. Enemy sniping continued and two reconnaissances of the RIVER ECAILLON made. Enemy sniping and machine gun activity prevented our line being further advanced. The Bn. took part in the attack on the ridge E. of the R. ECAILLON on the 24th. B and D Companies provided bridging parties for the 18th Bn. SOMERSET L.I. and the 1st Bn. THE HAMPSHIRE REGT. While A and C Companies pushed parties for mopping up the Yellow line (vide map) when captured. The remainder of B Company withdrew to the R.B. area when the attacking Battalions were in position. They pushed forward again at ZERO + 2 hours and consolidated the BLUE LINE.	O.O. 96 Appendix II

Army Form C. 2118.

1/4 B. The Hyde Regt
October 1918

WAR DIARY
or
INTELLIGENCE SUMMARY.
(Erase heading not required.)

Place	Date	Hour	Summary of Events and Information	Remarks and references to Appendices
HASPRES area	17th	25th	The parties from A and C Companies rejoined the Bn. in the BLUE LINE on being relieved by 2 Companies of the HAMPSHIRE REGT. Enemy shelling was not heavy and casualties were comparatively few. On the night of the 24th/25th the Bn. was relieved by the 1st Bn. THE HAMPSHIRE REGT. and marched back to billets in HASPRES.	Appendix 12
HASPRES	25th - 28th		This period was spent in resting and cleaning up in HASPRES. On Sunday 27th there was a parade service after which the G.O.C. spoke to the Officers and the B.g.C. to N.C.Os. of the Battalion.	
Front line (ARTRES) Section	28th - 31st		The Bn. left HASPRES at 14:30 hours on the 28th to relieve the 2nd Bn. LANCASHIRE FUSILIERS in the front line, as right Bn. of the Division, with a view to carrying out an attack on enemy positions E. of the R. RHONELLE the early morning of the 30th. The Bn. had to include a large Bridgehead. C, A, and I Companies formed the front line, B Company in support. Enemy artillery was very active during the night, especially on ARTRES and THE CHATEAUX. At Haspres the Bn. going in was 18 Officers and 538 other ranks. The 1st Bn. E. LANCASHIRE REGT were on our right and the 1st Bn. THE HAMPSHIRE REGT on our left.	O.O. 97 Appendix 13

Army Form C. 2118.

1st Bn. The Rifle Brigade
October 1918

WAR DIARY
or
INTELLIGENCE SUMMARY.
(Erase heading not required.)

Instructions regarding War Diaries and Intelligence Summaries are contained in F. S. Regs., Part II. and the Staff Manual respectively. Title pages will be prepared in manuscript.

Place	Date	Hour	Summary of Events and Information	Remarks and references to Appendices
Front Line (ARTRES Sector)	28th	3:15	On the evening of the 29th a strong patrol from C Company was sent a platoon for further reconnoitring from K 23 c 25.50 to K 22 d 8.8. Three Casualties Enlarging the bridgehead. These posts had been firmly established, one platoon of A Company took them over and came under command of O.C. 'C' Company. The company of 1st HAMPSHIRE REGT relieved E Company who moved back 2nd Battn. H.Q. moved to CHATEAUX in K 28 a. Enemy active on the left of B. company. Batalion H.Q. 2 Lewis guns. Operation postponed for 24 hours. The K 30/c operation was again postponed 24 hours. Enemy artillery fire slackened but Snipers and machine guns were active. The 31st was uneventful, enemy attack remained unchanged. Heavy rain fell during the assembly which in addition to being days of thick heavy sleet and general discomfort proved a great strain on the troops.	3 Casualties Reinforcements and Appendix 14

R. L. Adams Lieut. for
O. C. 1st Rifle Brigade

Comdy 1st Bn The Rifle Brigade

Appendix I

SECRET WARNING ORDER

O.C. "A" Company
(Repeated O.C. "I" Coy.)

It is highly probable that you will relieve the left Company of the 1st Somerset Light Infantry this evening.

O.C. "A" Coy. will take over, in addition, the three right forward posts held at present by "I" Coy.

"A" Coy. will draw their rations before leaving and will cary them forward to their new position.

All arrangements will be made between Os. C. Companies concerned.

Completion of relief will be wired to Battalion H.Q. by the code word "BOAT".

ACKNOWLEDGE

(sd) O. C. NAUMANN Lieut
A/Adjt   Mudu

2-10-18

SECRET

WARNING ORDER

O.C. "B" Company
(Repeated "I" Coy)

      It is highly probable that you will be relieved tonight by a company of the Hampshires, in which case you will hand over your two right forward posts to "I" Coy., i.e. the posts in the wood and will, after handing over the remainder to the Hampshires proceed to take up positions held by the Reserve Coy. at present occupied by "A" Coy.

      You should send an N.C.O. to "A" Coy. to take over dispositions, trench stores, etc. as soon as possible, who will also act as your guide tonight.

      Your ration limber will be stopped at the present Reserve Coy. dump and you will draw your rations from there on arrival in your new position.

      All arrangements for relief will be made by Company Commanders concerned.

      Completion of relief will be wired to Battalion Head Quarters by code word "BRIDGE".

                              (sd) C. C. NAUMANN Lieut.
9-10-18   A/Adjt Mudu

OPERATION ORDER No 86
by Lt.Col. G. W. LIDDELL, D.S.O.
Commdg 1st Battn. THE RIFLE BRIGADE

2nd OCTOBER, 1918

RELIEF I. The following reliefs will take place to-night:-
(1) "B" Coy. less the two forward posts in L'ECLUSE Wood will be relieved by the 1st Hampshire Regt.
The two posts mentioned above will be handed over to "I" Coy.
(2) "A" Coy. will relieve the left Coy. of the 1st Somerset-Lt. I. and also the 3 forward right posts of "I" Coy.
(3) After relief "B" Coy. will occupy the position formerly occupied by "A" Coy. and will become reserve Company.

All details of relief will be arranged by Officers Commanding Companies concerned.

BOUNDARIES II. Boundaries after relief will be:-
Right Battn Boundary:- K.27.Central, Q.1.b.4.0. - Q.7.c.0.0.
Left Battn Boundary:- Junction of Railway and Road K.20.a. 25.95., road to Cross roads K.19.c.9.1. - S.W. corner of Cemetery K.30.b.6.7. - N.W. corner of L'ECLUSE Wood - P.5.Central - P.5.c.0.0.
Inter Company Boundary:- Road junction K.31.c.15.50. - P.1.a.0.0.

RATIONS III. Rations for "A" Coy. will be drawn as usual and carried forward to the new positions.
The limber carrying "B" Company's rations will be stopped at the Reserve Company's dump and on Arrival "B" Coy. will draw them immediately.

TRENCH IV All Trench Stores will be handed over by "A" and "B"
STORES Companies, and taken over by "A" Coy from the 1st Somerset L.I., and receipts forwarded to Battalion H.Q. by the first run to-morrow.
"I" Coy. will hand over the 6 pairs of gum boots to "A" Coy. on relief.

V. ACKNOWLEDGE

(sd) C. C. HAUMANN Lieut.
Adjt
1st Battn. THE RIFLE BRIGADE

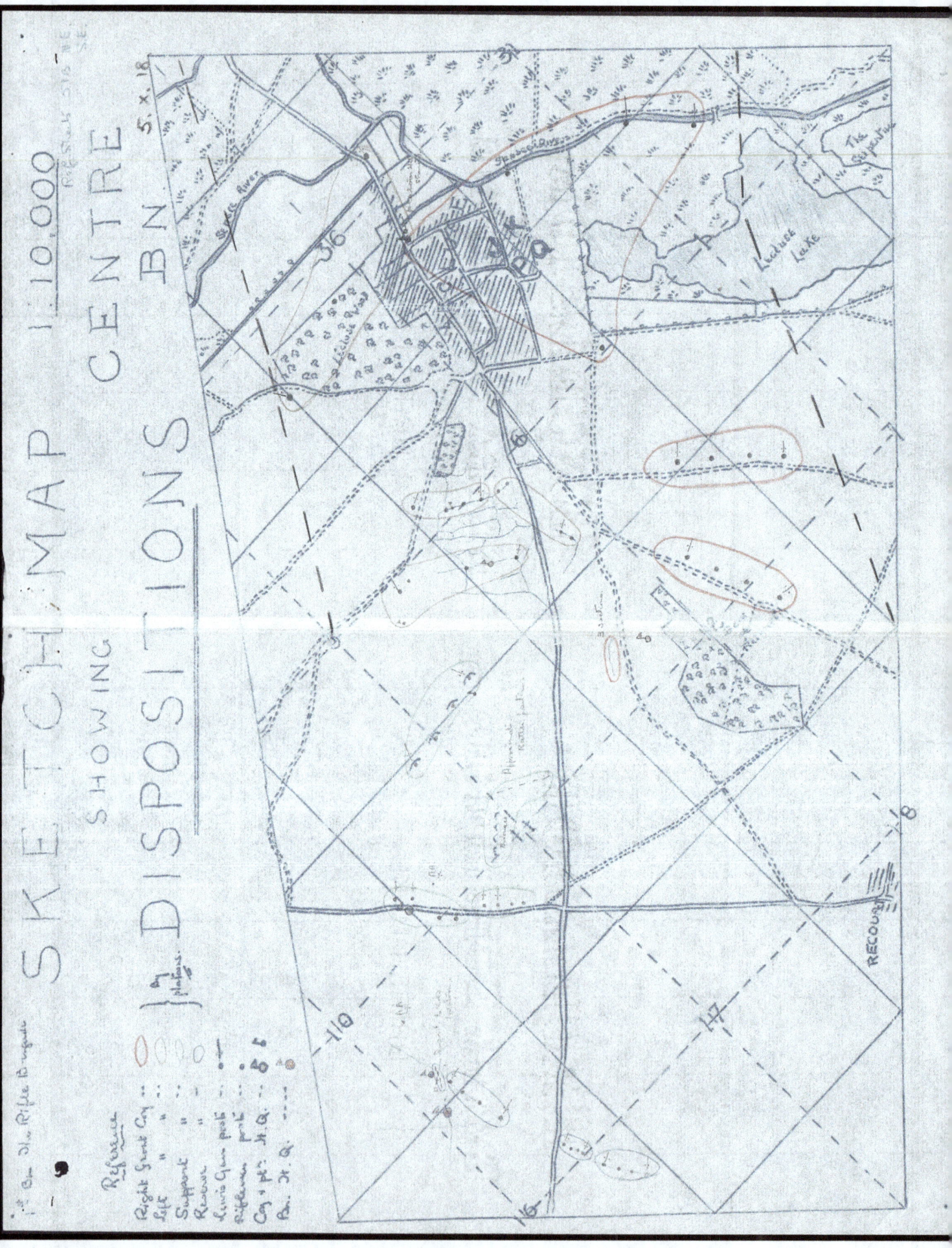

Appendix 2

SECRET

OPERATION ORDER No 27
by Lt. Col. G. W. LIDDELL, DSO.
Commdg 1st Battn. THE RIFLE BRIGADE
3rd OCTOBER, 1918

Ref. Sheet 51 B   Copy No

1. It is possible that the enemy carry out either a partial or general withdrawal on this front.

2. IN ORDER that the withdrawal does not take place unnoticed active patrolling and a close observation will be maintained, and when the enemy does withdraw immediate contact will be regained with him North of the SENSEE Marshes. No advance will be ordered on this front until troops holding the line North of the SCARPE move forward. Should it be thought that the enemy has withdrawn patrols will at once be pushed forward. It will then be ascertained whether

    (1) he is holding his line in strength, or
    (2) he has left isolated Machine Guns to delay an advance, and cause us casualties, or
    (3) He has evacuated his forward positions completely.

The action of the Battalion will be as follows:-

In the case of (1) and (2) above, report will at once be made to Battalion H.Q: it is probable that if the situation mentioned in (2) occurred, artillery support would be called for and a definite operation would be undertaken.

In the case of (3)
  (a) Bridgeheads will at once be established at J.36.b.55.50, North of L'ECLUSE and on the L'ECLUSE-HAMEL Road at Q.1.b.7.6.
  (b) After these have been established, the right Coy. will push one platoon over the SENSEE at Q.1.b.7.6. and will make good the line K.31.b.9.7. to K.32.b.1.3. making blocks on their right facing HAMEL as the Somersets will not cross at the same time as the Battalion. The left Company will have one platoon detailed off to pass over the bridge at Q.1.b.7.6. 20 minutes after the above mentioned platoon of the right Coy. has gone over: this platoon will push up the two lines of trenches in K.32 and K.25 towards TORTEQUENNE and will establish themselves in the most Northern line between K.25.a. and K.26.c.0.6.
  (c) After this line has been established the left Coy. will push forward through TORTEQUENNE and make good the high ground MONT BEDU, the line of the road running through K.25.b. and K.26.c. being established.

The right Coy. will push on over the crossing at Q.1.b.7.6. and make good the high ground in K.26. on the same line as the left Coy.

Throughout, very careful touch must be kept with the 1st Hampshire Regt. on the left: they will cross the SENSEE at J.34.b.40.30. and will establish bridgeheads at J.29.c.60.40. and J.28.Central. The Somerset Lt.I. will not cross the SENSEE, so special attention will be paid to the right flank.

The support and reserve Coys. will not move until orders are received from Battalion H.Q.

Any further advance beyond the line of the road in K.19.d. and K.25.c. will not be made without orders from Battalion H.Q: this, however, does not stop Company Commanders from sending out patrols to make good further ground: these patrols must be given a definite line to establish and will send back word as soon as they are on their objective.

3. BOUNDARIES Right Battalion Boundary: K.27.Central- Q.1.d.4.0. - Q.7.c.0.0.
    Left Battalion Boundary: Junction of Railway and Road K.20.a.25.95. by road to cross roads at K.19.c.9.1. - S.W. corner of Cemetery K.30.b.8.7. - N.W. corner of L'ECLUSE Wood - P.5.Central - P.5.c.0.0.
    Inter-Coy. Boundary: Road Junction K.20.b.9.1. to Road junction K.31.c.15.50 to P.12.a.0.0.

4. Information will be sent to Battalion H.Q. as frequently as possible.

5. ACKNOWLEDGE

(sd) C. J. NAUMANN Lieut.
Adjt 1st Battn THE RIFLE BRIGADE

Appendix 8

OPERATION ORDER No 88
by Lt.Col. G. W. LIDDELL, DSO
Commdg 1st Battn. THE RIFLE BRIGADE

4th October, 1918.

RELIEF   I.   The following relief will take place to-night, the night of the 4/5th:-

"C" Coy. will relieve "I" Coy. as left Front Coy.

After relief "I" Coy. will occupy positions evacuated by "C" Coy and will become Company in support.

All arrangements re guides, etc. will be made by Officers Commanding Companies concerned.

"I" Coy. will detail one N.C.O. to report at "C" Company's H.Q. at 3.0 p.m. to take over dispositions, and act as guide to his Company.

RATIONS   II.   Rations for "C" Coy. will be delivered as usual, and will be carried forward on the man.

Rations for "I" Coy. will be delivered at the Support Coy. H.Q. and will be drawn as soon as that Company has occupied its new position.

HANDING OVER   III.   All trench stores and dispositions will be carefully handed over and the receipts obtained for the former will be forwarded to Battalion H.Q. by the first run on the morning of the 5th.

Officers Commanding Companies will be careful to hand over all detail as regards defence and pursuit scheme personally.

RELIEF COMPLETE   IV.   Relief complete will be wired to Battalion H.Q. by the code word GLOVES and confirmed by runner.

V.   ACKNOWLEDGE

(sd) C. C. NAUMANN   Lieut.
Adjt
1st Battn THE RIFLE BRIGADE

Appendix 4

SECRET   OPERATION ORDER No 89
                 by Lieut.Col. G. W. LIDDELL, D.S.O.
                 Commdg 1st Battalion THE RIFLE BRIGADE
                       5th OCTOBER, 1918

----

1. **RELIEF**   The Battalion will be relieved by the 7th Canadian Battalion to-morrow night, night of 6/7th inst., as follows:-
"A" Coy. R.B. will be relieved by No 1 Coy. 7th Canadian Battn.
"C" " "   "   "   "   " No 3   "   "   "   "
"I" " "   "   "   "   " No 2   "   "   "   "
"B" " "   "   "   "   " No 4   "   "   "   "

2. **GUIDES**   Guides, one per platoon and one per Coy. H.Q. will report to Battalion H.Q. by 08.30 tomorrow.
                Guides as mentioned above and 2 per Battalion H.Q. will meet the incoming unit at the Cross Roads in SAUDEMONT P.30.a.80.85 at 18.00 (winter time).
                ROUTE:- SAUDEMONT - RECOURT - Cross roads in P.11.c.
                Order of relief will be "C", "A", "I", "B" and H.Q.
                2nd Lieut. C.B.CRAVEN will be in charge of these guides.

3. **MOVE**   On completion of relief the Battalion will move back to the HAPPY VALLEY area. The Q.M. will send the necessary party to take over accomodation: Stores and Companies will, as far as possible, be distributed as before: the taking over party will report to Battalion at present in occupation by 10.00.
                ROUTE back to HAPPY VALLEY area:- By tracks to P.15.b.8.7. thence via ARTILLERY TRACK to ETERPIGNY-HAUCOURT Road at P P.13.c.15.50 - MOULIN DU ROI Bridge - through REMY - REMY LANE - ARTILLERY BRIDGE O.11.c.5 .5. - Track to STIRRUP LANE - O.9.b.85.65 - STIRRUP LANE to Cross Roads O.8.d.15.15. The ARRAS-CAMBRAI Road will not be used. The Q.M. will arrange to have guides for all platoons, Coy. H.Q. and Batt. H.Q. at Cross Roads O.8.d.16.15 from 23.30 onwards (winter time).

4. **TRANSPORT**   The Transport Officer will arrange to convey all kits, blankets, etc. to the new area in day light on the 6th inst.
                One limber per Coy., One for Battalion H.Q. for the conveyance of Lewis guns, ammunition, officers' trench kit and mess stores, water tins, etc., will arrive at ration dumps at the following times:-
                  Battalion H.Q.   19.30
                  Company   20.00

5. **HANDING OVER**   All trench stores, bridges, boats, aeroplane photographs etc., will be carefully handed over and receipts obtained. Receipt of trench stores will be forwarded to Battalion H.Q. as soon as possible on 7th inst.
                The extra ammunition at present being carried will be left in the Line and will be handed over as trench stores.
                Picks and shovels will be regarded as part of the equipment of each man and will be brought out of the Line.
                All gum boots will be handed over.
                Dugouts, posts and the area around will be left thoroughly clean and all refuse buried.

6. **COMPLETION OF RELIEF**   Relief complete will be wired to Battalion H.Q. by the code word "DUCK" and confirmed by runner.

7.   Orders with regard to a march to BERNEVILLE on the 7th inst. will be issued later.

8.   ACKNOWLEDGE

                                                   (sd) C. C. NAUMANN   Lieut.
5-10-18   A/Adjt 1st Batt THE RIFLE BRIGADE

Appendix 5

SECRET

OPERATION ORDER No 90
by Lt.Col. G. W. LIDDELL. D.S.O.
Commdg 1st Battalion THE RIFLE BRIGADE
6th OCTOBER, 1918

MOVE 1. The Battalion will move by march route on the 7th inst from the area H.36.b., H.36.a and c. to billets in BERNEVILLE.

Order of march will be Battn H.Q., "B", "C", "I", "A".

An interval of 100 yards will be kept between Companies. Battalion H.Q. will march off from HAPPY VALLEY at 10.55 hrs in order to pass the starting point FEUCHY CHAPEL Cross roads at 11.40 hrs.

ROUTE:- SWORD LANE - FEUCHY CHAPEL CROSS ROADS - ARRAS - DAINVILLE - WARLUS - BERNEVILLE.

DRESS:- Fighting order without tools

The Transport will be drawn up facing West, head at FEUCHY CHAPEL Cross roads at 11.40 hrs, and from there will move in rear of the Battalion.

O.C. "A" Coy. will detail one platoon under an officer as baggage guard: this platoon will also act as stragglers' guard.

Throughout the march distances given in S.S.724 will be maintained.

At the second halt Companies will close up to Battalion H.Q. before the order to fall out is given. They will open out again on completion of the halt.

TRANSPORT 2. Four lorries will report at O.13.a.1.0. at 09.00 hrs on 7th inst. The Transport Officer will arrange to take these over and after loading Picks and shovels on will send them with a guide to HAPPY VALLEY H.30.b.3.3. by 09.45 hrs if possible.

All blankets will be rolled in bundles of ten and labelled: officers' kits, men's packs and tools will be dumped, together with blankets, at H.30.b.3.3. by 09.15 hrs. One man per Coy. will be left to look after his Coy's blankets, etc.

O.C. "I" Coy. will detail one platoon to load the lorries as soon as they arrive at the above mentioned point.

TRENCH SHELTERS 3. All trench shelters, tents, etc. in the HAPPY VALLEY area will be struck and handed to the Area Commandant ORANGE HILL, H.35.a. by 09.30 hrs. Receipts will be obtained and forwarded to Orderly Room as soon as possible on arrival at BERNEVILLE.

BILLETING PARTY 4. A billeting party consisting of 2/Lieut. C.B.CRAVEN, the 4 C.Q.M.Ss and one N.C.O. from Battalion H.Q. will report to Staff Captain at the Town Major's Officer at BERNEVILLE at 18.00 hrs.

DINNERS 5. The Battalion will halt for dinners at time and place to be notified later.

6. ACKNOWLEDGE

(sd) C. C. NAUMANN   Lieut.
A/Adjt 1st Battn THE RIFLE BRIGADE

Appendix 6

SECRET

OPERATION ORDER No 81
by Lt.Col. G. W. LIDDELL, DSO.
Commanding 1st Battalion, THE RIFLE BRIGADE

Ref Sheets 51C, 57C   10th OCTOBER, 1918   Copy

MOVE   1.   The Battalion will move to-day, 11th October, to the BOURLON - FONTAINE NOTRE DAME area by bus.
         Companies will move to the embussing point on the DOULLENS-ARRAS Road west of the turning to BERNEVILLE in the following order:-
         "I", "C", "A", "B", H.Q.
         100 yards interval will be kept between Companies.
         "I" Coy. will move off at 10.20 hrs.
         DRESS: Full marching order; L. gns, picks & shovels will be carried

EMBUSSING   2.   Major C.F.C. LETTS will be embussing officer for the Brigade and 2/Lieut. C.B. CRAVEN will report to him at the embussing point at 10.45 hrs.
         Debussing point FONTAINE NOTRE DAME.

ADVANCE PARTY   3.   Lieut. H. L. ROUTH will report to the Staff Captain at Brigade H.Q. at 08.30 to-day for billeting purposes.

BLANKETS etc.   4.   Blankets will be rolled in bundles of 10 and dumped by Companies near the road outside the huts at 0800 hours today. Two lorries will report at this time for conveying above and surplus Quartermaster's stores to the new area.

TRANSPORT   5.   Transport will move by road, staying one night at WANCOURT.

KITS, etc   6.   Officers' kits, extra mess stores will be dumped near the road outside the officers' mess by 08.00 hrs to-day. The Transport Officer will arrange for baggage wagons to collect these.

BILLETS   7.   Billets at present occupied will be left scrupulously clear and a certificate will be obtained by Companies from the Area Commandant or one of his representatives to the effect that billets have been left in a satisfactory condition.

RATIONS   8.   (a) Rations for consumption to-day will be carried on the man
         (b) Rations for the 12th inst will be delivered in the forward area.
         (c) In view of the fact that the Transport will not reach the new area to-night all available camp kettles will be taken on the busses or sent forward on the lorries to the forward area to-day.

DETAILS   9.   (a) Details will be located in ARRAS.
         (b) 2/Lieut. F.R.H. LEE will be in charge of Battalion details
         (c) 2nd Lieut. T.J. WOODSIDE, MC will report to Divisional Education Officer at the Town Major's Office, ARRAS, at 11.00 hrs to-day to take over accommodation.
         (d) Rations will be delivered in ARRAS from 12th inst onwards.
         (e) Blankets, officers' kits will be loaded on lorries arriving in BERNEVILLE between 14.00 and 15.00 hrs today. Packs will be carried on the men.

     10.   ACKNOWLEDGE.

Lieut.
A/Adjt 1st Battn THE RIFLE BRIGADE

Appendix 7

SECRET   OPERATION ORDER No 99   COPY No 12
by Lt.Col. G. W. LIDDELL, DSO
Commdg 1st Battn. THE RIFLE BRIGADE

Ref. Sheets 57c, 57b, 51a 1/40,000   13th OCTOBER, 1918

MOVE   1.   The Battalion will move to the ESCAUDOEUVRES area by march route to-day.
         ORDER of march:- "H.Q.", "B", "C", "D", "A".
         An interval of 200 yards will be kept between Companies.
         Distances laid down in S.S.734 will be maintained.
         Connecting files will be maintained throughout the march.
         HEADQUARTERS will move off at 08.45 hrs, in time to pass the starting point, F.3.d.4.5. at 09.00 hrs.
         ROUTE:- RAILLENCOURT - main ARRAS-CAMBRAI Road - Road Junction A.9.a.O.5. - Cross roads A.3.d.5.5. - Cross roads A.3.d.7.5. - RAMILLIES Road to S.24.c.5.4. - S.30.d.9.4.
         DRESS:- Marching order.
         Packs will be carried.
         PICKS & SHOVELS will be dumped at Qr.Mr. Stores by 07.30 hrs.
         Battle ammunition will be carried on the man.

ADVANCE PARTY   2.   1 N.C.O. per Coy., 1 for Battalion H.Q. and 1 from Transport will report to 2nd Lieut. C.B.CRAVEN at Battalion H.Q. at 07.15 hrs for billeting purposes.
         This party will meet the Staff Captain at ESCAUDOEUVRES Church, T.25.a.5.4. at 10.00 hrs.

TRANSPORT   3.   First line transport will move with the Battalion.
         "A" Coy. will detail one platoon as baggage guard.
         BLANKETS, officers' kits, will be dumped at Q.M. Stores at 07.00 hrs. These will be conveyed to the new area under arrangements as detailed in Brigade letter S 317, attached to Quartermaster's copy only.
         The Transport Officer will arrange for the mess cart to collect officers' mess stores before 08.00 hrs.

RATIONS   4.   Rations for consumption on the 14th inst. will be delivered in the new area.
         O.C. H.Q. Troops will send a guide to Brigade H.Q. on arrival in the new area to guide vehicles to the Battalion area.

         5.   ACKNOWLEDGE.

                           (sd) C. C. NAUMANN   Capt.
                           Adjt 1st Batt. THE RIFLE BRIGADE

DISTRIBUTION

Copy No 1 Commanding Officer
    "   2 2nd in Command
       3 Adjt.
       4 A/Adjt
       5 Intell. Offr.
       6 O.C. "A" Coy
       7   "   "B"
       8   "   "C"
       9   "   "D"
    10 T.O.
    11 Q.M.
    12 War Diary
    13   "
    14 File

Appendix 8

SECRET

Copy No 11

OPERATION ORDER No 93
by LT. COL. G. W. LIDDELL, D.S.O.
Commdg 1st Battalion THE RIFLE BRIGADE

IN THE EVENT OF A HOSTILE ATTACK

16th OCTOBER, 1918

1. It is probable that the 11th Brigade will support the 51st Division on the left of the Corps front, and the Battalion will occupy the Support area of the Brigade.

2. BOUNDARIES
    (i) <u>Between 10th and 11th Inf. Bdes (Right Bdy. of 11th Bde)</u>
    Railway from T.16.a.0.0. to N.36.d.0.0. (inclusive to 10th Bde) – thence IWUY – AVESNES-le-SEC road to O.89.Central (inclusive to 10th Inf.Bde) thence a line to O.12.Central.
    (ii) <u>Between 4th Div. and Right Div. Canadian Corps (Left Bdy of 11th Bde)</u>
    CANAL DE L'ESCAUT exclusive to N.23.d.2.0. – thence a line to railway at N.24.a.0.0. – thence N. along railway inclusive to its junction with the CANAL DE L'ESCAUT.

3. In the event of the Brigade moving forward to counter-attack the wire "Support 22nd Corps" will be sent round.
    Companies will AT ONCE move to the following area:-
        "B" and "I" Coys to T.5.c. and d. ("B" Coy will be on the left and "I" Coy. on the right.)
        "A" Coy. in close support in T.10.b. and T.11.a. and b.
        "C" Coy. will line the railway embankment in T.11.a. and b in the first instance, facing S.E. to guard the right flank.
    Battalion H.Q. T.11.a.2.4.
    Areas will be reconnoitred forthwith.
    The town of IWUY will be avoided as much as possible.
    The objective of any counter-attack will be the present front line.

(sd) C. C. HAUMANN Capt
A/Adjt
1st Battn THE RIFLE BRIGADE

DISTRIBUTION

O.C. "A" Coy.	No 1
"B" "	2
"C" "	3
"I" "	4
Commanding Officer	5
2nd in C.	6
Adjutant	7
A/Adjt	8
Intell. Offr	9
Transport Offr	10
War Diary	11
" "	12
File	13

Appendix 9

SECRET   OPERATION ORDER No 94   Copy No 12
by LT. COL. E. T. LIDDELL, D.S.O.
Comdg 1st Battn. THE RIFLE BRIGADE

17th OCTOBER, 1918

RELIEF 1.   THE BATTALION will relieve the 4th Battn YORKS & LANCS in the left support position of the left Brigade to-night.

DISPOSITIONS 2.   "B" and "I" Companies will be in the front line: "B" Coy. on the left and "I" Coy. on the right.
        "A" and "C" Companies will be in support, "A" on the left "C" Coy on the right.
        Battalion H.Q. will be at Q.27.a.5.0.
        Position of Aid Post will be notified later.

MOVE 3.   Battalion will move off from billets by march route in the following order:- "B", "I", "C", "A", Battn H.Q.
        Probable time of starting 14.00 hrs.   Exact time will be notified later.
        ROUTE: ESCAUDOEUVRES-IVUY main road
        As far as the RIEUX-IVUY road distances as laid down in SS734 will be kept, after which 100 yards will be kept between platoons.
        The Battalion will halt for teas in T.1.a.   The Transport Officer will arrange to have cookers at this point by 15.30.

BOUNDARIES: 4.   <u>Left Brigade Boundary</u>   The IVUY-AVESNES le SEC road and its continuation through O.12. Central to J.28. Central.
        <u>Right Brigade Boundary</u>   U.7.c.8.0. - U.2.Central.- O.34.Central - O.30.Central - P.20.Central.

GUIDES 5.   Guides for the Battalion, 5 per Company and two for Battn. H.Q. will be at track junction U.1.d.0.0. at 17.00

TRANSPORT 6.   Officers' kits, surplus stores, will be dumped by 14.00 to-day.   Transport Officer will arrange to collect.
        The Transport Officer will arrange for Lewis gun limbers to meet their respective Companies at track junction U.1.d.0.0. at 17.00.   Officers Commanding Companies will take these limbers on as far as possible, and then off-load.
        One limber for Battalion H.Q. will call for mess stores, orderly room boxes, signalling stores, etc. at 13.00 to-day, and proceed to the above mentioned rendezvous.
        Transport and Q.M. Stores will move to-day at the same time as the Battalion, to U.7.c.1.3.   A representative will be sent from Transport to take over before mid day.

RATIONS & WATER 7.   Rations for consumption to-morrow will be delivered at Battn H.Q. Q.27.a.5.0. at 12 midnight to-night.   Companies will send a ration party to Battalion H.Q. to draw these.
        Rations for consumption on the 18th inst onwards will arrive about 17.45 hrs.
        The exact location of Company dumps will be notified later.
        Filling point for water carts, Cross Roads U.13.d.0.5

TAKING OVER 8.   2nd Lieut. C. B. CRAVEN and one Officer per Company will report to Battalion H.Q. of the 4th Yorks and Lancs at Q.27.a.5.0. at 15.00 to-day.
        German anti-tank rifles, ammunition, defence schemes, aeroplane photographs and trench maps will be taken over. Duplicate of receipts, for these, together with a map showing dispositions with platoon areas marked, will be forwarded to Battalion H.Q. by 12.00 on the 18th inst.

                                                                       P.T.O.

- 2 -

TOOLS 9. The following tools will be drawn by each Company from the Qr.Mr.Stores this morning and packed on the L.G. limber.
10 picks, 36 shovels.
These will be required by Companies as accommodation is limited and those who cannot find accommodation will have to dig in immediately on sites selected for Posts by the Officers mentioned in para. 8.

REPORT 10. Completion of relief will be wired to Battalion H.Q. by the code word "PRESIDENT".

11 ACKNOWLEDGE

                            (sd)   C. C. NAUMANN   Capt
                                                     Act Adjt
              1st Battn THE RIFLE BRIGADE

DISTRIBUTION

Copy No 1 "O.C. "A" Coy
       2   "B" "
       3   "I" "
       4   "C" "
       5   Commanding Offr.
       6   2nd in Command
       7   Adjutant
       8   Asst Adjt
       9   Intelligence Offr
     10   Transport Offr
     11   Quartermaster
     12   War Diary
     13   " "
     14   File

B 1/1

AMENDMENT to OPERATION ORDER No 94

Ref. Paras 3, 7, 8, for "Q" in map reference read "O".
  Thus map reference will now read
  "O.27.a.5.0.

(sd) H. K. SHORT   2nd Lieut
  Asst/Adjt
1st Battn THE RIFLE BRIGADE

17-10-17

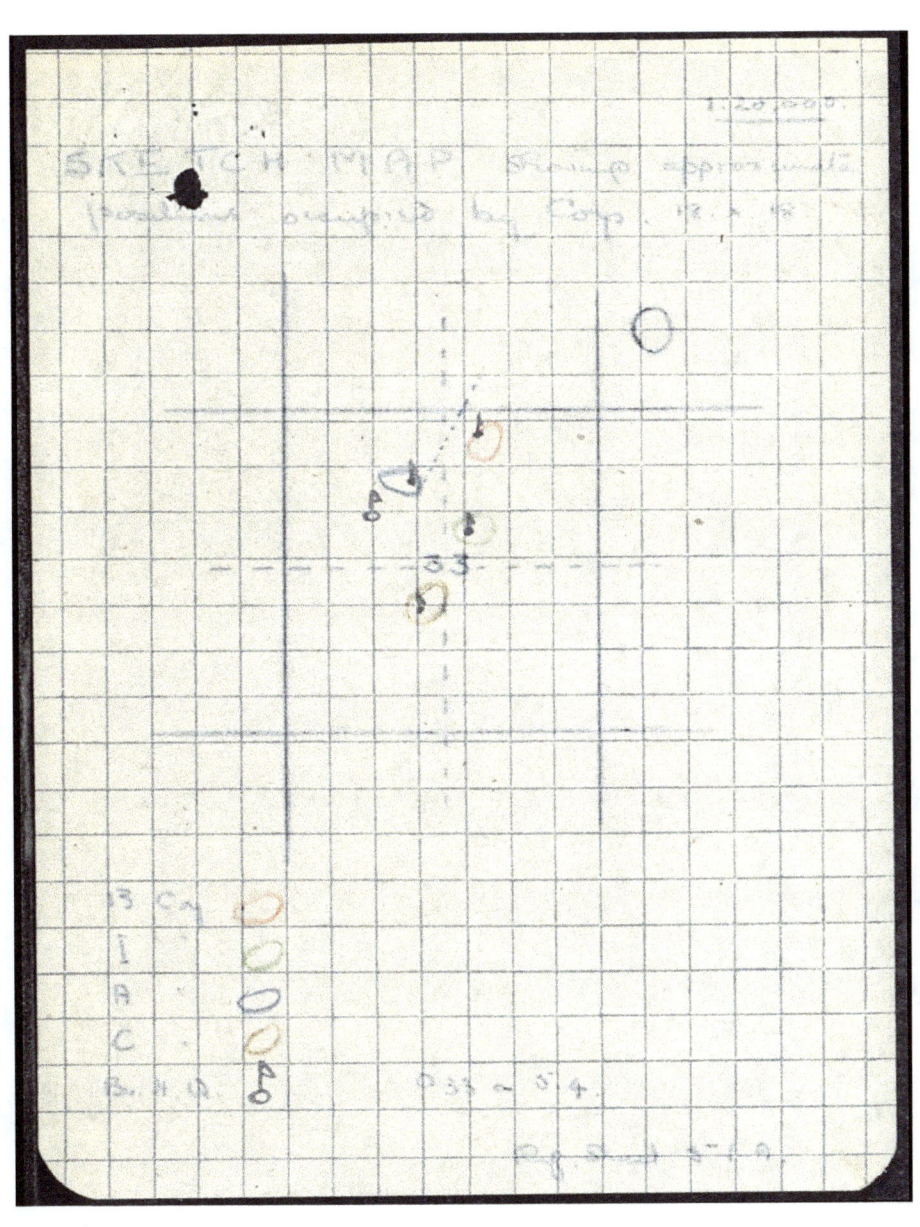

Appendix 10.

SECRET

OPERATION ORDER No 25
by Lt. Col. G. W. LIDDELL, D.S.O.
Commdg 1st Battalion THE RIFLE BRIGADE

19 - 10 - 18

OPERATION 1. The Battn will attack, capture and consolidate the NORTHERN portion of HASPRES and the high ground beyond.
The Battn will attack on a two Company front,: "B" Coy. will be on the left and "I" Coy. on the right: "C" Coy in support on the right and "A" Coy. on the left.
The advance will be made under an intense creeping barrage

ASSEMBLY 2. The Battn will assemble in the following area:-
"B" Company   ... O.25.c.
"I"   "   ... O.25.d.
"A"   "   ... O.22.d. and O.28.b.
"C"   "   ... O.29.a.
Battn. H.Q. will be at O.28.b.05.30 (N.28 billet)
Aid Post O.28.b.03.53.
All Coys. will be in position by 21.30 hours. Report to this effect to be sent to Battn. H.Q.
1st Hampshire Regt. will be on right and 4th Gordon Highlanders on left.

BOUNDARIES 3. LEFT BATTN. BOUNDARY O.31.d.7.5. - O.26.b.0.8. - O.19.d.8.6 thence railway NORTHWARDS inclusive to Left Division.
RIGHT BATTN BOUNDARY Road (exclusive) O.24.c.0.0. - O.24.b.7.5. - O.18.d.6.5. - P.13.c.6.8. - P.13.b.8.8. - P.7.b.8.0. - P.2.a.2.5.
INTER-COMPANY BOUNDARY O.24.c.5.0. - Road junction O.18.c. 10.35. (inclusive to "I" Coy.) P.13.a.4.8. - sunken road Northwards in P.7.c. (inclusive to "B" Coy.)

BARRAGE 4. At ZERO the barrage will fall on the line O.25.a.4.0. - O.24.c.0.7. - O.24.d.75.25. for 2 minutes.
It will lift back at the rate 100 yards in 2 minutes until the road P.19.a.5.0. - O.19.c.60.75 - O.18.c.80.85 has been reached at ZERO plus 30 minutes (FIRST OBJECTIVE). From this road to the river LA SELLE (SECOND OBJECTIVE) the Barrage will move forward 100 yards in 3 minutes; it will stop for 30 minutes 200 yards EAST of the River in order to give the Battn time to cross and form up on the EASTERN bank. It will then proceed at the rate of 100 yards in 5 minutes through the village till the railway (THIRD OBJECTIVE) is reached at ZERO plus 95 minutes. There the Barrage will stop for 15 minutes, after which it will move forward to the final objective O.13.b.90.15 - P.7.a.7.2. - P.7.b.5.9. - P.7.b.99.15. The Barrage will continue on the final line as a protective barrage for 15 minutes, when it will cease. It will only come down again if the S.O.S. signal is sent up.

ATTACK. 5. "B" and "I" Coys will, between 02.00 and 02.02 hours move as close up to the Barrage as possible. "A" and "C" Coys. will keep close up to the two leading Coys until well clear of the ridge in front of the original front line, after which the distances of about 100 yards will be kept.
On reaching the river "B" and "I" Coys. will immediately cross with the bridges provided - see Para 7 - and must be close up to the Barrage ready to go forward again when the 30 minutes has elapsed. After reaching final objective patrols will be pushed forward to gain observation.
"C" Coy. will push over as soon as "I" Coy. is across and will be responsible for thoroughly mopping up the village: the men of this Coy. will wear a band of sandbag material round the right forearm.
After mopping up the village "C" Coy will occupy a line from the cemetery P.13.b.2.7. - P.7.c.10.05. round the N.E. and N. of the village.
"A" Coy. will mop up the first objective and after cross the river behind "B" Coy. will send two platoons forward immedty

cont. on sheet 2

- 2 -

and occupy a line P.7.c.5.6. East and West of the road and the other two platoons will mop up the railway occupying a line - Cemetery P.13.b.8.7½ - P.7.c.10.05. until relieved by "C" Coy. when they will join the forward 2 platoons.

LIAISON POSTS 6. The following liaison posts will be established:-
By "I" Coy. at P.8.a.2.3.
" "B" " " O.12.b.8.1.
The posts will be at least 1 section strong.

BRIDGES 7. An R.E. Officer and 15 Sappers are allotted to the Battn for erecting bridges across the LA SELLE. The Officer will be under the direct command of Capt. W.H.P.SWAINE.
A carrying party of 1 Officer and 40 men will be supplied by the 1st Somerset L.I. to carry the four bridges (2 per front Coy) from the assembly position to the river. The parties carrying the bridges will move in rear of the support platoons of the leading Companies.

LIGHTS 8. As soon as the LA SELLE is crossed by the front Companies "B" and "I" Coys will each fire ONE GREEN VERY LIGHT.

COMMUNICATIONS 9. A Battalion advanced Report Centre will be established as soon as possible after ZERO, at about O.23.b.5.5. At Zero plus 2.30 hours this Report Centre will move to the sunken road at O.18.c.80.55. All messages will be sent to the Report Centre and Runners will be instructed to keep N. of the village.

CONTACT PATROL 10. Flares will be called for at :-
Zero plus 5 hours
"   "   7   "
"   "   9   "
Only the most advanced troops will light flares. A Counter attack aeroplane will be up from dawn onwards.

PRISONERS OF WAR 11. All prisoners will be sent back to Battalion H.Q. under a small guard: the above also applies to civilians.

CASUALTIES 12 (a) Estimated Casualty Reports stating Officers by name and Other Ranks by numbers will be sent to Battalion H.Q. at the following times:- Zero plus 5 hours
"   "   7   "
"   "   11   "
All casualties since Zero hour will be included in EACH of the above.
(b) A detailed Casualty Report will be sent in as soon as possible.

RATIONS 13. Rations for tomorrow will be carried on the man.

GREATCOATS 14. Greatcoats will be carried rolled round the haversack. All water bottles must be full before starting.

ANTI-TANK RIFLES 15. If possible 1 Anti-Tank Rifle and ammunition will be issued to each front line Coy. They should be carried forward by the support platoon.

ZERO 16. Zero hour will be at 02.00 hours on the 20th unless further orders are received.

BARRAGE TRACING 17. One copy of Barrage Tracing is attached to "B" and "I" coys Operation Order only.

ACKNOWLEDGE.

(sd) C. C. NAUMANN Capt.
Act/Adjt 1st Battn. THE RIFLE BRIGADE

19/10/18

AMENDMENT No 1 to OPERATION ORDER No 95

Ref. Para 4. BARRAGE
    When the Barrage reaches the final line, each gun will fire two smoke shells.

Ref. Para 4. BARRAGE
    There will be no protective Barrage.

    One section of 11th T.M.B. will be attached to "A" Coy. during the operations.

ACKNOWLEDGE

                                        (sd) C. C. NAUMANN Capt.
                                                    Act/Adjt
                                  1st Batt. THE RIFLE BRIGADE

19/10/16

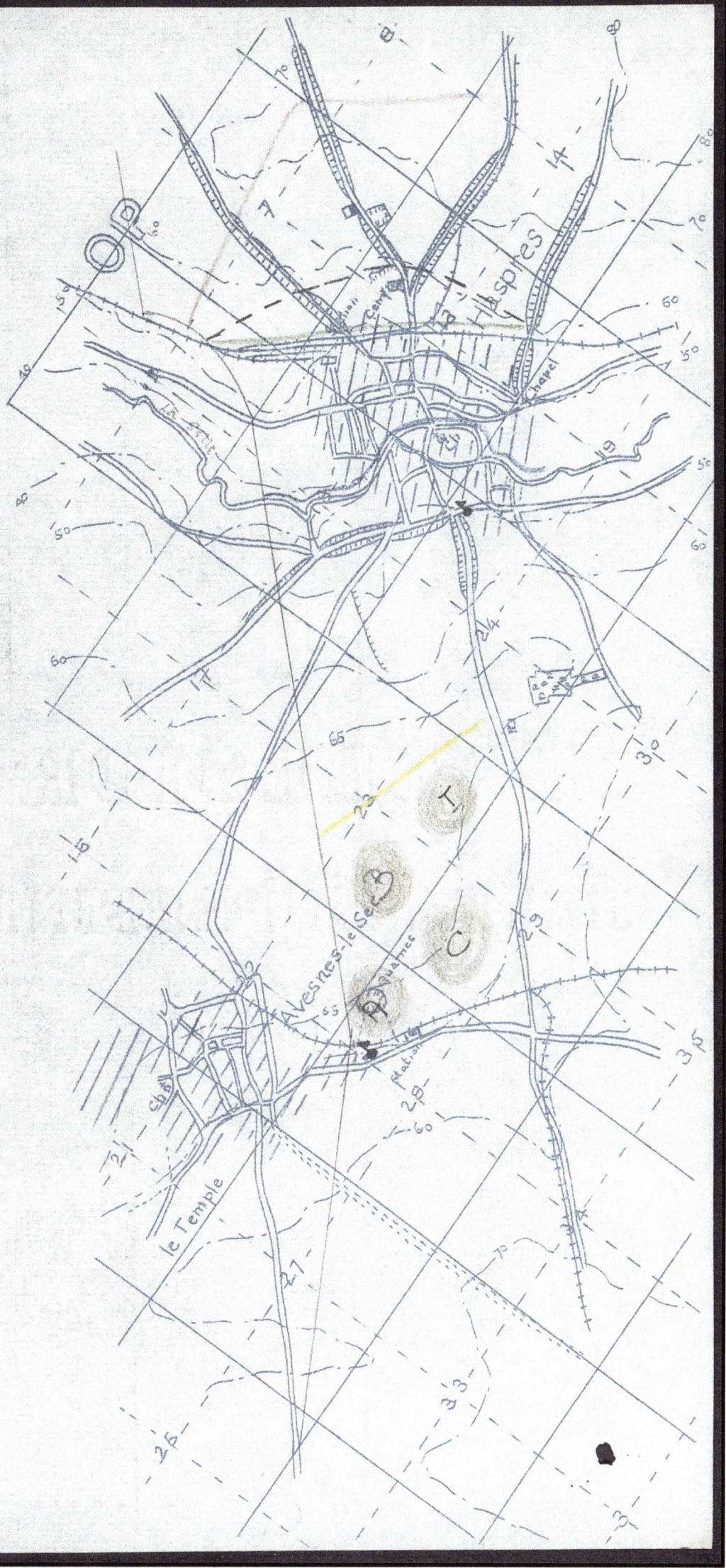

Appendix 11

SECRET

OPERATION ORDER No 20
by Lt.Col. G. W. LIDDELL, D.S.O.
Comndg 1st Battalion THE RIFLE BRIGADE

Ref SHEET 51a   23rd OCTOBER, 1918   Copy No

OPERATION   1.   The 11th Infantry Brigade will attack the enemy's position W. and E. of the river ECAILLON on the morning of the 24th inst. The 1st Somerset L.I. will be on the right and the 1st Hampshire Regt. on the left, with the Battalion in Reserve.

REORGANISATION   2.   The front will be reorganised on the night of the 23rd/24th:-
(i) The 1st Somerset L.I. will assemble in rear of the right front Coy., pushing forward posts to protect the assembly area. On completion "B" Coy will withdraw and assemble in P.S. area.
(ii) The 1st Hampshire Regt. will assemble in rear of the left front Coy.   "I" Coy. will withdraw on completion of relief to P.S area.

GUIDES   3.   16 guides from "B" Coy. for the 1st Somerset L.I. and 16 guides from "I" Coy. for the 1st Hampshire Regt. will report at Battalion H.Q. at 18.00 hrs to-day.

CARRYING PARTIES   4.
(i)   "B" Coy. will provide two parties each of 1 officer, 2 N.C.Os and 30 men for carrying bridges for the 1st Somerset L.I.   The first party will assemble at P.10.c.1.2. and the second party at P.9.b.2.7.   When parties are in position O.C No 1 party will report to O.C. right front Coy. 1st Somersets, and O.C. No 2 party to O.C. left front Coy. 1st Somersets.
(ii)   Ref. (i) "I" Coy. will supply identical parties for 1st Hampshire Regt. and instructions in the above sub para. hold good except that the No 1 party will assemble at P.3.b.2.3. and the second party at J.33.d.0.8.
     The above parties will move with the Coys. to which they are attached, and after placing the bridges across the river ECAILLON at the places selected by the Os.C. Coys of the 1st Somerset L.I. and the 1st Hampshire Regt. concerned will await the arrival at the river of the remainder of their Companies, vide para 6.

DETACHED   5. (i)   Two platoons of "C" Coy. will be attached to 1st Somerset L.I. and will move in rear of Support Coys. These two platoons will follow the 1st Somerset L.I. to the YELLOW LINE between J.35.a.40.25. to P.6.b.00.25., which they will mop up and, when released by "A" Coy. of the 1st Somerset L.I. will rejoin their Coy. in the BLUE LINE, vide para. 6.
(ii)   Two platoons of "A" Coy. will be attached to 1st Hampshire Regt. and will move as detailed in Para 5, sub para (i) as far as the YELLOW LINE between J.34.c.3.3. and J.33.d.4.8., mop that portion up and join their Coy. in the BLUE LINE vide para. 6.

ACTION OF BATTALION   6.   The remainder of "A", "B", "C", and "I" Coys. will move from the area P.8. between ZERO plus 100 and ZERO plus 120 minutes as circumstances allow, cross the river and start consolidating the BLUE LINE.
     The Bridging parties of "B" and "I" Coys will join their own Coys. as the latter cross the ECAILLON.

cont on sheet 2

- 2 -

ACTION 6. cont.
Battn   BOUNDARIES for Coys on the BLUE LINE
    "B" Coy. from Road Junction P.5.d.15.50 - P.5.a.1.1.
    "C" "   " P.5.a.1.1. - J.34.d.0.0.
    "A" "   " J.34.d.0.0. - J.34.a.0.7.
    "I" "   " J.34.a.0.7. - J.34.a.4.0. Road Junction inclusive.
    Battalion H.Q. and Aid Post will remain at P.7.d.5.3. and P.13.a.8.9. respectively, until further orders.

COLLECTING 7.   "B" and "I" Coys will each detail one N.C.O. and 6 men
POSTS   to be at P.10.c.6.9. and at J.33.b.4.1. respectively to collect all prisoners of war and send them under escort to Battalion H.Q.

ZERO HOUR 8.   Zero hour will be at 04.00 hours on the 24th.

    9.   ACKNOWLEDGE.

                      (sd) C. G. NAUMANN Capt.
                    A/Adjt 1st Battn THE RIFLE BRIGADE

SKETCH MAP 1st Bn. The Rifle Brigade.
SCALE 1:20,000.
TO ACCOMPANY O.O. No. 96

Appendix 12

O.C. "A", "B", "I" Coy

1.   "A", "B", "I" Coys will be relieved by two Coys of the 1st Hampshire Regt tonight. On the arrival of one Company, Hampshire Regt. the Coy. of this Battalion thus relieved will move out. On the arrival of the second Coy. Hampshire Regt. the remaining two Coys will move out. On relief Coys will move back to billets in HASPRES. Guides for billets will be at broken down railway bridge P.13.a.85.90 from midnight onwards.

2.   Lewis Guns, ammunition, etc. can be dumped 200 yards S.W. of cross roads J.33.b.4.1. One N.C.O. and one man per Coy. will be left with them to load them on the limber. On arrival at HASPRES limbers will deliver Lewis guns etc. at the various Coy. H.Q. It is possible that limbers will not be at the above mentioned place by the time Coys are relieved: Coys will not wait for them but after dumping L.Gs will push straight on to billets.

3.   Relief complete will be reported by runner to Battn. H.Q.

4.   "C" Coy. will be relieved under orders from O.C. 1st Somerset Lt.I.

                                                (sd) C. B. CRAVEN 2/Lieut.
                                                              for Capt.
                          Adjt 1st Bn THE RIFLE BRIGADE

24/10/18

Appendix 13.

SECRET   OPERATION ORDER No 97
by Lt.Col. G. W. LIDDELL, DSO.
Commdg 1st Battalion THE RIFLE BRIGADE

28th OCTOBER, 1918   Copy No 11

RELIEF   1.   The Battalion will relieve the 2nd Battn Lancashire Fusiliers in the front line, right sub-sector, to-night 28/29th inst., as follows:-
"C" Coy. will be the Right Front Company
"A" " " " " Left Front Company
"B" " " " " Right Support Company
"I" " " " " Left Front Company
Battalion H.Q. will be at K.32.d.45
Location of Aid Post will be notified later.

GUIDES   2.   Arrangements about guides will be notified later.

MOVE   3.   The Battalion will move off from billets as follows:-
"C", "A", "B", "I", H.Q.
"C" Coy. will move off at 14.00 hours.
An interval of 100 yards will be kept between platoons: Troops when on the road will march in file, but should be kept off the road as much as possible. Mounted officers will ride off the road except in villages and in enclosed country.
Battle ammunition will be carried up to the trenches. Jerkins will be rolled on the belt.
ROUTE:- Road junction P.13.b.25.45. - Road junction P.14.a.95.50. - P.10.c.45.90. - thence track to P.10.b.4.2. - Cross roads P.10.b.6.0. - Cross roads P.5.d.20.35. - CHAPEL P.12.a.5.9. - thence road to QUERENAING.

TRANSPORT   4.   Lewis Gun Limbers (1 per Coy.) and 1 limber for Battalion H.Q. will be loaded by 13.45. Lewis guns will be off loaded as far up as possible, and will be carried into the line from that point.
Three cookers will accompany the Battalion as far as Sunken Road P.6.c.5.0. - P.6.d.4.7. where a halt will be made for teas.
Officers' kits, surplus mess stores, will be packed by 12.00 hrs and the Transport Officer will arrange to collect.

RATIONS   5.   Rations will arrive at Battalion H.Q. to-night at 23 hours. Companies will be notified when and where to draw.
Instructions for the following days will be issued later.

ACKNOWLEDGE

                               Capt.
                               Act. Adjt

28/10/18   1st Battn   THE RIFLE BRIGADE

DISTRIBUTION

Copy No 1 Commanding Officer   9 Transport Offr,
2 Adjutant   10 Quartermaster
3 Asst/Adjt   11 War Diary
4 Intelligence Offr.   12 " "
5 O.C. "A" Coy   13 File
6 "B" "   14 Sig. Officer.
7 "C" "
8 "I" "

AMENDMENT No 1
to OPERATION ORDER No 97, dated 28/10/18

GUIDES will meet the Battalion at 17.00 hours at the Cross Roads in K.32.C.

(sd)   C. C. NAUMANN   Capt.
                         Act Adjt
28/10/18   1st Battn THE RIFLE BRIGADE

To accompany Dispositions. 1st Bn. The Rifle Brigade
O.O.97. 29.x.18.

Scale 1:20,000.
Sh. 51A N.E.

K

Artres

Notes.

O — C Coy. Bridgehead.
O — A Coy.
O — I Coy. ⟶ H.Q. in Chateau.
O — B Coy.

Bn. H.Q. at K.32.d.5.5.

Appendix 14.

CASUALTIES

OFFICERS

Oct 20	Capt. T. CARLYLE	Wounded (Remaining at duty)	
	2nd Lieut. G. A. LUKER	Wounded — ditto —	
	" " J. K. METHERELL	Wounded	
21	" " F. R. M. LEE	Wounded (Remaining at duty)	
	" " J. S. TIDBALL	Wounded	
22	" " W. G. KING	To Hospital	
24	" " G. A. LUKER	Wounded	
3	Lieut. W. H. GOSNEY	Transferred to 13th Battn The Rifle Brigade	

OTHER RANKS	Killed	Wounded	Missing	To Hospital
Oct 1st to 7th	1	8	-	
17th to 19th	-	1	-	
20th to 23rd	17	65	1	
24th	2	21	1	
28th to 31st	-	5	-	
	20	100	2	45

------::------::------::------::00::------::------::------::------

REINFORCEMENTS

OFFICERS and OTHER RANKS

Oct 3	...	2
6	2nd Lieut. G. A. MITCHELL	
	" " J. K. METHERELL	
	" " R. G. TARLTON	
7	...	21
8	...	17
9	...	2
13	...	6
14	...	12
16	Capt. F. H. FARMER	1
20	2nd Lieut. P. C. SOMERVILLE	1
24	...	24
25	2nd Lieut. A. E. SALTER (From Hospital)	
27	Lieut. A. E. ADAMS	
	" F. YOUNGHUSBAND	
	2nd Lieut. H. FINCH	
	" " G. D. CHAMBERLAIN	
28	...	3
29	...	3
30	...	1

TOTALS Officers 10   Other Ranks   93

Army Form C. 2118.

HONOURS & AWARDS

Date	Award	Recipient
14/10/18	BAR TO MILITARY CROSS	Capt. A.S.S. HERBERT, MC
	MILITARY CROSS	2nd Lieut. H.V. MORLOCK
	.....	Lieut. J.W. ALDRIDGE (MORC, USA)
1/10/18	BAR TO MILITARY MEDAL	20910 Cpl. A. CORNWELL, MM
		203482 Rfn. E. MARSHALL, MM
	MILITARY MEDAL	1364 Sgt. R.W. STONE
		8094 : T. MANN
		2715 Cpl. W.M. BAMBLETT
		260 A/Cpl. G. CARTER
		S/5104 : A.J. BARNES
		7094 Rfn. S. HASLAM
		200244 : E. NIXON
		203522 : A. SHEARD
		25859 : G. MAYER
		201404 : B. CLEALL
		200373 : T. KITE

DISTRIBUTION of BATTALION 31/10/18

OFFICERS	OTHER RANKS
In the Line	
Lt. Col. G. W. LIDDELL, DSO	
Capt. C. C. NAUMANN	
2nd Lieut. C. B. CRAVEN	517
" " W. G. WAYMOUTH	
Capt. J. A. TAYLOR	
" T. CARLYLE	
" F. H. FARMER	
Lieut. H. L. ROUTH	
2nd Lieut. R. WILSON	
" " E. J. PODBURY	
" " A. E. BOYLAND	
" " J. H. DAVIES	
" " C. KNOWLES	
" " A. E. SALTER	
" " G. A. MITCHELL	
" " R. G. TARLTON	
Lieut. J. W. ALDRIDGE (MORC, USA)	

At 1st Line Transport
Capt. G. BLAND
Lieut. & Q.M. C. MORGAN   118
Major C. F. C. LETTS
2nd Lieut. H. K. SHORT
Rev. A. J. BILLINGS (C.F.)

At S.S.135 Details
Capt. W. H. P. SWAINE
Lieut. W. H. SHOOBERT   87
2nd Lieut. C. A. BALDWIN, MM
"   "   F. R. M. LEE
"   "   R. C. LOVELL
Lieut. F. YOUNGHUSBAND
"   A. E. ADAMS
2nd Lieut. P. C. SOMERVILLE
"   "   G. D. CHAMBERLAIN

Otherwise Employed

Capt N.D.HARVEY On leave	4th Div H.Q.	7
Lieut G. J. COLE.MC "	" " Sig. Coy	5
" A. WAUDBY " "	11th Bde	13
2/Lt. W.E.G.LEGHORN,MC "	3 Sec 4 Sig Coy	10
" T.R.LECKIE 11th T.M.B.	11th T.M.B.	6
Lieut. G.T.KERSWELL Town Major	3rd Echelon	1
(Saulzoir)	4th Div Recep.Cp	3
2/Lieut. H. FINCH 4th Div.	1st Army Schools	7
Ammn. Column	4th Div "	1
" H. V. MORLOCK,MC 1st Army	G.H.Q.,L.Gn Sch	2
School	4th Div Ammn Col	17
" L. WATSON do	On leave	44
" A.R.BURRIDGE 4th Div	Agricultural Work	1
Salvage Coy	Rest Camp 1st Army	5
" W.J.WOODSIDE,MM G.H.Q.	4th Div Salv Coy	6
L.Gn School	Escort duty	2
" W. G. KING Hospital	4th Div Stragglers Post	3
" A.O.HUNTING On leave	Town Major's svt	1
	Absent without leave	1
	Hosp. svt to Offr	1
	Hospital sick	15
		151

WAR DIARY or INTELLIGENCE SUMMARY

1st Bn The R. W. Brigade

November 1918

Army Form C. 2118.

Place	Date	Hour	Summary of Events and Information	Remarks and references to Appendices
PRESEAU	1st - 2nd (cont)		At 05:15 hours on Nov. 1st the Battalion plus one Company of the 1st Bn SOMERSET L.I. attacked the enemy positions E of the RHONELLE RIVER. A and C Companies formed the front line, A on the left, B on the right, supported by I and B Companies respectively. The attached Company of the SOMERSET L.I. followed in rear of B Company. On our left flank were the 1st Bn THE HAMPSHIRE REGT. and on our right the 1/7 WARWICKS. The artillery put down a very heavy creeping barrage and the attack proceeded well, the objective being gained after meeting with but little resistance. Touch however was not maintained with the flanks and in consequence the enemy seized the opportunity for an immediate thing counter attack from either flank. This forced our troops back through the village of PRESEAU after some very severe fighting. Eventually a line was established with great difficulty on the high ground running from K 18 d 3.6. to K 24 b 4.5. Touch was gained with the troops on our left but the right flank remained exposed except for its protection afforded by some machine guns.	O.O. 98 and map Appendix I

Army Form C. 2118

1st Bn. The Rifle Brigade

WAR DIARY
or
INTELLIGENCE SUMMARY.
(Erase heading not required)

November 1918

Place	Date	Hour	Summary of Events and Information	Remarks and references to Appendices
PRESEAU	1st – 2nd (incl.) continued.		By this time companies had become very weak and the troops were out of communication. In the evening the Battalion was relieved by the 2nd Bn. SEAFORTH HIGHLANDERS and moved back for a few hours to K 23 b. During the day large numbers of prisoners and machine guns were captured. At 05.30 hours on November 2nd the attack was continued by fresh troops attached to the 11th Brigade and the Battalion moved up in support to the 1st KINGS OWN in the Rifle Wood sector. The sunken road in K 12 c was reached at Zero + 1½ hours. Touch was gained with the 1st SOMERSET L.I. on our right near the OLD MILL at K 18 b 3.2. At first the enemy was very active with his machine guns but later little shelling was experienced until the Battalion was being relieved by a company of the 4th Bn. SHERWOOD FORESTERS. On completion of the relief the Battalion marched back to billets in HASPRES.	O.O. 99 Appendix 2 O.O. 100 Appendix 3
HASPRES	3rd – 4th (incl.)		After the heavy fighting of the previous day and the three days holding the line before the attack, the troops were thoroughly exhausted. These two days were entirely devoted to resting, cleaning up and reorganization.	

1st Bn. The Rifle Brigade.

Army Form C. 2118.

WAR DIARY
or
INTELLIGENCE SUMMARY.

November 1918.

Place	Date	Hour	Summary of Events and Information	Remarks and references to Appendices
HASPRES	5th – 10th (incl.)		This period was devoted to section, platoon and Company training, particular attention being paid to "turn out", close order drill and arm drill. Two hours Physical Training was carried out under the Brigade "Physical on the 8th". On the same date the Brigade Efficiency Competition started. In the afternoon Signalling and Revolver Shooting Competitions took place. On the morning of the 10th the Transport was inspected and marks allotted for "turn out" to count towards the Brigade Competition. At the same time Companies were given one hour each on an improvised range just S. of the HASPRES – AVESNE-LE-SEC Road. On Sunday 10th that was a Parade Service in the Boy's School at HASPRES. In the afternoon orders were received for a move to SAULTAIN the following day.	
CURGIES	11th – 12th (incl.)		Accordingly on the 11th the Battalion left HASPRES for SAULTAIN proceeding by march route. The order of march was H.Q. B.T.A.C. H.Q. Coxes, the starting point (i.e. the bridge railway bridge) at 09.00 hours. En route a small flank guard and advanced guard scheme was carried out. The Battalion reached SAULTAIN about 13.30 hours but found that the billets allotted in the village of CURGIES some two kilometres further along the main VALENCIENNES – BAVAI Road. The Battalion reached its new billeting area about 14.00 hours.	O.O. 101 Appendix 4

1st Bn. The Rifle Brigade

Army Form C. 2118.

November 1918

WAR DIARY
or
INTELLIGENCE SUMMARY.
(Erase heading not required.)

Place	Date	Hour	Summary of Events and Information	Remarks and references to Appendices
CURGIES	13th	30—	From the 13th onwards an hour and a half and a half hour to two and a half hours of the day was set apart for Education or Training in Military Training. The men of the latter period was occupied by parades under the Regimental Sergeant Major and the remainder with Classes of instruction in Lewis Gun and Scouting, and training with Company and Platoon NCOs. The afternoons were devoted to recreation i.e. football, Cross Country Running &c. On the morning of the 14th the B.G.C. inspected the Battalion in marching order on the Battalion parade ground. On Sunday 17th there was a Brigade Parade Service at 11.00 hours immediately followed by a Battalion practice Ceremonial parade. On the 19th the Brigade Ceremonial practice was held on the open ground W. of CURGIES just S. of the CURGIES - SAULTAIN road. The Battalion took part in a Divisional Ceremonial parade at the old German Aerodrome at SAULTAIN on the morning of the 20th. The Division was drawn up in line to General Salute after which each Battalion marched past in Column of Companies. The Corps Commander Major R.G. Haviland DSO MC inspected the Battalion and took on General Command.	

Army Form C. 2118.

WAR DIARY
or
INTELLIGENCE SUMMARY.
(Erase heading not required.)

1st Bn. The Rifle Brigade

November 1918

Place	Date	Hour	Summary of Events and Information	Remarks and references to Appendices
CURGIES			On the 23rd. the transport & rear of the Battalion marched past & on the 27th. a Brigade Ceremonial parade was held & on the SAULTAIN aerodrome(four squares 105) by the Army Commander. The transport of the Division was inspected by the G.O.C. & the Battalion was highly complimented. On the 26th. the Division was inspected on the Army Commander.	Appendix 5.
			For Honours & Awards Reinforcements Distribution Casualties } See Appendix 5.	

E.M. Bidewell.
LIEUT. COL.
COMMANDING
1st Bn. THE RIFLE BRIGADE.

SECRET

Appendix 1.

OPERATION ORDERS No 98
by Lt.Col. G. W. LIDDELL, D.S.O.
Commdg 1st Battalion THE RIFLE BRIGADE

Copy No 11

30th OCTOBER, 1918

GENERAL PLAN 1. On the 31st, at a time to be notified later, the 11th Brigade will attack and capture the village of PRESAU and the high ground to the NORTH. For the above mentioned attack this Battalion will attack on the right and the 1st HAMPSHIRE REGT. on the left, with the 1st SOMERSET LIGHT INF. in support.

One Company of the 1st SOMERSET LT.I. will be attached to this Battalion.

The 1st Division will be attacking on the right.

BOUNDARIES 2. RIGHT BATTALION BOUNDARY:- K.99.a.e.7. - L.19.b.1.0.
L.90.a.0.7. - L.14.c.9.1.
LEFT BATTALION BOUNDARY:- Road junction K.23.d.3.3. - Road junction L.13.a.8.5. - Road junction L.13.a.0.8. - L.8.a.9.1.
INTER-COMPANY BOUNDARY:- K.23.d.9.1. - N.W.Corner of Wood L.14.a.3.4.

OBJECTIVE 3. Blue or Final Objective:- L.14.c.9.1. - L.14.a.4.5. - L.8.c.0.0. - L.7.Central - L.7.a.5.0. - K.6.d.8.5.

ARTILLERY SUPPORT 4. The attack will be carried out under an intense artillery creeping barrage by 18 pounders. This barrage will open at zero on a line 300 yards in front of the forming up line, and at zero plus 3 minutes will creep forward at the rate of 100 yards in 3 minutes, except in front of the Bridgehead where it will remain stationary till zero plus 15 minutes, when it will conform and move forward at the same rate.

On the line K.18.b.9.5. - K.24.c.15.45., it will become protective for 10 minutes. It will then move forward at the rate of 100 yards in 4 minutes for the next 400 yards, after which it will move at 100 yards in 5 minutes, except when it again becomes protective for 10 minutes on a line K.13.a.0.0. - L.19.a.6.4. In front of the final objective there will be a protective barrage for 10 minutes only.

DETAILS OF ATTACK 5. (i) "A" and "C" Coys. will be in front, "A" Coy. on the left and "C" Coy. on the right. "I" and "B" Coys. will be in support with "I" Coy. on the left and "B" Coy. on the right.

The Company of the 1st SOMERSET L.I. attached will move in rear of "B" Coy.

(ii) After the 10 minutes protective barrage on the line K.12.a.0.0. - L.19.a.6.4. "I" and "B" Coys will pass through the two leading Companies and go straight to the final objective.

(iii) "C" Coy. will then reorganise, and as soon as the protective barrage in front of the final objective has ceased, will push through "I" and "B" Coys. and exploit success as far as possible, and if possible capture hostile batteries suspected in L.8, L.7 and L.2. This Coy. will form an outpost zone in front of the whole Battalion front, special attention being paid to the right flank.

(iv) "A" Coy will follow behind "B" and "I" Coys. and mop up the village of PRESAU thoroughly, after which they will withdraw and consolidate the OLD MILL SPUR L.19.d. and K.13.c. relieving the attached Coy. of the 1st Somerset L.I. if circumstances permit.

(v) The Company of the 1st Somerset L.I. will follow in rear of "B" Coy. and will consolidate on the OLD MILL SPUR K.18.d. and K.13.c. until relieved by "A" Coy., when they will act on orders received from Batt. H.Q.

(vi) Great care will be taken to mop up isolated houses and small woods during the attack.

(vii) Battalion H.Q. will be at the CHATEAU K.23.a.7.4. during the attack.

(viii) AID POST will probably be at K.23.d.30.10. (present

- 2 -

Bridgehead Coy. H.Q.)

LIAISON POSTS 6. (i) "B" Coy. will form a Liaison Post of at least one section with the 61st Division at L.20.a.4.9.
(ii) A Liaison Post between Coys will be established at L.14.a.3.4.

ASSEMBLY POSITION 7. The Battalion will assemble in the Bridgehead area in order named in para 6 (i) South of road through K.23.c. and d. Companies will open to correct intervals when the Battn starts to move at zero plus 15 minutes.
One platoon of "A" Coy. will assemble on the right of the front Coy. of the HAMPSHIRE REGT West of the river and start with them at ZERO to ensure touch being maintained when the remainder of the Battalion moves at zero plus 15 minutes.

BEARINGS 8. Right flank of the Battn will march on a grid bearing of 69° (approximately 81 1/2 magnetic).
Left flank on a grid bearing of 57° (approx 69 1/2 mag.)
Centre, on a grid bearing of 63° (75 1/2 magnetic).
Great care will be taken to keep good direction and a small party per Coy. will be detailed for the sole purpose of doing so.

COMMUNICATION 9. (i) There will be a Brigade Visual Station in the CHATEAU K.22.a.7.4. Coys will endeavour to gain communication with this whenever possible. Call:- R.C.
(ii) Battalion Report Centre will be about K.23.b.8.2. in the Sunken Road to which all Coy runners will be directed. This R.C. will be connected to Battn H.Q. by visual and line.
Also an attempt will be made to obtain communication with Coys by visual from high ground at K.24.d.3.8. at ZERO plus 100 minutes. Call:- P.Z.

ZERO 10. ZERO hour will be notified later.

CASUALTIES 11. (i) Estimated Casualty Reports should reach Battn H.Q. at ZERO plus 4 hours; ZERO plus 8 hours. Reports will include all casualties since ZERO: i.e. The casualties reported in the zero plus 4 report will be included in the second report as well.
(ii) A detailed Casualty Report should be forwarded as soon as possible.

PRISONERS OF WAR. 12. Prisoners will be sent back under escort to collecting station, to be notified later.

ACKNOWLEDGE.

(sd) C. C. HAUSMANN Capt.
Adjt 1st Battn THE RIFLE BRIGADE

DISTRIBUTION

Copy No 1 Commanding Officer
2 Adjutant
3 Intelligence Offr.
4 Signal Offr.
5 O.C. "A" Coy
6 " "B" "
7 " "C" "
8 " "D" "
9 1st Bn HAMPSHIRE REGT
10 " " SOMERSET L.I.
11 War Diary
12 " "
13 File

SECRET   AMENDMENT No 1
                        To OPERATION ORDER No 98
----

1. Ref. para 4
    (a) A Barrage Tracing is attached to all Companies' copies.
    (b) Each 18 pdr will fire one round of smoke on arrival at a
    protective barrage and one round immediately before lifting
    forward: guns will quicken rate of fire immediately before
    moving forward from a protective barrage.

2. Ref. para 7.
    (a) All Companies will be in position by 02.30 hours tomorrow,
    and reports to this effect will be made to Battalion H.Q. by
    03.00 hours.
    (b) Companies will use the River crossings at the following
    times:-
            "A" Company   01.30 - 01.50 hours
            "B"   "   01.50 - 02.10   "
            "I"   "   02.10 - 02.30   "
            Coy. Somerset L.I.
            (attached)   02.30 - 02.50   "
    (c) Companies will assemble in absolute silence so as not to
    arouse the suspicions of the enemy.
    (d) All posts in trench K.23.c.3.3. - K.22.b.8.0 and posts
    from K.22.b.8.0 - K.22.Central will be withdrawn between ZERO
    minus 30 minutes, and ZERO minus 15 minutes.
    (e) Troops will dig in at the assembly position.

3. AID POST   The Aid post will be at K.22.d.90.10.

4. FLARES   Flares, when called for by the contact aeroplane, will
             be lighted by the most advanced troops only.

5. ZERO   ZERO hour will be at 05.15 hours on 1st NOVEMBER.

6. FLANKS   RIGHT Flank Regiment   2/7th WARWICK
             LEFT   "   "   1st HAMPSHIRE

7. AMMUNITION 2/Lieut. C. B. CRAVEN will be responsible for seeing that
             6 boxes of S.A.A. are sent to Battalion Report Centre as soon
             after zero as possible. These will be supplemented by a further
             6 during the day.
                  If necessity arises "C", "I" and "B" Companies will draw
             on this and will send a chit stating amount required to O.C. "A"
             Company who will send a party to draw from Report Centre and
             convey to the Coy. requiring it direct.

                                    (sd) C. O. NAUMANN Capt.
                                    Adjt 1st Battn THE RIFLE BRIGADE

Issued to all recipients of OPERATION ORDER No 98

31/10/18

1st Bn. The Rifle Brigade.

SKETCH MAP

To accompany O.O. no. 98.

Final Objective — — — — — — ———

Approx line held Nov. 1st — — — — ———

Approx Line of Bn
 in Support Nov. 2nd — — — — ———

Bn. Boundaries — — — — — ———

Bn. H.Q. — — — — — ⊙

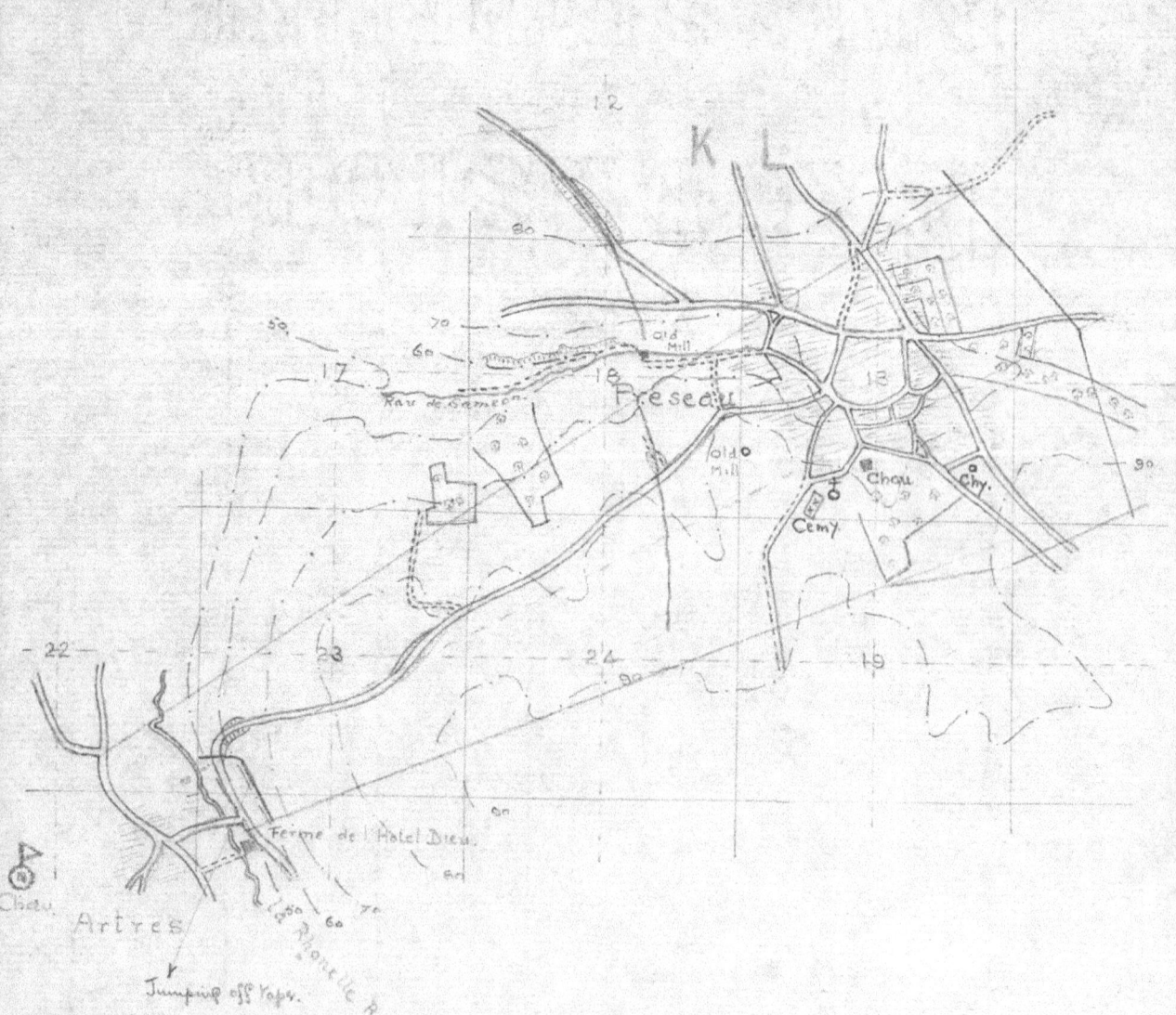

Bn. H.Q.
K 28 a 75.35

Ref. Sheet 51 A.

Appendix 2

SECRET   OPERATION ORDER No 99
                by Lt.Col. G. W. LIDDELL, D.S.O.
            Commdg 1st Battalion THE RIFLE BRIGADE
----

1. ATTACK   The attack on the BLUE LINE will be continued tomorrow, 2nd November. The Battalion will be in Support of the 1st KINGS REGT in the left sub sector.

2. POSITIONS.   One and a half hours after ZERO the Battalion will have taken up the following positions on the Road in K.18.c.:-
          "A" Coy (plus "B" Coy) from K.18.b.3.7. - K.18.c.9.1.
          "C" "   From K.18.c.9.1. - K.18.c.6.5.
          "I" "   "   K.18.c.6.5. - K.18.d.0.0.

3. ZERO   Zero hour will be 08.30 hours.

4. BATTALION Hd.Qrs will be at K.28.a.3.1.

5. AID POST   will be at the MILL: same as today.

6. RELIEF   Tomorrow night the Battalion will be relieved and will move back to billets, location to be notified later.

                 ACKNOWLEDGE.

                           (sd) C. G. NAUMANN, Capt.
Issued at 23.35   Adjt 1st Batt THE RIFLE BRIGADE
   1-11-18

       DISTRIBUTION

        Copy No 1   "A" (plus "B") Coy
               2   "C" Coy.
               3   "I" "
               4   Commanding Offr
               5   Adjutant
               6   War Diary
               7   " "
               8   File

SECRET   OPERATION ORDER No 100
                 by Lt.Col. G.W.LIDDELL, D.S.O.
              Comdg 1st Battn. THE RIFLE BRIGADE

1 **RELIEF** The Battalion will be relieved this evening by one
Company of the 8th SHERWOOD FORESTERS and after relief
will move back to billets in HASPRES.

2 **GUIDES** "A" Coy. will detail 3 guides (one for "A" and "B"
Coys and one for Coy. H.Q.), and "C" and "I" Coys each
one guide to report to Battn H.Q. by 16.00 hrs today.

3 **TRANSPORT** One limber for Lewis guns, Ammunition, Officers'
mess stores, etc. will be at Battn H.Q. from 19.20 hrs
onwards;   Coys will each detail one man to accompany
the limber.
        Chargers of "A", "C" and "I" Coys will be just
West of Railway Bridge K.27.d.70.35 from 19.30 hrs
onwards.

4 **TOOLS** As many tools as possible will be brought out and
there will be a limber for these at Battn H.Q. at the
same time as the L.G. limber.

5.**MOVE** Coys will meet guides for Billets at the Broken
Railway Bridge in HASPRES P.13.a.3.3.

6. **REPORT** Relief complete will be reported by runner, and
O.C. Coys. should call in at Battn. H.Q. to see the
Commanding Officer before proceeding further down.

7. **FLARES** S.O.S. Rockets, Flares, Very Lights, etc. will be
handed over and receipts obtained.

ACKNOWLEDGE

                          (sd) C. C. NAUMANN Capt, Adjt
                          1st Battn. THE RIFLE BRIGADE

Issued at 14.30
  9 - 11 - 18

SECRET

Appendix 4

OPERATION ORDER No 101
by Major C.F.C. LETTS
Commdg 1st Battn. THE RIFLE BRIGADE

10th NOVEMBER, 1918

1. The Battalion will move by march route tomorrow to the SAULTAIN - CURGIES area.

2. MOVE Order of march - H.Q., "B", "I", "A", "C".

H.Q. will pass the starting point, P.13.b.0.3., junction of railway with road, at 09.00 hours, and will keep 300 yards in rear of the transport of the 1st HAMPSHIRE REGT.

An interval of 100 yards will be kept between Companies.

As far as possible all troops will march off the roads, but where it is necessary to use the road troops will march in file.

ROUTE: MONCHAUX - MAING - PAMARS - Road junction E.34.d.5.6. to SAULTAIN.

DRESS will be Fighting Order. Jerkins will be worn: Waterproof sheets will be carried under the flap of the haversack.

First line transport will move in rear of "C" Coy. O.C. "C" Coy. will detail one platoon as baggage guard. This platoon will also act as a stragglers' guard.

3. DINNERS A halt will be made for dinners between MAING and PAMARS. Further details of this will be issued later.

4. STORES Officers' kits, Mess stores, etc. will be called for at
   PACKS the respective Company H.Q. at 07.30 hours.

Blankets will be rolled in bundles of ten. Packs and blankets will be dumped at the Q.M. Stores by 07.45 hours. Two lorries will report to Q.M. Stores for the conveyance of packs and blankets. The Quartermaster will detail a representative to report at Brigade H.Q. at 07.45 hours to take over these lorries.

5. ADVANCE An advance party of 1 N.C.O per Coy, 1 N.C.O. of H.Q. and
   PARTY 1 N.C.O. of Transport, will report to 2/Lieut. C. B. CRAVEN at Battn H.Q. at 08.00 hours. This party will report to the Staff Captain at the Church in SAULTAIN at 11.30 hours.

2/Lieut. C. B. CRAVEN will arrange for guides to meet the Battalion and conduct them to their billets on arrival.

6. MARCH Strict march discipline will be maintained throughout the
   DISCIPLINE march.

7. BILLETS All billets will be left scrupulously clean, and a certificate to this effect will be obtained from the Town Major by Coys, H.Q., T.O. and Q.M. and handed in to Orderly Room before moving off.

(sd) C. C. MAUDANN Capt.
Adjt 1st Battn THE RIFLE BRIGADE

DISTRIBUTION
Copy No 1 Comdg Offr.   6 O.C. "C" Coy
         2 Adjutant   8   "I" "
         3 Asst/Adjt   10 Transport Offr
         4 Intell. Offr. 11 Quarter Master
         5 Sig. Offr.   12 & 13 War Diary
         6 O.C. "A" Coy   14 File
         7   "B"   "

Appendix 5

CASUALTIES, ETC.

OFFICERS

1/11/18	Lieut G. J. COLE, MC	To England (Off Strength)
	Capt. T. CARLYLE	Wounded
	Lieut. H. L. ROUTH	Wounded
	2nd Lieut. G. KNOWLES	Wounded
	" " J. H. DAVIES	Wounded
	" " A. E. BOYLAND	Wounded
	Rev. A. J. BILLINGS	Wounded
	Capt. F. H. FARMER	Wounded (Remaining at duty)
	2nd Lieut. R. WILSON	Wounded (Remaining at duty)
5/11/18	" " T. R. LECKIE	Transferred to 11th T.M.Battery
6/11/18	Capt G. BLAND	" " 11th Inf. Brigade
	2nd Lieut. R. WILSON	To Hospital
19/11/18	" " W.J.WOODSIDE,MM	" "
26/11/18	Major C.F.G.LETTS	" "
30/11/18	2nd Lieut. W. G. WAYMOUTH	" "

Other Ranks

	Killed	Wounded	Missing	To Hospital
1/11/18	51	200	13	-
November	-	-	-	41

---------- oOo ----------

REINFORCEMENTS

Nov.	OFFICERS	and	OTHER RANKS
6	...	...	9
7	...	...	3
8	2nd Lieut. G. W. BOYD MOSS		
9	Lieut. F. BILLINGTON		
	2nd Lieut. R. STARK		
	" H. C. HAMILTON		
	" O. R. FERGUSON		
	" K. P. TILDESLEY		
	" L. W. MAGRATH		
11	...	...	2
15	...	...	17
18	...	...	2
20	2nd Lieut. T. HOWARD		50
	Major R. T. FELLOWES, DSO,MC		
21	...	...	6
22	...	...	27
25	...	...	7
27	Lieut. F. J. BROOKER, MM		3
24	Capt. A. HENDRY (RAMC)		

TOTALS   Officers 11:   O.Ranks 126

HONOURS and AWARDS

Date	Award	No.	Rank	Name
15/11/18	MILITARY MEDAL	B/98	Sgt.	SPIERS S.
		49260	Rfn.	HORNER, G.
		49308	:	HASTINGS, A
24/11/18	BAR to MILITARY MEDAL	203522	Rfn.	SHEARD, A.
	MILITARY MEDAL ...	17675	:	EVANS, W.H.
		1164	Sgt.	MAINEY, R.
		166	Rfn.	PLAYLE, A.
		6170	CSM.	GOODE, W.
		Z/1803	A/Cpl.	McGLYN, V.
		23771	Cpl.	MORRIS, A.E.

DISTRIBUTION of BATTALION 30 Nov. 1918

OFFICERS   OTHER RANKS

With the Battalion

Lt.Col. G. W. LIDDELL, DSO
Major R. T. FELLOWES, DSO, MC
Capt. W. H. P. SWAINE
  :   F. H. FARMER
  :   J. A. TAYLOR
  :   N. R. HARVEY
  :   C. C. NAUMANN
Lieut. F. YOUNGHUSBAND   618
  :   F. BILLINGTON   ----
  :   A. E. ADAMS
  :   F. J. BROOKER, MM
  :   A. WAUDBY, DCM
2nd Lieut. W.E.G. LEGHORN, MC
    "   A. O. HUNTING
    "   C. N. CRAVEN
    "   K. P. TILDESLEY
    "   P. C. SOMERVILLE
    "   F. R. M. LEE
    "   R. C. LOVELL
    "   A. E. SALTER
    "   H. V. MORLOCK, MC
    "   A. R. BURRIDGE
    "   C. W. BOYD MOSS
    "   L. WATSON
    "   C. BALDWIN, MM
    "   G. D. CHAMBERLAIN
    "   R. C. TARLTON
    "   G. A. MITCHELL
    "   L. W. MAGRATH
    "   H. C. HAMILTON
    "   O. R. FERGUSON
    "   R. STARK
    "   T. HOWARD
Hon Lieut. & Qr Mr C. MORGAN
Capt. A. HENDRY (RAMC)

Otherwise employed

Major C. F. C. LETTS   Hospital: 11th Brigade &
Lieut. W. H. SHOOBERT   Leave   depts,   14
  :   G. T. KERSWELL   "   : 4th Div.H.Q. &
2/Lieut. R. WILSON   Hospital: depts   5
   "   W. G. WAYMOUTH   Hospital: On Leave   20
   "   W. J. WOODSIDE, MM Hospital: 1st Army Schools   3
   "   E. J. PODBURY   Leave   ; Hospital   14
   "   H. K. SHORT   Leave   : 3rd Echelon   1
   "   W. G. KING   Hospital:
   "   H. FINCH   1st Army: 57
                            School :   ----
Lieut. J. W. ALDRIDGE (MORC, USA) :
                            Leave   :

1st Battalion THE RIFLE BRIGADE

Narrative of Operations   1st and 2nd November, 1918

1. At dusk on 31st October four footbridges were placed across the river RHONELLE by 2nd Lieut. TARLTON, ready for the right Company 1st HAMPSHIRE REGT. to cross. This operation was well carried out without incident.

2. At 01.00 hours on 1st November Companies began to move into the assembly position, the front line of which had been previously taped out. Companies crossed by the bridge near the mill at times laid down in Battalion orders and formed up, two Companies in front, two in support and "B" Coy. SOMERSET L.I. behind the right support Company. Companies were a little crowded and the left Companies could not take up their full frontage, but the result was that the whole of the enemy barrage was avoided.

3. At 05.15 our barrage opened, the main part of it bursting very well about 300 yards in front. A few guns were shooting short, however, and caused some 40 casualties before the Battalion moved at zero plus 15 minutes. These few guns shot consistently short throughout the operations, causing some casualties even in the support line companies.

4. At zero plus 15 minutes the leading Companies moved, extending out to their left to get touch with the platoon of the left leading Company which had formed up and started from the West side of the river in close touch with the HAMPSHIRE REGT.

5. It was misty and the smoke from the barrage added to the difficulty of keeping direction. The opposition encountered was patchy, some enemy posts making no resistance and a few fighting well. The advance continued satisfactorily until the second halt on a line just West of PRESEAU when the leading Companies were well up with the barrage and in good touch with the 61st Division on the right. Touch with the HAMPSHIRE REGT. on the left was not quite so satisfactory, but existed up to this time.

6. The advance was continued from this point punctually, and the leading Companies penetrated through the village meeting with little opposition. They reached their final objective on the Blue Line, but could obtain no touch on either flank on arrival there. The left support Company proceeded to mop up the village, - a large undertaking for one Company - while "B" Coy. SOMERSET L.I., now reduced to about 20 other ranks, began to consolidate a support line West of PRESEAU.

7. Before the consolidation of the front line was complete, and before the outpost Company had got out in front, a strong counter attack developed from the N.E. and S.E. The enemy, making use of the gaps in the line on either flank of the Battalion, entered the village from the North and could be seen crossing the high ground both North and South of the village, so that the three leading Companies were completely cut off. Enemy artillery fire was not great, but the Machine Gun fire was very heavy. At this time the mopping up Company had barely completed their task, and withdrew, according to orders, to consolidate a support position West of the village in conjunction with "B" Coy. SOMERSET L.I.

8. It is probable that "B" Coy. of the Battalion, having lost all its officers early in the attack, lost direction and very few of them were seen on the final objective and very few ever returned to the support position. The other two Companies, now very weak and trying to hold a front of about 1,400 yards, finding the enemy all

cont. on sheet 2

- 2 -

round them, turned and fought their way back to the support position through the village, where the remains of them were reorganized and helped "B" Coy. SOMERSET L.I. and "A" Coy. of the Battalion to hold the line and stem the counter attack.

9. At the commencement of the counter attack the S.O.S. signal was sent up six times but got no response for about half an hour, when the barrage came down on its old line East of the village. It was eventually brought back to a line on the Western outskirts of the village to help to cover the reorganisation of the support line. Machine Gun fire was extremely heavy during this reorganization, and intermittently during the rest of the day. On this line West of the village touch was obtained with the HAMPSHIRE REGT at the Old Mill in K.13.b., and the line was held. Troops on our right were some way further back and touch was not established till later in the day.

10. A number of casualties were inflicted on the Battalion by low flying enemy aircraft, about 15 of which were present. They were especially active during the counter attack.

11. The Battalion captured 9 trench mortars and a battery of field guns, though the latter and 3 of the former were lost in the counter attack. It is impossible to estimate the number of prisoners and Machine guns captured. About 100 prisoners were lost in the counter attack.

12. The Battalion was relieved by the Seaforth Highlanders after dark (and returned to a position K.23.b. and d.)

13. On the 2nd November by zero plus one-and-a-half hours the Battalion had moved by Companies and taken up a supporting position (along the road K.13.c.) behind the King's Own Regt. They were shelled intermittently in this position but suffered few casualties. The battalion was finally relieved by a Company of the 9th Sherwood Foresters after dark on 2nd November and returned to billets in HASPRES.

Lt.Col.
Comdg 1st Batth. THE RIFLE BRIGADE

Army Form C. 2118.

WAR DIARY
or
INTELLIGENCE SUMMARY.

(Erase heading not required.)

1st Bn The Rifle Brigade.

December 1918

Instructions regarding War Diaries and Intelligence Summaries are contained in F. S. Regs., Part II. and the Staff Manual respectively. Title pages will be prepared in manuscript.

Place	Date	Hour	Summary of Events and Information	Remarks and references to Appendices
CURGIES	1st–7th		During this period we were in the neighbourhood of the Curgies. Educational Drawing, its remainder of the mornings was set apart each day for Educational Drawing; its remainder of the time was spent in certain amount of Training, ceremonial parades, & talking. The training included several adjutants parades, junior N.C.O's parades under the R.S.M., & several parades under the R.S.M., for the new drafts. The Sunday Battalion Parade Services were held. The afternoons were invariably devoted to recreation while arranged off inter-company football & cross country running, & Battalion football matches.	
		3rd, 4th, 5th & mornings	On the 3rd, 4th, & mornings of the 5th, the Battalion was engaged in colouring the area S. & S.E. of Curgies. On the morning of the 3rd the 3rd Battalion Shooting Competition was fired	
			by the Battalion.	
		3.15	On the afternoon of the 5th H.M. the King, with H.R.H. Prince Albert, visited the 11th Brigade. The troops were ranked in sitting on sides of the road at the W. edge of CURGIES. On the arrival of His Majesty he was firstly cheered, & after the introduction of Commanding Officers, he passed down the road between the troops, & then returned & left amid loud cheers.	
		7.15	On the 7th a Brigade Ceremonial Parade was held.	

Army Form C. 2118.

1st Bn. The Rifle Brigade. WAR DIARY or INTELLIGENCE SUMMARY.
(Erase heading not required.)

December 1916. (continued)

Instructions regarding War Diaries and Intelligence Summaries are contained in F. S. Regs., Part II. and the Staff Manual respectively. Title pages will be prepared in manuscript.

Place	Date	Hour	Summary of Events and Information	Remarks and references to Appendices
CURGIES	8-14		The mornings were devoted to educational training. All companies made use of the bodeu hoty. The new draft had instruction in arms + squad drill under the R.S.M. Recreational training with inter-company football matches and cross country running was carried in the afternoons.	
		8th	Church parade.	
		11th	Presentation of medal ribands by Corps Commander in the Barn behind Transport.	
		14th	Fortnightly examination in General Education.	
	15-21		The first three mornings of the week, companies in turn for battalion at VALENCIENNES. The remaining three mornings did education (0900-1000), platoon and company training in advanced guards, while the new draft (arrived 14th Dec) received instruction in drill under the R.S.M. Afternoons devoted to recreation.	
		19th	Battn. advanced guard scheme.	
		20th	C.O's inspection of billets. Range at FORT ROCHAMBEAU at disposal of Battalion.	
		SPORTS		
		17th	Football match at MARLY v. 21st West Yorks. Result lost 1-0 goals.	
		20th	Football match v. 1st Hampshire Regt. Result lost 1-0 goals.	
	15th + 22nd		Battn. Church parades.	
	22-25		Educational training every morning (except Xmas Day & Boxing Day) from 0900-1000. Companies at disposal of company commanders for training for the remainder of the morning. Range at FORT ROCHAMBEAU used by companies in turn. Afternoons - recreational training under company arrangements.	
		25th	Xmas day Church Parade in I. Coys Barn at 1000. Dinners by companies at 1800 hours. All companies were visited by C.O. during dinner.	

Army Form C. 2118.

1st Bn. The Rifle Brigade WAR DIARY
or
INTELLIGENCE SUMMARY.
(Erase heading not required.)

December 1918 (continued)

Place	Date	Hour	Summary of Events and Information	Remarks and references to Appendices
	26th		No parades. Time spent in clearing up billets where Xmas dinners had been held.	
	27th & 28th		C.O. inspected Companies in the large BARN behind Transport lines. Inspection of billets by C.O. and 2nd in command. Sports	
			23rd 11th Brigade Race Meeting 1330 hours. Rugby Match v. 2nd Can. Fusiliers. Result 3 pts – 15 pts (Lost)	
			27th Boxing. Battn. Eliminating Bouts.	
	29–31st		29th Church parade in I Corps BARN. Educational Training 0900 – 1000 hours on 30th and 31st. A & C Companies at disposal of Coy. Commanders for Training on 30th. while I Coy used the range. 31st Battalion Shooting Competition. Result A.C.I.B. Afternoons recreation. Sports Brigade Boxing Competitions in Barn behind Transport lines. Inter Battn. Tug of war. Result Battn. won.	
	31st		Orders received to move to new area on Jan. 5th 1919.	

Ellicombe Lieut. Col. Commanding
1st Bt. The Rifle Brigade.

4TH DIVISION
11TH INFY BDE

1ST BN RIFLE BDE
JAN - MAR 1919

SERVED IN MESOPOTAMIA
18 IND DIVISION 53 BDE

4th Division

War Diaries

All Homits

1919

1st Bn. THE RIFLE BRIGADE. Jan - Mar 1919

WAR DIARY
or
INTELLIGENCE SUMMARY.
(Erase heading not required.)

January 1919
Army Form C. 2118.

Place	Date	Hour	Summary of Events and Information	Remarks and references to Appendices
CURGIES	1st - 4th		During this period one hour daily was devoted to Educational Training. The remaining two and a half hours being allotted to Company Commanders for the training of their Companies in drill, musketry and tactical exercises. The draft which had joined the Battalion in the latter part of December 1918 received its share of attention in all drill under the R.S.M.	
HAINE ST. PAUL	5th - 9th		On January 5th the Battalion with the remainder of the Brigade group moved by bus to the LA LOUVIERE area and the Battalion was billeted in the village of HAINE ST. PAUL. The following day was spent in arranging billets and cleaning up. On the morning of the 7th the normal routine was recommenced, the first hour being devoted to Education and Training and Company being at the disposal of Company Commanders for training to the remainder of the Time. On the 9th Paucalin was done in Gas Drill and Confusion rain 2 hours	Appendix I C.O.
HAINE ST. PAUL	10th - 13th		Sport. A series of Inter-Company Competitions were carried out in drill, route marching and general Companies finished up in the following order A.C.I.B. meeting.	

1st Bn. THE RIFLE BRIGADE

WAR DIARY
or
INTELLIGENCE SUMMARY.

January 1917
Army Form C. 2118.

Place	Date	Hour	Summary of Events and Information	Remarks and references to Appendices
HAINE ST. PAUL	14th – 20th		From the 14th onwards 2 hours and a half hours training was done daily, the mornings being allotted to company commanders for the training of their companies chiefly in platoon exercises. A football ground having been found recreational training was carried on each afternoon. On the 17th an inter-platoon football competition was started.	
HAINE ST. PAUL	21st – 31st		A new training programme was introduced in which a two days a week each company did 3 hours military training and on the mornings of two days 2 hours Lewis gun training and one and a half hours under the Company Commander. On the 22nd the G.O.C. the 4th Division payed an informal visit to the Battalion and visited the Orderly Room, Drunotillyalch Office, Reading Room and Quarter master's Stores. The Divisional Cross Country Run on Lt. 27th resulted in a win for the Battalion, beating the 2/Duke of Wellington's Regt by two points. The Divisional Boxing Competition took place at LA LOUVIÈRE on the 28th and 29th. The Battalion was well represented and won the Boys Fly Weight Competition.	

1st BN. THE RIFLE BRIGADE

WAR DIARY
or
INTELLIGENCE SUMMARY.

Army Form C. 2118.

January 1919

Place	Date	Hour	Summary of Events and Information	Remarks and references to Appendices
HAINE ST PAUL	21st – 31st (Cont'd)		On January 29th the Bn supplied the Divisional Guard at BINCHE. This guard turned out both the G.O.C. the 50th Division who remarked to our own Divisional Commander that our was the best guard that he had seen in either France or Belgium.	

E.M. Riddell Lt. Col.
Commanding
1st Bt. The Rifle Brigade

SECRET   OPERATION ORDER No 102   COPY NO
by
Lt. Col. G. W. LIDDELL, DSO.
Commanding 1st Battalion THE RIFLE BRIGADE.

Ref. Maps VALENCIENNES & NAMUR 1/100,000   2nd January 1919.

1. **MOVE**   The Battalion will move to the LA LOUVIERE sub-area on January 5th.
   The bus convoy will be drawn up along the CURGIES-JENLAIN road, facing VALENCIENNES: the head of the column will be at the S.E. edge of CURGIES. Busses will be numbered from the front. Numbers 35 to 68/are allotted to the Battalion. The convoy will proceed by the VALENCIENNES- MONSEBINCHE road.

2. **EMBUSSING**   The battalion will parade in Column of Route in order "I", "C", "A", "B" on the Battalion Parade Ground, facing the CURGIES-JENLAIN road, at 08.25 hours.
   DRESS: Full marching order: Steel Helmets: Box Respirators.
   The Battalion will then be told off into parties of 25, each in charge of an Officer or N.C.O. irrespective of Platoons or Companies, and marched to the Embussing point. The road must be kept clear while the Battalion is embussing Officers will be evenly distributed throughout the column.
   2nd Lieut. C. B. CRAVEN will act as embussing Officer.

3. **DEBUSSING POINT.**   The debussing point will be the PERONNES - FAYE - los-SENEFFE road, the head of the column being at the road and railway crossing, about one mile N.E. of the "L" in HAINE ST. PAUL.
   Orders for the march from the debussing point, will be issued verbally on arrival.

4. **TRANSPORT**   The Transport, plus baggage wagons (which will rejoin from 3/1/19 till 10.00 hours 6/1/19) will pass the starting point (level crossing at CURGIES STATION) at 09.33 hours on the 4th, and proceed via ROMBIES - QUIEVRECHAIN - BOUSSU TO JENAPPES, where it will stage for the night. One mounted representative from the transport will proceed in advance of the column with the Brigade Transport Officer, for the purpose of taking over Billets for the night.
   On the morning of the 5th, the Transport will proceed to HAINE ST. PAUL via MONS - HAVRE - BOUSSOIT - STREPY and TRIVIERES, passing the starting point (road junction quarter of a mile North of "S" in JENAPPES) at 09.30 hours.
   Throughout the march 100 yards distance will be kept between Transports of Units.

5. **OFFICERS' KITS and BLANKETS**   All Officers' Kits, except what they require for the night of the 4th/5th should be handed in to the Q.M. Stores by 08.00 hours on the 4th.
   All blankets and Officers' valises will be taken to the Q.M. Stores by 08.00 hours on January 5th. The personnel of the Q.M. Stores will load these on to lorries provided.

6. **LEWIS GUNS**   All Lewis Gun Limbers will be loaded up by 16.00 hours on January 3rd.

7. **ADVANCED PARTY.**   A billeting party consisting of Lieut. WAUDBY D.C.M. 1 C.Q.M.S. per Company and 1 Representative of Headquarters will report at Brigade Hd.Qrs. at 08.00 hours on January 4th On arrival at the new area they will report to Lieut. COLSON, Area Commandant, LALOUVIERE. Two days' Rations will be carried.

P.T.O.

5. ADVANCED PARTY cont.
They will prepare all indents for material required for constructing latrines, ablution benches, etc., and will meet their Companies at the debussing point on the 5th in order to conduct them to their Billets.

8. BILLETS (a) All Billets will be left scrupulously clean.
(b) Billeting certificates will be handed into Orderly Room by 18.00 hours on the 4th.

9. CLAIMS All claims should be forwarded to Orderly Room as early as possible. Before moving out certificates should be obtained from the owners of property occupied by the troops, to the effect that they have no claim to make.

10. STORES. All Soyer Stoves, palliasses or other stores on charge will be taken to the new area.

11. SANITATION Latrines and ablution benches will be constructed as soon as posable on arrival in the new area.

12. ARRIVING   Arrival in Billets will be reported to Battalion
    IN BILLETS Hd Qrs. as soon as possible.

(sd) C. C. NAUMANN Capt.
Adjt. 1st Battn. THE RIFLE BRIGADE.

DISTRIBUTION.

Copy No		
1	Commanding Officer.	
2	2nd In Command	
3	Adjutant	
4	A/Ajutant	
5	Signalling Officer	
6	Intelligence Officer	
7	Educational Officer	
8	Transport Officer	
9	Quarter-Master	
10	O/C. "A"	Coy.
11	" "B"	"
12	" "C"	"
13	" "D"	"
14	War Diary	
15	"	
16	File.	

1st Bn. The Rifle Brigade.   February 1919.   M2/2/39S

Army Form C. 2118.

WAR DIARY
or
INTELLIGENCE SUMMARY.
(Erase heading not required.)

Instructions regarding War Diaries and Intelligence Summaries are contained in F. S. Regs., Part II. and the Staff Manual respectively. Title pages will be prepared in manuscript.

Place	Date	Hour	Summary of Events and Information	Remarks and references to Appendices
HAINE ST. PAUL	1st — 28th		Throughout the month the Battalion remained billeted at HAINE ST PAUL and nothing very stirring occurred. Demobilization went on steadily all the month with the result that at the end we found ourselves with only 534 Other ranks and a very serious shortage of N.C.Os, due to the fact that a great many regular soldiers had gone home for their furloughs prior to joining the Post-Bellum Army. The time of those who remained behind was divided between training in military work and Education. Training consisted of about 6 hours Education and 10½ hours military work & Counting Chiefly of drill, musketry, route-marching and tactical exercises. In the afternoon some form of recreation always took place, usually football. Between the 2nd and the 14th an inter-platoon championship competition took place, it included Competitions at drill, boxing, football and shooting, and was won by No.4 platoon Commanded by 2/Lt. R.C. LOVELL. Other events which took place during the month were (1) An Educational Training Lecture on "Japan" by Lt. DIGBY on the 24th and (2) the XXII Corps race meeting on the 26th which was attended by about 60 Riflemen.	

AMENDMENT NO. 1.
To OPERATION ORDER No. 102
by Lt. Col. G. W. LIDDELL, DSO
Commanding 1st Battn THE RIFLE BRIGADE.
----

1. <u>OFFICERS' KITS</u>. With Reference to para 5 all Officers' Kits except what they require for the night 4th & 5th, will be handed in to the Q.M. Stores by 16.00 hours to-day, the 3rd., and not as stated, in the OPERATION ORDER No 102.

2. <u>COOKING ARRANGEMENTS</u> One dixie per Platoon and two for Head-Quarters will be taken off the Cookers before they start to-morrow morning. Companies will be responsible that these dixies are taken to the embussing point on the morning of the 5th and reach the new area.

3. <u>RATIONS</u> Rations for the 5th will be dilivered to the Quarter Master Stores tonight. The Quarter Master will arange for the necessary cooking to be done tomorro-w, so that the meat ration for the 5th can be issued out to the troops tomorrow night.

(sd) C. C. NAUMANN Capt.
Adjt. 1st Battn THE RIFLE BRIGADE.
3rd Jan 1919.
Issued to all recipients of Operation Order No 102.

1st Bn. The Rifle Brigade   February 1919

Army Form C. 2118.

WAR DIARY
or
INTELLIGENCE SUMMARY.

(Erase heading not required.)

Place	Date	Hour	Summary of Events and Information	Remarks and references to Appendices
HAINE ST. PAUL	1st – 28th (Cont?)		About the 20th it became obvious that it was no longer possible, owing to the shortage of Officers and men, particularly the former, to maintain 4 companies. Accordingly on the 22nd "B" and "C" amalgamated to form a new "C" Company and "A" and "I" to form a new "I". This operation was not hard, so difficult as anticipated and was easily completed in the day.	

E.H.Vidow / Lieut. Col.
Cmndg. 1st Bn. THE RIFLE BRIGADE.

2.3.19.

CASUALTIES etc.

OFFICERS:
                    NIL

OTHER RANKS:
    Evacuated Sick .. .. 27.

-----------------000-----------------

REINFORCEMENTS:

Feb.	OFFICERS	OTHER RANKS
2nd	... ...	1
5th	Lieut. F. V. KIBBEY: MC	
9th	... ...	1
10th	... ...	2
14th	... ...	1
15th	... ...	1
17th	... ...	1
18th	... ...	1
20th	2nd Lieut. J.R.LECKIE: 2nd Lieut. F.W.RAY	2
21st	... ...	1
22nd	... ...	1
25th	2nd Lieut. J.R.F.W. PENNY: DCM	
26th	... ...	1
27th	... ...	1

TOTALS   OFFICERS   4: Other Ranks   21.
==

-----------------000000000000-----------------

HONOURS and AWARDS

M.M.   No 7849 Rfn. A. ROWE

Army Form C. 2118.

DISTRIBUTION of BATTALION 28/2/19.

OFFICERS   OTHER RANKS

Lieut. COL. G. W. LIDDELL: DSO
CAPT. W. H.P. SWAINE
  "   G. BLAND

Lieut. N. G. DENTON   (attached)
Lieut. F. YOUNGHUSBAND
  "   A. E. ADAMS
  "   F. J. BROCKER: MM
  "   A. WAUDBY: DCM   534
  "   A. O. HUNTING
  "   G. B. GRAVEN
2nd Lieut. F. R. M. LEE
  "   R. G. LOVELL
  "   W. J. WOODSIDE: MM
  "   E. J. PODBURY
  "   H. K. SHORT
  "   G. D. CHAMBERLAIN
  "   G. A. MITCHELL
  "   L. W. MAGRATH
  "   F. H. RAY
  "   T. R. LECKIE
  "   J. R. F. W. PENNY: DCM

CAPT. REV. W. J. LEWIS (C.F.)

Otherwise employed.

Bt. Major R. T. FELLOWES: DSO, MC	Staff)	:To BOULOGNE)	
	College)	: (BOULOGNE&)	
	CAMBERLEY.):	COLOGNE EXPRESS)	3
Lieut. F. BILLINGTON	LA LOUVIERE	:Leave	22
	(TOWN MAJOR.)	:R.E. BEAURANVILLE ..	1
2nd Lieut. L. WATSON	4th Div. HQ "A"	:Division & Depts.	41
2nd Lieut. T. HOWARD	4th Div. A.P.M.	:Corps	2
Capt. F. H. FARMER	) Conducting	:4th Remount Depôt	6
Lieut. F. V. KIBBEY: MC	) parties	:Brigade	7
2nd Lieut. P. G. SOMERVILLE	) to	:G.H.Q.	1
2nd Lieut. R. G. TARLTON	) ENGLAND	:Courses of Instrction.	28
2nd Lieut. H. FINCH	) for	:R.T.O. MANAGE	8
2nd Lieut. H. G. HAMILTON	) demobiliza-	:ARMY. HQ.	1
2nd Lieut. O. K. FERGUSON	) tion.	:3rd. Echelon	1
2nd Lieut. R. STARK	)	:Hospital	8
			122

1st Bn The Rifle Brigade

April 1919
Army Form C. 2118.

WAR DIARY
or
INTELLIGENCE SUMMARY.
(Erase heading not required.)

Instructions regarding War Diaries and Intelligence Summaries are contained in F. S. Regs., Part II. and the Staff Manual respectively. Title pages will be prepared in manuscript.

Army 46

Place	Date	Hour	Summary of Events and Information	Remarks and references to Appendices
BINCHE	1st & 2nd		Completed handing over Motorisation Stores &c the 1st Bn South Wales Borderers	
"	3rd - 4th		During these two days we were trying to get all our detached from the Battalion back, in order to work up drafts for the 148th Prisoners of War Company on the 5th	
"	5th - 20th		On the 5th we just able to work up the drafts required (i.e. 3 Officers and 80 O.R.) for the draft which was sent to MANAGE by bus and from there to POPERINGHE by train. From the 5th until the 20th nothing of any importance occurred.	
BINCHE to DUNKIRK	20th - 23rd		The "Cadre" Battalion moved by bus & MANAGE leaving BINCHE about 16.00 B.O. 104 (Appendix I) and entrained at 16.30 for DUNKIRK. Detrained at DUNKIRK at 12.00 hours on 21st and bivouacked there. At 08.20 hours on the morning of the 23rd the "Cadre" embarked for DOVER on the S.S. ANTRIM. On arrival at DOVER we entrained for ALDERSHOT. The platform by the G.O.C. i/c ALDERSHOT COMMAND. and were met on and later marched up to OUDENARDE BARRACKS.	

F.W. Withey Capt
Commanding 1st Bn The Rifle Brigade

Appendix I

No 10.

OPERATION ORDER No 104
by Captain F. V. KIBBEY, MC,
Commanding 1st Battalion THE RIFLE BRIGADE.

19th April, 1919.

1. **M O V E:** The "Cadre" will move by bus to the railhead (MANAGE) on Sunday 20th inst. for the purpose of entraining for DUNKIRK. Final destination will be WINCHESTER.

2. **P A R A D E:** The "Cadre" will parade outside the "Cadre" Company Office ready to move off at 15.00 hours on Sunday.
   DRESS:- Full marching order, steel helmets carried under the pack straps.
   The embussing point will be the GRAND PLACE.

3. **E N T R A I N I N G:** Orders for entraining will be issued verbally at MANAGE. Train is due to leave at 18.00 hours.

4. **S T O R E S:** The Band Stores will be dumped outside the band store room ready for loading by 14.45 hours. The Band will supply their own loading party.
   All other stores including officers' kits, Mess Stores, Orderly Room boxes and blankets will be dumped ready for loading outside Q.M. Stores by 14.45 hours.
   "Cadre" Company will detail eight men to report to Q.M. at 14.45 hours to act as loading party.

5. **PERSONNEL SURPLUS TO "CADRE":** Officers and other ranks who have not been selected for the "Cadre" will not accompany the Battalion to MANAGE. Further instructions will be issued on this subject.

(sd). H. K. SHORT Captain,
A/Adjt. 1st Battalion THE RIFLE BRIGADE.

D I S T R I B U T I O N.
-:-:-:-:-:-:-:-

Copy No 1 Commanding Officer.
: : 2 Adjutant.
: : 3 Demobilization Officer.
: : 4 O. C. "Cadre" Company.
: : 5 C.S.M. "Cadre" Company.
: : 6 R. Q. M. S.
: : 7 Bandmaster.
: : 8) WAR DIARY.
: : 9)
: : 10 FILE.

Distribution of Battalion
on 24.4.19

Officers   Other Ranks

With the Battalion

Capt F. V. Kibbey M.C.
" H. K. Short
Lieut A. Wandby-Don   70.
2" R. C. Lovell

Otherwise Employed

Capt F. H. Farmer (Conducting Officer) Attached 1st Hants Regt
Lieut C. R. Craven (Leave)   do

Casualties

Officers :-   NIL
Other Ranks (Evacuated Sick)   10.

Reinforcements

April 19.   Officers   Other Ranks
6th.   1
13.   2
15.   1
20   2

                      NIL   6

Honours & Awards

NIL